Praise for Growing Up bin Laden

"There have of course been many books in English on Osama bin Laden, but this one is different. . . . Always interesting and highly readable, this is recommended for the many people who will wish to learn more about this man."

—*Library Journal*

"Compelling."

—*Booklist*

"*Growing Up bin Laden* is a critical missing corner piece of the Osama bin Laden puzzle, filled with astonishing secrets that could only be told by the al-Qaeda leader's loved ones. With Jean Sasson's expert help, Najwa and Omar must have dug deep in their anguished souls to find the courage to bring us these never-before-told revelations about the seeds of Osama bin Laden's extremism that ultimately created the most notorious terrorist of our time."

—Dalton Fury, *New York Times* bestselling author of *Kill bin Laden*

"Fascinating! Worth far more than dozens of intelligence reports, this enthralling portrait of Osama bin Laden, sharply drawn by his senior wife and favored son, captures as no other work has done—or could do—the degeneration of the world's most notorious terrorist from a loving, if stern, teenage husband to a fanatic who covered his cherished faith in blood. Skillfully framed by Middle East authority Jean Sasson, this book will grip you, make you shudder, and leave you better informed than presidents and generals have been."

—Ralph Peters, author of *Beyond Terror* and *The War After Armageddon*

"*Growing Up bin Laden* opens up a rare window into a hidden culture, giving the reader much to contemplate. . . . A fascinating example of how, in a family sharing genes and environment, fathers and sons emerge with different life missions. Osama, a compassionate and fun-loving young boy becomes today's most sought-after terrorist. Omar, raised in a world of violence, longs for peace. This is an unforgettable story."

—Betty Mahmoody, author of the *New York Times* bestselling book *Not Without My Daughter*

ALSO BY JEAN SASSON

NONFICTION

The Rape of Kuwait

*Princess: A True Story of Life Behind
the Veil in Saudi Arabia*

Princess Sultana's Daughters

Princess Sultana's Circle

Mayada, Daughter of Iraq

Love in a Torn Land: Joanna of Kurdistan

HISTORICAL FICTION

Ester's Child

For more information on Jean Sasson and
her books, see her Web site at
www.jeansasson.com

Growing Up bin Laden

OSAMA'S WIFE AND SON TAKE US
INSIDE THEIR SECRET WORLD

Najwa bin Laden, Omar bin Laden,
and Jean Sasson

St. Martin's Griffin ✹ New York

We dedicate this book to every innocent person who has suffered pain or lost their life in terror attacks throughout the world, and the families who continue to suffer and mourn them.

We pray for peace all over the world.

GROWING UP BIN LADEN. Copyright © 2009 by The Sasson Corporation. All rights reserved. Printed in the United States of America. For information, address St. Martin's Press, 175 Fifth Avenue, New York, N.Y. 10010.

Maps and other illustrations by Evan T. White

www.stmartins.com

Book design by Rich Arnold

The Library of Congress has cataloged the hardcover edition as follows:

Bin Laden, Najwa.
  Growing up Bin Laden: Osama's wife and son take us inside their secret world / Najwa bin Laden, Omar bin Laden, and Jean Sasson.
    p. cm.
  Includes index.
  Mother and son give us an extraordinary view of the private life of a man both loved feared by his family.
  ISBN 978-0-312-56016-4
  1. Bin Laden, Najwa. 2. Women Saudi Arabia—Biography. 3. Saudi Arabia—Social life and customs. 4. Bin Laden, Osama, 1957– 5. Bin Laden, Omar. I. Bin Laden, Omar. II. Sasson, Jean P. III. Title.
  HQ1730.B56 2009
  958.104′6092—dc22
  [B]

                                                          2009024037

ISBN 978-0-312-56087-4 (trade paperback)

First St. Martin's Griffin Edition: December 2010

10 9 8 7 6 5 4 3 2 1

Contents

Acknowledgments

Thank you, Omar, for your sincerity and integrity. Thank you, dear Najwa, for your sweet ways and your oh-so-careful responses to my endlessly intrusive questions at all hours of the day and night. Thank you, Zaina, for your devotion to Omar, and for your encouragement that Omar not give up to make this book happen.

Thank you, Liza, my indefatigable literary agent, for believing in this project when others who should have believed did not. I am a most fortunate author to have you represent me. And Frank, my literary attorney, I thank you for being a rock throughout my literary career, for sixteen years now. Havis, I thank you for your generous nature and unfailing help. To Chandler, foreign rights connoisseur, I thank you for falling in love with this story and for presenting it to publishers worldwide with that love in your heart.

A special thanks to my editor, Hope. Liza had told me you are one of the great editors, and working with you has proven to me that truth. Laura, you never let me down and were always there to answer my questions with a friendly word. I thank you and the many people at St. Martin's, who, like me, were pulled into this unique story and enjoyed exercising their skills to bring this important project to full fruit.

Thank you, my dear Hikmat, for your diligence in translating a seemingly endless stream of pages from English to Arabic and Arabic to English for my critical researches. And to you too, Amina, for pitching in when it seemed the translation stream threatened to crest and overflow. Evan, you were a pro from the first moment, and your illustrations add so much value to this work. You have my sincere thanks for never complaining despite the many tweaks on the road to perfection.

Thanks to those who care deeply about this book, as well as care about the other books I have written or planned projects yet to be written. This includes relatives Aunt Margaret and cousins Bill and Alice. My nephew Greg and his son Alec express sincere care by calling to check on my progress and well-being during the difficult days and nights of writing. Dear friends who graciously support me at every turn cannot go unnamed. I thank Alece, Anita, Danny and Jo, Joanne, Judy and her mom, Eleanor, Lisa, Maria and Bill, Mayada, Peter and Julie, and Vicki and her mom, Jo.

And, of course, once again, to my darling Jack, who gives me unconditional love while securing the perimeters of my life.

—Jean Sasson

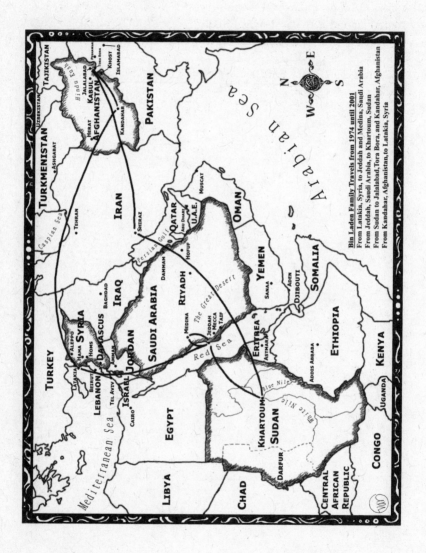

Bin Laden Family Travels from 1974 until 2001
From Latakia, Syria, to Jeddah and Medina, Saudi Arabia
From Jeddah, Saudi Arabia, to Khartoum, Sudan
From Sudan to Jalalabad, Tora Bora, and Kandahar, Afghanistan
From Kandahar, Afghanistan, to Latakia, Syria

A Note to the Reader

From the moment he came to the world's attention, Osama bin Laden has meticulously guarded even the most impersonal details about himself and his wives and children. This lack of private information about Osama bin Laden and his immediate family has fed the world's imagination ever since September 11, 2001.

While there have been many books published about Osama bin Laden and his al-Qaeda organization, this is the first book written from inside Osama bin Laden's family life, with personal accounts directly from his first wife, Najwa, and their fourth-born son, Omar. I want readers to know that nothing in *Growing Up bin Laden* has been filtered through the opinions of this writer. Memories of events, stories, and personal thoughts have come straight from Najwa and Omar to me. Although I was startled by certain revelations, I let the truth of the bin Laden family life unfold naturally. Like other members of the vast bin Laden family, Najwa and Omar are *not* terrorists. Neither has ever harmed anyone, but are in fact two of the kindest individuals it has been my pleasure to know.

It is important to remember that this book is about the private life of Osama bin Laden and his family. Please keep in mind that his son Omar bin Laden was a young boy until the time he lived in Afghanistan, and that Omar's mother, Najwa, lived in isolation during her marriage according to her husband's wishes. This is strictly a personal account of family life because much of Osama bin Laden's political, militant, and Islamic life was hidden from his wife and son, although it permeated their own lives in ways they did not always understand at the time.

During the turbulent years they were living with Osama bin Laden, Omar and Najwa were often occupied with survival rather than with keeping notes or diaries. They acknowledge that the timing and dates of family events may not always be exact, and ask that readers consider that the information in this book is essentially an oral history, and therefore subject to the omissions of memory.

Finally, although this book is the story of Najwa and Omar, and their recollections and views as they recounted them to me, the reader should understand that those clearly identified materials I have added to the narrative—this and other author's notes in the text and the Appendices at the end of the book— reflect solely my views and opinions and not those of Omar or Najwa bin Laden.

When seeking to deepen our knowledge of those who bring great harm to the world, perhaps we should be guided by the words of Sir Winston Churchill at the end of World War II:

> *Now that it is over we look back, and with minute and searching care, seek to find its criminals and its heroes. Where are they? Where are the villains who made the war? . . . We ought to know; we mean to know. Smarting under our wounds, enraged by our injuries, amazed by our wonderful exertions and achievements, conscious of our authority, we demand to know the truth, and to fix the responsibilities.*

People are not born terrorists. Nor do they become terrorists in a single stroke. But step by step, like a farmer preparing a field for planting, their lives unfold in a pattern that leaves them prepared to receive the seed of terrorism.

And so it was with Osama bin Laden. And the man, men, and events that planted that seed faded away. But the seed grew and the terrorist walked. And the man before, became the terrorist thereafter.

Najwa Ghanem bin Laden knows only the man. The West knows only the terrorist.

—JEAN SASSON

PART I

Early Days in
Saudi Arabia

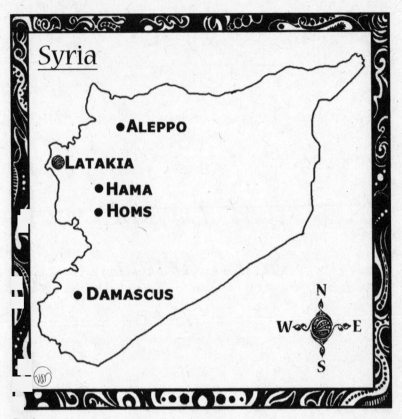

Syria

- •ALEPPO
- ⊙LATAKIA
- •HAMA
- •HOMS
- •DAMASCUS

Syria

Najwa Ghanem born in Latakia, Syria, in 1958
Najwa moved to Jeddah, Saudi Arabia, after her marriage in 1974
Najwa Ghanem returned to Syria, September 9, 2001

Facts on Syria:

Full Name: The Syrian Arab Republic
Ruled by: Republic: Baath Party
Head of State: President Bashar al-Assad
Capital: Damascus
Area: 71,498 sq miles
Major Religion: Islam with Christian minority
Major Language: Arabic
Population: 20 million
Monetary Unit: 1 Syrian pound = 100 piastres

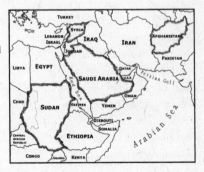

Chapter 1

My Youth

NAJWA BIN LADEN

I was not always the wife of Osama bin Laden. Once I was an innocent child dreaming little girl dreams. These days my thoughts often drift back in time and I remember the little girl that I was and the safe and happy childhood I enjoyed.

Often I've heard adults speak of their childhood with regret and even anger, glad that they have escaped the younger years. Such talk is baffling to me, for if I could, I would go back in time to the first part of my life and I would remain a little girl forever.

My parents and siblings and I lived in a modest villa in the port city of Latakia, Syria. The coastal region of Syria is lovely, with sea breezes and fertile land where lucky farmers grow fruit and vegetables. Our backyard was abundant with green trees bursting with delicious fruit. Behind our narrow seaside plain one could see the picturesque coastal mountains, with terraced hills of fruit orchards and olive groves.

There were seven people living in the Ghanem household, so our home was undeniably hectic. I was the second child born to my mother and father and enjoyed good relations with my older brother, Naji, and my younger siblings, Leila, Nabeel, and Ahmed. There was also a half-brother, Ali, a few years older than the children of my mother. My father had been married several times before he married my mother, fathering Ali with an earlier wife.

My closest sibling was Naji, who was one year older. Although I loved my brother dearly, he, like most boys, possessed a mischievous streak that caused me many moments of terror.

For example, I was born with a fear of snakes. One day, Naji used his pocket money to slip into the local bazaar to purchase a plastic snake, then knocked very politely at my bedroom door. When I answered, my brother gave me a roguish grin and suddenly thrust what I thought was a live snake into my hand. My piercing screams stirred the entire household as I dropped the snake to run so fast one would have thought I was riding on air.

My father happened to be home and rushed to deal with the crisis, almost certainly believing that armed bandits had come to murder us. When he finally realized that my hysterics were caused by Naji, who was proudly brandishing the fake snake, he stared long and hard at my brother before he began to shout a father's threats.

Naji remained unrepentant, crying out over Father's yells, "Najwa is a coward! I am teaching her to be brave."

Had we been able to see into the future, when snakes would become routine visitors to my mountain home in Afghanistan, perhaps I would have thanked my brother.

My favorite spot in the villa was the upstairs balcony, a perfect place for a young girl to escape to dreamland. I spent many enchanting hours lounging there with a favorite book. Generally, after reading a few chapters I would use my finger to hold the page and gaze outward to the street below me.

The houses in our neighborhood were nestled closely to one another, with small commercial establishments all around. I loved to observe the busy traffic of human beings rushing throughout the neighborhood, completing their daily tasks so that they might retire to their homes for an agreeable evening of dining and relaxing with their families.

Many of the families in our neighborhood had originated from other lands. Mine came from Yemen, a faraway country that was reported to be spectacularly beautiful. I was never told specifics as to why our ancestors had left, but so many Yemeni families have emigrated to nearby countries that it is said Yemeni blood flows throughout the entire Arab world. Most likely it was simple poverty that drove our Yemeni ancestors to sell their livestock, close their homes, abandon inhospitable fields, and leave behind forever old friends in familiar towns.

I can imagine my ancestors sitting in their home, the men, dashing with their curved daggers, possibly chewing the leaf of the qat tree, while the women, with black eyes intensified by kohl, listened quietly as their men discussed the challenge of parched land or missed opportunities. The old incense trade had died out, and the rains were too uncertain to grow reliable crops. With hunger pangs stabbing the small bellies of their children, my ancestors were likely persuaded to mount tall camels and trek through the green valleys brimmed by those high brown hills.

Upon their arrival in Syria, my ancestors established their home on the Mediterranean, in the large port city of my own birth and childhood. Latakia was noted in texts over two thousand years ago, described as having "admirable buildings and an excellent harbor." Framed by the sea on one side, and fertile land on the other, it has been coveted by many, and in the process was occupied by the Phoenicians, the Greeks, the Romans, and the Ottomans. Like all ancient cities, Latakia has been destroyed and rebuilt numerous times.

Up until the time I married and traveled to Jeddah, Saudi Arabia, my life experiences were limited to my family home, my school, my hometown of Latakia, and my country of Syria.

I was a daughter proud of her parents. When I was old enough to understand the things people said around me, I became aware of friendly talk regarding both the inner and outer beauty of my family. I was glad, of course, that we were respected for our good character, but my girlish pride was particularly pleased by talk of our handsome appearance.

My father worked in trading, which is a common way for Arab men in the region to make their living. I never knew much about my father's daily life, for daughters in my culture do not accompany their fathers to work. I do know that he was diligent, leaving our home early in the morning and not returning until the evening hours. His hard work ensured an ample living for his family. Looking back, I believe that my father had a soft touch for his daughters. He was firmer with my brothers, whose naughty ways sometimes made it necessary for him to be alert.

Mother remained in our home caring for our personal needs. She was a gifted cook and fastidious housekeeper. With a husband, three sons, and two daughters, her work was never finished. Much of her day was spent in the kitchen. I'll never forget the wonderful meals she prepared for her family, beginning with a delicious breakfast of eggs, cheese, butter, sweet honey with cottage cheese, bread, and jam. Our lunches might be hummus, made of chickpeas and spices, various vegetables fresh from the garden, newly picked tomatoes and cucumbers, mint-pickled eggplants stuffed with garlic, and pecan nuts. Our nighttime meal would be served between seven and eight. Our big eyes were often greeted by plates of mother's delectable rice with peas, stuffed grape leaves, okra and kibbe, a particularly popular dish for Arabs, which is basically ground lamb with bulgur wheat mixed with salt, pepper, onions, and other spices.

Of course my sister and I helped with the housework, although our duties were light compared to Mother's tasks. I kept my bed neat, washed dishes, and when I was not in school, was my mother's kitchen helper.

Mother was the chief disciplinarian for all the children. In truth, when I was a young girl, I was frightened of her strict rules regarding the social conduct of her two daughters. This is not unusual in my culture, for girls are the shining light of the family, expected to be perfect in every way, while it is anticipated that sons will sow wild oats. Should a female child behave badly, the entire family suffers enormous disgrace in the eyes of the community. Had I seriously misbehaved, it might have been difficult for my parents to find a family who would allow their sons or daughters to wed into our family. A girl's careless actions might deprive brothers and sisters of worthy marriage partners.

When I was a teenager, my mother did not agree with how I dressed. While she was a conservative Muslim woman, covering her hair with a scarf and wearing dresses that cloaked her from neck to ankles, I rebelled against such traditional dress. I resisted her pleas to dress modestly, even refusing to cover my hair. I wore pretty, colorful dresses that were not so old-fashioned. In the summer I rejected blouses that covered my arms, or skirts that hung to my ankles. I would argue with my mother if she spoke against my modern fashion. Now I am ashamed that I caused her such grief.

I remember how proud I was when I first went to school. I wore the usual girls' uniforms, which was a jumper when I was very young, though once I began secondary school, I could no longer ignore my mother and wore a jacket over my dress for modesty.

How I loved school! School expanded my small world from family members to new friends and teachers who had so much information crammed into their heads that I didn't know how their skulls kept from bursting. I was an inquisitive child, and read as many books as possible, mostly enjoying stories about faraway places and people. I soon came to realize how much I shared with other young girls my age, no matter where they might live.

In my culture school-age boys and girls rarely mix outside the family circle, so my school was for girls only. I came to know a number of impoverished students, and their poverty taught me one of the greatest lessons of life. I particularly remember one friend whose family was so poor that her father could not purchase school supplies or even food for the lunchtime break. Without considering how it might affect my situation, for my family was of modest means, I shared my money, my food, and my school supplies with my little friend. I felt the greatest rush of happiness at her reaction.

Since that long-ago day, I have learned that the joy of giving is more acute when sharing creates a personal hardship. It is easy enough to share when a person has plenty.

I recall a second friend, who was often on the verge of tears. I soon learned that her father had recently divorced her mother. My poor friend was not even allowed to even see her mother, but was forced to live with her father and his new wife. My sensitive heart ached for her situation, for every child wants their mother near. I realized that sharing does not necessarily mean the giving of money or goods; there are times that the greatest gift is to set aside one's own troubles and listen, to care about another's heartache.

I happened to meet this childhood friend by chance recently. My heart sang with joy when she told me that she had found happiness in the second part of her life. She took the veil out of choice, and she married happily. She didn't surprise me by saying that her children bring her the greatest joy.

While school was a mind-opening pleasure for me, there were other hobbies that added spice to my life. Contrary to many people's assumptions about the lives of conservative Muslim women, I was a skilled tennis player. Although I never owned special tennis attire, I would wear a long dress so that I did not expose too much of my legs while leaping about, slip on comfortable shoes, and practice for hours. My goals were to hit the ball just right, or return a serve with such power that my girlish opponent would be left standing with her mouth open in surprise. Yet in truth, the main thing was the sport. To this day I can still hear the laughter that would ring out when my girlfriends and I played tennis.

I also loved riding my colorful girl's bicycle. Once again I would select a long dress so I would not expose my legs to bystanders, then run out of the house with my brothers and sister to pedal up the gentle slopes of Latakia. We would squeal with laugher as we flew past surprised neighbors on the way down. Other times I would ride my bicycle to the homes of my girlfriends or nearby relatives.

For many years I experienced great joy as a fledgling artist, painting portraits and landscapes on canvas and smooth pieces of pottery. I spent hours mixing the colors and making the pictures pleasing to my artist's eye. My siblings were impressed enough by the quality of my paintings to predict that Najwa Ghanem would one day become a world-famous artist.

These days I am unable to enjoy such pursuits, but even now, as a mother alone with many responsibilities to my young children, I still derive some small pleasure from using my imagination. In my mind I often paint beautiful scenes or strong faces conveying great intensity, or I imagine my muscles being stretched tight from cycling up and down a steep hill, or even winning a tennis match against a faceless opponent.

I suppose one might say that Najwa Ghanem bin Laden is an artist without paints, a cyclist without a bicycle, and a tennis player without a ball, a racket, or a court.

My siblings had their own hobbies as well. We all liked musical instruments and it was not unusual for guests to hear a guitar strumming from some hidden corner of our home. My older brother even gave me a present of an accordion. I am sure I was a funny sight, for I was slim and delicate and the accordion better suited to the hands of a hefty musician.

The best time was the summer, when relatives would come to stay in our home. Most of all, I took pleasure in visits from my father's sister, Allia, who lived in Jeddah, Saudi Arabia. My Auntie Allia was lovely in every way, inspiring awe in everyone who met her. Since she dressed so fashionably when visiting us, I was surprised to learn that back home in Saudi Arabia she wore the hijab, which means full cover for a woman, including her body, face, and hair. In Syria, however, she wore modest but elegant dresses that covered her arms and legs. She also wore a flimsy scarf over her hair but did not cover her face.

Auntie Allia was known for her kindness even more than she was for her style and charm. Whenever she heard of a struggling family, she would secretly provide for their upkeep.

I overheard my parents speak quietly of her first marriage to the very affluent Mohammed bin Laden, a wealthy contractor in Saudi Arabia. Because of his special friendship with King Abdul Aziz al-Saud of Saudi Arabia, Auntie Allia's first husband had become one of the wealthiest men in a country brimming with wealthy men.

The marriage was brief and my auntie had only one child from Mohammed bin Laden, a son named Osama. After her divorce, my auntie married Muhammad al-Attas, a Saudi man who worked for Auntie Allia's first husband. Attas was known to be a caring husband to my auntie and kindly stepfather to my cousin. Never have I heard a hard word spoken against my auntie's husband. Together the couple had four children, three sons and one daughter.

I knew them all very well, for the entire family accompanied my auntie when she visited relatives in Latakia. We had many meals together in our home, occasions I remember as being particularly festive, with lighthearted talk and laughter. Osama, of course, was part of the group. My cousin, already a year old at the time of my birth, was always in my life.

Once I became seven or eight years old, memories began to stick. Osama seemed much more than a year older than I, perhaps because he was such a serious, conscientious boy. He was a mystery to his cousins, yet we all liked him because he was very quiet and gentle in his manners.

In describing the young boy Osama that we all knew, I would say that he was proud, but not arrogant. He was delicate, but not weak. He was grave, but not severe. Certainly he was vastly different from my very boisterous brothers, who were always teasing me about one thing or another. I had never been around such a soft-spoken, serious boy. Despite his serene demeanor, no one ever thought of Osama as being weak-willed, for his character was strong and firm.

When Auntie Allia and her family visited, the entire family would sometimes take day trips to the mountains or the seashore. During such family jaunts, we kids would run about with excitement, racing each other on the beaches, playing hide and seek, or tying a rope to a tree and then making a swing or jumping the rope. I remember how thoughtfully Osama would select juicy grapes, handing them to me to eat off the vine. My brothers meanwhile might be shouting gleefully that they had found some crunchy pecans lying under the branches of the tree. Other times we all might climb short-trunk trees to pluck sweet apples or thrust our hands through bushes laden with tart berries. Although Mother warned us about snakes, I was so happy to be playing with my cousins that even my fears didn't hinder my activities.

There were sad moments, however, including September 3, 1967, when my cousin Osama's father, Mohammed, was a passenger in a small airplane that stalled and crashed. At age sixty-one, Osama's father was killed, along with several other people.

My cousin was only ten years old, but he had greatly loved and respected his father. Osama had always been unusually restrained in his manner and in his speech, but he was so stricken by the death of his father that he became even more subdued. Through the years he spoke little of the tragic incident.

My mother's voice was hushed when she told me about Osama's loss. I was so shocked I couldn't react, but I did retire to the balcony to reflect on my love for my own father, and the emptiness I would feel without him.

When they were young, my brother Naji and Osama sometimes got themselves into trouble. Once they were camping and on a whim decided to go for a long walk, hiking to Kasab, a town in our Latakia Province, close to the Turkish border—and managed to walk themselves right across the border into Turkey. In our part of the world, straying into another country can result in serious consequences, with careless travelers disappearing forever.

A Turkish army officer spotted the strangers on his territory. As he yelled excited threats and pointed his weapon, Naji and Osama exchanged a single glance, then turned and ran faster than horses until they reached a garden. Thankfully the Turkish guard did not follow them clear into another country.

On another occasion, Naji and Osama went to Damascus, the ancient city that is the capital of Syria. Osama always enjoyed long walks more than most, and after a brisk hike, the two boys and their friends found shade under a tree. They were tired and a bit hungry. You might know that the tree just happened to have branches heavy with succulent apples. Tempted at the sight of the fruit, Naji and his friends climbed the tree, telling Osama to stay behind as a look-out. Naji said later that he knew that his pious cousin would probably balk at plucking apples from a tree that was not his, so he didn't want Osama participating in the actual pilfering.

The boys scrambled up the tree, but before they had time to gather a single apple, a mob of men started running in their direction, shouting angrily while whipping leather belts in the air.

"Apple thieves!" the men yelled. "Come out of the tree!"

There was nowhere to escape, so my brother and his friends slowly retreated from the safety of the bushy limbs to face their challengers. As their feet touched the ground, the men began to beat them with those strong leather belts. In between gasps, Naji yelled for Osama to "Run away! Run away as fast as you can!"

Osama was their guest, and it was important that a guest not be harmed. Also, Naji knew how dearly Auntie Allia loved her firstborn son. My brother did not want to return home with bad news about Osama.

At Naji's urging, Osama dashed away from the confrontation. For some reason the owners decided it was of the utmost importance to capture the fleeing boy, so they kept after Osama until they caught him, threatening him with their belts. Alone, without the protection of his relatives or friends, Osama was set upon by one of the largest men, who leaned forward and bit Osama's arm, a bite so strong that Osama carries a slight scar to this day.

Osama pulled the man's teeth from his flesh and pushed him away, then faced those angry men: "You had better leave me alone! I am a visitor to your country. I will not allow you to beat me!"

For some reason Osama's intense expression made those men turn away. They lowered their belts, staring at him for a few minutes before saying, "You are being released only because you are a guest to our land." By this time, my brother and his friends had made their escape. With Osama in the clear, the apple thieves were allowed to reunite and return to a place of safety. Osama's wound was cleaned and bound and thankfully he did not suffer from an infection.

Those happy days of childhood years passed too rapidly, and as I entered my teenage years, unanticipated emotions began to swirl between my cousin and me. I was not sure what was happening, but knew that Osama and I had a special relationship. Although Osama never said anything, his brown eyes lit with pleasure anytime I walked into a room. I trembled with excitement when I felt my cousin's intense attention. Soon our hidden emotions would rise to the surface and change our lives forever.

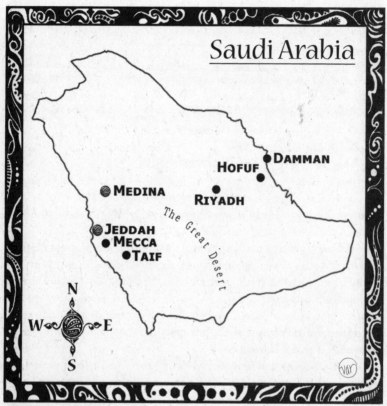

Saudi Arabia

Kingdom of Saudi Arabia
Osama bin Laden born in Saudi Arabia in 1957
After marriage to Osama in 1974, Najwa lived in the country
from 1974 until the end of 1991
Cities where the bin Laden family lived: Jeddah and Medina

Facts on Saudi Arabia:
Full Name: Kingdom of Saudi Arabia
Ruled by: Monarchy: al-Saud family
Head of State, Prime Minister,
Custodian of the Two Holy Mosques:
    King Abdullah bin Abdul Aziz al-Saud
Capital: Riyadh
Area: 864,968 sq. miles
Only Religion: Islam
Major Language: Arabic
Population: 24.8 million
Monetary Unit: 1 Riyal = 100 halalah

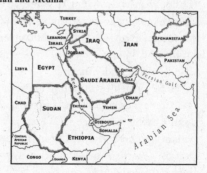

Chapter 2

Married Life

NAJWA BIN LADEN

Most girls marry young in my culture. Around the time I became a teenager, my stirring heart drew me to think of marriage to Osama. While I knew little of adult lives, I liked everything about him, from his looks to gentle manner and his strong character.

It is common for Muslim women to marry their first cousins; such unions are widely favored because they keep families intact without a threat to inherited wealth, if that is an issue.

From the way he looked at me, I believed that Osama liked me, too, yet nothing specific about affection or marriage was ever openly discussed. Serious talk about love and marriage between the two of us would have been improper until our parents had given their approval, but with Osama, everything moved slowly.

Osama's silence soon grew annoying. I wanted him to say *something*, to confide that he was going to approach our parents about an engagement. But Osama remained stubbornly proper! In fact, when he would engage me in small talk, he seemed to have difficulty expressing himself. I remember staring up into his kindly eyes, tartly thinking to myself that my cousin was shyer than a "virgin under the veil."

Finally, when I was around fourteen years old, Osama found his courage. It was after a long summer visit to my family's home in Syria, when we had been around each other every day. Once they returned to Saudi Arabia, he discussed with his mother the idea of an engagement. Auntie Allia was pleased at the prospect of a marriage between her son and her brother's daughter, which would draw our two families even closer.

In my Muslim world, women generally are the ones to begin the often tedious process of arranging marriages. From the time a son is born, this mother will attend female social functions with the idea of finding a suitable bride. A careful mother will consider only a girl from a good family, who is healthy and physically attractive. Once an appropriate prospect is found, the two mothers will initiate marriage discussions. If the mothers are satisfied, the fathers are brought in to settle the dowry, which can involve jewelry or even cash. At some point the potential bride and groom are told about each other. Since males and females usually trust their parents' decision about a marriage partner, it is rare for a child to say no; but if it happens, the parents should not force the issue.

Fortunately, such detailed planning was not necessary in our case. Not only had Osama and I had been around each other since we were children, but Auntie Allia was also inclined to allow her strong-willed son to make his own decision about marriage. She discussed the idea with my parents, who leaked the information to me.

I have never been told the particulars of that conversation, and it would be considered disrespectful to ask. To my surprise, while my heart was leaping with joy that Osama wanted to marry me, my mother argued against the match. Her lack of enthusiasm was not due to any dislike of Osama but to something more basic: She did not want me to move so far away.

Mother pleaded, "Najwa, please do not agree to this marriage. I want you close, daughter. If you go to Saudi Arabia, our visits will be as rare as expensive jewels."

For a moment I stared at my mother without responding. She was right; once I was settled in Saudi Arabia, my visits home would be rare, for in those days people did not travel as frequently as they do now. I could understand my mother's sadness, as it is one of the great joys of an Arab mother to see her children and grandchildren on a routine basis.

Marrying Osama also meant that my life would change in other, more dramatic ways. After moving to Saudi Arabia, I would be wearing the face veil. And Osama was so conservative that I would also live in purdah, or isolation, rarely leaving the confines of my new home.

Although I knew that my response would not please my mother, I replied firmly, "It is my life, Mother. I will decide. I love him. I will marry him."

I have always been strong when I decide on an action. No one would keep me from marrying Osama.

And so it came to be that I was married in 1974, when I was fifteen, but soon to turn sixteen. My husband was seventeen.

On my wedding day, I was young in years but mature and certain in my thoughts. I was not apprehensive. All was perfect. My wedding dress was elegant and white. My hair was chic and perfectly styled. I knew that I looked as beautiful as I could look. My desperate wish was that my groom would be pleased with my appearance.

Although most weddings in Syria were flamboyant events, my wedding was purposely small and subdued, held in our family home and entirely appropriate for the conservative beliefs of the man I was marrying. We took special care to seat female guests on one side of the room, and male guests on the other side. After the brief ceremony, the segregated wedding party sat down to an abundant dinner of the usual Syrian dishes, barbecued meat, crushed wheat with pigeons, grape leaves, and kibbe. There were many desserts, but I felt no hunger, eating little. The entire evening felt dreamlike: I was a woman married to the man I loved.

Everything lively was banned. There were no musicians present to strum their instruments or to sing their songs. Those with dancing feet were instructed to remain motionless. Laughter and jokes were discouraged. The evening never progressed beyond small talk. Yet I was happy, for I could tell from the sweet expression on Osama's face that he was pleased with me and satisfied with my choices. And so it was that my life progressed from childhood into adulthood by the end of that evening. I was a married woman in every way.

There were disappointments. Even though Osama and his family remained in Syria for a short time so that we could become accustomed to the change in our relationship, I was distressed to learn that my husband must return to Saudi Arabia without me. My official travel documents were not yet ready. Such documents took time, even though I had married into one of the most influential and wealthy families in the kingdom. Instead, I would remain in my parents' home, still a schoolgirl, waiting for approval of my new status as a Saudi citizen, the wife of Osama bin Laden.

My mother was much more pleased than I was about the delay. I was excited at the idea of living in a new country, and yearning to start my new life as a married woman.

The next few months were terribly unsettled, as I tried in vain to concentrate on my studies, while eagerly waiting for letters from Osama. From the words he wrote, I believe that my young husband was as eager for me to join him as I was to be with him.

Finally, just as I thought I could not abide the separation any longer, the day arrived when my father informed me that my Saudi Arabian residency and travel documents had been approved. Osama and his family could soon arrive back to Syria to escort me to Jeddah, as it would not be proper for me, a Muslim woman, to travel without a guardian.

Since I had packed long before, there was little for me to do but wait for my husband and his mother and stepfather. I was told that my father would be accompanying me as well, to reside in Jeddah until I was settled.

The knock on the door could not come soon enough. Finally they arrived! Although we were still shy with each other, one of the happiest moments of my life was when I saw my husband's face. We would be leaving for Jeddah in a day or two.

On the morning of our departure, I was filled with energy, dashing about, rechecking my bags, and saying my goodbyes over and over. Although I knew that nothing would ever be the same, I simply could not restrain my happiness. At some point, I did notice the dejected looks on the faces of my family, and made an attempt to curb my enthusiasm at leaving. I did not want to wound my cherished family, most particularly my dear mother. Still, when the final moment came to say goodbye, I was in a bit of a rush to start our journey.

I was about to embark on my first airplane ride, yet I didn't feel a spark of fear. Ever since I was very young, I have been convinced that my life is in God's hands. This belief keeps my nerves steady.

Although I had no fear of death, that day *was* a momentous one in my life, with everything changing in the blink of an eye. From that moment, my husband would be the head of our family. For the most part, his decisions would rule my life and the lives of any children we might have. From now on, I would lead a restricted life, leaving behind the possibility of driving an automobile or working in a job outside the home.

Then there was the dreaded veil. This was also the day when I first draped the black veil over my face and body. Although I was modestly covered in a simple dress with long sleeves that reached midway between my knees and ankles, this was not conservative enough for Saudi Arabia, a country where no part of a woman's flesh or hair should be seen by a man outside her immediate family.

I was prepared for the inevitable, for my Auntie Allia had presented me a gift of the flowing black cloak, called an abaaya, a black scarf, and a thin face veil. The abaaya is simple with full sleeves, open in the front without any buttons or clasps. Although I did not drape the costume over my clothing while we were still in Syria, I followed Auntie Allia's lead and covered myself within a short time of boarding the plane.

There I sat, swathed in black from head to toe. Since Saudi women who live in the cities do not expose their eyes, my entire face was covered along with everything else. Suddenly I felt myself smothering, suffering panicky thoughts about what would happen when it was time to leave my seat. Would I be able to see well enough to walk safely through a crowd? What if I stumbled and fell, crushing a small child?

Just then, I looked over at Osama and he smiled. My husband seemed very pleased that I had taken to the veil without too much excitement, although it felt strange to carry on ordinary conversations through a face curtain. Being young, I found it difficult to swallow my giggles, but somehow I managed.

Soon our plane landed, and I braced myself for the challenge of walking about with my eyes covered. Thanks to God that I have been blessed with firm footing as well as good vision and could see clearly enough through the thin fabric of the face veil. I fluttered about in the black curtain without harming myself or any innocent bystanders.

I stood back with Auntie Allia while our husbands dealt with the formalities of entering the kingdom. Soon we were in the long black automobile that would take us through the city and to my husband's home.

Even though I could see Jeddah only through the black gauze of the veil, I was not disappointed in the city that has been called the "Bride of the Sea." Everything about Jeddah is beautiful, from the blue sea to the wide boulevards and the distinctive homes. Besides, after growing up on the port city of Latakia, I am fond of having the sea as my neighbor.

For centuries Jeddah was nothing more than a small settlement serving as a pilgrim port, a gateway to our most holy city of Mecca, which is located forty-seven miles inland. But when Europeans discovered their desire for Arabia's frankincense and myrrh, Arabian traders rose to the occasion, building ships and seaports for the incense trade.

In 1945, thirteen years before I was born, Jeddah's population was said to be 25,000 people. By the time I made Saudi Arabia my home in 1974, Jeddah was a cosmopolitan city of one million citizens.

Osama told me that Jeddah was growing too fast, that the city had begun to feel overcrowded, especially during certain Muslim holidays, when at least a million pilgrims descended to double the population. But even though it was not the time for pilgrimage when I arrived, I could instantly see that Jeddah throbbed with excitement. I would later learn that the oil boom had brought a burst of energy to the port city, which grew to two million souls only six years after I landed there.

I was most looking forward to see the home where my husband had grown up, and was not disappointed. Auntie Allia's home was located in the Mushraf area of Jeddah, a comfortable neighborhood with a number of shops and mosques nearby. My new home was a lovely two-story house that, although not elaborate, was a perfect place for us to begin married life. I was pleased to learn that Auntie Allia and her husband had made arrangements for Osama and me to have an entire floor to ourselves, which gave us our privacy.

I remember feeling as much at ease in my new home as if I had lived there for many years. While I was so busy settling in that many of the details of those early weeks are now a blur in my mind, I do remember that it was a lovely time for me.

My daily life was so radically different from my childhood in Syria that my husband allotted much of his time to patiently explaining how important it was for me to live as an obedient Muslim woman. "Najwa," Osama said, "for me, you are a prized pearl who must be protected." Smiling reassuringly, he promised, "Just as the hard shell of the sea protects the exquisite pearl, I will be the hard shell protecting you."

I felt proud that Osama wanted to protect me, as he slowly brought me to an understanding of the reasons behind the need for a female's isolated life. I never objected because I understood that my husband was an expert regarding our faith.

My husband and I decided that I would not continue with my formal schooling, although I privately educated myself on religious matters with my husband's assistance. Osama was so well versed that he made a good teacher. Osama's own father had been a devout Muslim who demanded that his sons honor the faith. None had heeded their father's counsel more than Osama.

For this worthy purpose I spent many hours sitting in our pleasant garden, eagerly reading the Koran, Islam's most sacred text, which contains the revelations that were given by God to the Prophet Mohammed (May peace be upon him). The Hadith is also very important, and is called "The Traditions," or written reports of Prophet Mohammed's words and deeds. Although many scholars and clerics can recite the teachings by heart, I was surprised that my young husband could recite both sacred texts without referencing a single page.

I wanted to be able to do the same.

Jeddah, an alluring city of contrasts, continued to be a great pleasure for me. The heartbeat of old Jeddah was still alive. There were many traditional homes with charming small balconies bolstered with lattice screens to shield the women of the household, who could entertain themselves by sitting quietly and looking out upon the busy streets, being observers of life rather than participants. Some people said that in the old days the enclosed balconies were welcome sanctuaries, protecting occupants from insults and robberies.

Those old homes contrasted with the new world that was racing to embrace Saudi Arabia. Modern mirrored buildings sparkled in the Jeddah sun. Behind all that costly glass, bustling newcomers lived near proper ladies closeted behind their latticed windows, ladies who must have wondered what their safe and comfortable world was coming to.

My husband made the decision to employ domestic help to assist me with general housework and kitchen duties. The woman he hired was a pleasant Ethiopian maid named Zamzam, whom I believe was delighted to acquire a position in a home where she was respected.

Early each morning my husband would awaken without any help from a clock, rising before the sun as effortlessly as if it were noontime. He would leave our home quickly to walk to the neighborhood mosque, as the muezzin, or the cleric, called out from loudspeakers that believers must come to prayer. Unless one has heard the haunting cry to prayer, it is difficult to imagine, but it sounded like music to my ears.

Allah Akbar! (God is most great!) Allah Akbar! Allah Akbar!
I bear witness that there is no God but Allah.
I bear witness that there is no God but Allah.
I bear witness that there is no God but Allah.
I bear witness that Mohammed is the Apostle of Allah!
I bear witness that Mohammed is the Apostle of Allah!
I bear witness that Mohammed is the Apostle of Allah!
Come to prayer! Come to prayer! Come to prayer!
Come to success! Come to success! Come to success!
Allah Akbar! Allah Akbar! Allah Akbar!
There is no God but Allah!

Luckily for the Saudis, the government had decreed that a mosque would be constructed in every neighborhood, so no one had to walk a long distance to fulfill his Muslim duty of praying five times a day. Prayer time is very specific and greatly cherished as a time set aside that all Muslims should pray to their God. Every shop and every business in the kingdom closes during these times.

The *Fajr,* or dawn prayer, is called between the first light on the horizon and sunrise. Religious men keep watch so that the perfect moment is not missed. *Zohr,* or the midday prayer, is called at noon. This prayer cannot end until the sun has traveled five-ninths of its journey toward sunset. *Asr* is the afternoon prayer, followed by *Maghrigb,* which must be said between sunset and the time the light on the horizon completely disappears. *Isha* is the final prayer of the day, to be said from the time the light of the sky turns yellow until it becomes completely dark. This is our longest prayer.

While Osama was at the mosque I would say my prayers at home, sometimes praying in our bedroom, or our sitting room, or on our balcony. Women do not pray in neighborhood mosques in Saudi Arabia, but every Muslim knows that there is no need for a special place to pray. A Muslim can bow down on the sidewalk and pray to God.

Our religion has many requirements, but my husband and I met our obligations gladly. It is gratifying to the heart when one pleases God with the proper devotion.

Osama would not be long at morning prayers. When he came home, we would eat breakfast. His tastes were simple; he was as contented with a piece of bread with oil or thyme as he was with the finest cuts of meat. "Najwa, do not worry," he told me. "Whatever is available and what God gives me, I thank Him for whatever He provides." Of course, I made certain that he had a good breakfast of cheese and bread and eggs and yogurt. And I knew from childhood that Osama did have a preferred food, which was zucchini stuffed with marrow. That dish soon became my own favorite.

I was determined to give my husband healthy foods because his days were long and strenuous. Not only did he attend school, where it was important for him to concentrate on his lessons, but he also worked for his family's business, the huge Saudi bin Laden Group. My husband was very serious about doing a fine job, so he often stayed late at work.

After breakfast, we would talk for a while before Osama would change from his white thobe, the Saudi costume that resembles an ankle-length shirt and is appropriate for prayer or other daily activities, into a western-styled school uniform of a freshly ironed white shirt and gray trousers. I was proud that my husband was quite tall, but his height made it necessary to have all his clothes, including his school uniform, made by a special tailor. He was very particular about his appearance, and when he left our home my eyes told me that he was a picture of perfection.

I would watch him leave our living area, feeling empty inside that he would be gone for the entire day. Osama was a student at the Al-Thager Model School, a secondary, or high school, for boys only. Although I never went inside, my husband drove me past on several occasions, when I saw that it was a modern building with two stories near the downtown area of Jeddah. Osama was proud that the school was a special project of Saudi Arabia's third king, King Faisal, who had overseen the school's progress until his tragic assassination in 1975. Osama had first enrolled when he was eleven years old, and he would be graduating in 1976, two years after our marriage.

Osama said that he was attending one of the best schools in Saudi Arabia, and that courses were of high standards so that the graduates could advance from there into any good university. Many of the instructors were from England, so Osama was well spoken in that language. At the time we married, he was taking the usual courses of mathematics, biology, history, and of course, religion.

When school was over, he would take up his duties at the family construction company. Despite his position as a bin Laden son, Osama would do the most difficult and dangerous work alongside his men. He knew how to drive the biggest equipment, including huge machinery with giant shovels that scraped out mountain roads. He actually worked on paving roads, although he said that he most enjoyed digging safe tunnels through the hard rock of the mountains in the Saudi desert.

Despite his youth, his older brothers felt so confident in his abilities that they made him a supervisor at a special construction project at Abha, a Saudi town a few hours' drive south of Jeddah. To save travel time, most people would fly from Jeddah to Abha, but I never brought it up because Osama had lost his father in a plane crash. Besides, my husband had enough money from his inheritance to buy the latest model automobile and loved seeing how fast it could go. "Do not worry," he would tell me. "The trip is safe and easy. My father personally supervised the road construction from Jeddah to Abha, so the road is the best." I knew Osama was telling me the truth, for I had heard others in the family discussing that fine road; but I also knew the trip took him less time than most because he drove too fast. But I quieted my tongue about such matters, for my husband was not one to welcome a female with opposing opinions.

Once Osama had departed for school, I followed a specific routine. After getting dressed for the day, I would enjoy a cup of tea with my Auntie Allia while we discussed everything from the latest news about the royal family to the details of redecorating her home. I listened with special interest whenever she told me little secrets about the huge bin Laden clan, and I repeated to her the things I had heard from Osama. Although she had not been a member of the family in nearly fifteen years, she still knew much of their personal stories.

I was slowly learning about the bin Ladens, although I was shy when attending family events, for I was one of the newest and youngest brides. I sat quietly and listened while the older wives talked. Looking back, I imagine the more experienced wives must have worried that I didn't have a thought in my head, but that was not the case.

I remember a time at one of the women's gatherings when one of Osama's older sisters related a family joke that three of the bin Laden sons were "crazy and sick people." The sister laughed as she said, "Crazy number one is the sky, and he is Salem the pilot, who is so reckless piloting his plane that everyone worries that each flight will be his last. Crazy number two is the sea, and he is Laden who sails heedlessly in his boat, causing the family to fear that he will one day disappear in the folds of the sea, or be lost to a boating accident. Crazy number three is the land, and he is Osama who drives his automobiles too fast in the desert and then leaps out of his car to climb mountains that are too rugged for any human being. We fear Osama will kill himself by his rash motoring.".

I knew that the women were joking and that my husband and his brothers were not crazy, although sadly enough the fears of the bin Laden women came true when Osama's older brother, Salem, died a few years later in an airplane crash.

In addition to new cars with big engines, my husband treasured nature more than anyone I have ever known. Nothing brought him more satisfaction than having a full day to take a speedy drive to the desert, where he would leave his automobile while he took long walks. He was highly interested in everything made by God, down to the smallest plant and the smallest animal put on our earth.

After visiting with my Auntie Allia, I would take my Koran and devote a few quiet hours in our family garden to further study of our religion.

Sometimes I would telephone my mother to catch up on family events in Syria. Although I experienced moments of melancholy at being so far away from my parents and siblings, the sadness did not linger because I knew I was exactly where I belonged, at my husband's side.

Later in the day I would spend time on my various hobbies. I was particularly interested in planning the home that Osama and I would have after we started our family. Looking at pictures of elegantly decorated homes, I dreamed of the day when I would have the opportunity to furnish and beautify my own home. Osama had smilingly assured me that I would be in complete charge of the decorations.

Soon after arriving in Jeddah, I had also become interested in sewing my own clothes. Although my dresses were simple, I enjoyed studying fashion magazines and selecting the designs I liked, then carefully drawing a pattern on thin paper. If I had the suitable material, I would very cautiously cut the fabric and sew the pieces together. Otherwise, I would send our driver to purchase materials and supplies. Making our confused driver, who had lived most of his life in a small village in Yemen, understand the importance of the specific weight and color of feminine fabric was never easy. I smile today when I think of those torturous conversations, although it was not funny at the time.

But such was life in Saudi Arabia; we women remained in seclusion most of the time. I was rarely frustrated, but on occasion I felt my nerves frayed and needed different scenery. When that happened, Auntie Allia would volunteer to escort me on a rare trip to a commercial establishment to select a supply of pretty fabrics.

Such outings had their own frustrations. I often read postings on the windows and doors of women's dry good shops declaring that women were forbidden to enter. Most Saudi-owned shops were managed by men from other countries such as Pakistan, India, or other Arab lands. Even if females are allowed to enter the store, most Muslim women did not feel comfortable conversing with a man not of their family.

Despite such obstacles, sometimes I would meet with success and my reward would be a lovely dress to wear for my husband or to exhibit at one of the female family functions. Other times I would be forced to discard the dress and the pattern in our garbage bin.

I still painted on canvas, although less than before.

I still read, but because of my goal to become more knowledgeable about my faith, I mainly read religious teachings.

My hobbies kept me busy even though I was alone for many hours each day. Often I exhausted myself by mid-afternoon and required a long nap. I trained myself to wake up with ample time to attend to my appearance before my husband came home for the evening.

Once Osama returned, we would lightly discuss his day and mine, and then we would have our evening meal. Sometimes we ate alone but more often with Auntie Allia and her family, which was very enjoyable. Of course, we would break off social talk for all the required prayers, with the men dashing off to the mosque and the women praying at home.

After family time, my husband often joined other men for impassioned discussions of political or religious topics. It is common in Saudi Arabia for men to spend the evenings with their male friends, rather than with their wives and families. The men will gather in various homes on different evenings of the week, where the men have a special room that is all their own. They will drink tea or coffee and some will smoke cigarettes and enjoy the camaraderie of their peers.

Like all women in Saudi Arabia, I would never attend such gatherings, but would remain with the women of the house. By the time my husband returned late at night, everyone would retire.

The best time for me was the sleeping time.

After a year or so of living in Jeddah, I had girlfriends I had met through my Auntie Allia. We would visit in each other's homes on occasion and sometimes discuss our husbands and our mothers-in-law. I was one of the few young brides who had no complaints about my husband, our marriage, or my mother-in-law.

One of the many blessings in my life was that we lived near Mecca, the Blessed, the most holy city for Muslims, which was only about fifty miles from my new home. I held Jeddah in great affection, but Mecca was the city I loved most.

Our Prophet Mohammed was born in Mecca, and Islam's most holy mosque, the Grand Mosque, is the heart of the city. Because of this, Muslims from every corner of the world spend long hours dreaming of the day when their happy eyes will see the blessed city and their feet touch the sandy soil.

Osama was eager to take me there soon after I arrived in Jeddah—for the obvious reasons, but also because he was proud that the rulers of the kingdom had chosen his family to maintain the holy mosques in Mecca and Medina, which was the greatest honor for a Muslim.

I remember my high excitement on the short drive to Mecca. To travel there from Jeddah takes only an hour, and less with Osama at the wheel. Mecca is

910 feet above sea level, so the highway slowly climbs to that elevation. Nothing had prepared me for the sensations that gripped me at the moment the city dipped into sight and I spotted the vista all Muslims ache to see.

Soon my feet were on the ground. In a dreamy daze I walked in the direction of the great mosque. To my despair, I soon found myself distracted. Although it is not a requirement to wear the veil at the holy mosque in Mecca, I did so in deference to Osama's wishes.

I had not yet become accustomed to wearing the veil. Although Saudi women familiar with the abaaya appear svelte and elegant, those new to the veil and cloak are not so graceful. The face veil is kept in place by hairpins, while the abaaya is held closed with the right hand, giving the wearer a lot to coordinate. In my inexperience, I remember being worried that I might accidentally expose my face or my garments underneath the cloak. I first adjusted my face veil under my head scarf, then tightly grasped the edges of the cloak with my right hand. As I walked through the huge mosque area, I prayed that I would do nothing to create attention, humiliating myself before other worshippers.

I was sure that I looked the fool, hanging on to my garment and placing each step with great care. Suddenly, in that most holy place, an unwelcome comic image popped into my mind. I remembered a story I had read as a child about a big black bird who is tricked into dropping the cheese. That children's fable swirled around and around in my head as though an automatic switch had been flipped. As desperate as I was to savor this sacred moment, I could not get the fable out of my thoughts:

> *There was once a big black crow sitting high up in the trees.*
> *In her beak she had a nice, round cheese.*
> *Along came a fox, as clever as they come,*
> *"Mmmmm," he thought. "I'd like to have a bite of that cheese."*
> *"Oh crow," called the fox, "if your voice is half as beautiful as those*
> *fine feathers I see, it would please my ears to hear*
> *you sing a little melody."*
> *Well the crow had never heard anyone say such a nice thing.*
> *So, she opened up her beak and she began to squawk and sing.*
> *Down came the cheese into the waiting mouth of the fox.*
> *"Oh no! You have my cheese," squawked the crow.*
> *Meanwhile, the fox was licking his lips.*
> *"You got the compliments, and I got the cheese!*
> *It's a fair enough trade!"*

Did my lack of grace made me as conspicuous as a big black crow? The idea brought forth fears, followed by giggles. I struggled with my secret thoughts until the emotional impact of the mosque and my nearness to God helped to calm my mind and erase the bizarre image. I lumbered on, graceless in the midst of so many Saudi women who glided along as elegantly as skilled ice dancers.

By the time I located the spot delegated to female worshippers, the black bird had flown. Never did I reveal my tactless thoughts to my husband, who would have been angered by such irreverence. I felt humbled as I knelt to say my heartfelt prayers to God, knowing that he would forgive me for my sins both great and small. Such awe filled my soul that my eyes overflowed with fat tears that rolled down my cheeks.

Within a year of my marriage, my body began to feel strange. I confided in my Auntie Allia, who told me that all the signs made it clear that I was pregnant.

Expecting a child was the loveliest feeling I had ever known. Osama was very happy about my news, and like all Saudi men he expressed his sincere wish that our firstborn be a son. A son for our first would be nice, I thought to myself, but I had always wanted a small daughter so that I might dress her in frilly dresses and braid her long hair. But in truth, like most mothers, I wished for nothing more than for God to give me a healthy baby.

Everyone was more than joyous about the upcoming event. My husband and his family remained solicitous about my health and state of mind for the entire nine months, so I was a pampered expectant mother. There was nothing I needed that I did not receive. I gave thanks to God that I did not suffer during the months before my first child was born. My parents were told and they were pleased as well, although sad that they would not be with their daughter during the happy occasion.

After having such an easy pregnancy, I was surprised by the degree of difficulty and pain of childbirth. I did not go to the hospital but was attended to at our home by a well-trained midwife. The birthing was so excruciating for me that my anxious husband announced, "From now on, Najwa will be taken to a hospital for the birth of our children."

Never have I been so happy to see a face as I was to see the face of our firstborn. He was a healthy baby, thanks be to God for His blessings. We named our little son Abdullah and were in high spirits that he was with us. That first birth was a long time ago, in 1976, but I do remember that there were some problems with his feedings. I was a young and inexperienced mother and did not have the answer for all questions. Happily all was resolved over time and Abdullah grew into a healthy toddler.

After Abdullah was born, Osama hired a second Ethiopian maid by the name of Naeemah. What happy days those were! We were a young couple without the usual worries of so many newlyweds. We had our healthy son, we enjoyed close relations with both sets of parents, and we had enough money for our needs. We were blessed.

How I wish we could have stayed in that happy place forever.

We were so occupied with our young family and my husband was so involved with his work and his schooling that the time passed as rapidly as a strong wind. Everything seemed the same to my heart and mind, yet everything was changing.

Within a year of his birth, Abdullah was a precocious toddler and I was pregnant once again. In 1978, the same year that I passed from being a teenager and turned twenty, we were blessed with a second son, Abdul Rahman.

In early 1979, I found myself pregnant again, feeling that God would surely bless me with a daughter this time. Many Saudi wives envied me, for sons are most prized in my culture; still, I secretly dreamed of a little girl.

My husband, who would soon be twenty-two years old, was attending college at the King Abdul Aziz University. His main course of study was in economics and management, although he took a particular interest in his religion classes. My husband also devoted time to the charity work that is so important to a true believer.

Even though I have never been involved in public life, I did overhear various discussions of events shaping the world. I heard something about the troubles in Iran, a Muslim nation near Saudi Arabia, where protesters were unhappy with the Shah and instead favored a religious government. Sure enough, in January 1979, the Shah and his family were forced to flee, making way for a Muslim cleric by the name of Khomeini to rule the large country.

As my husband became older and more educated, I noticed that a new and broader awareness of the outside world began to occupy his mind. He would occasionally comment on his disappointment in the politics of the world, and in particular on the fact that Islam was not held in greater respect. No one in our family took umbrage at his new political awareness and religiosity; Osama was highly praised for his keen interest in supporting Islam.

One evening he arrived home with a surprise announcement: "Najwa, we are going to travel to the United States. Our boys are going with us."

I was shocked, to tell you the truth, as this was the first occasion I would accompany Osama on a trip. At that time Abdullah was a toddler and Abdul Rahman was still a babe in arms, less than a year old. Pregnant, and busy with two babies, I remember few details of our travel, other than we passed through London before flying to a place I had never heard of, a state in America called Indiana. Osama told me that he was meeting with a man by the name of Abdullah Azzam. Since my husband's business was not my business, I did not ask questions.

I was worried about Abdul Rahman because he had become quite ill on the trip and was even suffering with a high fever. Osama arranged for us to see a doctor in Indianapolis. I relaxed after that kindly physician assured us that Abdul Rahman would soon be fine.

When people make the unexpected discovery that I have visited the United States, I am sometimes questioned about my personal opinion of the country and its people. This is surprisingly difficult to answer. We were there for only two weeks, and for one of those weeks, Osama was away in Los Angeles to meet with some men in that city. The boys and I were left behind in Indiana with a girlfriend whom I would rather not name for her own privacy and safety.

My girlfriend was gracious and guided me on short trips out of her home, for I would have never ventured out alone. We even went into a big shopping mall in Indianapolis.

I was surprised that the landscape looked very flat, and so different in many ways from Saudi Arabia. As far as the people, from what I experienced on that brief outing, I came to believe that Americans were gentle and nice, people easy to deal with. As far as the country itself goes, my husband and I did not hate America, yet we did not love it.

There was one incident that reminded me that some Americans are unaware of other cultures. When the time came for us to leave America, Osama and I, along with our two boys, waited for our departure at the airport. I was sitting quietly in my chair, relaxing, grateful that our boys were quiet.

Suddenly my instinct warned me to look around. Sure enough, I saw an American man gawking at me. I knew without asking that his unwelcome attention had been snagged by my black Saudi costume, consisting of a face veil, head scarf, and abaaya. That curious man was exhausting himself pacing back and forth in front of me.

Little could he know that under the veil, my eyes were fastened on him, too. That funny man was wearing out his shoes coming one way and then going another, each pass bringing him closer to me. With a jaw dropped open in surprise, and curious eyes growing as large as big bugs popping from his skull, he actually stopped to gape at my veiled face. I did not react, of course, even though he took enough time to stare at me from every possible angle.

I wondered what my husband was thinking. I took a side glance at Osama and saw that he was intently studying the curious man. I knew that my husband would never allow the man to approach me, so I was not worried about what would happen.

Later when my husband and I discussed the incident, we were both more amused than offended. That man gave us a good laugh, as it was clear he had no knowledge of veiled women, or that the Muslim woman under the black cloak covered her face and body because she chose to do so.

We returned to Saudi Arabia none the worse for our experiences.

Thankfully Abdul Rahman's health was improved, and I had an easy time when my third child was born. Sa'ad came to us as a smiling baby. Of course, Osama received many congratulations to be the father of three sons in a row.

Other dramatic events occurred during that year of 1979, bringing much worry to Muslims, although to tell you the truth I was so busy with three babies that I noticed little of the world outside my four walls.

One significant event adversely affected my own family, including the lives of my children born and yet to be born. In December of 1979, the Soviet Union invaded Afghanistan, beginning a brutal occupation against our Muslim brothers. Although many Saudis and Muslims from other lands were dismayed by the attack, my husband appeared more agitated than most. He constantly sought news of what was happening in Afghanistan, whether from Muslim sources or international news media. The more he learned, the more anxious he became.

I had no idea what might be happening in that faraway land, but whatever it was, my husband was highly affected. When I gathered my nerve to press for information, Osama simply said that a great evil had taken over a Muslim land. He was more upset than I had ever seen him regarding stories of innocent Muslim women and children who were being imprisoned and tortured to death.

The accounts he knew but refused to share must have been horrific, for it seemed that my husband's heart had been burned to a crisp.

By this time Osama was an adult in every way, and his reactions were those of a man who knew what he must do. He was at the forefront of the Saudi campaign to offer assistance to our beleaguered brethren in Afghanistan. In the beginning, his busy campaign emphasized the gathering of money to support the tribal leaders in Afghanistan who were fighting a full-fledged war against the invader. There were successful money drives at the mosques, and within the bin Laden family unit, for they were a very generous family. All wanted to contribute, but few worked harder than Osama to raise funds on behalf of the Afghan victims.

Soon, the war in Afghanistan began to take over my husband's life.

Osama made plans to travel to Pakistan, a neighboring country to Afghanistan where many Muslims were gathering. My husband said that he would take the charity funds he had collected and purchase food, medical supplies, and weapons. After arriving in Pakistan, he would organize trucks and drivers to deliver the supplies to the Afghan fighters.

Before Osama left on his trip, he surprised me by purchasing a large twelve-apartment building in Jeddah, not too far from the home of his mother, which he said would be our new home. My feelings were mixed; I was glad because our growing family needed space, but sad because I had grown accustomed to the company of his mother and her family, all of whom I loved.

Osama took me to see our new building located in the Azazia Village 8, close to Macarona Street. The building was nicely built out of pale colored stone. I was rather astonished by the size, thinking to myself that I could never have enough babies to fill up that huge building.

When we went inside I saw that the apartment had many plain rooms that were simply decorated with traditional Persian carpets and Arabic-styled cushions lined up against the walls. I had always fancied our home to be adorned with draperies and furniture and special decorations, but who knew when Osama would return from Pakistan? It would be impossible for me to go around the city alone to purchase new furnishings.

Soon after our outing, Osama arranged for the family to move into the new building, then left Jeddah for Pakistan.

Although my husband never failed to be a kindly partner, I could see that his mind was overflowing with business not connected to our home or to our children. I was supportive always, and I yearned for success on the battlefield for two reasons: one, that the Afghans could live without danger and rebuild their shattered nation, and two, that my husband and the father of my children might come home so we could resume the life we had once known.

And so it came to be that I found myself alone with three babies.

Fortunately, I was unaware that we would never return to an ordinary life. From that time on, Osama was away from Saudi Arabia more often than not. That huge building never became the elegant home I had envisioned during those early years of marriage.

Even with maids to help with my three boys, and a driver responsible for acquiring our supplies, my life resembled a fast-moving spinning wheel. I did not want to miss a moment of my sons' baby days, so I was often fatigued. Adding to my exhaustion, I found myself pregnant again in July of 1980.

The fourth child I carried kicked with such enthusiasm that I suffered from the inside out. Surely, after three sons, it was time for a dainty female, yet it was hard to imagine the baby inside me that was bursting with abundant energy was a delicate girl. Surely the child must be male!

Thankfully Osama was careful to mark the date in March 1981 and return home from Pakistan to be by my side when it was time for me to give birth. When I told Osama that I must go to the hospital, he was as excited as he had been with our first three. My husband was a man on a mission; he settled me in his automobile and raced to the Bukshan Hospital, driving through Jeddah neighborhoods at such a speed that familiar structures appeared as a blur.

Despite the intensity of the labor pains racking my body, I felt myself the luckiest woman in the world.

A Note Regarding Osama bin Laden's Political Activities

JEAN SASSON

During the years that Najwa married, moved to Saudi Arabia, and began having children, Osama bin Laden completed his high school education at the Al-Thager Model School in Jeddah, and in 1976 enrolled in the King Abdul Aziz University in Jeddah, where he studied economics and management. Najwa says that, despite reports claiming otherwise, Osama never graduated from the King Abdul Aziz University, but left three or four years after enrolling, only a few terms before graduation. His personal awakening had roused him to move on to the political movement sweeping the entire Middle East.

Actually, throughout Osama's formative school years, the Muslim Middle East underwent an Islamic awakening, called the Salwa. The beginnings of the Salwa could be traced to the 1967 war with Israel, when Egypt, Jordan, and Syria suffered a demoralizing military defeat. That's when many thousands of young Arab men began to question their leaders and the internal problems of their countries, as well as their losses to Israel. The Islamic awakening would gain in strength when many young Arabs began to demand change.

Although Osama was politically quiet during these years, his passion for Jihad, or holy war, was forming. During this time Osama met his first mentor, the activist Palestinian teacher and writer Abdullah Azzam, who inspired him to devote his life to something other than increasing the bin Laden fortune.

Abdullah Azzam was born in 1941 in Hartiyeh, Palestine, at the time the British were occupying his country. He attended school in his home village before studying at the Khadorri College, then worked as a teacher in Jordan before obtaining his BA in Sharia law in Damascus. When the Israelis occupied the West Bank after winning the 1967 Six Day War, he fled to Jordan, where he joined the Palestinian Muslim Brotherhood.

From Jordan, Abdullah Azzam became a part of the Palestinian resistance coalition, but grew contemptuous of Arab rulers, believing that the current rulers were too comfortable maintaining the status quo. Abdullah Azzam was adamant that the Middle East map drawn by Great Britain and France after World War I should be redrawn by Arabs.

Then in 1978, simmering troubles in Afghanistan ignited into a fire. After pushing for greater influence in the region, the Soviets backed a coup in Afghanistan to install a purely communist government. A second coup toppled the communist puppet government, and the Afghan president and most members of his family were assassinated. A Russian-backed president was put on the throne. Soviet tanks and troops fully invaded Afghanistan in December 1979.

Almost immediately, Muslim guerrillas launched a Jihad against the Russian atheists. The United States, Great Britain, and other Muslim nations supported the guerrillas. The Soviets were surprised by the heavy resistance, and would soon take heavy losses.

Enticed by Abdullah Azzam's political message, Osama was mentally ready to respond to the Soviet invasion of Afghanistan. Soon afterward, he left college to devote his time to working on behalf of the Afghan resistance fighters, known as the Mujahideen. Abdullah Azzam was his partner, and the two men met in Peshawar, Pakistan, on the border of Afghanistan, working closely to organize a method of delivering food, medical supplies, and weapons to the Mujahideen.

Chapter 3

Mother of Many Sons

NAJWA BIN LADEN

I soon discovered that my fourth child was indeed yet another son. Although I suffered a flash of disappointment when the doctor failed to announce the birth of a daughter, everyone around me was so overjoyed that my face flushed pink with pleasure. I reminded myself that many are the women in Saudi Arabia whose heartfelt prayers for sons go unanswered.

Boys are so favored in Saudi Arabia that a woman who gives birth only to sons is considered to be blessed by the hand of God Himself. Now that I had four sons, I witnessed many envious faces.

My husband and I named our fourth-born Omar Osama bin Laden. From the moment I looked into that baby's soulful eyes, I admit to a certain special tenderness. Although I had loved all my children with a full heart, something about Omar tugged at my core. Perhaps that is why I nursed Omar longer than my other children.

My husband was deeply pleased. He repeated more than once that the birth of our children was in God's hands, and that Omar was from God, another blessing in our growing family.

Soon my husband took yet another trip to Pakistan to support our Muslim brothers in Afghanistan. Some trips lasted for more than a month, giving me extra time to amuse myself with little Omar. One day I noticed that Omar's blond hair was growing. Without thinking, I began to braid and pull Omar's hair into various chic styles, some fashions resembling the braids I had seen knotted into the tails of some of my husband's horses.

Omar was such an unusually beautiful baby that my urges took me further than hairstyles. I found myself designing and sewing little girl dresses, using Omar as my model for the clothing. It seemed a natural step to leave him in those sweet little clothes; after all, he was only a tiny baby who knew nothing of what he wore. Before long I was outfitting him entirely in little girl clothes. Pink was the best color for him because the shade looked so juicy up against his skin, as smooth and soft as velvet.

What fun I had with that precious baby! I was encouraged when my girl-friends declared that Omar grew more beautiful with each passing day. No one around me expressed criticism, so I failed to realize the consequences of my actions until my husband came home. As soon as Omar toddled into the room, my husband noticed Omar's long hair and feminine attire. My stomach fluttered with nerves as I watched to see what Osama might do or say.

At first Osama's face wore a puzzled expression as he squatted to the floor and tugged with his slim fingers on Omar's curls and girlish costume. He looked at Omar, then back at me, and back at Omar once again. Osama's long fingers brushed the pretty dress on our son and quietly announced, "Omar, this dress you are wearing is for a girl. You are a boy." He lightly brushed Omar's hair with his hand. "This hairstyle is for a girl. You are a boy."

My heart plunged in dread, for never did I seek my husband's displeasure. In fact, I was known to be the most obedient wife.

Finally my husband gazed up at me. He did not shout, but spoke even more softly than usual, his voice as smooth as silk. "Najwa, Omar is a boy. Put him in boy clothes. Cut this long hair."

I nodded mutely and did as I was told, at least temporarily.

My entertaining fantasy was over, at least when my husband was home. But I was still feeling naughty inside, at least on that one issue. As soon as Osama returned to Pakistan, my rebellion once again crept to the surface. I was so easily enticed by Omar's beauty that I instinctively pulled those girly dresses over Omar's head. My small joy continued until the afternoon when my husband walked into the house unexpectedly and I was caught in the act of admiring a pretty pink dress on Omar, whose hair was bouncing with curls.

Osama did not speak. He stood staring, his expression telling me that from that time on I should not tempt fate. And so I let go of my little sin, once again cutting Omar's hair into a boyish style and quietly folding away those little girl dresses. Yet hope remained alive that one day a daughter would grace our home to fill out those precious dresses.

Although there were many happy occasions, that was also a time filled with worries. After Omar was born, my husband began spending too many long weeks in Pakistan. When I accidentally overheard him tell other family members that some of his trips now included Afghanistan, I felt ill to think of the father of my children being in physical danger. Yet I did not dare complain, for my husband had made it abundantly clear that it was not my place to comment on anything outside our home.

We did not have a television, for my husband did not believe his family should be corrupted by such images, yet I learned through conversations with girlfriends and other members of my limited circle that my husband had become a well-known Saudi hero. I heard silly talk that many people wanted to inhale the very air that Osama breathed.

While it was no surprise that he and his brothers in the large bin Laden family gave much money to the cause, because the devout are well known to be generous when it comes to Muslim charities, everyone was astonished that a wealthy bin Laden son actually risked death or injury on the front lines.

Without knowing the specifics of my husband's military or political life, I felt keenly that there was danger in that Afghan air. Every day I prayed that God would keep him safe for me. I knew that my worries were not unreasonable after he returned to Jeddah with red raised scars all over his body. My own eyes told me that he continued to involve himself in dangerous missions, for he was wounded more than once.

I was also alarmed when Osama confessed that he had learned to fly a helicopter. After observing my anxious expression for a few days, my husband brought in a large round stick and placed it in my hands.

"Now, Najwa," he instructed, "hold the stick comfortably with your two hands, like this, and slowly move it around while you walk through the room."

I did as my husband said.

"Is that difficult for you?"

"No," I admitted.

"Then do not be worried about my safety. To pilot a helicopter is as easy as moving that stick."

On another occasion when I asked a few questions, he ordered, "Najwa, stop thinking."

That was that! Afterward, I tried to push away any thoughts of what Osama was doing when he was not by my side.

But one day when he was in a particularly good mood, he told me a little story that he had found amusing. Elated that he was finally sharing something of his adventures, I sat at his feet as solemn as an entranced child, so immersed in his story that I felt myself a participant in his adventure.

"There was one night that we went on a particularly dangerous mission inside Afghanistan, near the Pakistani border. The terrain in that mountainous region is so rough we could travel only by horse. There was an ongoing battle and our men needed armaments. Our mission was to deliver weapons to our fighters as quickly as possible, so we had to travel an exceptionally perilous route. Our horse train was so close to the Russian soldiers that if they lifted their eyes to look to the perimeter of their camp they would see us. We knew that we must pass through that enemy area as quietly as a feather falling from the sky.

"But there was a special worry. One of our fighters was riding a noisy little horse who was a talker. My, how that horse enjoyed whinnying. My men and I discussed how we were going to keep our talking horse quiet. Finally my closest friend on the mission had a clever idea. He took a small sack out of his bag, a sack made of coconut hair. He nodded at me with a small grin on his face, waving that rough sack. I had no idea how he thought that might solve the problem, but found out when he leaned forward, balancing himself close to the little horse face. The next time our talker opened his mouth, my friend pushed the sack in his mouth. Feeling the pressure of the sack, the startled horse quickly closed his mouth.

"Anytime the horse thought to open his mouth to talk, in went the sack. I had to force myself to look away or I would have laughed, alerting our enemy to our position."

My husband, who was the most serious person I've ever known rarely expressed even the most casual amusement, but suddenly he chuckled at the memory. I giggled, too, imagining the surprised expression on the little face of that chatty horse.

Other times I listened carefully as he spoke with our older sons about his military life. I cannot recall the date, or even the ages of our sons at the occasion, but I do remember once when he had been home for several weeks and enough time had passed that the tension in his mind and body was not so acute. He was sitting with a cup of tea and called our older sons into our sitting room, inviting them with his hand to sit. Knowing that most little boys dream of becoming soldiers, he had decided to share something of his life with them.

The boys looked a bit nervous. Their father was usually too busy for his sons, so they were worried as to why they had been summoned, afraid they had committed some act of disobedience and were about to be punished.

Although it was improper for me to sit in a circle of men, even if that circle was composed of my husband and sons, I remained in the room, busying myself with one thing or another so that I might overhear their talk.

My husband was in quite the rare good mood, entertaining our boys with his tale. "One night we were fighting and out of nowhere came a Russian helicopter. It was difficult to escape uninjured when such a thing happened on the battlefield.

"On that night we were in a specific region in Afghanistan where there was a large flat area where the terrain slowly gained in altitude until the ground reached some mountain caves. I was inside a cave when I heard the approach of a helicopter. I moved to the mouth of the cave to observe our exposed fighters.

Caught in the open, without time to seek shelter, I knew that there was little any of us could do to save them. I was fated to stand and watch a massacre, or so I thought.

"My heart pounded as I watched my fighters scatter. When the helicopter gunner began to fire upon my men, fighters began to dart from side to side. Some of them began to run backwards, then forwards. I was pleased to see that they had remembered their training as they had been told to keep a moving target. With such rapid, unpredictable movements, our brave fighters were not giving the Russian gunner an easy shot."

I glanced at my young sons. Being immature boys, they felt the excitement of it all, rather than the danger. Their faces were bright with wonder, hearing from their father about life and death during a heated battle. Their boyish minds were imagining those fast-footed soldiers dashing to and fro under the lights and bullets of the deadly machine.

My husband looked around at our boys, satisfied by their reaction to the story.

"That helicopter gunner was full of fighter heat. He was resolved to kill every man on the ground. Finally the battle became so intense that bullets flashed through the air like a fiery storm. Several of my soldiers were so disoriented to be caught out in the open that they stopped running. I watched as they kneeled in the sand. For a short moment I thought they were going to offer prayers. But instead they began frantically scraping holes in the dirt. Then they leaned forward to bury their heads in those small holes. They reminded me of insects going underground. They even patted the dirt around their heads."

Several of my boys let out a whoop of laughter, imagining those warriors with their heads buried in the sand.

Osama explained further, "The strange sight of all those posteriors in the air caused the helicopter pilot to fly away. Possibly he thought they were digging a new weapon out of the sand."

Our boys laughed boisterously, happy to be pulled into their father's adventurous life.

On another occasion, my husband expanded on his adventures, his soft voice louder than usual. Once again, I listened quietly.

"You boys have heard me speak of Abdullah Azzam. He was the best coordinator, organizing rallies and meetings all over the world, gathering charity, recruiting Muslims to go to Afghanistan to fight against the Russians. After recruiting, Abdullah would travel to the war zone and fight on the front lines himself."

I suddenly remembered that Abdullah Azzam was the man my husband had met in America when we had paid a visit to that state of Indiana. He was not only very smart, but very brave, according to my husband.

"On this past trip I was with Abdullah Azzam on the front line in Afghanistan. Suddenly our position was attacked by one of those dreaded helicopters. Missiles began flashing in every direction. We knew we would be killed unless we could find shelter.

"Suddenly God provided refuge! I saw two openings in the rocky mountainside. There were two small caves, very near to each other. Abdullah Azzam must have seen them at the same moment as his feet and mine grew wings as we raced across the battlefield. I don't know why but when I dashed into one cave, Abdullah Azzam ran into the other. I looked back as soon as I had safe shelter to see a missile perfectly hit the cave where Abdullah Azzam had gone. The missile triggered a landslide bringing down mounds of dirt and stones that completely clogged the entrance of the cave.

"I rushed to the mound of dirt and rocks and began hurling debris and burrowing through dirt. I had hardly made a crack in the rocky mound before the helicopter returned, once again making the air hot with flashing explosives. I was forced to retreat once more, although careful to keep my eyes on the mound of stones hiding the entrance. The firing would eventually cease and I would rescue Abdullah, or so I thought. But God had other plans."

Osama glanced at our sons, asking, "Do you know what happened?"

Our boys quietly murmured "La, la." (No, no.)

"I saw a miracle. God sent a second missile to hit the exact entry spot at the cave where Abdullah Azzam was trapped. That second explosive opened up the cave as cleanly as if it had been carved out by expert diggers." He nodded, remembering. "Abdullah Azzam came walking out of that God-made crevice as calmly as a man going to a picnic!"

My boys were awed by the thought of God's miracles.

A few days afterward, Osama informed me that he had plans that he believed would make me happy. He said that on his next trip to Peshawar, the city in Pakistan that was his base to gather supplies and organize fighters to be sent into Afghanistan, he was going to find a home suitable for our family. He had decided that on occasion, when our oldest boys were not in school, the family would go with him to Peshawar.

I had never been to Pakistan, but was eager to make the trip, wishing that we could accompany him sooner, rather than later.

For the past three years, Osama's life had resembled that of an industrious bird flying from one roost to another. He would fly from our home in Saudi Arabia, to Peshawar, in Pakistan, and from there dip into Afghanistan to connect with the Arab fighting forces on the ground. When he felt it vital to return to Jeddah, in order to raise additional funds for the fighters or work with his brothers in the bin Laden business, he would come back to us. But even when he was in Jeddah, his time with his family was severely limited; nearly every waking moment was crammed with important meetings regarding the battle against the Soviets or the construction business.

I was pleased to hear that we would be spending some time in Pakistan. I had grown weary of staying in Jeddah while my husband was away for months at a time; and our growing sons needed their father, particularly our youngest, the toddler Omar, who seemed to miss his father more than all the other boys combined.

By this time Osama and I had been married for eight years. Although there were tensions connected with his work in Afghanistan, for the most part, we had a sun-drenched marriage. I was more than pleased with my husband, and his behavior made it clear that he was equally happy with me.

How could I know that our married life would soon change forever?

Chapter 4

Born the Son of Osama bin Laden

OMAR BIN LADEN

Since the time I could observe and reason, I have mainly known my father to be composed, no matter what might be happening. That's because he believes that everything of earthly life is in the hands of God. It is difficult, therefore, for me to imagine that he became so excited when my mother told him it was time for me to be born that he momentarily misplaced his keys.

After a frantic search, I'm told that he settled my mother hastily in the car before spinning off at a reckless rate of speed. Luckily he had recently purchased a new automobile, the latest Mercedes, because on that day he tested all its working parts. I've been told it was golden in color, something so beautiful that I imagine the vehicle as a golden carriage tearing through the wide palm-tree-lined boulevards of Jeddah.

Within a short while after that chaotic journey, I made my appearance, becoming the fourth child born to my parents. I had three brothers who came before me, Abdullah, Abdul Rahman, and Sa'ad.

Mother has often reminded me that I was her most trying pregnancy, causing her genuine discomfort with my never-ending kicks. She had taken those months of my intense activity as a warning sign, in the same manner that scientists monitor a restless volcano. Mother knew that her fourth-born was going to have a forceful personality.

I was only one of many in a chain of strong personalities in our bin Laden family. My father, although quiet-natured in many ways, has always been a man that no other man can control. My paternal grandfather, Mohammed Awad bin Laden, was also quite famous for his strength of character. After the premature death of his father, who left behind a grieving widow and four young children, Grandfather bin Laden sought his fortune without a clue as to where he would end up. He was the eldest at eleven years.

Since Yemen offered few possibilities in those days, my grandfather bravely turned his back on the only land and the only people he had ever known, taking his younger brother, Abdullah, with him to join one of the many camel caravans trekking through the area.

After traveling through the dusty villages and towns of Yemen, they arrived at the port of Aden. From there they sailed a short distance across the Gulf of Aden to Somalia, on the African continent. In Somalia the two bin Laden boys were employed by a cruel taskmaster, known for his furious outbursts. One day he became so annoyed at my grandfather that he hit him on the head with a heavy stick.

The injury resulted in the loss of sight in one eye. My grandfather and uncle were forced to return to their village until his recovery. The following year they set out once again, this time traveling in the opposite direction, north to Saudi Arabia. I'm sure they were eager to stop at many outposts, but nothing seemed to have the magic they were seeking. The two boys, young and unlettered, lingered only long enough to earn sufficient money to stave off hunger and to continue what must have seemed an endless journey. Something about Jeddah, in Saudi Arabia, appealed to my grandfather, because that walled city on the Red Sea marked the end of their arduous voyage.

I once heard that a penniless man can only go up in the world. That was certainly true for my Grandfather bin Laden, who was poor, yet full of energy and determination. He felt no shame in tackling any honest labor. Jeddah was the ideal place for such a character, for the city and the country were at an economic turning point. In the early 1930s my grandfather's vigor, strength of mind, and attention to detail caught the attention of an assistant to King Abdul Aziz, the first king of Saudi Arabia, who had recently won many tribal wars and formed a new country, the Kingdom of Saudi Arabia.

King Abdul Aziz was known for his brilliance in getting the best out of men. He knew that he needed many smart, hardworking men to help modernize the kingdom, for his citizens were in need of hospitals, roads, businesses, and homes. The king was frustrated because he had many plans, but few competent builders to bring his plans to completion.

The assistant who had noticed the quality of my grandfather's work recommended him to the king. My grandfather genuinely liked the impressive king, who was physically and mentally strong. When the king asked my grandfather to make certain repairs, he was quick to do the work to the king's liking. With the success of that first job, other jobs came his way.

No one knew it at the time, but Saudi Arabia was set to become one of the richest and most influential countries in the world. After the 1932 formation of the kingdom, and the 1938 discovery of oil, the kingdom entered building boom never before witnessed. When the king wanted a new building or new roadway constructed, he turned to my grandfather. My grandfather's diligence and honesty so pleased the king that he was put in charge of the most coveted job for a believer, the expansion of the Grand Mosque in Mecca.

Everyone in our family knows that our Grandfather bin Laden had two main passions: work and women. He was extremely successful in both arenas. His ethic for hard work and total sincerity won him the complete trust of the king. With hard work came financial rewards, which enabled my grandfather to satisfy his second passion: women.

In my culture it is not uncommon for men, particularly the very wealthy and the very poor, to have four wives simultaneously. My grandfather was soon so rich that he not only married four women, but continually emptied several of the four marriage positions so that he could fill the vacated slots with new wives.

With so many wives and ex-wives, my grandfather had so many children that it was difficult for him to maintain a relationship with each child. As was the custom, he did give extra attention to the eldest sons, but most of his children were seen only on important occasions. This did not mean he did not follow the progress of his children; he would take time out of his busy schedule to make cursory checks to ensure that his sons were advancing in school or that his daughters married well.

Since my father was not one of the eldest sons, he was not in a position to see his father regularly. In addition, my grandfather's marriage to my father's Syrian mother, Grandmother Allia, was brief. After my father's birth, his mother became pregnant by Grandfather bin Laden for a second time, but when she lost that baby to a miscarriage, she asked her husband for a divorce. For some reason, the divorce was easily given and my Grandmother Allia was free, soon remarried to Muhammad al-Attas and becoming the mother of four more children.

Despite the fact that his stepfather was one of the finest men in Saudi Arabia, my father's life did not evolve as he wished. Like most children of divorced parents, he felt a loss, for he was no longer as intimately involved with his father's family. Although my father was never one to complain, it is believed that he keenly felt his lack of status, genuinely suffering from his father's lack of personal love and care.

I know how my father felt. After all, I'm one of twenty children. I've often felt that same lack of attention from my father.

My father was known to everyone in and out of the family as the somber bin Laden boy who became increasingly occupied with religious teachings. As his son, I can attest to the fact that he never changed. He was unfailingly pious, always taking his religion more seriously than most. He never missed prayers. He devoted many hours to the study of the Koran, and to other religious sayings and teachings.

Although most men, regardless of their culture, are tempted by the sight of a different female from the ones in their life, my father was not. In fact, he was known to avert his eyes whenever a woman not of his family came into his view. To keep away from sexual temptation, he believed in early marriages. That's the reason he made the decision to marry when he was only seventeen years old.

I'm pleased that my mother, Najwa Ghanem, who was my father's first cousin, was his first wife. The position of the first wife is prestigious in my culture, and that prestige is tripled when the first wife is a first cousin and mother of a first son. Rarely does a Muslim man divorce a wife who is a cousin and the mother of the firstborn son. My parents were bound by blood, marriage, and parenthood.

Never did I hear my father raise his voice in anger to my mother. He always seemed very satisfied with her. In fact, when I was very small, there were times that he and my mother secluded themselves in their bedroom, not to be seen by the family for several days, so I know that my father enjoyed my mother's company.

I understand his loyalty to my mother because she was a devoted wife and a wonderful mother. Her love for her children was indestructible. Although she was married to a wealthy man, and during the beginning years of their marriage had several housemaids assisting her, she personally took care of many of our needs, even hand-feeding us when we were sick.

In eyes as a son, my mother was a perfect mother.

My father was a different story. Although I cannot simply order my heart to stop loving my father, I do not agree with his behavior. There are times that I feel my heart swell with anger at his actions, which have harmed many people, people he did not know, as well as members of his own family. As the son of Osama bin Laden, I am truly sorry for all the terrible things that have happened, the innocent lives that have been destroyed, the grief that still lingers in many hearts.

My father was not always a man who hated. My father was not always a man hated by others. There was a time when many people spoke of my father with the highest accolades. History shows that he was once loved by many people. Despite our differences, I am not ashamed to admit that I loved my father with the usual passion of a young boy for his father. In fact, when I was a young boy, I worshipped my father, whom I believed to be not only the most brilliant but also the tallest man in the world. I would have to go to Afghanistan to meet a man taller than my father. In truth, I would have to go to Afghanistan to truly come to know my father.

I do have fond memories of my childhood. One early recollection involved teasing about a man having more than one wife. Many times when my father was sitting with his male friends, he would call out for me to come to him. Excited, I would follow the sound of his voice. When I would appear in the room, my father would be smiling at me, before asking, "Omar, how many wives are you going to have?"

Although I was too young to know anything of men and women and marriage, I did know the answer he was seeking. I would hold up four fingers and gleefully shout, "Four! Four! I will have four wives!"

My father and his friends would laugh with delight.

I loved making my father laugh. He laughed so seldom.

Many people found my father to be a genius, particularly when it came to mathematical skills. It was said that his own father was a numerical genius who could add up large columns of numbers in his head.

My father was so well known for the skill that there were times that men would come to our home and ask him to match his wits against a calculator. Sometimes he would agree, and other times not. When he would good-naturedly accept the challenge, I would grow so nervous that I would forget to breathe.

Each time I believed that he would fail the test. Each time I was wrong. We were all staggered that no calculator could equal my father's remarkable ability, even when presented with the most complicated figures. Father would calculate lengthy and complex figures in his head while his friends struggled to catch up to the math whiz with their calculators. I'm still amazed and have often wondered how any human being could have such a natural ability.

His phenomenal memory fascinated many who knew him. His favorite book was the Koran, so on occasion he would entertain those who would ask by reciting the Koran word for word. I would stand quietly in the background, often with a Koran in my hand, checking his recitation carefully. My father never missed a word. I can tell the truth now, that as I grew in years, I became secretly disappointed. For some strange reason, I wanted my father to miss a word here and there. But he never did.

He once confessed that he had mastered the feat during a time of great mental turmoil when he was only ten years old, after his own father had been killed in an airplane accident. Whatever the explanation for his rare gift, his champion performances made for many extraordinary moments.

I have bad memories, along with the good. Most inexcusable in my mind is that we were kept as virtual prisoners in our home in Jeddah.

There were many dangers lurking for the ones who had become involved in that increasingly complex quagmire that had begun with the Soviet invasion of

Afghanistan two years before I was born. My father had become such an important figure in the struggle that he had been told that political opponents might kidnap one of his children or even murder members of his family.

Because of such warnings, my father ordered his children to remain inside our home. We were not to be allowed to play outside, even in our own garden. After a few hours of halfhearted play in the hallways, my brothers and I would spend many long hours staring out the apartment windows, longing to join the many children we saw playing on the sidewalks, riding their bikes or skipping rope.

My father's piety made him strict in other ways. Although we lived in Jeddah, Saudi Arabia, which is one of the hottest and most humid cities in a country that is known for its hot climate, my father would not allow my mother to turn on the air-conditioning that the contractor had built into the apartment building. Neither would he allow her to use the refrigerator that was standing in the kitchen. My father announced, "Islamic beliefs are corrupted by modernization." Therefore, our food spoiled if we did not eat it on the day it was purchased. If my mother requested milk for her toddlers, my father had it delivered straight from cows kept on his family farm for just such a purpose.

My mother was allowed to cook her meals on a gas stove. And the family was permitted to use the electrical lighting, so at least we were not stumbling around in the dark, using wax candles to light dark rooms, or cooking food over an open fire.

My siblings and I hated such impractical directives, although my mother never complained.

There was one place where the sons of Osama bin Laden lived a fairly normal life. That was on our farm, located only a short drive south of Jeddah. Father built a family compound on the farm. The land was vast and the compound was large, with many buildings. The family homes were all painted a lovely soft peach to blend in with the calm color of the desert. There was a mosque on the compound because my father could not miss the five required daily prayers. My father's favorite building at the farm was the stables especially built for his beautiful horses.

My father loved the outdoors. He very carefully laid out an orchard, planting the area with hundreds of trees, including palms and other varieties. He also created a costly man-made oasis, cultivating reeds and other water plants. My father's eyes would sparkle with such happiness at the sight of a beautiful plant or flower, or pride at the spectacle of one of his prancing stallions.

It's good we had that farm to play on, because toys were forbidden, no matter how much we might beg. Father would give us some goats to play with, telling us that we needed nothing more than God's natural gifts to be happy. One lighthearted time he came walking in with a baby gazelle.

My mother was not pleased when my brothers and I slipped the gazelle through an open window and into our farm home. The coat of the gazelle was shedding, and when my mother found gazelle fur on the furniture, she raised her voice, which was unusual for her. Later we realized that she was pretending to be angry because we caught her secretly smiling at our antics.

I remember once when Father was given a baby camel as a gift. We were enthusiastic to have it on the farm, but soon realized that it was too young to be taken from its mother. The poor baby was so lonely and cried so pitifully that my father decided to take it to one of the farms belonging to his brother. But the baby camel was attacked by the other camels there, so he couldn't share their home. We never knew the outcome of the sad story, but I was haunted by that baby's misery for many days, as I have always loved animals and become terribly sad if one suffers.

Then one day one of my father's half-brothers arrived unexpectedly at our farm, his vehicle stuffed with toys! Never had we been so excited. For us, it was Eid (a Muslim holiday similar to Christian Christmas celebrations) a hundred times over! My father hid his anger from his brother, but not from us, remaining annoyed until all those toys were destroyed. But our uncle's kindness had made for one of the happiest days of our lives. Looking back, I suppose that our uncle felt sorry for us.

My father relented when it came to football—or soccer as Americans call it. When he brought a ball home, I remember the shock of seeing him smile sweetly when he saw how excited his sons became at the sight of it. He confessed that he had a fondness for playing soccer and would participate in the sport when he had time.

There was a second game, called the "hat game," that we sometimes enjoyed with my father. I'd bounce with glee when my father would instruct my oldest brother to go outside and mark the ground for the hat game. My brother would mark a line in an area of the yard where the sand was intentionally compacted to be nearly as hard as concrete.

My father would follow to place a man's hat on the line. Then he would go to the opposite side of the line and stand there, looking serious as he sized up his competition, his young sons.

My brothers and I would gather to stand in a row on the opposite side of the line, equally serious. The point of the game was to defeat your opponent in retrieving the hat, then run safely back to the starting line. Each person competed separately. At the countdown, the first boy in line would dash to grab the hat.

My father, watching from the other side, would wait until his opponent moved to race to the hat, pick it up, and return to the finish line. My father's goal was to catch the boy before he touched the finish line. My father had impossibly long legs, and was trim and fit, but his young sons could run as fast as the wind. Despite our ability to move quickly, my father was always the winner, because my brothers and I made it sure of it.

In my culture, we take care never to defeat someone who is older, and certainly never enjoy a victory against our fathers. Therefore, out of respect, my brothers and I always slowed our pace to make certain our father could catch us before we returned safely to the line.

For me, there was a sting attached to the game; I didn't think it was fair to pretend, to let someone win. Without confiding in my brothers, one day I decided that I was going to defeat my father by grabbing that hat and making undue speed back to the base. I would not let him catch me.

The next time we played the game, I knew that I would win. Until my turn came, the races went as usual, with my brothers allowing our father to catch them. But I roared off, fast and nippy, making it quickly to the hat, turning to race back to the base line. My father was shocked when he realized I was running too fast for him to catch me. He sailed through the air and I felt his hands as they made contact with my feet. But I slipped away with a few clever twists. I heard my brothers cry out when our father landed on the compacted dirt on his elbows.

Taking the full impact of his dive, he damaged his elbows and dislocated his right shoulder. The expression on my father's face told me that he was in legitimate pain. I hung back, shocked and dazed that I had caused the disaster. I was frightened to watch as my father was loaded into an automobile to be taken to the hospital in Jeddah.

Even after the initial medical treatment, we were told that my father would have to endure cortisone injections and physiotherapy for the next six months. The painful injury was serious and meant that he could not even travel to Pakistan, to return to his important work for Islam.

My brothers were annoyed with me, for they had grown to dislike my father's presence in Jeddah. They wanted him to return to Pakistan, for they said he was too strict when he was around us.

You might have guessed by now that my father was not an affectionate man. He never cuddled with me or my brothers. I tried to force him to show affection, and was told that I made a pest of myself. When he was home, I remained near, pulling attention-gaining pranks as frequently as I dared.

Nothing sparked his fatherly warmth. In fact, my annoying behavior encouraged him to start carrying his signature cane. As time passed, he began caning me and my brothers for the slightest infraction.

Thankfully, my father had a different attitude when it came to the females in our family. I never heard him shout at his mother, his sisters, my mother, or my sisters. I never saw him strike a woman.

He reserved all the harsh treatment for his sons.

Despite his cruelty, I so loved my father that I could not restrain my joy each time he returned from a long trip. As a child, I had little understanding of the situation in Afghanistan, although I overheard men speak of their dislike for the Russians. Yet I didn't hate the Russians because they occupied Afghanistan. I hated the Russians because they took my father away from me.

I remember one particular time when he had been away for longer than usual. I was desperate for his attention. He was sitting on the floor quietly studying intricate military maps. Hoping that he would not order me from the room, I watched him as he carefully laid his map flat on the floor, his earnest face puckered in thought, meticulously studying every hill and valley, mentally preparing for the next military campaign.

Unable to restrain myself a moment longer, I suddenly ran past him, laughing loudly, skipping, shifting my feet in various clever positions, striving to capture his attention. He waved me away, saying in a stern voice, "Omar, go out of the room." I darted out the door and stared at him for a few moments; then, unable to hold back my childlike excitement, I burst back into the room, laughing and skipping, performing a few more tricks. After the fourth or fifth repetition of my bouncing appearance, my exasperated father looked at me. He studied my dancing figure for a minute, then ordered me in his quiet voice, "Omar, go and gather all your brothers. Bring them to me."

I leapt with glee, believing that I had tempted my father away from his military work. Now I was certain that he would leave behind his worries to join his young sons in a game of ball. I smiled happily, running as fast as my short legs would take me. I was proud of myself, thinking that I was the only one with enough spark to remind him that he had young sons.

I gathered up each of my brothers, speaking rapidly in an excited voice, "Come! Father wants to see us all! Come!"

I failed to notice that my older brothers were not so eager to gain our father's attention.

I was still hopeful of good times even after my father ordered us to stand in a straight line. He stood calmly, watching as we obediently gathered, one hand clutching his wooden cane. I was grinning happily, certain that something very special was about to happen. I stood in restless anticipation, wondering what sort of new game he was about to teach us. Perhaps it was something he played with his soldiers, some of whom I had heard were very young men.

Shame, anguish, and terror surged throughout my body as he raised his cane and began to walk the human line, beating each of his sons in turn. A small lump ballooned in my throat.

My father never raised his soft voice as he reprimanded my brothers, striking them with the cane as his words kept cadence, "You are older than your brother Omar. You are responsible for his bad behavior. I am unable to complete my work because of his badness."

I was in the greatest anguish when he paused before me. I was very small at the time and to my childish eyes, he appeared taller than the trees. Despite the fact I had witnessed him beating my brothers, I could not believe that my father was going to strike me with that heavy cane.

But he did.

The indignity was unbearable, yet none of us cried out, knowing that such an emotional display would not have been manly. I waited until he turned his back to walk away before running in the opposite direction. I could not face my brothers, knowing that they were sure to blame me for bringing our father's cane down on their backs and legs.

I went for solace in the horse stables, seeking out my favorite horse, a beautiful white Arabian mare called Baydah. She was about fourteen hands high, with a coal black tail and mane. I thought she was a queen, with her strong, proud stance. Baydah loved me, too, and could pick me out from a large crowd, galloping to me to pluck a juicy apple from my fingertips. I remained with Baydah for hours, so stricken that I could not think coherently. As the sun began to leave the sky, I forced myself to return home, for I was too frightened to cause a further ruckus. I slipped in without notice, wanting to avoid my brothers, who surely blamed me for their beatings. Once in bed the dam of sorrow burst with sudden and unexpected loud wails coming from deep within.

My cries were so loud that my worried mother came into the room and asked, "Who is that crying?"

Mortified, I buried my head in my pillow so that the sounds of my misery might be muffled.

Now that I am an adult, I believe that perhaps my father had too many children at too young an age. Or perhaps he was so entangled with his war work that our importance failed to register against such a massive cause as fighting the Russians.

During my childhood, I can recall one magical moment when my father held me in his arms. The charmed incident was connected to prayer time.

When Father was home, he commanded his sons to accompany him to the mosque. One day when we were at the farm, the sound of the muezzin's call to the midday prayer rang out. My father in turn called out for us to join him. I was excited, looking upon prayer time as a wonderful excuse to be near my father. On that day I failed to slip on my sandals, which we always kept by the front door, a custom in our country.

At midday, the sands are blistering hot. Running about without sandals, the bare soles of my feet were soon burning. I began jumping about, crying out from the pain. My father stunned me when he leaned his tall figure low, and lifted me into his arms.

My mouth went dry from disbelief. Never could I recall being held in my father's arms. I was instantly happy, leaning in close. My father always used the marvelous incense called Aoud, which has a pleasing musklike scent.

I looked down at my brothers from my favored high perch and grinned, feeling jubilant, like the privileged dwarf atop the giant's shoulders, seeing beyond what the giant could see.

I was only four or five years old at the time, but I was stocky. My father was tall and thin and, although fit, was not very muscular. Even before we reached the mosque door, I could sense that I had become a heavy burden. He began breathing heavily, and for that I was sorry. Yet I was so proud to be nestled in his capable arms that I clung tightly, wanting to remain in that secure spot forever. Too soon he deposited me on the ground and walked away, leaving me to scramble behind him. My short legs failed to match his impossibly long strides.

Soon my father appeared as elusive as a distant mirage.

Chapter 5

Marriage Surprises

NAJWA BIN LADEN

At the time I became pregnant with my fifth child, Osama chose to raise an unexpected topic; he said he was thinking of taking a second wife. Although polygamy is a recognized practice in my culture, few women dance with joy when they contemplate sharing their husband with another woman.

Despite my unease at his suggestion, I understood that I was more fortunate than many. I had heard of Saudi husbands who marry other women without even discussing their plans with their current wife. So I felt relieved when Osama promised not to bring another woman into our lives unless I agreed with his decision.

I believed that Osama wanted to take a second wife in order to follow the actions of our Prophet. Our Prophet Mohammed was twenty-five years old when he married his first wife, Khadijah bint Khuwaylid. Khadijah was fifteen years older than her husband, yet the marriage lasted for twenty-five years, during which time the Prophet did not take another wife. Upon Khadijah's death, Prophet Mohammed did marry other women, although a number of his wives were older women whose husbands had died on the battlefield and needed the protection gained through marriage. Scholars believe that Prophet Mohammed married between twelve and thirteen women over the course of his lifetime.

The reference for the number of legitimate wives is clear in our holy book, the Koran, in Sura 4:3:

> *If ye fear that ye cannot act with equity towards orphans, take in marriage of such women as please you two or three or four. But if ye fear that ye cannot act equitably (towards so many), marry one only, or the slaves which ye shall have acquired.*

Based on this verse, it is the opinion of Islamic scholars that a believer may marry four wives, but no more. And, a man may not marry more than one wife if he cannot treat all equally, which is the tricky part.

Despite my strong religious beliefs, and my complete faith in God, I am still a woman, and I was wavering over Osama's plan to bring another female into our lives. In my culture, wives of the same man are expected to become friends, and for their children to play with one another.

My husband calmed me by telling me again and again that if I did not approve, he would not take other wives. His heart could not bear to hurt my heart about such a matter. My husband said that he would leave one of the most important personal decisions of his life entirely up to me.

I knew that few wives in Saudi Arabia would receive such respect and consideration. So I allowed the idea to burrow in my mind.

For some months the subject of Osama marrying another woman remained a big topic of discussion between us. One evening, my husband revealed his deepest thoughts, confessing that his aim was purely to have many children for Islam. Hearing his words, I suddenly found myself becoming more relaxed about the idea. My husband was not seeking a second wife out of unhappiness with me, but for the greater good of Islam.

At the end of that exchange, Osama realized that I was seeing the wisdom of his taking other wives. He gently reminded me of a very significant truth. "Najwa, if you are contented in your heart for me to take a second wife, you will gain in heaven. It is certain that your life will end in paradise."

My heart finally became tranquil, feeling for certain that my understanding attitude would intensify righteousness in my own life. That is when Osama felt comfortable enough to set about taking a second wife. I did not ask, nor receive, permission to have a voice in the actual selection of Osama's second wife.

And so it came to pass that Osama married again. I did not attend the wedding, but the ceremony was conducted as our faith demands. His second wife was a Saudi woman with the first name of Khadijah, the same name of a woman who married our Prophet. I was told that Khadijah was of the highly respected Sharif family, descendants of Prophet Mohammed. She was a few years older than Osama, well educated, and a teacher of girls at a school in Jeddah.

Anytime a Muslim follows Prophet Mohammed's actions, it is a good thing. Therefore, I was gracious as I welcomed Khadijah into our large home where she was assigned her own roomy apartment, although to be honest I will say that it took some time before I easily accepted that now I would share my husband equally with another woman.

From that day forward, Osama said that he must obey the teachings of Islam regarding multiple wives. Khadijah and I would be treated the same. This meant that everything of my husband would be shared equally—his thoughts, his time, and even gift giving.

As exacting as he was about every Islamic requirement, I knew that Osama would alternate evenings between our home and the home of his new wife. And as a good Muslim wife, I knew I must accept the situation with a clean feeling and a good heart. Otherwise, I would not be rewarded in heaven.

Yet I was not prepared for the quiet feeling in our home on the nights Osama did not make an appearance. As a woman who rarely stepped outside the walls of my home, I missed my husband and the excitement his arrival brought. Striving to be a good Muslim, I fought my feelings of emptiness, for I knew that what my husband was doing was sanctioned by Islam.

My children were instructed to honor and respect my husband's second wife, and I taught them to call her "Khalti" or "auntie mother's side."

Everything came together in a smooth manner, and soon Osama's second wife and I were enjoying routine visits where we would share books, or read together, or even take some of our meals together. I benefited from Khadijah's company and looked forward to our hours together. Over time we became friends.

No long afterward, I gave birth to my fifth son, Osman. I was so contented to look upon his sweet face that for the first time I did not mourn at my failure to have a daughter.

One year after their marriage, Khadijah bore her first child, a little boy named Ali. Therefore, from the day of Ali's birth Khadijah was called by the honorable title Um Ali, which means mother of Ali. Likewise, I had been called Um Abdullah from the first moment my son was born. Those familiar with my husband called him Abu Abdullah, for a man is also titled by his first son's name.

From that time, Khadijah and I had our children in common. My youngest sons became Ali's playmates.

Not so long after Ali's birth, Osama arranged to take his family to Pakistan for the first time. Several years had passed since Osama had first promised to arrange a home for us in Peshawar, but pregnancies and his second marriage had delayed our journey.

As Osama's two wives and six lively sons boarded a commercial flight in Jeddah to fly to the Peshawar international airport, I was eager to see what my husband had been seeing for the past five years.

Compared to the restraint of Saudi Arabia, Peshawar felt like a colorful place for a Muslim city, with people in various ethnic costumes traveling around in garishly painted buses and taxis. Being accustomed to isolation, I thought the city looked dazzling. After the Russians invaded Afghanistan in 1979, Peshawar had become a virtual refugee camp for the Pashtun of Afghanistan, so there were even burqa-clad women shopping in the sidewalk bazaars. The burqa serves the same purpose as the abaaya, which is to cloak a modest Muslim woman from head to toe, although the styles of the two costumes are different. While the Saudi abaaya is black, a burqa can be pastel blue, yellow, brown, or other colors. The design is quite showy, with a lattice screen covering a woman's eyes, while there are embroidered designs on the front, and tiny pleats billow out from the back.

Osama had found a beautiful villa with enough room for his growing family. Although enjoying the change of scenery, Khadijah and I continued to live in virtual isolation, with our family life carrying on as usual, while Osama continued his business outside our home, even making frequent trips into Afghanistan. I was pleased that Osama devoted more time to our sons, and on one or two occasions, he even took our eldest, Abdullah, who was eight years old, with him into Afghanistan.

After spending three summer months in Peshawar, Osama said that he would escort us back to Jeddah, for our two eldest sons were already enrolled in school. Since the trip had gone well, from that point it was not unusual for us to spend our summers in Peshawar.

A year after the birth of Khadijah's first son, Ali, I found myself pregnant yet again. This time, after five sons, I was certain I would have a daughter. Although my husband was even more involved in the war in Afghanistan, he returned to me in Jeddah for the birth. When the sixth child turned out to be another boy, we gave him the most special name for a Muslim, which is Mohammed.

My six sons, together with Ali, made the bin Laden home decidedly lively. I'm sure that many men were in awe of my husband and his house of seven sons.

Soon after Mohammed was born, my husband approached me regarding his desire to take a third wife. According to my husband, the time was coming when Islam would need many more followers, and he wanted to have more sons and daughters to carry forth the message of God. On this occasion Osama suggested that he would be pleased if I would find him a suitable wife. After thinking on the subject for only a few days, I agreed. My heart told me that if I did this important thing for him and for Islam, my love for my husband would live and grow even more.

Surely God was guiding me in this important duty, for within a few weeks of our conversation, I met a lovely Saudi woman from Jeddah. Her name was Khairiah Sabar, and she was a highly specialized teacher of deaf-mute children.

For me, it was important that the women my husband married were devout. Khairiah was very religious, but she had other qualities that drew me to her. From the first moment my eyes saw her charming face, I liked Khairiah. Every new discovery about her religious life and her fine Sabar family increased my affection. I went back and forth between Osama and Khairiah's family, reaching the routine agreements of dowry and other points, so that I could arrange their engagement.

By the time their wedding came to pass, I had grown to love Khairiah as a precious sister. My sincere feeling for her has grown with each passing year.

I helped to settle Khairiah into her separate apartment in our large home. Her fresh presence added to my pleasure, and we spent many hours reading and discussing the Koran and other aspects of our religion.

While Osama's third wedding had made 1985 exciting, 1986 was more settled, at least for the wives and children. For the first year in a long time, there were no new babies born during the calendar year.

For the wives, our main concern was the care and happiness of our little children and the running of the household. We were expected to supervise the housemaids and tea girls, as well as keep our children on their schedules, as the oldest had reached school age. With three wives, seven active boys, some of whom were attending school, many housemaids, tea girls, cooks, and drivers, our home was a busy beehive. It mattered little that our home was a huge dwelling, with twelve large apartment areas, for with so many people scurrying about to complete their many duties, the human traffic created deafening noise and action, even on a day of routine pursuits.

Osama's wives used to joke that our Jeddah home was a virtual mini-U.N. with people employed from the Philippines, Sri Lanka, Africa, Egypt, Yemen, and many other countries. Even though Osama had arranged for several drivers to transport our sons to school and to shop for our groceries and necessary items, all three wives were busy keeping everything organized.

As Osama's first wife, considered to be the most important wife in our Muslim society, I was given much respect by everyone around me, including his two new wives. Yet I never felt myself above Khadijah or Khairiah. Osama's wives had become my friends. Conflict was unknown among the wives of Osama bin Laden.

Once again I became pregnant in 1986. I was earnestly hoping that Khairiah would announce a pregnancy, but that happy day had not yet come.

Around that time my husband came to me and announced that he would soon be taking a fourth wife. He did discuss his thoughts, although he did not ask for my express approval or participation. Besides, I felt that to find Osama one wife was quite enough.

Osama's new wife was the sister of one of his Saudi fighters in Afghanistan. The family was from Medina, and her name was Siham. I did not attend the ceremony, although I helped Osama's wife to become settled in our home.

Shortly after his fourth wedding, Osama told us news that I would have never expected. Our family would be moving to Medina, two hundred miles northeast of Jeddah, because Osama would be supervising a bin Laden construction project in that city.

While I liked living in Jeddah best, Medina is a significant city in Islam because Prophet Mohammed fled there when he was initially driven out of Mecca by unbelievers; it is the site of the Prophet's home and of his tomb. Medina is known to Muslims as "The Radiant City" or "The City of the Prophet," and is so holy that it is second only to Mecca in the hearts of all Muslims.

Our routine days ended with Osama's announcement. Chaos ruled as we organized our personal items for Osama's packers.

In the beginning of our married life Osama was quite generous, but as time went on, he grew austere, believing that to be a good Muslim one must embrace simplicity. With this new way of thinking firmly in place, Osama decreed that our home furnishings should be plain, our clothing modest in number, and our food simple. The only area where Osama splurged was on his automobiles, which were always the latest models. Therefore, Osama's wives and children never acquired the masses of household goods or personal items loved by many people of the modern world. Despite this, the family was so large that even the bare necessities of life filled many packing boxes.

Although I loved Medina, for who could not love a city special to our Prophet Mohammed, I was not excited about leaving Jeddah. That was where I felt most comfortable, with my Auntie Allia and her family nearby, as well as a few girlfriends. The family farm used for weekend jaunts was only a short distance away. The four-hour drive to Medina was enough to discourage casual visits to Osama's family or spontaneous trips to Osama's farm. Since I was pregnant, I was not happy about being away from familiar territory when my child arrived.

But there was nothing I could do to alter the situation.

In Medina we moved into a spacious villa owned by my husband. It was huge, at least four times the size of a normal home, with four large stories. But with four wives, soon to be eight children, and many servants, our family easily filled most of the space.

As Osama's first wife and the mother of his firstborn son, I lived on the top level, but each wife had her own separate floor, including bedrooms, bathrooms, sitting areas, and kitchens. While the excitement of living in the City of the Prophet never ceased, it soon became clear that most members of the family missed Jeddah.

My seventh child soon livened up our lives, however.

Despite the move, my pregnancy had been calm. After giving birth to six sons, pregnancy had become routine in my life. I had finally accepted that I would be the contented mother of many sons. I had even trained my thoughts not to drift to the pastel tints of the girl's clothes locked away in a storage bin.

Osama made certain he was home at the time I gave birth and once again we took a predictable dash to a hospital in Medina. Thankfully, my labors were becoming easier and the baby came quickly. Through a fog I heard my doctor speak, bringing me news that brought forth a gasp. After thirteen years of marriage and six sons, Najwa Ghanem was the mother of a baby girl! A thrill of anticipation swept throughout my body. The feeling in my heart was like no other when I looked upon a face so sweet I felt I was gazing at pure sugar.

Osama seemed pleased as well, but said that his happiness came from witnessing my elation. We named our darling girl Fatima, a favored Muslim name for girls because the Prophet had named his daughter Fatima.

I felt myself in a rush to return home with my precious daughter so that I could dig into those boxes of girly clothes. What joy! That first year with my little daughter was one of the happiest of my life.

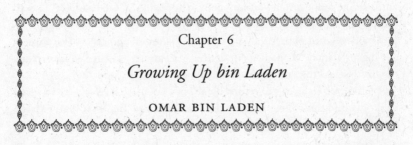

Chapter 6

Growing Up bin Laden

OMAR BIN LADEN

The children of Osama bin Laden felt it normal for our father to marry women other than our mother and to bring those women to live in our home. I was two years old when my father married his second wife; four when he married his third wife; and six when he married his fourth wife.

I thought little of the fact there were four women living under one roof, and that all four women were married to the same man, my father. My mother's demeanor appeared positive so there was no reason for her children to respond in any other way. In fact, my mother sweetly taught us to respect the women my father married.

There are many reasons that multiple wives are viewed so favorably in Saudi Arabia. Culturally, Saudi culture is dominated by men. Although there are a few token women in organizations that deal with women's issues only, it is men who make all the important decisions. When it comes to private life, it is true that some women make personal rulings regarding the organization of their households, but their actions are based on the hope of pleasing their husbands.

In our home, the wives of my father were instructed on the behavior that was expected of them and their children, although my mother has said that her husband often discussed personal matters with her before making a final decision.

This patriarchal system has been in place in the Arabian Peninsula since the beginning of time. In ancient days, men married as many women as they pleased, with some men marrying hundreds of women. When a man wearied of a woman, he could desert her without any legal obligations. The same was true regarding female babies. It was not unusual for unwanted female offspring to be buried alive. Quite simply, females were property of males and could be discarded at the will of the man who was in charge of their destiny, whether that man was her father, husband, uncle, or son.

After Prophet Mohammed laid the formation of the Islamic faith, women's lives vastly improved. Islam forbade the killing of baby girls. Females were provided with specific financial rights, including the right to own property. Islam limited a man to no more than four wives, with the important stipulation that he must care for each wife in exactly the same manner.

Some Islamic scholars believe such a relationship with four wives is essentially unachievable, and that was the rationale behind Prophet Mohammed's limiting provision. Other scholars have varying opinions, with a large number saying that it is entirely possible for a fair-minded man to treat four wives identically. For this reason, Saudi men remain free to marry up to four wives.

I have always liked the opposite sex. I was not yet in school when I first realized that love between a man and woman was a very powerful emotion. Women were on my mind, for my father had recently taken another wife.

I first fell in love when I was very young. Despite my immaturity, I was struck so strongly that I felt as though a bolt of lightning had collided with my heart. My love was an "older woman," a beautiful eight-year-old girl who was the daughter of my mother's friend. She was tall, with chestnut-colored hair that reached to her waist, lush olive skin, and exotic doe-shaped black eyes. Her physical magnetism was so potent that I just stared at her. Nothing came of it, of course, due to my youth.

Meanwhile, I found great joy in horses and riding. My father, a natural horseman who had ridden since childhood, introduced his sons to his love of horses at an early age.

The first time I rode a horse was when I was four or five. I was with Abdullah, my oldest brother, who was nine or ten at the time. My father had trusted his firstborn son with the honor of easing his youngest into the world of horses. Abdullah felt the responsibility keenly.

I remember little of that day, other than the basics. I do recall being carefully positioned on a saddle with Abdullah behind me. Being on a horse for the first time, I became excited and quickly lost my balance. I was a strapping child, and grasped my brother's arms and neck with such force that I took him with me as I fell to the hard dirt under the horse's hooves. Thankfully the mare was accustomed to children, and managed at the last minute to dance around our small bodies.

My brother was shaken by the fall and more than a little worried that he would be blamed if his baby brother was injured, so he announced that we had "learned enough about horses for one day."

Although I had taken an early spill, I was eager to try again. Within a year or two, I was riding bareback with my brothers.

Occasionally I also rode with my mother. My mother liked riding, although she faced two obstacles. First, she was pregnant during most of my youth, and knew that horseback riding would be dangerous for her and the child she was carrying. Second, she could not be seen riding horses by any men outside our immediate family, so her outings had to be carefully planned.

Horses became the center of my life. I hated the fact that my father had given permission for me to ride only the gentlest horses in his stable, and was eager to ride the most powerful stallions, like my older brothers.

I can't recall my age when I first rode a stallion, but I know I had been riding for only a few years when my three older brothers and I accompanied our father and a group of seven friends into the desert. The adults were riding horses. For some reason I can't remember, my father's sons were following along in a four-wheel drive.

Suddenly, our driver came to a skidding stop; one of my father's friends had been thrown from a rambunctious horse. Thankfully, the man was not badly injured and was able to limp away from the incident, but he decided to continue the day's journey in the automobile. That's when our father galloped up with the reins of the rider-less horse dangling from his fingers. He bent down, glanced into the car, and asked, "Who wants to ride?"

My three older brothers avoided our father's eyes. I was surprised, thinking that it was a great opportunity. Already bold for my years, I leapt out of the automobile, declaring, "I will! I will ride!"

Never had I been allowed to ride such a big, powerful horse, and was afraid my father would say no, but he shrugged his agreement. I was so small he had to dismount to lift me into the saddle. Despite my size, I was feeling quite the big man, excited that the time had come when I could prove my excellent horsemanship.

The shock came quickly. Before I was even settled in the saddle, my father and his friends abruptly galloped away. Without prompting, my big stallion shivered in excitement and leapt forward after the other horses. Had my horse wings? I wondered, because I was flying through the desert so rapidly that I couldn't tell which way I was going, positioned so high above the ground that I felt myself atop a mountain. Clinging for dear life, I tried every trick I knew to stop the horse, but the stallion ignored every command of his tiny passenger. In fact, rather than slowing his pace, my horse gained momentum. Too late I learned that although I was a proficient horseman for my age, that didn't mean I could handle any situation. I screamed for my father, *Father! Stop the horse! Stop the horse!"*

Thanks to Allah that my father finally heard my cries for help. He turned around and came to me, skillfully plucking the horse reins out of my hand, slowing the stallion to a full stop.

I tried not to show my immense relief, although I silently admitted that my riding skills were not yet perfected. I jumped down from that frisky stallion, determined to walk the remainder of the journey. Deeming that I was safe, my father and his friends left me in the dust. Soon the automobile transporting my brothers passed me. Sensing that they were enjoying my plight, I took care not to make eye contact with any of my brothers. The vehicle slowly cruised past.

Too soon, riders, horses, and the car disappeared into the haze of the desert. I was completely alone, my small hands grasping the reins of a horse that I knew I could not control. I felt a nervous lump thumping in my throat.

Suddenly something spooked the stallion. He reared to his full height, front legs bucking, back legs dancing, his intense power heaving the reins. I gripped the reins in a vain attempt to keep him in check, and although strong for my age, I didn't have the muscle to restrain him, or even to hold on to the reins. The horse gave one final buck before zipping away. Terrified of the consequences if I lost one of my father's prized stallions, I dove for a stirrup, miraculously seizing it with my hand. I held on tight, feeling my knees and feet sting as I was roughly dipped back and forth to the ground, yanked through sagebrush, dirt, and small stones.

My wild ride ended when the stirrup broke loose. The world around me stilled. I was crumpled in the dirt, sputtering sand and coughing dust, but still clutching the broken stirrup. When I looked at my escaped charge, I got a final view of the stallion's haunches and tail as he moved like the wind. The unbearable had happened. Not only had I been unable to control one of my father's prize stallions, I had lost the horse. I sat quietly, looking around, wondering what to do next.

Soon the desert came alive with a welcome clatter. Our worried driver had circled back to check on me. I jumped to my feet. Over the din of the automobile I could hear the sounds of my brothers' laughter. The car pulled along beside me. I was so ashamed that I didn't know what to do, so I tried to pretend I didn't have a care in the world.

My father soon came galloping back, surprising me with his visible concern for my well-being. When I haltingly revealed what had occurred, my father let out a rare laugh, giving my brothers the courage to laugh so hard that they exposed their teeth, which was not allowed in our family.

The noise of the car engine failed to muffle my brother's guffaws. Everyone was laughing at me, other than our Yemeni driver. How I loved that kindly man. He had been our driver since I was a child, and although he had children of his own, he took a special interest in us. I shot him a look of appreciation.

As my brothers continued laughing, my humiliation ballooned. Not wanting my father or brothers to know that I was ashamed, I began laughing with them. Soon I found myself unable to stop laughing, my merriment at such an excessive pitch that tears rolled out of my eyes and down my face.

There was only one bit of good news in that most unpleasant day. After abandoning me to my fate, Father's stallion had raced back to the farm, where we later found him impatiently waiting for us at the stable gate.

The older I became, the more surprises I learned about how the sons of Osama bin Laden were expected to live. As we all discovered, my father had a lot of unusual ideas about what he called the "evils of modern life."

For example, my brothers and I all suffered from asthma and had endured many serious bouts during our youth, particularly while playing sports in the hot desert climate. On a number of occasions, I had been rushed to the hospital and connected to oxygen. Concerned that my brothers and I were repeat asthma patients, the doctors advised our father to keep a supply of Ventolin on hand and to have his children use an inhaler, but my father was adamant that we not take modern prescription drugs, no matter how serious our affliction.

Regarding all things except modern transportation, our father decreed that we must live just as the Prophet had lived whenever possible. Since modern medicines were unknown in those ancient days, we were not to take them. In fact, unless one of us was near death, my father refused all modern medical treatment.

His recommended treatment for asthma was for us to break off a piece of honeycomb and breathe through the comb. This did little good, but still our father would not relent, first making his claim about the life of the Prophet, then warning us that Ventolin would destroy our lungs.

Often I felt as though I was struggling to breathe through a straw, but unless death came knocking, my suffering was ignored. When Abdullah grew older, he heard about Ventolin and sneaked and purchased a supply. He gave me permission to use his inhaler.

I did so at the onset of the next attack. After two puffs, my life was transformed. Mother eventually discovered that we were disobeying our father's orders by using inhalers, but thankfully she never reported our defiance to our father. Mother only cared that we were no longer suffering.

Until we were teenagers living in Afghanistan, none of us had ever met anyone who shared our father's severe views. From the time we were old enough to talk, my father made it clear that we were expected to adhere to specific rules as to how a Muslim boy should live.

Like children everywhere, we tried to circumvent those rules at every opportunity. For example, Father forbade us to drink fizzy drinks that came from America. How we loved the forbidden! We obeyed his decree regarding American products so long as he was in sight, but heartily consumed Pepsi-Cola and other soft drinks whenever we got the chance.

There were other unexpected rules that had nothing to do with his aversion to western products. From the time we were toddlers, he demanded that we be given very little water. As we grew older, he reinforced the importance of drinking water only when absolutely necessary. He explained that his children should be "tough" and "patient," so we must set our minds to resist nourishment of any kind for as long as possible.

Identical rules were set in place for his daughters, but he left our mother in charge of instilling discipline in them. My sisters were more fortunate because our mother found it impossible to resist the cries and pleas of her little girls for water or food.

Even when we were very young, our father would transport his sons into the dry desert outside the Jeddah farm, adamant that we accompany him on long walks, even though we were all given to asthma attacks. His harshest ruling was that we could not drink any water until we returned from our hike. We were told that we should not even "think" about water. Of course, anyone knows that walking in the desert dangerously depletes the body of liquids. In fact, the government tells visitors to the deserts in Saudi Arabia to consume as much water as they can.

The sons of Osama bin Laden were taught the contrary, that we must train ourselves to remain for long hours in the desert without any liquids. Bin Laden sons must learn to be physically immune to inhospitable desert heat, to make our bodies and minds strong and sturdy. We were repeatedly warned that we must be prepared to face desert warfare when the infidel West attacked the Muslim world, a belief that first developed in his mind when I was a baby and grew with every passing year.

There were so many of these sessions that most of them have merged in my memory, although I do recall one specific trip when my father announced, "Today we are going to add rigorous training to our program. We will include mountain climbing. I have selected an area where there are many steep hills." His soft voice dropped. "There will be no water until we descend the hills." Despite this, we knew that he often carried a small container of water in case anyone collapsed from the heat.

My brothers and I were downcast at the prospect, but did not protest. We had tried reasoning with our father before. Instead of a useless argument, I decided to prepare myself mentally.

Off we went with our driver, who was always ordered to accompany us on such jaunts, obediently trailing in our father's footsteps. Up we walked, the searing Saudi sun beaming down on our heads, our legs soon becoming tight with the steep incline. No one could keep pace with my father. He had physically trained himself since youth. Although he was not a man of muscles, no one could hike with the relentless persistence of Osama bin Laden. After observing him on many desert excursions, I had the childish thought that my father could circle the globe without a moment's respite or a drop of water.

By the time we were halfway up the high hill, our poor Yemeni driver's eyelids were mere slits. I watched as his face paled, his steps slowed, and his breath became labored. His voice was pitiful when he croaked out, "Water . . . I must have water . . ."

At first my father ignored him. He relented only when the poor man, who was of an age that white hairs were sprouting in his beard, slumped to the ground and commenced begging. "I will die without water, Sheik Osama. I will die. Just a drop, please, one drop . . ."

I was so relieved when his thirst was quenched that I let out a rush of breath. Unfortunately, our driver's water hysteria grew contagious. Soon one of my older brothers began to weep, believing that he, too, would perish without a drink of water. I walked steadily, staring at my feet, yet listening as one by one my brothers gave in, beseeching my father for a small sip of water.

My father clicked his lips in disappointment as he rationed the water, giving each of my brothers a few sips. I studied his expression, so bland with insensitivity. Boiling anger heated my heart and mind even more than the desert sun! I decided I would rather die than beg. It would serve him right if he had to tell my mother that he had killed one of her sons.

With my pounding head keeping time with my loud heartbeat, and my throat so parched that my tongue began to swell, I refused to allow the words I longed to shout escape from my lips. Never have I wanted water with such intensity. But I never faltered. I walked steadily until I took that final step at the base of the hill.

I looked at my father in triumph. I had passed his inhuman test. I had not pleaded for water. The two of us were the only ones who succeeded in making it to the base of hill without taking a drink of water.

Looking back, I know now that my father was surprised that one of his youngest sons on the trail was the last male standing.

There were other absurd rules regarding our conduct. We were allowed to speak in his presence, but our voices must be kept low and our words carefully measured. In other words, we should not "over-talk." We were told that we must not become excited at any situation. We should be serious about everything. We were not allowed to tell jokes. We were ordered not to express joy over anything. He did say that he would allow us to smile so long as we did not laugh. If were to lose control of our emotions and bark a laugh, we must be careful not to expose our eyeteeth. I have been in situations where my father actually counted the exposed teeth, reprimanding his sons on the number their merriment had revealed.

The older sons of Osama bin Laden were all adversely affected by our father's fanaticism. As a child, Abdullah, the firstborn son, never sought friend-ships with other boys, preferring a solitary life. His greatest joy was riding a motorbike. When we were at the farm, Abdullah would leap on his motorbike and disappear for hours, his hair blowing in the breeze as he vanished into the desert.

My next brother, Abdul Rahman, born in 1978, was a solitary personality, often sitting on his own and staring without purpose. I remember when he was a young boy, he would go on a wild frenzy of activity, destroying household items or perhaps seeking tamer pursuits, such as playing with pieces of paper for hours on end.

Whatever was the problem, I believe that Abdul Rahman was unable to draw the usual boundaries between himself and others. For example, even though he was enthralled with animals, particularly horses, there were times in his childhood when his personality would alter and he would become cruel to the very animals he professed to love. This trait first manifested itself when Abdul Rahman was very young.

My father had also noticed trouble during Abdul Rahman's younger years and once shared a disturbing incident with me: "Omar, I remember visiting my mother when your brother was a toddler. Mother's pet cat walked into the room. Abdul Rahman rushed to grab the cat. He held her hard between his hands. I did not know what he was thinking to do, and then in a big surprise, Abdul Rahman bit the cat. Before we could pull the cat from Abdul Rahman, the poor cat clawed your brother and scampered away. We believed it to be a passing incident, but later in the evening I caught Abdul Rahman stalking the cat. Moving quickly, he got her in his grip once again, biting the cat yet again until it shrieked from the pain."

My father shook his head in sorrow, saying nothing more.

Sa'ad, the third son, was Abdul Rahman's opposite. Sa'ad was a natural comedian and enjoyed talking more than any human being I have ever known. He chatted expansively about the most inane topics, anything that popped into his head, whether it was about the newest baby goat, or the latest trick performed by one of the baby siblings, or perhaps it might be the consistency of the yogurt he had eaten at breakfast. Sa'ad frequently appeared out of con-trol with his endless chatter, sometimes confiding intimate personal informa-tion that no one wanted to hear.

Such boundless liveliness brought Sa'ad constant trouble, for of all the chil-dren, he was the one who continually failed to abide by our father's strict rules of conduct. Sa'ad's limbs moved as fast as his tongue. My brother never walked anywhere. He ran endlessly—until one day he ran straight into the path of an automobile.

This happened when our father was in Afghanistan and we were in Jeddah.

Our Yemeni driver, who had been left in charge, had walked with us to the neighborhood mosque. As always, Sa'ad was running far ahead of everyone. He was in such a rush that he foolishly failed to look before he crossed the road. There was a sickening thump as Sa'ad collided with a moving automobile.

We ran to the accident. Everyone at the scene was agitated, but no one more than the driver of the car, who was employed as an engineer for the family firm and had been driving a company car. When that poor man understood that he had struck a son of Osama bin Laden, he became overwrought, as did our driver, who was responsible to our father for the safety of his sons. I'm sure that both men were already envisioning the loss of good jobs, or perhaps long jail sentences, for drivers involved in automobile accidents with injured parties can be held in prison while waiting for a ruling.

My brothers and I circled Sa'ad's prostrate body. Not even the accident had silenced Sa'ad's tongue; my brother was muttering and wailing. It was soon concluded that his injuries were probably not severe. We watched as an ambulance rushed Sa'ad off to the hospital while our driver ran home to tell our mother of the accident.

We kids hung around to learn what might happen next.

Much to the driver's good fortune, the police captain left the incident to the bin Laden family. The driver was plainly relieved, until he realized that our father was yet to be told, and his worry heated up yet again. I can't remember who made the decision, but someone in authority for our family resolved that since Sa'ad had survived without serious injury, our father could live without knowledge of the incident, at least so long as he was in Afghanistan.

Happily for all, by the time Father returned to Saudi Arabia, Sa'ad had fully recovered from his injuries. Although Father was shocked to learn that his son had been struck by an automobile, he held no earthly being accountable. "The accident was not the driver's fault," our father said. "It was God's will that Sa'ad be hit. It was God's will that Sa'ad survived. We can thank God."

While it is difficult for any human being to accurately describe their own personality, I know enough of myself to be convinced that the life my father decreed for his sons also shaped me negatively.

The years before I started primary school were the best of my life. I greedily devoured my mother's full attention before my younger brother Osman was born, at least when my father was away in Pakistan and Afghanistan. After Osman was born, my brother consumed much of my mother's attention. That is when I began to spend more time with our Yemeni driver, the kindly man I have spoken about earlier.

When our father was away, our mornings would start with the first prayer of the day. Afterward, our mother would be waiting with a simple breakfast of bread, cheese, and eggs. At the end of breakfast, my brothers would be taken to school by our driver. After Osman was born, I began going along for the ride.

At the time I felt sad that I could not attend school with my brothers, for I was lonely when they were gone. After returning home, I would sometimes play with the driver's children, who lived with their parents in my father's home. If I grew bored, I would go to my mother and follow her around for a while before she put me down for a nap. After my nap I would have lunch with my mother. Generally we ate salads and chicken and rice.

After lunch our driver might take me with him on his errands to purchase food and personal items for our family. Later in the afternoon we would return to the school to collect my brothers.

As the years passed, I became even more solitary. I read books alone. I played with the animals alone. A born lover of all animals, I got a thrill from studying any birds that might alight in our garden. When we traveled to the farm, there were many animals to observe or to play with. I became so accustomed to being alone that I began to relish solitude. When our family traveled, I enjoyed finding an isolated corner for my bed, but too often my father noticed and he would order me to put my bed next to my brothers.

With my willful personality, I tried my parents' patience many times.

On one of those occasions, I wanted to go to the shops to buy myself something special. I knew from experience from observing our driver that a person needed coins to exchange for goods. I didn't know how I might find myself some coins. Suddenly I had a flash of memory: My mother kept a few gold coins in a bedside cabinet in her bedroom. Those coins were gifts from family members presented each time she gave birth to a son.

I was deceitful, watching to see when mother busied herself. At my first opportunity, I dashed into her bedroom, opened the drawer to the cabinet, and spotted two large gold coins. Now I know that each coin was worth about 1,000 Saudi riyals, or around $300 each.

I ran out of the house, slipping through the front door, and made my way to a shop I routinely visited with our driver. The owner of the shop was from Egypt, a very nice man who hid his surprise when I came trotting through the door. I felt quite the big boy when he politely asked me what I needed. I pointed to some candies and a soft drink and some colored pencils, all items specifically forbidden by my father. I paid the shop owner with the two stolen coins. Successful with my mission, I crept back into our home, hiding my goodies so that my brothers would not demand a share.

I was unlucky that a few days later my father had business in that shop. When he walked in, the Egyptian pulled out the coins and gave them to my father, along with the news that his young son Omar had come on an unsupervised visit to make some unusual purchases.

My father was so pleased by the man's honesty that he presented him with one of the coins as a reward. Of course, my father was not pleased with me. I was punished severely for my deceit and thievery. Yet his harsh punishment failed to put a stop to my naughty behavior. Before long I suffered from the shopping bug again. As before, I tiptoed into my mother's room to look for money. This time I found paper money, and took about 500 Saudi riyals.

Knowing that my father had alerted his employees to keep a special watch for me, I realized the difficulty of slipping out unseen. I went into one of our bathrooms and scrambled out the window, sliding down a drainpipe before crossing the garden. I was relieved to see that the large metal gate was unlocked, saving me from a dangerous climb over the tall wall that enclosed our home. I ran to the shops, but was disheartened to discover them closed. The hour was later than I realized.

I retraced my steps, and returned the money to my mother's secret place. Wanting to brag about my adventure, I stupidly confided in older brother Abdullah. Abdullah looked at me sternly before marching to my mother to inform her of my midnight journey. I escaped serious punishment only because Mother was incapable of being tough on any of her children, even when we deserved a reprimand.

When my father learned of my escapades, he called me a "little villain" and ordered his men to install a barbed wire fence on top of the wall that circled our grounds. My father's men were diligent to make the fence "rascal-proof," as they called it. The fence was erected in the shape of a Y so that it would be impossible to scale. Proud of their work, they congratulated each other, talking about how the sheik's son would never scale such a fence, adding that the cleverest thief would never rob the bin Laden home.

We were locked in and the world was locked out.

Within the week I had made my first of many breakouts, discovering that if I climbed the wall under the gatehouse where the guards were posted, there was one spot where I could hang by my legs and fling my upper body onto the street lamppost, first catching with my hands and then easily sliding down that post until my short legs hit the sidewalk.

When the fence builders discovered I had cracked the "rascal-proof fence" to make daily escapes, they were humiliated. After that incident, my father began keeping me by his side anytime he was in Jeddah, taking me everywhere he went, claiming that his fourth son was the one who led the others into mischief because by this time my brothers were beginning to emulate me.

My brother Osman was the next one born after me. For years he was the smallest of the sons, but one day he starting growing and couldn't stop, growing fat, remaining overweight for several years. Then Osman began a rapid weight loss and became skinny, growing in stature until he reached the same height as our father. Osman was such a quiet boy that he never saw the purpose of a joke; in fact, the telling of a joke would make him angry, leading him to walk away to sulk. He was religious, but not so overly religious as our father. He did resemble his brothers in one way, as he liked animals and often rode horses.

Mohammed was the baby son for years, concentrating on playing. Little Mohammed yearned for toy cars, but because our father forbade toys, we older boys made it our business to slip to the stores and purchase play cars for our baby brother.

As the first girl after five sons, our baby sister named Fatima was a novelty, a pet whom we all loved. She entertained the family for hours as she first learned to crawl and then to walk. My mother had dreamed of a daughter for so many years that she loved playing with Fatima and dressing her in frilly clothes. She had a beautiful face and her hair was curly and grew so long that it hung down her back. As she grew older she watched our mother and copied everything she did.

I often studied my father's conduct with the younger siblings. He appeared to enjoy lounging on the floor and rolling around with the babies, allowing Mohammed and Fatima to crawl on his head and chest. He even hugged and kissed them. I couldn't recall my father being so affectionate when I was a baby, although my mother claimed to remember such moments.

Soon after my father married his fourth wife, I learned that our entire family was moving to Medina. I was not troubled in the least because I was too young to realize the implications of leaving Jeddah.

Chapter 7

Moving to Medina

OMAR BIN LADEN

In the beginning, Medina was an exciting place to live. My eyes bulged when I caught sight of the enormous villa—even bigger than our large apartment house in Jeddah—that would be our home. But disappointment loomed. The exterior of our new home appeared a mansion, but we discovered that the interior was simple to the point of being stark. The vast floor space was empty other than a few inexpensive Persian carpets on the floor, cushions lined against the walls, and thin mattresses for sleeping.

I often wondered why our beautiful mansions were so plainly decorated. Once I asked my mother and she confessed that when she was a young bride she had dreamed of having a lovely decorated home. But she had long ago left those dreams behind.

My father's frequent absences, added to her almost continuous pregnancies, had left her without the opportunity to decorate in the early years of their marriage. Then, after they moved into their own home, my father had changed his opinion and decreed that his family should live the simple life. He said that he would not allow her to spend his money on elaborate furnishings.

Remembering the stark furnishings of that Medina home, I would classify my mother's living quarters as penthouse living without the luxury.

Although we were together as a family, most members of the family missed Jeddah. Only Siham, our father's fourth wife, who came from Medina, seemed happier there, because she could see her family more often. The rest of us had left our hearts in Jeddah, the only city we had known, within a short driving distance of our beloved family farm. Never had we imagined how forlorn our life would become without the freedom of those weekend breaks on the farm.

Still, there were a few good moments in Medina. I recall an amusing incident that occurred shortly after we moved to the city.

My wittiest brother, Sa'ad, and I were bored, pacing through our empty home in search of something entertaining to occupy our time. At the welcome sound of a knock on the villa door, we hastened to see who was visiting. We found three veiled women, hands extended, begging for money.

Saudis by their nature tend to be generous, but are more so during religious holidays. Therefore, underprivileged Saudi women stroll through wealthy neighborhoods, knocking on doors, making their case for charity during such times.

Sa'ad and I were both young, and neither of us understood exactly what we should do, especially since we had no coins to give them. At first we indicated that they should leave, and then Sa'ad suddenly changed his mind and declared, "Wait! You can't leave!"

I gazed curiously at Sa'ad, as did our veiled visitors. They looked at us through their black coverings for a few minutes, but then all turned to go at the same time.

Sa'ad's voice became urgent. "No! You can't leave!" he cried again. He paused, then shouted, "Our father wants to marry you!"

Calling to mind that my father did seem to enjoy having many women around, I thought Sa'ad's idea was sound. "Yes!" I chimed in. "Our father would like to marry you!"

Sa'ad and I opened the door as wide as possible, indicating with our hands that the women should come inside and make themselves comfortable for a wedding.

Seeing that we were serious, the veiled women turned and fled, moving as fast as their black veils and long abaayas would allow.

Panicked that potential brides for our father were escaping, Sa'ad and I ran after them. Sa'ad launched his nimble body in front of the bewildered women, his voice pleading, "Come back! You must come in! It's true! Our father wants to marry you!"

Thinking how excited our father would be to gain three wives in one go, I was determined not to let them escape a second time.

Becoming agitated by the crazy episode, those poor women pushed us aside and ran faster than before. The last we saw of them, their black abaayas were flapping.

There was another incident that seemed humorous at the time, but that was because we were ignorant of the actual danger. One of my brothers spied a pigeon nest in one of the round planters built on the outside of a fourth-story window. Always looking for a new pastime, we made it our business to keep watch. Soon enough, there were two eggs that hatched into two baby pigeons. Each day we would take a survey of the chicks.

One morning the mother pigeon did not return on schedule, and we decided that we must save those baby chicks. To reach the chicks in the planters, we ran up the stairs and onto the roof, where Abdul Rahman volunteered to swing from the roof to the fourth-floor planters. Once in place, he reached into the nest to pluck out the baby pigeons. My brothers and I watched Abdul Rahman tottering about while clutching the baby birds and trying to climb back to the roof. But we were so hyper that we quickly lost interest and found another pursuit. We rushed off without considering our brother, locking the door from the roof to the staircase.

Like many Saudi homes there was a round shaft in the center of our home, reaching from the bottom floor to the roof. Soon Abdul Rahman was shouting at us from the top of that shaft. Rather than climbing back up four flights of stairs to unlock the door, we yelled for him to jump.

Abdul Rahman hesitated. My brothers and I set up a chorus, "Jump! Jump! We will catch you! Jump! Jump! Jump! We will catch you!"

We didn't realize that if Abdul Rahman listened to us and jumped, he would suffer serious injuries or possibly even death. Pain and death were simply not on our minds that morning, although we knew about pain from our father's beatings and had heard about how many humans went from life to death in just a moment. After death, some people even went to a frighteningly hot place called hell. Our religious instructors often concentrated on the terrors of hell, so we had no desire to make a trip there.

We truly believed that Abdul Rahman could make the leap from the roof down to the ground floor without pain or death. We would reach out and catch him.

Becoming convinced by our chants, Abdul Rahman put down the chicks and took the plunge. At the last moment, he thought better of the plan, instinctively grasping the edge of the high floor while his fast-moving feet found a tiny ledge on the inside wall.

We were laughing and screaming all at once, "Let go, Abdul Rahman! We will catch you!"

I have no idea why our mother, or one of our three aunties, did not respond to the uproar. Looking back, I suppose that my father had trained them so well to remain behind locked doors that they ignored all that went on beyond them. Thankfully, our cries alerted one of the family drivers, who dashed in the front door to check on the commotion. Our driver looked where we were gazing to see Abdul Rahman hanging. The driver, hands to his head, gasped loudly before letting out a few screams and then ran as fast as he could, taking three steps at a time to reach the top where he grabbed Abdul Rahman's hands, struggling to heave him back to safety.

Excited by the hullabaloo we had created, we followed our driver up the stairs, where we found the poor man visibly shaken. He gave us a rare scolding, saying that he had nearly toppled over with Abdul Rahman, and had that happened, both would have died when they hit the hard marble floor four flights down. Luckily our driver had saved the day.

Another personal milestone occurred for me in Medina. I turned seven and was enrolled in the Obaiy bin Kahab School, beginning the daily school trek with my older brothers. I had longed to go to school with my brothers for years, and despite their warnings that I was the lucky one to remain at home, I never believed them. I thought perhaps they were having so much fun that they wanted to cut me out.

Too late I discovered that my brothers had not misled me. School was an instant torture, because our family name created vicious animosity from our teachers. I was shocked to learn that I was hated for being a bin Laden.

The bin Ladens were known to be among the most prosperous and influential families in the kingdom. Rarely did the middle- or lower-class Saudi have an opportunity to be around a member of my grandfather's fabulously wealthy family. Perhaps the teachers were privately seething at the bin Ladens' riches and influence. Whatever the reason, when they had a chance to take out their jealousy on us, they did. Despite our desperate attempts to please those teachers, nothing helped to deflect their anger. I remember one teacher who announced in class that my family's wealth and influence would not affect his conduct. That man was the worst, and taunted me more than the others.

It was particularly painful because some students mimicked his actions. One gang of boys even threatened my brothers and me with rape! There were times we had to fight to protect ourselves or, if caught alone, run like the wind.

Teachers in Saudi Arabia have the legal right to cane any student, and some of them exercised that right. Our grades were often lowered, sometimes marked as failing, even when our work was of high quality. There were times when the beatings and hazing became so unbearable that we pleaded with our father to enroll us in schools where our name would not attract such hostility.

My brothers and I questioned why the sons of Osama bin Laden were sent to public school when our father, uncles, and sons of our uncles attended only the best private schools. While our cousins were being prepared for a life of privilege, we were being sent to substandard schools that would hamper our future. Indeed, our futures were fixed by those inferior schools. Not only were the teachers cruel, but we were receiving an inadequate education.

Had our father made a strong complaint to the school, the teachers would have adjusted their behavior. But he was strangely unmoved by our dilemma, lecturing us on his stern beliefs: "Life has to be a burden. Life has to be hard. You will be made stronger if you are treated toughly. You will become capable adults, able to endure many hardships." When no one stood up for us, the teachers grew even bolder.

Because of my early school experiences, it was one of the happiest days of my life when I learned we were returning to Jeddah in 1988, a year after moving to Medina. All I could think was: I will escape the Obaiy bin Kahab School! My brothers tried to warn me that the school in Jeddah would be more of the same, but I brushed their warnings aside, believing that nothing could be as bad as the school in Medina.

Every day was a torture until our belongings were packed and we were all loaded into large vehicles for the return move. I was smiling so widely when I saw Jeddah that one of my younger brothers warned me that he could see too many of my teeth. When he began to count them, I stopped smiling. Nevertheless, I remained happy, for those cool Jeddah sea breezes felt like a healing balm.

I soon discovered that my brothers had not lied about the school in Jeddah. I became so desperate that I spoke to my mother of the abuse. She was horrified, but I believe afraid to speak to our father, who was adamant that he would make every decision about his sons.

It's a miracle that none of us was beaten to death. I don't know about my brothers, for it is a subject matter so painful that we do not approach it, but the extreme cruelty those teachers meted out upon my body and my mind scarred me for life.

The only happy moment I recall was the time that I submitted a painting that was chosen to hang on the school wall. I had never received any positive recognition in school before. My mother was pleased as well, thinking that I had inherited my artistic streak from her, and I believe that to be the case.

While school remained a source of constant misery, there were other changes in our life. For as long as I could remember, my father had been flying back and forth to Pakistan and Afghanistan for the cause of Jihad.

Jihad is a religious duty of Muslims, meaning struggle in the way of God. Jihad can be violent or nonviolent. Nonviolent Jihad means a struggle within, such as those who fight their baser impulses to live a righteous life. In my father's case, the concept of Jihad included violent, armed struggle against the Soviet army that was oppressing a Muslim land.

When a Muslim believer is called to engage in armed struggle, that believer becomes known as a Muhahid. A group fighting together against oppression is called Mujahideen. The best known Mujahideen were the soldiers who fought in Afghanistan, including my father and his band of Arab fighters. In fact, the movement to fight the Russian invaders in Afghanistan became so popular that the United States under Presidents Jimmy Carter and Ronald Reagan helped to finance the Mujahideen with President Reagan publicly praising the Mujahideen as freedom fighters.

In those days, my father was a great hero to the West, too.

Suddenly there was excited talk that the impossible had happened: The Soviet army was pulling out of Afghanistan—defeated by a ragtag group of Mujahideen, some who were led by my own father!

I remember speculating on what my father might do with his spare time, since his life had been totally focused on that faraway war for so many years. To my surprise, my father became busier than ever, for he was in great demand as Saudi Arabia's war hero. The Saudi government as well as private Saudi citizens had donated enormous sums of money to the Afghan cause. Additionally, many Saudi men had volunteered to fight on the battlefields in Afghanistan, with many Saudi fathers and sons grievously injured, or even dying. After such sacrifices, Saudis felt they had a huge stake in the war.

Everyone in the country celebrated the Islamic victory. As the face of those heroes, he was greatly revered by many Saudis and by Muslims in other lands. Many men wanted to meet him, to hear about his personal experiences on the battlefields. Although my father did not seek special attention, he did agree to give talks at the mosque and at private events.

Our lives grew more routine, something none of us had ever known. Our father was like other fathers, going to work each day at the family business, although he was still intensely occupied with our Islamic faith, and spent much time meeting with others about his obligations as a believer.

Happily for us, for a year or so he became less ill-tempered, though his sons were still expected to conduct themselves in a manner excessively solemn. Despite our father's uncompromising rules, I was disturbed to hear my older brothers complaining that the only times they had tasted freedom was when our father was away, fighting the Russians. They were sorry that the war was over!

When I was a child, I wanted nothing more than my father's companionship and approval. But those years had long passed. Although I still revered my father and desired his approval, I was no longer in need of his companionship. After giving the matter much thought, a sad reality struck me. My older brothers had spoken a truth I could not deny: Life *was* more agreeable when my father was far, far away.

Chapter 8

Many Children for Osama

NAJWA BIN LADEN

In 1988 another girl, Kadhija, was born to Osama's newest wife, Siham. And so it came to be that our family consisted of four wives and nine children. The following year brought the blessing of two additional children to our ever-growing family. Siham had a quick second pregnancy, giving birth twice in two years as she welcomed her first son, baby Khalid. From that time Siham was happy to be known as Um Khalid.

Most exciting for me was that my sweet friend Khairiah, Osama's third wife, gave birth to her first child, a little boy named Hamza. Khairiah now also wore the highly prized mantle of being known as Um Hamza.

We could all proudly say that we were the mothers of sons, which is an important distinction for a woman in Saudi Arabia.

Suddenly Osama traveled less frequently to Pakistan and Afghanistan. I felt my spirits lift when told that the long war in Afghanistan finally ended. The Soviets were out of Afghanistan as of February 15, 1989, which was particularly auspicious because it was also Osama's thirty-second birthday. Although Muslims do not celebrate birthdays, Osama said that he felt that day was filled with the most important gift, that the war he had fought for so long had finally been won.

For me, the most important gift was the thought that my husband could now resume the life of an industrious Saudi businessman. No longer would Osama be a warrior. No longer would I spend hours filled with worry that I might receive a message that my husband had been killed on the battlefield.

I was told that my husband was a hero in many Muslim eyes. But Osama seemed a reluctant hero, failing to enlighten me of the many awards received and of the widespread adoration that put his name on the tip of many tongues.

Osama soon settled into his routine of going to work in the mornings and coming home in the afternoons, although he now had four wives and alternated his time with each family. This meant that my husband came to me only once every four nights. When we all went to the farm, he would alternate our time with us there as well.

Osama was certainly achieving his goal of having many children for Islam. In fact, 1990 brought three more babies into our busy lives. This was the year that Osama's second wife, Khadijah, had her second child and second son, Amer. During this same season, two other pregnancies occurred nearly simultaneously, with an amusing conclusion.

It came to be that I was pregnant with my eighth child at the same time my husband's fourth and newest wife, Siham, was pregnant with her third child, although Siham was due a few months later than I.

As usual, Osama was in attendance when the time was near for me to give birth. As God would have it, the moment I began to have labor pains, one of the maids dashed from Siham's apartment with the news that her mistress was in premature labor. At first we thought perhaps Siham's pains were not real labor, for her child was not due for another two months. But we soon realized that was not the case.

The circumstances were beyond belief. Had I not been feeling so poorly, I would have smiled watching my husband struggle to settle two pregnant women into the backseat of his new Mercedes.

The drive was surreal as Siham and I sat side by side, clasping our stomachs, wanting nothing more but to gain some relief from the pain. As might be expected, there was a bit of bedlam at the hospital as the staff dashed about trying to admit two women into labor rooms at the same time. There was such a commotion that several of the nurses had no idea that we were all together.

The most humorous moment arrived after a bright-eyed nurse witnessed Osama dashing from my room into Siham's. The woman was a dainty Filipina, yet she was very bold, scolding my physically large husband, telling him that he must remain in his wife's room. That little nurse warned him, "You will get into serious trouble for peeking at another woman!"

I'm sure she was astonished when an excited Osama shouted out, "I am not illegally peeking! These two mothers are both my wives."

As for me, I was very pleased to learn that I had a second daughter, a girl we named Iman. In a house with so many males I had fretted that my delicate first daughter, Fatima, felt isolated.

Siham was also the mother of a daughter named Miriam, but because she delivered too soon, little Miriam needed extra care, staying in the hospital for a week longer than her mother.

The end of 1990 brought less happy news, when the president of Iraq invaded his neighbor, Kuwait. At the time I was afraid for everyone in the region, but being a woman whose only business was the home and children, there was nothing I could do but be anxious. I know certain facts now only because my grown sons shared information with me. They told me that their father was so convinced that the Iraqi army would walk across the Kuwaiti border to Saudi Arabia that he gave speeches warning of the danger. But no one else believed the Iraqi president would be so foolish.

War came to the region, but I buried my head in the sand like those soldiers Osama had described in Afghanistan. I took care for my children and did not doubt that my husband would protect us.

After the war ended and Iraqis ran through the desert and back into their own country, we all assumed that calm would return. That was not the case, at least not for my family. I noticed that my husband's demeanor grew more serious with every passing month. He made the unusual arrangement for me to travel alone with my youngest children to Syria, telling me to remain there for a nice long visit. When I asked why he thought I should leave Saudi Arabia at such a tension-filled time, he told me, "Najwa, the time may unfurl into years before you see your parents and siblings again."

And so it came to pass that Abdul Rahman and I took my daughters, Fatima and Iman, for a holiday in Syria. While I was worried about the events in Saudi Arabia, I did enjoy sharing my little daughters with my parents and siblings and other relatives. Although I had visited Syria on holidays, the visits were not as frequent as we would wish.

While the visiting time was as sweet as candy, as the time passed and the day drew near that I would say goodbye, a strange feeling kept visiting me. I would be cheerful one moment and suddenly a dark cloud would be cast over my heart, like someone had tossed the "unhappy net" over me. In the past when I left after a holiday in Syria, all of us would say our goodbyes in the midst of joyful talk, reminiscing about the good times we had enjoyed at the beach or in the mountains.

But during that goodbye I had a difficult time finding a smile. I didn't share my strange concerns. I just knew something terrible was going to happen to me or my family. Indeed, before I saw my family in Syria again, something wildly unexpected would happen, not only to me and my children, but to many other people in the world. But I was a woman confined to her home, so there was nothing I could do to alter anyone's future, not even my own.

A Note Regarding Osama bin Laden's Political Activities

JEAN SASSON

During these same years that Najwa continued having more children and Omar reached an age when he grasped that his life was different from those of other children, Osama bin Laden was fully involved with the conflict in Afghanistan. The war changed, with the Russians occupying the main cities and the Mujahideen fighters (of which Osama was a part) waging a guerrilla war. In fact, from 1980 until 1985, there were nine main Russian offensives resulting in heavy fighting.

In 1985, Abdullah Azzam and Osama established a formal office, called the Services Office, where Muslim volunteers were sent for training and then to fighting units in Afghanistan. Osama was no longer content to limit his activities to raising money and organizing the delivery of supplies, but expanded his participation in Jihad by helping to establish training camps, building roads, and forming his own fighting unit manned by Arab fighters. By this time he was a participant in the battles, risking his life alongside his men, and suffering injuries.

Osama also met the main Egyptian Jihadists who inspired him further. All were of the same mind, wanting to remake the Muslim world as soon as the Soviets were defeated. These men would later become some of his most devoted followers, including Mohammed Atef, Dr. Ayman al-Zawahiri, Abu Ubaidah al-Banshiri, Abdullah Ahmed Abdullah, and Omar Abdel Rahman, the blind cleric from Egypt.

Because Osama was in Pakistan and Afghanistan more than he was in Saudi Arabia, he arranged a family home in Peshawar, Pakistan, so that his wives and children could join him for summer visits. Osama introduced his firstborn son, Abdullah, to the conflict in Afghanistan, bringing him to the fighting camp in Jaji, where the young boy was exposed to great danger. Osama received unexpected criticism from his family and other Jihadi leaders, including Abdullah Azzam, for doing so, yet it was only the first of many instances when Osama would push his unenthusiastic sons to the forefront of his personal passion for Jihad.

In April 1988, nine years and four months after the Soviets first invaded Afghanistan, representatives of Afghanistan, the USSR, the United States, and Pakistan met to sign an agreement calling for the Russian army to pull its forces out of Afghanistan. Afghanistan and Pakistan agreed to stop interfering in the other's political and military affairs. And the United States agreed to end its support for the Afghan anti-Soviet groups.

Osama's mentor, Abdullah Azzam, made the case for an extensive foundation from which believers could launch their struggle for a perfect Islamic world. In full agreement, Osama called for the planning meeting that would be named al-Qaeda al-Askariya, which translates to "the military base," and was later shortened to al-Qaeda, "the base," or "the foundation." The first meeting was held at his family home in Peshawar, Pakistan, in August 1988.

The founding members decreed that Osama's al-Qaeda organization would be a global crusade, having both an Islamic arm and a military arm, so that the organization could support Islam with violent and nonviolent means. Goals included ridding the Muslim world of western influence, overthrowing monarchies and secular governments, and making Islam the only religion in the world. As the war in Afghanistan wound down, Osama found more time to devote himself to the Islamic goals of al-Qaeda.

After Osama assumed a leadership role in the movement, there were tensions among some of his followers, most noticeably between Abdullah Azzam and Dr. Ayman al-Zawahiri, with both men competing for Osama's support, financial and otherwise. While Abdullah Azzam was not in favor of violence against fellow Muslims, Zawahiri had no such scruples. As time went on, the tensions between the two men grew problematic for the movement.

On February 15, 1989, the last Russian soldier departed Afghanistan. Osama and his fighting men claimed a great victory. Tragically, with the departure of the Russians, the Afghan warlords commenced quarreling, each faction determined to gain leadership of the war-weary country. Osama made some efforts to bring the warlords together, but his efforts were unsuccessful.

After the war ended, and al-Qaeda was looking to move their movement global, there were attempts on Abdullah Azzam's life. On November 24, 1989, Azzam and his two sons were killed when three land mines detonated as a motor caravan was taking them to the mosque in Peshawar to pray. There have been many speculations as to the guilty party, but most believe Zawahiri to be the mastermind of the assassination.

When Abdullah Azzam died at age forty-nine, he was likely the only person who might have cautioned Osama against future attacks against the Saudi rulers and the Americans.

Osama soon returned to Jeddah, Saudi Arabia, a man whose political, religious, and militant vision had been fully awakened. From that time on, he continued to push for the growth of al-Qaeda, and was actively meeting with other Arabs who held similar views.

Chapter 9

The Nightmare Begins

OMAR BIN LADEN

The regional calm brought by the end of the Soviet-Afghan war on February 15, 1989, did not last. Not unexpectedly, my father was one of the first to sound a new alarm because his mind was like an antenna set for regional news, especially attuned to all things Muslim. Despite the fact that Afghanistan's woes had kept him engaged for over ten years, he remained watchful, carefully following the events related to the Iraq-Iran war. That 10-year war had begun on September 22, 1980, the year before I was even born, and had come to an exhausted conclusion on August 20, 1988, six months prior to the cessation of hostilities in Afghanistan. There was no clear victory for Iran or Iraq, and my father began monitoring the business of Iraq, believing that Saddam Hussein was so dissatisfied with the result of that war that he would not remain silent.

My father had never been a supporter of Saddam Hussein due to the dictator's secular rule over a Muslim land. My father often mocked Saddam Hussein for "not being a believer." There is no bigger insult for a Muslim. My father also scorned Saddam's aggressive character, saying, "The leader of such a large army will never stop looking for war."

My father was so concerned that a debt-stricken Saddam might be tempted by the wealth of his rich neighbors that he took his private thoughts about Saddam public, beginning a dangerous habit of using the mosque and audiotapes to make his feelings known. The audiotapes were widely distributed to the Saudi population, creating little ripples of displeasure from the royal family, yet their disapproval remained a private affair.

Regretfully, my father's warnings came true. Beginning in February of 1990, strong words began to fly from Iraq to Kuwait City and Riyadh, with a cash-desperate Saddam Hussein demanding that the Kuwaitis and Saudis forgive the $40 billion in loans given to him to fight Khomeini and the Iranians. Saddam's neighbors had been generous in supporting the Iraqis against the Iranians, for both governments had become increasingly uneasy with the antagonistic militant stance taken by the Khomeini government against the Sunni-led governments in the area. Iran is a Persian Shiite country, while most of the Gulf nations are Arab Sunni. There have been hostilities between the two sects and the two nationalities since the earliest times in history. But the Kuwaiti and Saudi governments rejected his request and Saddam became aggressive, demanding an additional $30 billion in interest-free loans: "Let the Gulf regimes know, that if they do not give this money to me, I know how to get it." That's when the Iraqi dictator put his huge army on the move, positioning 100,000 trained soldiers on the Kuwaiti border. When questioned, he claimed that his army was conducting training exercises.

King Fahd reached out to bring all the parties, including Saddam, together at an emergency meeting in Jeddah on July 31, 1990. Unfortunately, the meeting ended with additional insults rather than a solution. That was the night my father said that war was imminent.

At dawn on August 2, 1990, Saddam Hussein's army invaded Kuwait, easily occupying the small country. My father repeated: "Saddam will attack Saudi Arabia for possession of the oilfields in the eastern province. This will happen as soon as his military consolidates its hold on Kuwait."

I was ten years old. For the first time I truly grasped the concept of war, and that war could come to any nation. That was also when I recognized my father's standing as a war hero so revered that his actions generally went unquestioned. He was the only civilian in Saudi Arabia allowed to drive cars with blackened windows, or to strap a machine gun across his shoulder and walk through the streets of Jeddah. From then on, I began to take note of what was happening in our region of the world and my father's reactions to the events.

My father's mind began to prepare for the possibility of war within the kingdom. One day he returned home with supplies of heavy-duty adhesive tape, instructing his sons to help him cross the windows to save them from shattering if Saddam dropped bombs on the city. He arranged for extra stocks of food, candles, gas lights, handheld transceivers, and battery-battered radios. He even purchased military-quality gas masks for everyone in the family. We kids treated the gas mask lessons as a game, but our father had never been more serious, predicting that Saddam would not hesitate to use chemical or biological weapons, as he had done on the Iranians.

Once our home and family were ready, he turned his attention to the farm, stockpiling gas, food, and large trucks there. He had come to the conclusion that our farm would be the best military base, believing that the royal family would call upon his military skills when Saddam attacked.

He even purchased a speedboat to be used if he had to take his family to safety. The boat's engine was removed and replaced by a more powerful one, then it was docked at the bin Laden marina at Jeddah's harbor. I was taken aback when my father mentioned that he had named the boat in honor of Shafiq al-Madani, a war hero who had died in the Afghan-Russian war.

Certainly Shafiq al-Madani was a champion in my young eyes. I had met the man when my father had taken his family to Pakistan for the summer. I was only eight years old at the time, and as usual, looking for activity. Some of my father's men were organizing the loading of two trucks with food and other essentials for the training camps in Afghanistan. My brothers and I were thrilled when the men asked us to assist in the loading. I gave a little twitch when I caught a glimpse of a soccer ball in the stack of goods. I wanted that ball for myself. I gathered my courage to ask one of the men, "Are they going to play football at the soldiers' camp?"

The man answered, "Yes, they will play with it."

I said, "I don't think they will," and then lifted the ball in my hands, hoping to make a quick getaway before he could react.

The man's voice was stern. "Yes, they will," he said, snatching the ball from my hands and throwing it back into the truck.

At that time, a man about twenty years old came forward and retrieved the ball, tossing it to me, saying, "Catch!"

I caught it, so excited that I couldn't restrain my glee.

He smiled. "You keep it. It's yours."

I couldn't believe my good luck. I asked his name and he said, "Shafiq al-Madani." I never forgot his kindness, and can see his face today if I think about him. He was not very tall, but looked wiry and tough, with short black hair, a thin beard and long sideburns. Yet he had a sparkle in his eye, deriving genuine pleasure from my joy.

A few weeks later I was struck by sadness when my father told me that the man named Shafiq al-Madani had been killed in the war. During a battle, Shafiq and two other men had ventured into the dangerous area between the Russians and the Afghans, and walked directly into a line of tanks and heavy weapons. The three men quickly retreated, but the Russians followed.

Knowing they were outnumbered and escape was impossible, Shafiq volunteered to cover the men as they fled, saying all would die unless one remained behind. The two men protested, but Shafiq insisted. As the men were dashing away, they heard many shots and at the top of the ridge turned back to see Shafiq lying dead, his gun still clasped in his arms.

My father was particularly sad because he remembered a melancholy exchange with the young man only a week before he died. Shafiq said that, "Oh Sheik, my one prayer to God is that He not dig a grave for me in Afghanistan. I can die all right, but I don't want to be buried in the ground."

My father remembered the young hero when purchasing the boat, wishing that Shafiq could have lived to ride the waves, rather than be buried in a dirt hole in Afghanistan. I admit I had visions of our family making a daring escape from invading Iraqi troops by launching the boat named *Shafiq al-Madani*.

Perhaps Saudi Arabia would not be attacked and my father could take me out on the *Shafiq al-Madani* for a pleasure ride rather than a wild escape.

My father was a patriot in those days, loyal to his country and his king. My father already knew that he had displeased the Saudi royal family with his public comments about Saddam, so he cautioned his employees: "If any of you are ever attacked or even arrested by the police or soldiers, do not protest. Raise your arms in surrender and go in peace. Do not run away. Do not defend yourself. I will see to your freedom."

Time and again my father repeated, "The bin Laden family supports the royal family. My own father was a trusted friend of our first king, Abdul Aziz. Now the sons of our father support Abdul Aziz's sons."

As a son of Mohammed bin Laden and a war hero, my father still maintained loose contact with the royals. Convinced that Iraq would cross the Kuwaiti border to invade Saudi Arabia, he approached the royal family with his ideas. During that tumultuous time he met with a number of princes, but most importantly, called on the powerful interior minister, Prince Naif bin Abdul Aziz al-Saud, who was a full brother to King Fahd bin Abdul Aziz al-Saud. My father offered the royal family his services in fighting Saddam, volunteering to bring in twelve thousand well-armed veterans from the Afghan war still under his command. He assured Prince Naif that he could have his soldiers equipped to defend Islam's holiest land at lightning speed. All he needed was royal approval.

As is the Saudi way, no important decisions are taken hurriedly. The royal family did not say yes, and they did not say no, but told my father that they would get back to him.

Meanwhile, Saddam increased the tension by making hateful public statements about the Saudi rulers and menacing our borders with his huge army. American leaders arrived in the kingdom with great fanfare, attempting to convince the royal family to allow the U.S. military access to Saddam from our land. To my father's shock, he soon discovered that his offer to defend the kingdom had been ignored.

He learned through the Arab media that it would be a huge coalition of military forces, led by the United States, that would defend Saudi Arabia. My father believed that his fighting force could trounce Saddam. I heard him demand in great anger, "Are Saddam's armies more powerful than the mighty Russians? No!" He muttered, "We do *not* need the Americans!"

While my father announced his bitter feelings to family and friends, he did not speak out in public, for he remained a loyal supporter of the Saudi royal family. For too many years the bin Laden and al-Saud families had worked closely for the advancement of Saudi Arabia. Yet the rejection was distasteful, for he had told family, friends, and acquaintances that he had offered his military services to the royal family.

There was another important issue besides pride. In my father's mind, the whole of Saudi Arabia was Islamic holy land and should not be contaminated by the presence of Christian or Jewish soldiers from America and other western nations.

Since the formation of the Jewish state in 1948, few Muslims considered America a friend to the Arabs. Now, many besides my father were convinced that the American government was using the crisis as justification to establish their forces in Saudi Arabia so that they might use our country as a base to flood the region with their unwelcome secular views.

My father's loyalty to the royal family soon changed.

I was enjoying a fine day because my father had invited me to accompany him on his routine appointments in Jeddah. We were walking from one business to another when my father was approached by a trusted employee, a man who appeared noticeably tense even to my youthful eyes.

The man whispered in my father's ear.

My father's face paled.

I'm certain that my face paled, too, when I heard that government forces had raided our Jeddah farm earlier that morning. We heard that heavily armed Saudi troops had surrounded the farm before arresting our farmworkers and the war veterans.

Since my father's return from Afghanistan, he had arranged for approximately one hundred of his former Mujahideen fighters to be given visas to live in Saudi Arabia, where he settled them on our Jeddah farm. Many of those men had been refused entry to their own countries for one reason or another, and I believe that is why my father brought them to Saudi Arabia.

Our employees and the war veterans followed my father's instructions by peacefully holding up their hands and following orders. Despite their humble behavior, we were told that they were taken away to jail. All the supplies my father had so carefully gathered were confiscated. After months of work and millions of Saudi riyals, nothing was left.

My father was so furious that he could not speak. But he could still move rapidly. I ran to keep up with his long strides as he rushed to his office in Jeddah.

From there he placed a telephone call to Crown Prince Abdullah, the half-brother of King Fahd, and the man who would one day be king, Inshallah (God willing). I listened quietly as he recounted the details of the raid to the prince.

Their conversation was brief. My father said that Crown Prince Abdullah had known nothing of the raid, but promised to investigate the matter and return with an explanation. My father thought highly of the crown prince and felt in his heart that he had been hearing the truth. Still, the sting of the incident had altered my father's feelings forever, starting him on a tragic road that would destroy many lives.

He became even more angry when no further explanation was forthcoming, although my father had ongoing conversations with several high-ranking princes who said they represented Crown Prince Abdullah or King Fahd. We were relieved when the royal family ordered the release from jail of our farmworkers and my father's war veterans.

During the fall of 1990, members of the American military surged into Saudi Arabia. While many Saudi men were offended by the sight of a mainly Christian western army defending their honor, they were doubly traumatized by the full realization of what it meant to be protected by America and other western allies: The Kingdom of Saudi Arabia was flooded with female soldiers.

At the first sight of a capable-looking female soldier, my father became the most outspoken opponent of the royal decision to allow western armies into the kingdom, ranting, "Women! Defending Saudi men!"

No insult could be worse! My father became frustrated to the point of declaring that he could no longer accept the pollution he claimed hung in the air above any non-Muslim. He let loose with a barrage of criticisms, verbally attacking the royal family, the Americans, the British, and anyone else he believed was working against the good of Islam.

My father spoke at the local mosque, sent out flyers, and made audiotapes, all criticizing the government, which he claimed was making Saudi Arabia a colony of America. The royal family became increasingly unhappy, rightfully so, for they were responsible for the well-being of all Saudis, and had made the wise decision not to put the country's fate in the hands of my father and his twelve thousand Mujahideen, despite the fact no one denied that the men were brave fighters.

Although I loved my father, and had difficulty criticizing him, I must say that I believe the royal family behaved responsibly, and for the good of all Saudis.

My father was not appeased when the fight to dislodge Saddam's military from Kuwait was a great success, ending quickly with very little loss of life. In fact, the easy victory seemed to anger him further, making me believe that he would have preferred defeat by a Muslim sword to victory at the hands of the infidels. His fury intensified once the Gulf War ended and it became clear that some American soldiers would remain in Saudi Arabia. He spoke from the mosque, saying, "The continued presence of American soldiers is proof that my prediction of secular pollution has begun in earnest."

I do not know all the details, for I was still young and my father did not consider me his confidant. Yet I sensed from my father's dissatisfaction that an unwelcome change was coming to my family.

Of course, I know now that my father initiated a quarrel with the royal family. Although they calmly and wisely attempted to defuse the squabble, my stubborn father rebuffed their appeals for rational dialogue, magnifying his complaints until a small sore finally festered into an ulcerated boil. His attacks became so unreasonable that the royal family finally threw up their hands in exasperation. Prince Naif, the minister of the interior, informed my father that he was forbidden to leave the kingdom. In Saudi Arabia, such a government action is generally the first step to losing one's freedom. Was prison in my father's future?

My father's elder brothers struggled to bring him to a place of peace, reminding him of the loyalty our family owed the royal family, but my father was immovable, refusing to modify his activities.

Tension filled our household. Every aspect of our personal lives revolved around our father. When he became disgruntled, his displeasure trickled down through the family circle to every wife and every child. In the midst of the crisis, my father unexpectedly ordered my mother to take Abdul Rahman and her two young daughters and travel for a long holiday with her parents and siblings in Syria.

Except for Abdul Rahman, all the sons of my father remained in Jeddah. Then one day my father simply disappeared without telling us anything. We were informed by one of his employees that Sheik Osama had left the kingdom for some business. My brothers and I wondered how he had accomplished the impossible. Remembering his powerful boat *Shafiq al-Madani*, I hoped that my father had not made a daring escape without me.

I was relieved to learn that was not the case. My father had convinced one of the princes to allow him to depart the kingdom in order to attend to some important business in Pakistan, giving that kindly prince his word that he would be back in the kingdom before he was missed.

We waited for my father's return, but we waited in vain. When my mother returned from Syria, the family was further informed that our father was never coming back and we were leaving as well. From now on, we would be living in Africa.

I looked around at our home. I cared little about personal items and could think of nothing beyond my favorite horses stabled at the ranch. What would happen to the beautiful mare Baydah? Or to our favorite stallions, Lazaz, a chestnut Arabian with a white blaze, and Adham, who was also white with a black mane and tail? Adham was my father's special horse, a warrior horse fit for a king.

I was soon given the heartbreaking news that Baydah would be left behind, because there were Saudi laws forbidding Arabian mares to leave the country. My only consolation came from hearing that we would be allowed to take Lazaz and Adham. There was no law restricting the export of stallions.

Yet had I known what the future held for those two beloved horses, I would have done anything necessary to keep them safe in the sands of the kingdom.

Sudan

Sudan:
Osama bin Laden moved his family to Sudan in late 1991
Osama bin Laden expelled from Sudan in mid-1996
Omar bin Laden accompanied his father on the trip out
Osama bin Laden moved his three wives and children to Afghanistan in late 1996

Facts on Sudan:
Full Name: Republic of Sudan
Ruled by: Provisional Government-Republic
Head of State: President Omar Hassan
    Ahmad al-Bashir
Capital: Khartoum
Area: 966,757 sq miles
Major Religions: Islam and Christian
Major Languages: Arabic, Nubian, and others
Population: 38.6 million
Monetary Unit: Sudanese dinar

PART II

Our Life in Khartoum

Chapter 10

To Africa

NAJWA BIN LADEN

I believe that God decides all things. My faith sustained me even as I was boarding the Saudia commercial flight leaving Saudi Arabia, a country that I had grown to love with the same intensity as I loved Syria, the land of my birth.

My steadfast devotion to God was linked with my confidence in my husband. I trusted my husband too, too much. My mind had always confirmed to my heart that all of his ideas and plans were for the benefit of his wives and children. After all, for the past seventeen years Osama had made each and every important decision for his family. There was no reason for me to be wary of anything my husband told me or chose for me.

My unquestioning trust resulted in a consoling influence, which I am certain was reflected on my face. Ever since I was a child, I have been incapable of feigning an emotion I do not feel. My serene manner shaped my children's demeanor, too. They mainly expressed curiosity and happiness, most of them looking on our flight and journey as an adventure altering the routine of school and home.

While our personal items were being transported by cargo ship away from Saudi Arabia's long shores, my husband's family was soon airborne, lifting into the indigo-colored skies of Jeddah to soar over the open desert.

There were eighteen of us. Each wife had been assigned seats with her children in various parts of the airplane. While there were passengers unknown to us between our sections, we took no note of those travelers. We exchanged many glances, looking forward or backward, peeking through our veils, silently inquiring if all was well with the others. Over the years the wives of Osama had become uncommonly dear to one another, considering we were married to the same man.

Osama's first family was comprised of me and our eight children. Abdullah, a dear boy who cared deeply for his younger siblings, was fifteen years old at the time. Abdul Rahman, my second son, who was known to exert himself at whatever might catch his fancy, was thirteen. Both older sons were very quiet, behaving responsibly.

Chatty Sa'ad, often called the "joker" by his brothers, was twelve years old. As usual, high-strung Sa'ad appeared delighted to have a captive audience, making conversation with anyone who would listen.

My most sensitive child, Omar, who at the tender age of ten was beginning to prove himself an earnest and sincere adviser to his siblings, was sitting rigidly with a tense expression on his face. My mother's instinct told me that Omar was still troubled over the fate of our mares on the farm. My fourth-born son loved animals and was always worried over one creature or another.

Eight-year-old Osman and six-year-old Mohammed were frolicking in youthful high spirits. Both were wiggling and giggling over something or other.

My four-year-old daughter, Fatima, was perched daintily beside her mother. Dear to my eyes was my one-year-old daughter, Iman, who copied every movement made by her older sister. My little daughters were such a profound joy for me.

Osama's second family was Khadijah and her children. She had established herself only a few aisles away from me with her well-loved sons, Ali, who was a very serious and sweet seven-year-old boy, and Amer, her cherished two-year-old.

Osama's third family was my closest friend in our "wife-family," Khairiah, who was keeping close watch over Hamza, her active three-year-old boy, who was full of charming tricks.

Osama's fourth family consisted of Siham and her three children. There was Kadhija, her pretty four-year-old daughter; Khalid, her happy three-year-old son; and finally, little Miriam, the premature baby who had been born the same day as my precious Iman, but who was now healthy, thanks be to God.

And so it came to be that four wives and fourteen children were on their way to their one husband and one father.

My husband's face kept appearing in my mind. I was keen to see Osama, for it had been some weeks since he had mysteriously departed from Saudi Arabia. I had been told few details since that time, other than his startling instruction: "Najwa, do not leave one dish in Saudi Arabia."

I knew that Osama would be waiting to greet us when we arrived at our destination. I prayed that God's plans included just resolutions to all the problems my husband was facing, and that God would see fit to hand him the keys to the newly locked doors of Saudi Arabia. Then we might return to the home we had just departed.

My musings, along with my two active girl babies, kept me so occupied that two hours passed rapidly. Soon the pilot of the plane announced that we must prepare ourselves for landing.

I gazed through the small porthole window as we drew closer to our new home, Khartoum. Since I had never visited the country I would now call home, I was struck with curiosity.

Pressing my face against the window, I could vaguely see through my veil and noticed the bare ground rising up beneath us. Teeny buildings and thread-sized roads slowly grew in size. My eyes promptly saw that Khartoum was vastly different from Jeddah.

The previously small town of Jeddah had become a thoroughly modern city over the past ten years, boasting tall contemporary buildings and the most modern highways. In contrast, Khartoum appeared to be comprised of sun-baked, mud-brick buildings, none higher than a few stories. I could not be certain from my viewing spot, but many of the roads appeared to be unpaved. As we drew near to landing, the dirt and dust began to increase.

While it was true that the desert was always encroaching upon Jeddah, Saudis made it a goal to push the creeping sand back, hindering its stealthy crawl into the city streets. That did not seem to be the case in Khartoum. I thought perhaps the Sudanese did not possess the financial resources blessed upon Jeddah.

I knew a few facts. Sudan was the largest country in the African continent, with an Islamic government. Egypt was a neighbor, as well as Ethiopia and Eritrea, two countries I knew something about due to conversations with some of our tea girls, smart young women we had left behind in Saudi Arabia to work for other lucky families. Because Sudan was so vast in size, the country claimed a host of border-linked neighbors: Egypt, Eritrea, Ethiopia, Kenya, Uganda, Congo, the Central African Republic, Chad, and Libya. Just as in Saudi Arabia, the Red Sea bounded one side of Sudan.

Khartoum, the city where we were landing in the plane, was the capital of Sudan, although it was a relatively young city, being founded in 1821. The White Nile, which flows down from Lake Victoria, and the Blue Nile, which flows west from Ethiopia, come together in Khartoum as twins, but leave the city as one, flowing north into Egypt, where it became famous to the world.

My girls gave a little jump and giggled when we felt the airplane wheels hop along the bumpy runway. Fatima joined me when I peered once more out the windows, gazing at the scenery consisting of open fields of dirt and sagebrush. There were a few dust-laden trees that seemed so out of place one would wonder if they had unexpectedly popped out of the ground. We observed men and women scurrying about simple homes in small settlements. The Sudanese women were wearing loose, vivid-colored dresses with matching head wraps.

Most of the men were wearing the traditional jalabiya, which is an ankle-long gown, with tagias (skullcaps) on their heads. Others were dressed in the sirwal and ragis, which are baggy pants and thigh-length tunics, generally of the same pastel color.

I had a brief thought about those people and the sort of lives they were living, but I lost sight of them as we pulled closer to the terminal, a concrete building about three stories high. At the landing time, I had to concentrate on my children.

Carrying Iman in my arms and encouraging Fatima to remain by my side, I motioned for my six sons to stay nearby. There was a rush as everyone pushed to the door of the airplane and onto and down the steps the airport workers had rolled up to the door.

The moment I stepped outside the door, I recognized my husband's tall figure standing beside a long black car that one usually associates with very important visitors, or VIPs. Well-armed security guards were circling the area. The car windows were blackened for privacy, an Osama family custom. There were other similar cars in a line, all waiting to carry my husband's large family to our private homes.

I walked near to my husband. I knew him so well that without his speaking a word I could see that he was relieved that we had arrived safely. We exchanged little other than a nod and a casual greeting. Muslim men and women do not express emotion or touch physically in public, even after marriage of many years and many children.

Everything had been arranged beforehand. Because of my husband's influence, there was no requirement for our family to endure the formalities of passport control and customs.

The moment everyone was settled in the long black cars, security cars surrounded our motorcade and our drivers sped away from the airport. While my little daughters were leaping about with excitement to be out of the restraints of the airplane seat belts, I took occasional glimpses out the dark windows, getting a closer view of Khartoum.

Soon we pulled into a posh area where I saw that many attractive homes had been recently constructed. I was informed that we would be living in that community, a well-to-do suburb of Khartoum known as al-Riyadh Village. The houses were all nice-sized and built closely together.

Osama had arranged for four houses in al-Riyadh Village for the family and for his men who guaranteed our security. The house where his family would live was fine enough, a large house with three stories. As always, I lived on the top story, with my wife friends residing in various apartments below me.

My oldest sons were quick to choose their living space, while I made the decisions for the little ones. All in all, I was relieved and pleased, knowing that so long as we were all together all would be well. My husband resided that first night in my private apartment. His presence was agreeable to me.

After two weeks, we had settled into a routine that in many ways resembled our life in Saudi Arabia. My husband arranged for two local women to help with the home and children, although Osama had lately been hinting that I should take care of my children by myself. In my culture, the men of the family make all the important decisions, but I believed that with eight children, some of whom were toddlers and babies, I required assistance. On this point I was quietly determined, and in the end Osama arranged for the two native girls, who were very helpful and more than pleasant.

Each morning we would rise with the sun to say our first prayers of the day, and then would return to sleep. After resting for a short time, we would make certain that the boys were not late for school. As was the custom in Khartoum, our sons would have breakfast there.

I was glad to hear that Osama had arranged for the oldest boys to attend a very good private school. I knew by that time my sons had been miserable with the public schools they attended in Jeddah and Medina. In Khartoum, they would be attending the Al-Majlis Al-Afriiki Ta'leen Alkhaas, or the African Council for Special Teaching. The school was open for six days a week, every day but Friday, which of course is our Islamic holy day when the routine of daily life is suspended for twenty-four hours.

Seeing my handsome sons in their regulation school uniform erased nearly a generation of time. My thoughts swirled back to the early years that suddenly seemed so far away. I felt the ache of those days when I was a young wife, dolefully watching my young husband in his carefully pressed school uniform as he left me to miss him while he was attending to his work and his schooling.

Now our handsome sons were following in their father's steps. Abdullah, Abdul Rahman, Sa'ad, Omar, Osman, and even our youngest son, little Mohammed, created a clamor each morning as they leapt to don their dark green trousers and light green colored shirts. If their father was not staying with me, they were permitted to make a lot of noise. I would smile, watching as they became too boisterous and fell over each other, rushing from my living quarters to meet Ali, Khadijah's oldest son. Together all seven of the boys would run a foot race to the curb of the compound area to wait for a white school bus.

My apartment was very quiet after my six sons emptied out, leaving me with my two girls, Fatima and Iman, who were as calm as a blue sky after the passing of a sandstorm. My daughters and I would eat a nice leisurely breakfast, and then I would take up important playtime with them, for they were still too small to learn to read the Koran or to help me with chores. We might play hide-and-seek if I was feeling up to it.

Afterward, my maids would continue to play with my girls so that I might stretch and exercise. As I grew older and stiffer, I was discovering the importance of becoming more physically active. After exercise time, I might do some sketching, as I still derived much pleasure from drawing faces and, most especially, expressive eyes. After putting away my pencils and paper, I would read for a while, mainly concentrating on the Koran. Every morning the four wives of my husband would visit each other and chat for a while and then read religious texts together.

We had a very large private garden with grass, flowers, and short trees with fat trunks. Nearly every day when there was no one else around, and it was not too hot, I would take the younger children into the garden and watch them there. Sometimes the other mothers would bring their little ones out to the garden and we would guard over our playful children.

With so much to do, the morning passed quickly and the boys would return one hour after the noon time. After their mental and physical exertions, their stomachs would be empty, so I would make certain the cook had prepared a good lunch. Afterward, I might enjoy a nap. My girls often slumbered with me but the boys were left on their own as they were getting older.

My husband was not a believer in modern playthings for our children, but boys without toys will find many activities to pursue. Once I remember waking up from a nap and looking out the windows of my apartment to see my sons busily engaged constructing wooden tree houses in those short trees in the garden. The tree houses emerged as elaborate constructions with walkways from one tree house to the other. Where they located the large pieces of lumber I do not know, but some of my husband's employees probably provided my sons with the building materials.

After completing the tree houses, they lived in those make-believe homes for many long hours. Many times I would observe each boy perched in his house in the tree, to my mind resembling a big bird, staring at the blue sky or over the large walls surrounding our home. Sometimes they would devote whole days of their free time doing nothing but sitting and staring. What dreams they were spinning I will never know.

I observed yet another special project for many weeks as they put together an oven under the ground, installing pipes for the air to transfer. Afterward they set out on a project of growing kidney beans. Once mature, they picked those beans fresh from the plants and cooked them in various dishes.

Since moving to Khartoum, Osama had more time for his children. My husband devoted hours explaining to his sons the importance of growing fine vegetables and other produce on the land. He set an example with his many farms growing corn and soybeans and even sunflowers. Perhaps that is where the boys got the idea to grow those kidney beans.

Whatever the reason, I was glad to see the boys entertaining themselves. They had led such isolated lives when we lived in Saudi Arabia that now their boyish games and pursuits created gladness in my heart. They grew bold, sometimes escaping from the al-Riyadh compound to explore our neighborhood. I believe that my husband was mainly unaware of their daring adventures. Knowing they were good boys who needed some little freedoms, I chose to remain silent, although I would have never lied to my husband had he asked me directly.

There were other good things about living in Khartoum. I was happy that my husband did not travel so much, and that he seemed more at ease tending to his many important projects. He had arrangements with high officials in the Sudanese government to build roads and factories and various businesses, including the farms I mentioned. Osama's favorite undertaking was working the land, growing the best corn and the biggest sunflowers. He had seriously overworked his mind to discover new ways of producing the largest sunflowers in the world. Nothing made my husband happier than showing off his huge sunflowers.

I smile when I remember those rewarding days. In fact, some of my fondest memories are the times when the corn or the sunflowers were ready to be harvested and off we would go to one of the farms, usually to al-Damazin, which was south of Khartoum. The outings reminded me of the days when we used to load up the family to visit our Jeddah farm.

The sunflower harvest was the most fun. I would select a big pair of scissors and be happy to settle myself in a caravan of big black automobiles. Once at the farm, Osama would arrange the timing so that there would be private hours when his wives and children might work harvesting the sunflowers without concern that we would accidentally mingle with strangers. Although we wives would wear our customary veils, when no one else was in the vicinity our veils might slip away from our faces because we were concentrating on clipping the sunflowers. Of course, if we heard any human voices unfamiliar to our ears, we would quickly conceal our naked faces.

Some of those enormous sunflowers were many times the size of our heads. I often studied those huge plants in admiration, knowing that Osama was the reason for such beauty. Those are the best memories, to be busy and part of a worthy mission to produce something practical.

There were other times we traveled to a place called al-Kuttiya. The trip was very long and the roads unpaved, so the roadway created many thrills. When it was the dry season we stirred up dust storms and when it was the rainy season the dust had been turned into mud, and our vehicles often became bogged in the gummy muck. Everyone would groan in frustration at the delay. In truth we were not as displeased as we appeared because our lives were so quiet that we minded little to be trapped on the road.

Omar and his brothers would struggle to push the wheels free so that we might continue our trip. For some reason the sight was very funny to me and the other wives, watching our strong sons heave and push and strain. Sometimes the eager driver would push too hard against the gas pedal and the mud would sling in many directions. We would giggle under our veils watching the boys leap about, trying in vain to escape that airborne mud.

On the way to the farm in the south, the boys would sometimes call for the caravan to stop at a certain area that only they knew was favorable for hunting. They would leave the women and the small children in the cars while they slipped away to hunt for food. There was a special big turkey that was most exceptional, and loved by all family members. Our boys were excellent hunters and never failed to shoot several. Once we arrived at the cottage area, we would boil the turkeys, then pull away their feathers. It was a bit sad to eat them because those turkeys were quite attractive with their white-dotted feathers.

Other times Omar would call out for us to stop because his keen eyes had caught sight of a special tree that produces delicious fruits. The name of the tree is lost to memory but we would eagerly watch as Omar climbed the tree and selected the best fruits. My sweet son would present them to me so I could save them to eat once we arrived to the farm.

At the farm there were a few lovely huts, like little cottages. They were small and round, with tall thatch roofs shaped like a big ice cream cone. Those round huts had been constructed in the middle of a forest of big trees where large groups of monkeys lived. Those monkeys were more fun than a circus. The entire monkey family would become animated at our arrival and would amuse us with songs and dances. After watching the entertaining monkey show for a while, we would enter the cottages to settle ourselves for a much anticipated holiday that generally lasted four nights, or until Osama said it was time for us to leave.

The cottages were masterfully constructed from dried tree pieces, twigs, foliage, and small branches. Osama had arranged for numerous cots to be placed in the cottages so that all had their assigned beds. Osama also arranged for us to have mosquito nets to drape over our bodies, Osama warned us about malaria, which is a deadly disease in that part of Africa, particularly for small children. I was serious about draping those nets over my smallest children.

Mainly I liked the delicious mangoes that grew on trees right outside the cottage. I have happy memories of sitting at the door of the cottage, watching my children play under the twinkling stars while eating some of those juicy mangoes.

It was more common for us to take trips to Osama's small horse farm, which was only a short distance away from our home in al-Riyadh Village. While the men of the family occupied themselves with the horses, the women enjoyed the private swimming pool. Once the men had gone for their rides and our seclusion was assured, some of the wives and daughters would take a cool dip. Of course we did not own swimming costumes, but we would splash in the pool while wearing our long dresses.

My older boys learned much while we lived in Khartoum because their father began to treat our eldest sons as young men. Osama would even take the six older boys along when he would go out on a special project. I remember the times they accompanied him in order to observe the building of a railroad. My sons were excited to tell me that Osama had explained the smallest details from how the rails were constructed, and the steps taken by the engineers. They were convinced that their father knew everything.

My husband had a dream that his many sons would one day be in charge of his numerous businesses in Sudan.

There were other unusual experiences. From the time our eldest sons were young boys in Saudi Arabia, Osama had focused on training them to endure long periods in the desert without outside assistance. One day Osama informed us that the state of the world had brought him to the conclusion that his wives and daughters must also be trained to become patient and courageous.

He came up with plans to help all the members of his family achieve strong, resilient characters. How he thought of those unique ideas remains a mystery to me. But when the notion struck, he would arrange transportation to take his family out of Khartoum to the edge of an undeveloped area. We were not allowed to take our usual supplies for an overnight trip, although we would notice shovels and other tools for digging stacked in the backs of the vehicles.

Once we arrived at an isolated place in the desert, we were told that we would be staying overnight under the stars. Osama said, "While on this training mission all must limit liquids and other nourishment." Additionally, we would not be provided with any modern conveniences such as beds or blankets. We were most surprised when Osama said, "I did not bring mosquito nets, but do not worry. Mosquitoes rarely come into the desert."

While the wives and daughters watched, Osama directed the biggest and strongest boys to use the digging tools to excavate hollows large enough for a human to stretch out lengthwise when sleeping.

Meanwhile, Osama was preaching: "You must be gallant. Do not think about foxes or snakes. Remember, you are in training. Challenging trials are coming to us. There will come a day when you will not have a shelter over your head. You will not have a blanket to cover your body."

I blinked, wondering if snakes were common to the area.

Osama gestured at the holes taking shape in the ground. "Each one of you will sleep alone in a dirt hole."

No one protested, not even our babies. Everyone did as told, slowly easing our bodies into those dirt holes, waiting for a long, long night to pass.

Remember that countries like Sudan are boiled by the sun during the day, but the moment the sun drops from the sky, the desert is cold.

I heard a soft voice complain about the night chill.

Osama advised the complainer to "cover yourself with dirt or grass." He paused, then called out from his hole, "You will become warm under what nature provides."

Although uncomfortable with the idea, for who knew what insects were using that sand as their homes, I finally grew so chilled that I did cover my body up to my waist with dirt and grass. It's true that nature will provide warmth, just as Osama said, although I preferred my bed and blanket back in my apartment in Khartoum.

As I lay in that hole covered with dirt, staring at the starlit sky above, I reminded myself that my husband knew much more about the big world than any of us. We were all pearls to my husband, and he wanted to protect us.

And, who knew? Perhaps the scary time would come when my children and I would find ourselves running from aggressive warriors, thankful for the lessons we had learned from Osama. Wouldn't everyone be surprised when my children and I popped up alive because we knew how to endure the harsh desert climate without water supplies or without benefit of modern conveniences?

Of course, I did not want my little children to suffer thus, so I said many prayers to God, asking that such a thing should never come to pass.

Chapter 11

Family Affairs

Our oldest sons became young men during the Khartoum years. They excelled in sports that young men enjoy, soccer and martial arts, and other similar hobbies. All our sons were good swimmers; in fact, the boys used to swim across the Nile River for fun. This is no small feat, for the Nile may be narrow but its waters are tricky with unexpected currents. The Nile was near al-Riyadh Village, so it was not uncommon for them to go there with their father for a swim. Other times they would ride out into the desert to race some of their father's automobiles. All our sons were taught to drive automobiles by age eight, which is expected in Saudi Arabia. They became skilled hunters, easily capturing animals in traps or killing them with one shot.

I remember once when they built a trap to try to capture the hawk that goes by the name of the Shaheen. I knew about the Shaheen hawks from the time I was a small girl because Arabs favor that predatory bird above all others. Shaheens are trapped alive in the open desert to be trained to swoop to earth to catch rabbits, quails, and other small creatures. I've been told that they are very particular how they pick up their prey and actually present their owners with the creatures without taking a bite, or even making a scratch. I know little else because I am not a hunter woman.

Much of what we had been accustomed to changed during those Sudan years, but mainly for the boys. The women of the family remained inside our homes and focused on our female activities, as we had always done, and always would. My daughters, Fatima and Iman, were still very young, so they were contented scampering around in our large home, mimicking their mother in her daily routine. Both girls provided a lot of amusement to our household as they were of the age to perform a lot of cute baby tricks. Osama took a lot of joy from those baby girls and let them crawl the length of his long body and even tweak his beard. Those were very happy times, rare moments I had not witnessed for many years. Watching my husband and our daughters, I thought perhaps all might work out well for the bin Laden family in Africa.

There were scary times as well. For the first time in our married life, Osama became so ill that I feared for his life. Mysteriously, he contracted malaria. From where we could not guess, as anytime he was in an area that mosquitoes were known to inhabit, he always used a mosquito net.

His sudden illness was a big fright for me because my husband was famous for being the most healthy man in the world. In fact, up until that time, I cannot recall his ever making a single protest of pain, not even of a minor headache or toothache.

He had been traveling for business and soon after returning complained of a fever and nausea and pains in his joints. For the first day or two, we believed that he had contracted a strain of flu. But he became too sick, shivering with chills one moment and sweating with fever the next. Soon Osama had difficulty standing. He even turned a peculiar shade of yellow. But even after turning yellow, he refused to visit a doctor of medicine. Soon, though, Osama concluded that there was no other explanation other than he had been bitten by a female mosquito carrying the malaria.

My own heart thumped loudly at his diagnosis, for I knew the outcome for many malaria victims. After he returned home, he was so feverish and ill that he had no thoughts of further protecting himself. I suppose he was bitten again. Those new infected mosquitoes spread the disease to other family members. My four oldest sons, Abdullah, Abdul Rahman, Sa'ad, and Omar, followed their father, coming down with the same scary symptoms.

My poor sons reported being dizzy and short of breath, with painful joints and pounding heads. Although I served food and water, nothing I could do would ease their discomfort. Poor Abdul Rahman became dangerously ill. The wretched look on Abdul Rahman's face finally brought Osama to the conclusion that he must seek medical treatment for himself and for our boys. Weak though he was, he roused everyone sick and had them transported to a local clinic.

I was saying many prayers as I watched them disappear from our home, and many more prayers during the brief time they were away. Thanks be to God, after receiving special medical treatments, including fluids that were pumped directly into their veins, all of them returned, weak but alive. That's when Osama told me that he had been informed by the doctor that there was no guarantee of evading malaria, despite using a nightly mosquito net. On occasion, mosquitoes would bite victims even before dusk. There was really no way to be completely safe unless one wore a mosquito net over one's body throughout the entire day.

Perhaps that is why we females were less likely to be bitten, for we never left our home without being covered from head to toe in our customary abaayas.

A good day came at the end of our first year in Khartoum when my father traveled to Sudan for a holiday. His jolly face was the best view I had enjoyed in many months. Although I remained at home with my daughters, Osama escorted my father to the most interesting sights in Khartoum, which I was told had a modern central city, although the outskirts were very simple. Most pleasant of all were the relaxing hours when my father sat with me and shared news of my mother, siblings, and other relatives living in Syria.

I hoped that my dear father could return at least once every year for similar holidays. Yet within a short time of my father's visit to Khartoum, I received the most alarming telephone call from a family member in Syria whispering that my father was bedridden with a lung infection. We Arabs break bad news very slowly as not to shock loved ones; therefore it took some time for my relative to confess that the lung infection was quite serious, and in fact, was lung cancer.

My father had loved the smoking evil since the time he was a young adult. Those cigarettes had finally turned on him. My father was unable to fight the spiteful disease and quickly lost the ability to live a normal life. He was suffering with pain that put him to bed.

To my dismay I learned that even after being diagnosed with lung cancer, he could not force back the desire to smoke. I was told that he had lost so much of his body weight that he was all bones with a little skin, and that he was in so much pain that he had to fight not to cry out. Yet, there he was, a gravely ill patient reclining in bed with a cigarette hanging from his lips. That habit carried on until the moment of death; he stubbornly clenched a cigarette between his teeth until God called him away.

Since I was unable to travel from Sudan to Syria, it came to pass that my beloved father died without his daughter Najwa by his side. This was a big hurt in my heart because any daughter feels close to a father who is so caring. I was helpless, so far away in Africa. I could only pray to God for Him to bless my father's soul and to put him in white paradise.

Despite my knowledge that God knows best for all of us, I have never erased the sadness from my heart, even though my husband, Osama, reminded me that God decides all things and that whatever God decreed should be celebrated.

I was also nudged by the premonition I had suffered when last visiting Syria, during the time our family had not yet left Saudi Arabia. I remembered the dark foreboding surrounding me, strong feelings that something terrible was going to happen to someone. Now I wondered if perhaps God Himself had forewarned me of my father's death.

We had other visitors from the family. Some of Osama's siblings and their spouses came to visit, which was a happy occasion for us all. Even Auntie Allia and her husband, Muhammad al-Attas, traveled to Khartoum for two lovely visits. Osama was in a particularly light mood when his mother was in his sight. He adored showing her the city that was now our home, as well as his farms so that she would know what her son was producing for Sudan and for the world. Although Allia, like me, wanted all the troubles to go away so that her son and his wives and children could return to Saudi Arabia, she did not protest to me or to Osama because she knew she had no way of changing the situation.

There were not so many pregnancies among my husband's four wives during the four years that we lived in Khartoum, only three in fact. Siham, Osama's fourth wife, was first, giving birth to her fourth child, and third daughter, Sumaiya. Then Osama's second wife, Khadijah, became pregnant soon after our arrival in Sudan. Khadijah had her first daughter, and last child with my husband, a little girl named Aisha.

The family was in for a shock. Shortly after little Aisha joined our growing family, Khadijah chose to return to Saudi Arabia. My husband agreed with her plan. Many people have speculated about their divorce, but there are special secrets in every family, secrets that I would never dishonor myself and my family by unveiling. All I will say is what is already known, that Khadijah returned with her three children to Saudi Arabia, where she lives to this day. Khadijah was sorely missed by her sister wives, and I am certain that my sons pined for Ali and Amer, for the boys had been playmates from the time they were toddlers. Other than Ali, who came back to Khartoum for a visit to Sudan when he was eleven years old, Khadijah's children were gone from our lives forever.

With Khadijah's departure, we suddenly were only three wives and thirteen children.

Happily, I became pregnant with my ninth child in early 1993. Osama said that I should travel to be with his mother, Allia, in Jeddah to give birth in the fine hospital using the excellent female doctors there. When given the opportunity, I always chose to be attended by a female physician because of my womanly shyness.

A short time before the estimated time for birthing, I learned that Osama would be unable to travel with me into Saudi Arabia. Although disappointed, I was not surprised, for I was aware that past problems kept my husband out of the kingdom. So it was necessary for Osama to select our eldest son, Abdullah, who would turn seventeen during the year and was of a responsible mind-set, to be my guardian.

You may or may not know that Muslim women are forbidden to travel alone. Our traveling companions cannot be just anyone, but must be a suitable guardian, called a mahram, who can only be a male family member whom the woman is forbidden by religious law to marry. Blood mahrams include a woman's grandfather, father, brother, husband, son, grandson, or nephew; and there are in-law mahrams, such as a father-in-law, son-in-law, stepfather, or stepson. There is one last group of men with whom a woman can become mahram. If any woman acts as a wet nurse, she becomes the child's milk mother, or rada. Blood mahrams apply to this group of people associated with the milk nurse, including milk mother husband, father, brothers, sons, uncles, and so on.

While I was pleased to return to Jeddah, I was despondent at the idea of leaving my family in Khartoum. Despite that hint of sadness, there were many joyful moments in Jeddah. I was delighted to see that beautiful city once again. I had visits from girlfriends not seen in a long time. Allia and her children, as always, were the kindest hearts, taking care of my every need. My friends and family would even take an afternoon walk in the family garden with me, something many Saudis avoid due to the tremendous heat generated by the desert sun.

Before I left Khartoum to travel to Jeddah, Osama had decided that if our child was a son, he should be named Ladin. As soon as I was well enough to travel, my eldest son, Abdullah, ushered his mother and baby brother, Ladin, safely back to Khartoum.

Everyone loved Ladin because he was such a pretty baby and had special cute ways. After our return to Khartoum, for some reason my husband changed his mind and decided that Ladin should be renamed Bakr. Although Bakr is his proper official name that appears on all his documents, the name Ladin stuck with the children and with me. Of course, such a situation created confusion for our little boy, but I told him that he was so special that he must have two names, and that seemed to satisfy him.

I came to see that additional women would be joining our family as the wives of my husband, Osama. A year or so after Khadijah and Osama divorced, my husband married another wife. But this new marriage ended quickly because of a secret. Being on paper only (meaning not consummated), she did not come into our close family group. Therefore, our family unit remained for a time as it was, with three wives and their fourteen children.

Life changes. Things alter. Such matters were out of my hands. But I was at peace, for as a believer, I leave all things to God.

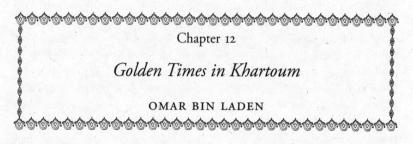

Chapter 12

Golden Times in Khartoum

OMAR BIN LADEN

Who could have known that the happiness I was seeking was waiting for me in African Sudan? When my feet touched the dusty soil of Khartoum, I was only a child of ten, but soon to turn eleven. My father met us at the airport with a huge entourage, which was not unusual. I noticed that many of the men accompanying my father were Mujahideen soldiers from the days of Afghanistan, while others were impassioned followers of my father's beliefs, so all carried a reverence for him.

Happily for his sons, their deference trickled down to us. He was the prince, or so they said. In fact, few people outside our world understand the high degree of love the Arab masses expressed for my father. Although he had to depart Saudi Arabia, his exile came about due to his disagreements with the Saudi royal family, not with ordinary Saudi citizens.

We were to live in a neighborhood called al-Riyadh. Our personal home was a beige-colored house behind walls of the same color, the same kind of concrete block enclosures we had left behind in Saudi Arabia. There was a large beige metal gate. Several of my father's men rushed to open it so that our large family might enter the grounds.

I exchanged a few glances with my brothers and I knew that we were of the same mind. We were looking at my mother's new prison, for she basically lived in purdah, a state of almost total isolation when females socialize only with family members, and rarely if ever leave private dwellings. For her entire married life my mother was allowed to leave her home only when we were traveling to visit relatives, or transferring to another family home, such as our farm on the outskirts of Jeddah. I believed that the large house would be my prison as well. The children of Osama bin Laden enjoyed very few ordinary freedoms, although in comparison to the women of the house, we were as free as birds.

As I studied the exterior of the dwelling, I realized the Osama bin Laden family was coming down in the world. Our new home was decidedly smaller and more modest than the spacious mansions we left behind in Saudi Arabia, yet it was larger than any home I had viewed on the trip from the airport. The house appeared to have three separate floors so I hoped it was large enough for four wives and many children.

My father led the way.

My older brothers and I quietly followed in our father's footsteps, for we knew that he had no patience with children who failed to conduct themselves as adults. Even the smallest siblings walked in silence. Our veiled mother and aunties followed behind us because it is our custom for women to follow men.

After entering the yard, Father walked through the double wooden door painted a dull brown color. Of course he had already made every decision about who would reside where. We were told that the room on the right was the family's guest room if any relatives might come to visit and on the left was the apartment for Auntie Khairiah, mother of the toddler Hamza. She had the smallest apartment because she had only one child, but it was still ample with a living room, bathroom, and kitchen along with two bedrooms. The remaining space on that floor was our father's study and private office.

Marble stairs took us to the second floor. Both Auntie Khadijah and Auntie Siham had generous-sized apartments on the second, or middle, floor.

Climbing to yet another level, the third and top floor, always my mother's favorite position in any home, we came to our family's living quarters. There we found four bedrooms, a living room, bathrooms, a third kitchen, and a stairway leading to the rooftop. As in Saudi Arabia, Sudanese homes were built with flat roofs, an area serving as an open living space.

The house was rather disappointing for our tastes, but there was nothing to do but settle in and hope for the best. Undoubtedly, we were mischievous boys and the moment our parents locked the door leading to their private area, we burst into action, eagerly exploring the various rooms and good-naturedly quarreling over sleeping arrangements, although we were cautious to keep our voices low to keep from provoking our father's legendary temper.

The house was plainly furnished, which wasn't a surprise. Our father always scorned anything elaborate when it came to his family, often stating that we should not be pampered, and we were not. There were cheap Persian carpets on the floor and beige curtains on the windows. There were blue cushions placed seatlike along the walls, in the manner common in many Arab homes. There were no decorations, not even one picture hanging on the walls, although we did notice evidence of our father's work tacked up on the walls of his study on the lower level. We tried to make sense of some maps and plans for the roads and factories he was currently building, but could not. As usual, his study was crammed with hundreds of books, both in English and Arabic, mainly to do with religion and military matters. Our father spoke and wrote fluent English because his own father had decreed that his children should be highly educated.

When we finally retired, we found that there was not enough space for all of us to have conventional beds, so we slept on mattresses tossed to the floor, ending with wall-to-wall mattresses in the bedrooms. In the morning it was necessary to roll our mattresses for storage in order to walk around in the room.

The attached outdoor garden was generously laid out, with plenty of space for a group of boys to play. Unlike Saudi Arabia, which has little in the way of garden vegetation, there were some trees, thick bushes, and flower beds dotting the edge of the garden. In fact, everything on the physical grounds of al-Riyadh Village was to our liking, including a large empty lot a short distance from our home that we hoped to use as a soccer pitch.

Things were looking up.

Despite these early positive signs, worries nibbled at my mind. What about the mares we had left behind? When would our stallions arrive in Khartoum? Would our father purchase additional horses in Sudan? Would I find friends in this new environment? Would I be required to attend public school?

School was my principal concern. What if my Sudanese school experiences deteriorated into something even more hideous than I had already endured in Saudi Arabia? I prayed that our father was too occupied with his businesses to find a school for us.

Within a few days my brothers and I received the sobering news from one of our father's drivers that we had already been enrolled in school. But when we learned that we would be attending the finest private school in all of the country, the Al-Majlis Al-Afriiki Ta'leen Alkhaas school, our spirits lifted.

When we were fitted for our school uniforms, I noticed that they were in much the same style as the uniforms worn by the Sudanese military. Later I was told that the Sudanese government had a policy that young boys should be trained to be soldiers.

We were thrilled when we learned that we would be picked up in our compound by a school bus. The lucky six to attend the school with me were my full brothers Abdullah, Abdul Rahman, Sa'ad, Osman, and Mohammed, the youngest to be registered at age seven. Eight-year-old Ali, our half-brother who was the firstborn son of our Auntie Khadijah, was also enrolled at the same school.

The first day of school we were anxious but excited. After prayers we rushed home to slip off our thobes and put on our uniforms. The moment we were properly dressed, we dashed to the bus stop to wait for the bus we were told to expect. A very long white bus appeared promptly at 6:30 A.M. Schools in hot climates begin and end early, with school hours from seven in the morning until one in the afternoon. We clamored aboard to receive the biggest shock of our lives. There were girl students on the bus!

My brothers and I thought we must have boarded the incorrect bus. Almost instantly we saw that there were boys as well, all dressed in uniforms identical to our own. Not knowing what else to do, we stumbled forward, noting that the girls and boys were not sitting together.

Even so, such a thing would never have been allowed in Saudi Arabia, where everything in public life is segregated by sex, including weddings, parties, restaurant seating, and schools. In Saudi Arabia the girls have their schools and the boys have theirs. Should a girl require a course taught only by a man, the only way she is allowed to take the course is by satellite or pre-taped video. I have been told about some highly conservative female students who even wear their veils when viewing a male teacher on tape.

Many Muslims believe that if an unrelated male and female are in the same room together, there are really three creatures in attendance, the third being the devil himself. Nothing good could come from such mixing, or so we Saudis are taught.

In Sudan, the female students were required to sit on the left side of the bus and the male students on the right. My brothers and I hurriedly found seats, saying little as we glanced around the bus. I admit I cast my eyes more than once on the girls' section but noticed that most of the girls were careful to keep their eyes chastely averted from the boys. Occasionally a bold girl might lift her eyes and her face would crinkle with a shy smile, but for the most part they talked and laughed among themselves. Never did I find the courage to attempt a conversation. I soon realized that the bus driver seemed to have eyes in the back of his head and was quick to reprimand any student who made an attempt to converse with the opposite sex. My father's stern image gave my imagination a quick visit. I believed that once he discovered that his sons would be in close proximity with girls not of our own family, we would be unceremoniously pulled from the school.

Would the first day be our last?

My father frowned upon formal education for females. His own daughters were not allowed to attend school, but instead were taught some basics at home by Auntie Khairiah, who was an educated woman.

I wondered if we might share our classrooms with the opposite sex. If so, I knew our school outing was doomed. Thankfully that was not the case, although we did catch fleeting glimpses of the girls as they changed classes. Everything was relaxed on the playground, giving the girls courage to slip away from their assigned area to venture into ours. Surprisingly, none of the teachers sent them back where they belonged. Yet if any boy tried to sneak onto the girls' playground, he would be reprimanded and marched back to our section of the yard.

Our new world was strange, indeed.

To our great relief, students and teachers alike were friendly and respectful. Our Sudanese school routine was simple but enjoyable. Due to the early hour, all the students were fed breakfast upon arrival. After our simple morning meal of boiled eggs, cheese, and flat bread, we once again attended prayers, for the government of Sudan was an Islamic regime. Classes followed, with classroom teachers who were firm, soft-spoken, and kindly. No instructor sneered that we would not receive good grades even if we earned them. No instructor threatened my brothers or me with a caning. No instructor encouraged the other boys to tease us.

Shortly after nine each morning, students were given a break when we were free to meet other boys and to purchase a snack from the school canteen. Since our father had banned American soft drinks, my brothers and I were sure to purchase a can of cold Pepsi and a packet of crisps, or potato chips.

Since our school was one of the most expensive private schools in the city, many students came from wealthy families. Yet there were others whose families were of the professional class and in a few cases the poorer working class. Even if it meant pinching pennies and saving from their small family budgets, Sudanese parents made extreme efforts to give their children a good education. That meant there was a varied assortment of boys at our school, making the experience much more interesting, at least to me.

There were sports and games before the day ended. For the most part, my brothers and I greatly enjoyed playing with the Sudanese students, who were friendly. Yet there was one schoolyard game that I've never forgotten, mainly because it required a brutality that was undetected in all other activities.

The boys would be selected for two teams. There was an assigned safe area. The teams would line up at a distance from the safe area with the goal being for various players to reach the safe area by outrunning the members of the other team. If one was unlucky enough to be caught, he would receive a physical beating. Those whippings were not your typical schoolyard thrashings. No, the physical poundings were painfully meaningful. Those slow of foot came away with black eyes, bent noses, and massively swollen lips.

From the days when my aim was to outrun my long-legged father in the hat game, as well as my time in Saudi Arabia when schoolyard bullies had chased me, I had learned to fly like the wind. As I studied the brutality of this new game and the distance I would need to sprint to safety, I knew I must run faster than ever before. When my turn came, I could have easily qualified for the Olympic trials. My feet practically flew over the playground and I outran them all.

I often asked those boys why they participated in such a violent game, but their only responses were affable grins and convincing talk that the game was steeped in their culture. The Sudanese believed that boys must not only be schooled, but should also be strong and hard, and that nothing toughened a body like a good beating. Obviously adults shared the boy's opinions, because teachers would observe without interfering even when a boy was beaten bloody. No parents came to the school to complain about their injured children. Years later when I heard of the brutal Sudanese wars and the fighting among the various tribes, I understood that Sudanese boys really did need to learn physical endurance. In real life adult male Sudanese fighters ripped into each other with the ferocity of hungry lions.

After all that strenuous activity, we would all board the bus at one o'clock in the afternoon for a pleasant ride back to al-Riyadh Village. The same boys who had beaten each other silly on the playground maintained a perfect demeanor. I was astounded. In my Arab world such a beating would have never been forgotten, leading to years of fierce reprisals between entire families and even whole tribes. In the land of my birth, brutal tribal wars have been ignited over less.

The new country we now called home was fascinating. I enjoyed staring out the bus windows at the noisy street scenes. Colorfully dressed Sudanese appeared to be celebrating. Not only did men mingle with women, but such boisterous public gatherings are unknown even among men in Saudi Arabia. In the country of my birth, everything of life is hidden behind the privacy of high walls.

Besides regular school, we older boys had additional classes back home. Our father had employed three instructors to teach his sons, each teacher highly qualified in such subjects as world affairs, math, geography, history, and Arabic. One of the three was a Moroccan, whose expertise was religious training. All three men were patient and kindly and we boys respected them greatly.

The lessons were given in the guest house, which was one of our father's villas used mainly to lodge his numerous visitors from the Muslim world and from Europe. The guest house climbed three spacious stories, with twenty-two large rooms and a square footage much larger than our family home. The house was painted a light pink shade with a distinctive shiny black gate.

Inside the guest house there was a special room set aside for teaching, where my brothers and I spent three hours of each afternoon. Tired of too much school, I retained little of what I read, dreaming of freedom to watch the sunset or play soccer.

In addition to our private residence and the guest house, our father had two other houses in the al-Riyadh Village area, all close to our family home. Those two villas were large as well and served as housing for some of our father's many employees, mainly administrators, drivers, or security guards, with most of the men former Mujahideen veterans of the Russian-Afghan war. My father had not only employed the same veterans who had lived on our farm in Jeddah, but had brought in others. The ones who did not live in our area were scattered around the country in other housing.

Other than the few men who had worked on our father's farm outside Jeddah, we had rarely been around our father's soldiers. Besides, I was too young during my years in Saudi Arabia to fully comprehend everything I witnessed. Suddenly, I began to understand more of my father's world, with its vast business and political interests, and people from many countries paying homage. It was in Sudan that I believe our father began to think of his sons as potential future partners, and it was there that we were first invited to take a peek into his convoluted world of politics and commercial activities.

After spending more time with our father at his offices, we began to meet the Mujahideen and slowly learn something of their life histories. That's when we discovered that few of those former soldiers were allowed to return to their own nations.

Every soldier had an interesting story.

While the Afghan-Russian war was raging, governments in the area assisted my father and other organizers by sending groups of young men to fight at the front. The youthful soldiers were full of ideals, being given every reason to believe that they would be rewarded for giving up their schooling, their careers, and possible marriages, all to answer the call to violent Jihad, to assist their Muslim brothers in need. During their fighting years, they were showered with talk of glory, but after winning a war that everyone had told them was impossible to win, their governments discarded them. Some soldiers' passports were not renewed, while others trying to go home were turned away at the borders.

Their countries' leaders apparently feared that the Mujahideen had gained too much knowledge in the art of resistance and war. Perhaps if they returned, they would be a danger to a repressive regime.

Those brave warriors suddenly discovered that they were men without a country. Desperate for jobs, they turned to my father. Although his own life was in such turmoil that he had to flee his own country, all were given jobs, with good salaries and housing. Many veterans told my brothers and me that our father was the only one who never forgot them and never broke a promise.

Many of the hardened soldiers became our father's security guards, zealously protecting him and his family. Those burly soldiers looked as though they could kill my slim father with their bare hands, yet they treated him with awe and respect, standing humbly in the background, never speaking until he spoke. Although our father didn't ask for their reverence, they worshipped him with their whole hearts, driven by the desire to please him.

As sons of Osama bin Laden, we were the beneficiaries of that worship. To protect Osama's family, every man would have sacrificed his own life.

We were cautious of those guards at first, for their loyalty to our father made us believe that our father's eyes were in their heads. We were too young to realize that we needed protecting, that there were people in the world who wanted our father dead, and if we were killed during the process, so be it. We believed that everyone on earth—except for those teachers in Saudi Arabia—revered our father, because most we met loved him to the point of worship. "Your father is the prince," we heard again and again.

Although our father had scores of men watching out for his sons, living in a busy neighborhood made it easier for us to evade the guards. Activity around our home was usually brisk, so we slowly learned ways to melt into the crowd or to slip away when the guards were busy with one thing or another.

Over time, we gained even more freedom. The Sudanese shackles we had so feared were slowly loosened. Did our father finally trust us? Or was he so busy with his various projects that we skipped his mind? I never knew the answer to that question.

To be sure, our father was engaged in many business interests during those years in Sudan. He once astounded us by saying, "Sudan is our home now. I will live out my life in this land." I remember how odd I felt at hearing his words, wondering how he could bear a permanent break with the land of his birth.

But with his loyalties now attached to Sudan, my father became enthralled with a goal of bringing the impoverished country up to modern standards. From his time in Saudi Arabia, he had seen real economic prosperity and he wanted that success for Sudan. Without the oil wealth of Saudi Arabia, he surmised that fertile areas of Sudan would be the solution to bring the African nation out of poverty. In fact, the land region south of Khartoum to the border of Ethiopia was popularly known as Sudan's bread basket. That is the area where my father had numerous farms, growing many different kinds of vegetables and sunflowers. He also became involved in construction work, farming, and horse breeding.

Soon after arriving in Khartoum our father informed us that he had already purchased a horse farm. It was nothing elaborate like our farm near Jeddah, yet it was only fifteen minutes by car from al-Riyadh Village, so we went to the stables at least once a week. He had purchased a few horses before we arrived, and the stallions exported from Saudi Arabia brought the number to seven. I was delighted with every horse, with my favorite being the stallion named Lazaz, one of the horses my father had managed to bring from Saudi Arabia. The beautiful Adham was set to arrive in Khartoum as well.

Lazaz, which most Muslims will recognize as the name of Prophet Mohammed's horse, was a pure Arab stallion with a chestnut mane and tail with a contrasting white blaze and three white socks, on his left foreleg and both back legs. Lazaz was a proud stallion, not the sort of horse that encouraged casual play. His greatest joy was running with his harem of mares and any interruption was a challenge for his human handlers.

I remember the day Lazaz was nearly killed for threatening my father.

Lazaz had recently arrived on a transport from Jeddah and was feeling frisky, for he had not been ridden in several months. He was prancing in a circular enclosure, eager to get away for his own horsey business. My father thought the time had come to take him out for a brisk ride. Lazaz had other ideas. When my father tried to saddle Lazaz, the stallion reared tall on his back legs, dancing, angry, ready to attack. My father, who was a great horseman, was equally unwavering in his aim to reclaim Lazaz.

They were fighting it out, a determined horseman and his equally determined stallion. My heart was in my throat because Lazaz and my father had enjoyed many days of horse-and-rider camaraderie, but now they were sudden adversaries, unequal in strength, but so similar in willpower.

Nothing my father could do calmed Lazaz. He repeatedly attacked my father, the fury in his eyes flashing threats of violence. Suddenly I noticed that one of my father's friends had loaded and lifted his weapon, his barrel aimed directly at Lazaz's head. The faithful man was taking no chances that Osama bin Laden might be crushed by a horse, no matter how valuable or beautiful a stallion Lazaz might be. Thankfully my father saw the man's action out of the corner of his eye, even as he was busy trying to keep away from Lazaz's striking hooves. My father, who loved horses more than any man, shouted, "No! Go! Bring more men!"

Someone did as he was told and soon the enclosure was filled with five or six men, none, other than my father, accustomed to taming horses.

But eventually poor Lazaz was cornered and secured. On that day my father ordered Lazaz's ear to be "twitched," which means a short loop of rope is attached to a piece of wood that is put around the muzzle of a horse and tightened until it is painful. Arabs believe that the tightness releases a chemical that subdues a difficult horse.

Before long my father had returned Lazaz to the point that he could be ridden, and from that day, for so long as we lived in Khartoum, Lazaz was relatively content.

I am sorry that in addition to his good activities, I know now that my father continued to be involved with his militant activities, although due to my young age I was not privy to specifics.

Meanwhile, our father remained convinced that as Muslims, we should live as simply as possible, scorning modern conveniences. Although we were allowed to use the electric lights in our villa, all were forbidden to use the refrigerators, electrical stoves, or the cooling or heating systems. Once again, our mother and aunties were forced to cook meals for their large families on portable gas burners. And, with Sudan's hot climate, all suffered without air-conditioning.

None of the children agreed with our father regarding these ideas, although his wives refused to express their opinions. In fact, when we knew our father had traveled out of Khartoum, my older brothers and I would sneak to turn on the refrigerator, or even flip the switches for the air-conditioning. But our mother was so terrified that our father would discover our rebellion that we would soon go back to his rules.

I overheard some of his faithful Mujahideen quietly complaining because they were not allowed to use the modern conveniences either. Those men had lived a harsh warrior's life for too many years, and saw no reason for needless suffering when surrounded by modern conveniences.

Even when guests from wealthy Gulf countries arrived to stay in the guest house, my father's rules were not relaxed. Many times I saw prosperous businessmen and royal princes sweating profusely, some of them made cranky by the impossibly high temperatures. After hearing numerous complaints, my father finally purchased a supply of small hand fans made from woven grass, which the Sudanese sold in the open market. I had to stifle my laughter watching those high-ranking visitors frantically fanning the warm air around their heads and bodies.

My brothers and I spent much time scheming on how to flee the al-Riyadh neighborhood so that we could escape our father's mad world. Being active boys formerly accustomed to living the life of prisoners, we began to test the boundaries of our newfound freedom, lingering out of our family villa home for longer and longer periods each day.

In the beginning we were only brave enough to hang about in the family garden. Looking for anything to fill the empty hours, we asked some of our father's workers for construction materials to build houses in the garden trees. Those men were agreeable, finding us what we needed. Our tree homes became quite elaborate with each boy having his own personal space.

Our unexpected liberation tasted sweet! Suddenly we had freedom to play games or hang around the neighborhood, just as the children in Jeddah and Medina used to do, the "freedom kids" that we had watched with such envy.

We even had money to spend, something new and tantalizing for us, although we did not obtain the money in a purely honest way. Our father was of the opinion that his children should never be given money, not even for school snacks. We needed pocket money for basics, but he said, "No. You need to suffer. Hunger pangs will not hurt you." Improbably, our father was different from so many fathers who wanted nothing but the best for their children. Our father appeared to relish seeing us suffer, reminding us that it was good for us to know what it felt like to be hungry or thirsty, to do without while others had plenty. Why? He said that we would end up being the stronger. Those with plenty would grow up weak men, unable to defend themselves.

His was an opinion that found no agreement with his sons, but of course, we were not allowed to oppose our father. If we protested, there was no possibility for a calm discussion between a father and son; instead, he would quietly order us to stand to be beaten. His wooden cane was his favorite weapon, but there were times he became so excited when hitting his sons that his heavy cane broke into two pieces. When the cane snapped, he rushed to grab one of our sandals by the door, using that to bash us.

It was not unusual for the sons of Osama bin Laden to be covered with raised red welts on our backs and legs.

In the past our drivers in Saudi Arabia would feel for our pitiful situation, coming to see that our father was cruel. Those poor drivers tried to compensate, being gentle and kind, and slipping us small amounts of change, money they could ill afford to give. But in Sudan, we had no such luck. The men working for our father did not live as closely to our family and were unaware of our personal situations.

Being clever boys, however, we found methods to obtain a little pocket change.

In those days our mother had an allowance from our father, so she had money to spare. From the early days of her marriage she had acquired a habit of concealing money in her bedroom. She would tuck bills under magazines, in books, or in drawers. We knew all her hiding places. My brothers and I would take turns looking out for our mother while one brave boy would dash into her room for a quick search.

Since Mother never once mentioned mislaid money, we concluded that she recognized our needs, yet would not go against our father's wishes to actually give us cash. Rather than disobey our father, she left currency where she knew we could easily find it. Were this not her intent, I'm sure she would have spread the alarm that her money was being stolen.

After finding her stashes, we would slip from the house and dash to some of the small markets scattered throughout our neighborhood. There we would splurge on snacks and soft drinks. We were never discovered, much to our relief, for we knew the penalty for outright disobedience.

With our newfound funds we even took up a hobby. We became interested in pigeons, for it was a popular pastime in Sudan. We had heard that the village close to our compound was the best place to purchase high-quality pigeons. Luckily we had personal means of transport, because our father had decreed that the oldest boys could have bicycles. This had happened shortly before we left Saudi Arabia around the time I was nine years old. Before then, we could not have bicycles or any kind of mechanical transportation. I remember pleading with my father for a bicycle or a motorbike, telling him that I must have one for short trips. I'll never forget his words, "If you need to travel, Omar, travel on a goat."

But for whatever reason, one day he simply changed his mind and commanded one of the family drivers to purchase Abdullah a motorcycle, a Quad, and that the rest of the boys could have bicycles, the most expensive that money could buy. That was one of the happiest days of our young lives. We had so loved our bicycles that we had brought them with us from Saudi Arabia. They proved to be very handy in Khartoum. In fact, we were going to use them to venture out and seek pigeons for sale.

My older brothers and I conspired as to how we might start a pigeon family. We plotted as carefully as if we were going on a military campaign. We knew that we had to wait until our father was out of the city for he did not like us to leave the neighborhood. We began noticing when the security gate guards took a break. Soon we realized that most of the guards took lengthy breaks from their posts during the hottest hours of the day. We waited until our father left on a trip before gathering our bikes to wait until the sun was noontime blazing. Sure enough, one by one, the guards drifted away, going to their villas for a cool drink and a nap. That's when we jumped on our bikes and burst through the unguarded entrance from al-Riyadh Village.

We pedaled furiously, traveling the highway with the wind in our faces and our hair blowing. Freedom had never tasted so sweet. Our mission was successful because we found what we were looking for in the adjacent village. Pigeons were famous there and we seriously looked over them all before purchasing our first breeding pair. That first pair was very expensive, costing us 5,000 Sudanese pounds. But we had become bolder over time and took larger amounts from our mother's stashes. Still, she never inquired about missing money, so we *knew* that she *knew*.

Although our mother's life was one of extreme seclusion, and she was a wife who obeyed her husband's every wish, when it came to her children she found ingenious methods to help us bend our father's too stern rules. Never was a word spoken about such matters, for she would never go directly against our father, yet she helped us to survive our bleak lives. My mother was a very wise woman in such situations.

Our pigeon hobby escalated. One small cage with two pigeons soon grew to larger cages with new breeding pairs. Oldest brother Abdullah was not so interested in pigeons, for some reason, but Abdul Rahman, Sa'ad, Osman, and I became obsessed. We personally built our cages. Then we helped Mohammed build his cages, because he was so young at the time. Before long the entire garden was filled with pigeons in cages. We loved those pigeons, spending many hours taking care of their needs and celebrating when little pigeons hatched. We neglected to worry about how our father might react to our hobby, although we felt that he wouldn't forbid it since pigeons are popular with many Muslims. Besides, in the beginning stages of our hobby we once noticed him when he arrived at the house to visit our mother. On that day he had casually glanced at the one small cage and the first two breeding pigeons. His expression didn't change and he just kept walking, so we let our guard down.

Then one day he walked into the garden and paused. Disbelief crossed his eyes. His face flushed a bright pink color as he studied the massive cages, pigeon houses, and what looked like hundreds of pigeons. Father was visibly shocked.

Knowing we were in for big trouble, my brothers and I attempted to hide, but he spotted our timid selves lurking in the background.

With anger sparking like lightning in his eyes, he said, "Come here."

We moved slowly, believing that we were going to feel the effects of his heavy cane.

He didn't shout, but the fury in his soft voice was scary. "What is this?" He gestured with his hand. My voice stuck in my throat, and without giving us a moment to respond, he ordered, "Get rid of every pigeon. If those pigeons are not out of the garden by nightfall, I will personally slit the throat of each one."

With an angry glare at each of us, he turned on his heels and walked away, his tall figure rigid with rage.

My brothers and I knew that he was capable of killing them all, so we scrambled to find them a home. After pleading with one of the family's drivers, he agreed to help us transport our pet pigeons to one of our father's many farms. Those pigeons were gone by nightfall. What happened to them after that, we never knew.

Of course, we were sad to lose our pets, as we had grown to love each and every feathered friend.

Certain people were as taboo as those pigeons. There were some Sudanese that our father would not allow us to meet. We didn't know that he had a rule against socializing with Christians until we got into trouble trying to meet them.

We noticed the Christian children soon after arriving in Khartoum. The family, consisting of a mother, father, and several sons and daughters, lived in a house across the street from our own. They were hard to miss for they were fair-skinned. They also behaved differently, children sauntering about with a relaxed ambiance. We Muslim kids lived our lives in fear that we might accidentally commit a forbidden act.

We had observed those Christians for some time, but didn't have the courage to introduce ourselves. Then one evening my brothers and I were startled when we spotted the Christian children leaving their home. They were dressed in funny costumes that made them look like ghosts and monsters and other strange creatures. Those curiously dressed kids were also balancing small orange pumpkins on a stick. Each pumpkin had been cut so that they appeared to have a face. A candle was placed inside the pumpkin. We noticed that some Muslim children living in the compound were allowed to join them and to go to the soccer pitch where they had a party.

Never had we seen such a sight. Anyone in Saudi Arabia who appeared in public dressed as ghosts and goblins would have been arrested, tried, and imprisoned as witches, possibly put to death. We watched with envy as those children moved through the streets, kids in comical costumes carrying lighted pumpkins. They were laughing and playing around, making a lot of noise. (I became an adult before I discovered that what the little Christian kids were doing was called celebrating Halloween.) My brothers and I longed to join in the fun, but of course, our father disapproved of anyone walking around looking like a monkey or a monster, so we were forbidden to mix in. Still, we thought we might later sneak out and meet those interesting children, but little did we know that our father had passed the word to his security guards to keep us apart from those children.

One afternoon a few weeks later we watched as those Christian kids came outside to play. We thought our chance had come. So we ran outside, hoping to meet up. Just as we were about to introduce ourselves, one of our father's armed security guards came running at us with such hostility that we drew away in fright. That man was shouting in the most horrible angry voice that any of us had ever heard, *"Get in the house! You are not allowed! Get in the house, NOW!"*

He was so heated with rage that I thought he might shoot at us. My father's men were so neurotic to please their "prince" that nothing would have surprised me.

We took no chances. We ran into our house and the Christians ran into theirs. We were later told that we had almost committed a double taboo, because we were not allowed to play with girls *or* with Christians, *ever*.

That was that!

Not so long after arriving in Sudan we suffered a bit of a family shock. Auntie Khadijah left Khartoum to return to Saudi Arabia. She had always been kindly to all the children of her husband. Most disappointing for me was that Ali left with her. Aware of my father's traditionalist beliefs, I was surprised, for many believers insist upon maintaining control of all their children, no matter the child's age. Auntie Khadijah was fortunate to keep custody of her three children, and in particular Ali and Amer, her two sons.

I was only a child so I never knew their private reasons for divorce, although I speculated as to the cause. Perhaps my father had become too radical for Auntie Khadijah, for although I was too young at the time to fully understand the dangers attached to his uncompromising and militant behavior, I'm sure his adult wives were much more aware, particularly Auntie Khadijah, who was an educated woman.

Perhaps she left because she found no pleasure or reason for trips into the wasteland to spend nights in a burrow in the ground. Or perhaps she grew weary of being confined to her home, unable to go to a shop or visit other women. Her only companions were my mother and other two aunties. There were many reasons that might have prompted her to ask for a divorce and depart Sudan.

After she departed our father acted as though she had never been of our family, yet nothing was ever quite the same after she left. Although we kids adjusted to our Auntie Khadijah's absence, we missed Ali. We had been playmates for many years and had been taught to be loyal to all our half-siblings.

Ali was the oldest child of Auntie Khadijah and was considered of an age he could return to visit his father. His one visit to Sudan a year later was awkward and brief and he never returned. Neither did he visit us in Afghanistan.

But we were active boys with boundless energy, so we recovered from the change. After our father forbade us our pigeons, we scouted around for other activities to fill our time. The Nile was only a few minutes away from our home and we desperately wanted to go and take a swim there. Much to our pleasant surprise, our father agreed to our idea and even accompanied us. Who would have guessed that he wanted a swim, too?

Twisting wormlike through Sudan and Khartoum, the slim Nile was deceptive to a swimmer's eyes. My brothers and I always spurred the others on, taunting until all dove into the dark waters and swam for the opposite shore.

The waters were rough and the distance longer than it looked.

Yet none of us would admit fear to the other, so in the process we all became excellent swimmers, and avoided any serious problems. However, one of my father's friends nearly died by drowning. On that day we were all swimming when suddenly that foolish man excitedly leapt into the water like a teenager. Before we knew it, the strong current was washing him away. We all began to shout, alerting our father. None of us could catch up with the man. The last we saw he was in a water panic, his head bobbing up and down, his arms desperately flailing. When he disappeared from view, we assumed the Nile would become his watery grave. But there was a happy surprise when some Sudanese fishermen found the poor man splashing and crying out for help some distance downriver. They were kind enough to bring him back to us. We were all smiles when we saw that he had survived. My stern father said that he had acted like a fool, and advised him, "Steer clear of the Nile," and I believe that he did.

Our father even allowed us to take our beloved horses for Nile swims to give them a treat from the heat. Our father's friends loved to hang on to the horses' tails for some strange reason and we would pull them across the Nile. At other times our father gave the order for his cattle to be led to the Nile and we enjoyed riding their backs or splashing them with the cool water. Those cows seemed to like the Nile as well as we did.

One funny episode occurred when my father had one of his Egyptian employees build a boat. The boatman's building skills were less than my father believed, as the finished boat proved a big disappointment. The boatman claimed to have coated it with some special substance that made it go very fast, and indeed, that appeared to be the case, for on the day of the big launch, the boat proved impossible to control, spinning one way and then another before lurching forward at a high rate of speed.

It just so happened that our father had claimed the right to captain the boat. We stood in amazement as the boat moved so rapidly that our father was quickly swept down the Nile. Alarmed men loyal to my father began slapping the water with their palms, loudly yelling, "*The prince is in trouble! The prince is in trouble!*"

Father's men ran to a neighbor by the name of Osama Dawoud who owned a very fast boat. Luckily, the man was home and quickly gave chase, catching up with father's boat to tie it to his racer so he could tow it back. I remember standing on the banks of the Nile while watching the return, and was astounded to see that our father was so ashamed to have lost control that he actually slipped out of the boat and into the water to hide. He hung to the back of his boat, concealing his face, not wanting anyone to witness his humiliation. For someone so powerful, our father could be extremely sensitive.

But he was accustomed to being number one in everything he did. He was the most skilled horseman, the best driver, the greatest boater, the fastest runner, and the top marksman. He simply couldn't bear the thought of looking foolish. From that day, his sons and employees were forbidden to mention that motor craft. I was told that he gave that boat to a surprised Sudanese who just happened to be standing nearby. I fear it gave the poor man many wild rides.

Sometimes we might return to the Nile after dark, finding swimming in the river under a starry sky a magical experience. After exhausting ourselves we would fall down on our backs and stare in wonder as the radiant moon snaked its way across the big sky. The moon's reflection in the ancient Nile was one of the most beautiful sights I have ever seen.

Abdullah seemed to enjoy the Nile more than most, and many times I witnessed my brother sitting on the banks of the Nile, looking dreamlike into the distance.

Abdullah is five years older than me but looks little like me. He is around six feet one, slim, with dark frizzy hair and dark complexion. Abdullah, like his brothers, was always serious. Given any chance to work, no one could match him for endurance. In the beginning of our time in Khartoum, Abdullah, who was the firstborn son of my parents, was responsible for the behavior and safety of his younger siblings, both male and female. This is routine in the Islamic world, where the eldest son is respected by all, as he is considered the head of the household when the father is absent. Of course, when Abdullah was young during our years in Saudi Arabia, this was not an issue for our father's drivers and employees were in charge when our father was away fighting in Afghanistan. But by the time we arrived in Sudan, Abdullah was fifteen years old, soon to be a man, and although our father had security guards watching our home as well as the al-Riyadh Village compound, our father and mother looked to Abdullah to supervise us. If our father expected Abdullah to imitate his actions, I'm sure he was disappointed. Abdullah ruled lightly, as he was the opposite of our difficult father. Although our father was a quiet figure, and generally spoke softly, his patience hung on a short thread. He was easily angered and could reach a point of violence in an instant.

But Abdullah was patient and kind and quietly encouraged all the siblings to get along. I'm sure that we often caused Abdullah exasperation, but no matter what silly things we might do, I can't recall Abdullah ever expressing displeasure with his younger charges.

I've often thought how different our lives could have been had our father taken parenting lessons from Abdullah, for I was certain that my brother had the character and personality to be a kind and understanding father.

Chapter 13

The Scent of Death

OMAR BIN LADEN

A day of terror started out like any other. We said our morning prayers, changed into our uniforms, attended school, returned home to eat, then played around until the Asr prayer. After prayer, we trekked to the guest house for our religious lessons. Our three instructors were waiting for us, with our Moroccan teacher taking the lead on that day.

After a brief lecture on Koranic texts, we were gathered in a circle, quietly studying, when a bullet whistled through the open window and fell at Sa'ad's feet. Sa'ad was quick to tell the teacher, "Sir, someone is attacking us."

The teacher knew the happy-go-lucky Sa'ad very well and had reason to believe that Sa'ad might be playing a little joke. He kindly told Sa'ad not to worry, that he believed the sound had originated from an electrical spark. "Continue your studies, Sa'ad. I will investigate the matter."

My ears had perked up because I had been hunting for years and my familiarity with guns left no doubt that Sa'ad was right. Someone was firing a weapon and indeed a bullet had whizzed through the window and into the room.

By that time Sa'ad had lifted a cartridge from the floor and held it aloft between two fingers. "Teacher, it was a bullet. See, I have it here," he stated proudly, for once being taken seriously.

Our teacher's eyes popped as he exchanged looks with the other two instructors, who by that time had jumped to their feet. I'm sure they all realized simultaneously that we were under attack and three scholars without weapons were in charge of the safety of Osama bin Laden's sons. Before they could say anything, a barrage of gunshots reverberated throughout the guest house, with bullets zipping through the window. The younger boys began to cringe and cry.

I knew that we must move away from that open window, and so did our Moroccan teacher, who shouted, "Come, boys! Come!"

Our instructors hurried us out of the teaching room and into the hallway. Just at that moment, our Moroccan teacher let out a gasp. He had been shot! He stumbled at the powerful force that hit his shoulder, but kept upright, rushing us out of the back of the villa to a small building so close it could have been connected to the main structure. He yanked the door open, and all three teachers began pushing boy after boy to the center. The building itself was tiny, with room for only four or five people, but somehow our teachers crammed ten human beings inside. The teachers followed, pushing their bodies up against an unsecured door without a lock. Our instructors motioned for us to keep quiet, and the older boys began an effort to comfort the little ones so that their cries would not give away our hiding place.

There we were, squashed like sardines in a can, when we heard the gunfire coming closer. A thought flashed through my mind: If we were discovered, we would be the easiest target for an assassin. Stacked against each other like logs, one bullet could easily smash through several bodies. Any gunman could kill two or three of us at the same time.

Obviously those gunmen wanted to kill someone, and perhaps they had been told to assassinate the entire Osama bin Laden family. My dread increased when someone from the outside began to push his body against the unlocked doors. But we were so crammed we were like a big, immovable block.

Without uttering even a sigh, the teachers held their positions, knowing that they would die first if the gunman shot through the door. But after a few heart-stopping moments, we heard the assassin no more, perhaps because one of our father's guards had rounded the corner giving chase. The gunfight continued for another thirty minutes or so, with the shooting slowly diminishing until all was quiet.

We wanted to rush outside, to dash home, to check on our parents and younger siblings, but our teachers refused to move from the door. Our legs and arms were numb because we could not move an inch in any direction. Thankfully, we soon heard a call from a member of our father's security patrol who was hunting for the sheik's sons, shouting that it was safe for us to come out.

Recognizing the man's voice, we started to file out, then thought to check on the teacher who had been shot as we were scurrying away from the teaching room. To our relief, we found that the bullet that had struck him had been halted by the thick shoulder pads in his jacket. We had our first laugh, happy that our teacher was a smart dresser and the bullet had done nothing more than bruise his shoulder.

My brothers and I ran like rabbits to find our father, who we learned had escaped death only because he had stopped to talk to Abdullah on the way to our school.

My father had felt so secure in Khartoum that he had discontinued his usual precautions of alternating his schedule, becoming a man of habit. Obviously his enemies had discovered that fact. Each afternoon our father walked to the guest house to satisfy himself that his sons were busy with their religious training. But on that one day our eldest brother, Abdullah, had some business he wanted to discuss with our father.

As my brother grew older, his discontent at our situation increased. He was particularly disturbed that our family could not make use of the refrigerator in our villa, for maintaining a supply of fresh foods was extremely difficult.

Although Abdullah had been on a campaign for some time, my father refused to relent when it came to using modern appliances. That just happened to be the day Abdullah decided to push the issue. Their heated discussion delayed my father.

While Abdullah was unable to convince our father of our need for refrigerators and other appliances, he did save our father's life.

Over the next few weeks we discovered how the assassination attempt had unfolded. Four gunmen had gained access to our area earlier in the day and were poised in a pickup truck beneath a large tree opposite the guest house. Why they went undetected, I was never sure, but many residents in the neighborhood were diplomats and government officials who retained security guards of their own. Basically, the al-Riyadh Village was an armed camp with men from various countries watching over their charges. I suppose it was an easy matter for four new faces to go unnoticed.

Those men had been told that while Osama bin Laden might be early, he would never be late. After waiting impatiently for more than an hour after their set time to attack, they grew increasingly uneasy that their target must have arrived at the guest house much earlier than usual. Without a real plan, they began to fire wildly at the villa where we were studying, concentrating on open windows in the hopes they would hit Osama bin Laden by pure chance.

Our father heard the commotion and instantly grabbed his Kalashnikov, the Russian AK-47, one of the first assault rifles. My father had decreed that none of his fighters should ever be without his AK-47. At the sound of the shots, he ran up to the roof of our family villa, where he fired upon the assassins.

Once the firefight started, all the security forces in the area responded with a fierce barrage of gunfire heating the air. The assassins were heavily outnumbered, and their carefully laid-out plan to pump Osama bin Laden full of bullets and make a quick getaway turned to dust.

One of the men fled the neighborhood. A second man hid in the mosque.

The third jumped behind the wheel of the pickup and started the engine. The fourth dove into the back of that same pickup. The driver careened through the streets, desperate to make his escape through the diplomatic area.

Surrounded by a small army of men, they didn't have a chance.

During the attempted getaway, the driver was shot and killed.

The hired assassin in the back of the truck was shot and wounded.

The one hiding in the mosque was shot and killed.

The one who fled the neighborhood was caught and killed.

The wounded would-be-assassin was taken to the hospital where he made a full recovery. After recuperating, the government hanged him by the neck until dead.

I never saw any of the wounded or dead men, although I would have liked to do so. Our father would not allow my curiosity to be satisfied. I did hear many tales of that day because some of our father's guards were wounded.

One man's story I remember particularly well, as he repeated it to anyone who would listen, even though his own words branded him a coward. When the shooting first started, he locked himself into a room in the guest house. But, as he proudly told us, his only thought was of our father and so he loudly prayed, repeatedly pleading with God Himself, "God save the sheik! God save the sheik!" None of us was rude enough to bring up the obvious, but I often wondered if he was so worried about my father why did he hide? He should have rushed out to shoot the assassins who were there to murder my father.

There were many wild speculations as to who was behind the assassination attempt. Some thought it was a revenge attack from the Russians for my father's actions in Afghanistan. Others believed that one of the Afghan fighting factions had sent the men to kill our father.

After an investigation, the Sudanese government declared that the assassins had been hired by the Saudi government. My father was convinced, although I did not know what to believe. Certainly my father had deeply angered our Saudi rulers. Later I came to the conclusion that it was not the Saudi government, for they continued to make attempts to convince him to return to the kingdom. Why would they try to kill him when they were more interested in bringing him back into the fold?

My father even confided that the royal family had offered him several high government positions. The only requirements were for him to cease his criticisms of the royal family, give up his militant activities, and return to live peacefully in the country of his birth.

My father was an uncommonly stubborn man, scorning the generous offer.

Later, various high-ranking princes had visited, urging him to return to the peace he could find in Saudi Arabia. Even bin Laden family members were sent to persuade my father that he was on a dangerous path. My father loved his family and did not become angry with them, saying that they had no choice but to go along with the royal family, but his answer was a disappointing and unfailing no.

As a last resort, King Fahd sent word for my father to expect a personal telephone call from the king himself. My father refused to take his call, which is a great insult in our part of the world. No one refuses an order from the king!

After that, the former friendly relationship between my father and the Saudi royal family was completely destroyed. After hearing these stories, I thought to myself that my father was busily covering himself in thorns so thick that no one would be able to cut through to help him, or to help his innocent family, who had no voice in any of his decisions.

Up until that day in Khartoum, my brothers and I had not fully grasped that there were people in the world who wanted our father dead. To our young minds, our father was a highly celebrated hero. Suddenly I saw a bit more of the full picture, beginning to realize that not everyone agreed with my father's violent message that the Islamic world was in extreme danger and that all Muslims should attack before they were attacked. For the first time I sensed that our father was addicted to an aggressive pattern of thought that would endanger us all.

Our lives changed immediately after the attack. From that day forward, al-Riyadh Village was surrounded by a wall of security men and Sudanese police. Because of the increased danger, we were banned from leaving the village. There would be no more bicycle rides to neighboring villages. Never again would we roam the nearby shops and neighborhoods. Most tragic of all, we would never again be enrolled in school. And so it came to be that I finished my public schooling at age twelve, which proved to be a disaster for my future. The sons of Osama bin Laden would receive religious instruction and home tutoring only.

Once again we became prisoners, confined to a very small and boring corner of Khartoum.

Abdullah was our leader, so long as he remained with us. But we had always known that Abdullah would be the first to marry, and potential brides were easily discussed throughout the years of our youth. So it was no revelation that when Abdullah turned seventeen arrangements were made for him to marry the daughter of Tiayba Mohammed bin Laden, who was our father's half-sister through his father, Mohammed.

Once the date was set, Abdullah left without a moment's fanfare. There was no send-off party, no pre-wedding celebration. My brother bade our parents a brief and calm farewell, with our father saying little and our mother telling him, "Take care, Abdullah. Go with God." He packed a few things in one bag, said a casual goodbye to his siblings, and then was taken to the airport by one of my father's drivers.

I noticed little at the time, because I believed that Abdullah was coming back to us. Before long, however, we were informed that Abdullah would remain with his wife in Saudi Arabia. Although my father was disappointed, because he had a vision of his sons taking over his empire, he said little about the matter. As usual, my father hid his hurts and disappointments from us.

Even then, I knew that my brother was lucky to have escaped the complicated existence of the Osama bin Laden family. Had I known it would be years before I would see Abdullah, I hope I would have told my brother how much he meant to me.

After Abdullah left, Abdul Rahman rose to the eminent position of the oldest son, as our father said that was the way it should be. Yet my older brother did not have the traits necessary to manage so many lively siblings; and besides, from his youth, Abdul Rahman had little awareness of anything but his horses. Sa'ad, the third-born son, remained such a lighthearted joker that no one could take him seriously, not even the youngest kids in the family. Soon the mantle of the most responsible son quietly fell upon the fourth-born: me. My shoulders were not yet broad enough for such a duty, as I was only twelve years old when Abdullah left. Yet I endeavored to muster up the good judgment to assume the role.

First we had lost Auntie Khadijah, Ali, Amer, and little Aisha. Now Abdullah was far away. Who would be next?

Realizing that only adults ask such questions, I suddenly knew that my childhood was over.

The hard times were upon us, and from that moment on, any chance of happiness evaporated. We soon learned that the Saudi government had revoked our Saudi citizenship and frozen my father's assets. Although he had some money in Sudan and a few other places, he lost access to his huge bank accounts in the kingdom. With limited funds, many things would change. Our homes in Jeddah and Medina and the Jeddah farm were all confiscated, including our personal belongings and even our horses and livestock.

We no longer had official connections to Saudi Arabia.

Panic set in. If not Saudi, who were we? I wondered. Our great-grandparents had originated from Yemen. Did that mean we were now Yemeni? My mother had been born in Syria. Could I possibly be Syrian?

Our father gathered our family to tell us that from that time on, we were Sudanese! Our father said, "The Sudanese government has graciously bestowed Sudanese citizenship upon us all."

I was devastated. While I liked many things about the Sudanese, I was a Saudi and knew it. In my heart, I always remained Saudi Arabian, although official documents said otherwise. Much to my horror, when I studied my Sudanese passport, I saw that my birth name had been changed. I was now Omar Mohammed Awad Aboud! My last name was no longer bin Laden! Even my birth year had been changed from 1981 to 1979, for whatever reason, I have never known.

Our small world was shrinking day by day. After the assassination attempt, my father grew edgier, behaving as though every government in the world, other than the Sudanese, was his devoted enemy. By this time I reached fourteen years, I was becoming uncomfortably aware that my father was heavily involved with more dangerous political issues than I had ever imagined. How I wished that he would limit his activities to raising the biggest sunflowers the world had known! But I knew that I was dreaming and that he would never change. In fact, his passion for Jihad was expanding.

There were many troubling signs. My father began to meet more openly with militants he knew from Afghanistan. Some of the groups felt the call to Jihad against various Middle Eastern as well as western governments. My father's group was al-Qaeda, which at the time was mainly interested in clearing Muslim nations of outside influences.

There was also the al-Jihad group, headed by Dr. Ayman Muhammad al-Zawahiri, which focused on overthrowing the Egyptian government. I was not often in Dr. Zawahiri's presence, and for that I was glad. From the first moment I met the man, he left me feeling unsettled, despite the fact my father respected him.

I do acknowledge that Dr. Zawahiri was a man of high intellect. He was born in Egypt in 1951 into a well-to-do family. His father was a respected professor and pharmacologist, while his mother came from a very wealthy family. My father told me that the young Ayman had a rare gift for learning. As a young man he was a bit of a dreamer, loving poetry and hating fighting and bloodshed. Few would have believed that such a peaceful young student would embrace violent Islam, but he was influenced by an uncle who was a follower of the most radical Islamic beliefs. Cooperating with other students to form underground cells calling for the establishment of an Islamic state, Zawahari found his purpose in life, the struggle against secular authority.

Egyptian students were in the midst of a restless period, and various forbidden cells merged with others, forming a larger group known as the Egyptian Islamic Jihad, or al-Jihad. Zawahari was a member, although his studies continued even as he plotted the overthrow of the Egyptian government. Despite his political activities, he excelled in his lessons, graduating as a medical doctor, specializing in surgery.

Zawahari married a woman equally pious and supportive of her husband's ideals. Her name was Azza Nowari.

Zawahari was so deeply entrenched in the Islamic movement, that when President Anwar Sadat was assassinated in October 1981, he was arrested. Tried and convicted, Zawahari was given a prison sentence of three years. After being released in 1984, he traveled to Jeddah, remaining there for a year. Sensing that an important Islamic movement was being born in Pakistan, he traveled on to Peshawar. Using his medical degree, he worked in one of the many Red Crescent medical centers, treating wounded Afghan refugees.

During this time, he reconnected with other Egyptian Islamic Jihad members, increasing his revolutionary fervor. Soon he was the proclaimed leader. While in Peshawar, he allied with my father's friend and mentor, the Palestinian activist Abdullah Azzam. Through Abdullah Azzam, he met my father.

I believe that it was during this time that Zawahari began plotting to tap into my father's wealth. In fact, I have heard that he became Azzam's competitor for my father's financial contributions to the cause of Islam.

At the end of the war, when my father returned to Saudi Arabia, Zawahari went back to Egypt. But he was unable to stay out of trouble, almost immediately renewing his efforts to overthrow the Egyptian government led by President Hosni Mubarak. There were several failed attempts by Zawahari's group against various government officials. But their plans backfired when a number of innocent Egyptian civilians were killed in the assassination attempts. That's when the Egyptian populace turned on the once popular Islamic radicals.

No longer welcome in Egypt, Zawahari traveled to the United States, where he became one of the many radical Muslims on a popular speaking circuit, all attempting to raise money for their organizations. Some said that Zawahari falsely claimed that the money raised would go to wounded Afghan children. But there were so many radical Muslims speaking for money that Zawahari did not collect the large sums he had envisioned. That's when he heard that my father had fled Saudi Arabia, and was living in Sudan, a country with an Islamic government friendly to radical groups.

I was sorry that Zawahari tracked my father to the Sudan, and once again linked himself and his organization to my father and to al-Qaeda. I felt that nothing good could come from the association.

Lastly, there was the al-Gama'a al-Islamiyya group, led by Omar Abdel Rahman, a blind Egyptian cleric. Since he was in prison in the United States, his son was the local organizer in Khartoum. But the old man's spirit still encouraged his followers.

I heard all about him. Abdel Rahman was born in 1938 in Egypt. Afflicted with childhood diabetes, he lost his sight when a young child. He was given a Braille version of the Koran and developed a keen interest in Islamic teachings. Despite his blindness, he went on to graduate from the famed al-Azhar University in Cairo, gaining his degree in Koran studies.

While in university, Abdel Rahman developed an interest in and became a member of the al-Gama'a al-Islamiyya. He quickly emerged as the leader. Calling for a purely Islamic government, he denounced the Egyptian government. He even issued a fatwa calling for the overthrow of President Anwar Sadat. When Sadat was assassinated, Abdel Rahman was arrested for issuing the fatwa and spent three years in Egyptian prisons awaiting trial. While awaiting trial, he was tortured. Although he was acquitted, the Egyptian government expelled him. He traveled to Afghanistan, where all the radicals appeared to be gathering. There he met up with his former schoolteacher, Abdullah Azzam. Through Abdullah Azzam, he met my father.

Abdullah Azzam's assassination in 1989 was a tragedy, for he often calmed the violence brewing in radical believers.

After the assassination, the blind Abdel Rahman traveled to New York to establish himself as head of Abdullah Azzam's organization. Despite the fact Abdel Rahman was listed on the U.S. terrorist list, he was given a visa and allowed to enter the country.

The blind cleric traveled throughout the United States and Canada, recruiting support for the Islamic cause to overthrow secular governments. He was a brazen speaker, calling for supporters to ignore American laws and to kill American Jews. He aggressively ordered Muslims to attack the West, and to "tear it apart, destroy their economy, burn their companies, eliminate their interests, sink their ships, shoot down their planes, kill them on the sea, air, or land."

In fact, his followers were behind the 1993 World Trade Center bombing. Abdel Rahman was arrested in June 1993, approximately a year after we arrived in Sudan. That's why his son was running his organization. But the blind cleric's incarceration became a rallying cry for Islamic militants worldwide.

Put simply, all three groups focused on various aspects of restoring Islamic Jihad, although the two Egyptian groups were rabid regarding their goal of overthrowing the Egyptian government so that an Islamic government might be put in place.

The al-Jihad and al-Gama'a al-Islamiyya groups had brought their families to live in Sudan as well. At first our father had kept us isolated from everyone but our own family members, but increasingly he allowed us to mix with the teenage sons of those leaders. There was one particular boy who was my age and enjoyed the same sort of activities. He was the son of Mohammed Sharaf, an important man in the al-Gama'a al-Islamiyya group.

There was a sickening incident when someone targeted my friend, the son of Mohammed Sharaf. That young man was abducted and brutally gang-raped by a group of men. The rapists added insult to the attack and injury by snapping photographs of the young man during and after the rape.

My poor friend managed to escape with his life and returned to his father, Mohammed. Shockingly, those damning photographs ended up in the hands of Dr. Zawahiri, the leader of the al-Jihad group. Dr. Zawahiri was incensed, believing that the teenage boy was somehow at fault. There were pictures to prove it! In our world, sex between men is punishable by death. So a second horror was awaiting my friend when he was arrested by the group leaders, put on trial, and condemned to death.

My father was uninvolved with anything to do with this incident, although he used the episode to remind us that he had always kept his sons under guard and close at home to ensure that such things could never happen to us. He reminded us that many people would like to harm him through his young sons.

I was so sad that my father refused to approach Dr. Zawahiri about the incident, and to save my friend's life, as I believed in those days that my father could accomplish anything he wanted.

Mohammed Sharaf knew the truth. That good father strongly defended his son, telling Zawahiri that his son was an innocent victim. But no one wanted to believe that they had wrongly condemned an innocent boy. And so it came to be that Dr. Zawahiri ordered that my doomed friend be delivered to his offices. My friend was dragged into a room with Dr. Zawahiri, who shot him in the head.

For days I was frozen with shock and grief that an innocent person might be murdered at the hands of those he had believed offered protection. I fretted over the terrors my friend had endured in the last days of his young life—first to be brutally gang-raped, then to be falsely accused of having illicit sex, then to have his last image be that of a gun placed to his head before his world turned dark and his life on earth ended.

Creeping memories reminded me that I, too, could have suffered the same fate. Threats of rape were the preferred method of intimidation by the bullies at my former schools in Jeddah and Medina. I had never told anyone of the threats, for I was ashamed to be so menaced, but now I couldn't help but wonder that if such a thing had happened, would I have forfeited my life for another's crime?

For the first time I also realized that some of the men surrounding my father might be dangerous even to the sons of Osama bin Laden. Such men had danced with brutality since they were young, and now malice was mixed in their blood. I had always recognized this, yet felt immune to their cruel impulses. But Mohammed Sharaf was one of the most prominent leaders. If his son could be raped and murdered, my brothers and I could be targeted as well. From that time on we were very vigilant as to whom we trusted, and for the first time had a glimmer of understanding of why our father felt that his young sons must be kept secure.

One question kept troubling me: Why would my highly educated and soft-spoken father hang about with such ruffians, even if they were faithful to his cause? I really could not understand.

Although most of the veterans who had followed my father from the days of the Afghanistan-Russian war never exhibited criminal conduct, there were a few who bore watching. One of the men had murdered a puppy, while another buried a dog alive. A third slaughtered a beloved pet monkey.

Because of our Islamic teachings, few Muslims are fond of dogs. Our own Prophet suggested that it was best to avoid dogs. Despite this religious instruction, my father had ordered some German shepherd watchdogs from Germany and he often kept those dogs nearby. My brothers and I made friends out of some of the neighbor's pets, as well as stray dogs that hung around the al-Riyadh Village, by saving some leftovers and feeding them. In the beginning our acts sprang from boredom, but as time passed, the cuteness of the puppies tugged at our hearts. Each of us soon had our favorites.

My preference was a dog named Bobby. He was a rich ginger and white color, medium in size, with funny floppy ears. Bobby had a wife named Shami. Those two loved each other and seemed to be sexually faithful. There was another dog we named Lassie and she tried to tempt Bobby, but he was uninterested at first. Since Lassie was more beautiful than Shami, we would try to encourage Bobby and Lassie to mate because we wanted puppies out of those two beauties.

Eventually this happened and Lassie became the mom of some beautiful pups. Then one day my favorite of the pups began to foam at the mouth. I called one of my father's war veterans, hoping we could take the pup to the local veterinarian, but that veteran decided on the spot that the pup had rabies. He said he couldn't shoot it, otherwise the entire neighborhood would spark to life, but he would have to kill it. Before I knew what was happening he had dragged in a rope, climbed a tree, tied one end of the rope to a branch and the other around my pup's neck. He called on my brother Abdul Rahman to hold one end of the rope, ordering him not to let go. Poor Abdul Rahman, not knowing any better, did as he was told. I was just a kid and stood there protesting in vain while my pup hung by the neck until it died.

A second veteran became so annoyed with the large number of stray dogs hanging around the neighborhood that he dug a hole in the ground and made a trap. When one particular dog fell in the trap, he rushed to beat it over the head with an iron bar, then pulled the dog up and threw it in his car and drove its carcass to the edge of the desert and discarded it there.

We were sad but didn't know what to do. We knew our father would take the side of his war veterans. We were helpless witnesses to anything an adult might decide to do.

Imagine our surprise a few weeks later when our pet came limping into the mosque door, pitiful, minus an eye and with other visible injuries, but alive. After that close call, we kept feeding her until we left Khartoum.

Nothing was more bizarre than the fate that befell our beloved pet monkey.

By this time, our father had acquired much land throughout the country. One of his farms was at Damazin, south of Khartoum, nearby the Ethiopian border. The cone-shaped huts where we sometimes visited were set close to a jungle with various primates that seemed to enjoy entertaining visitors. There was one particular female monkey who had the cutest baby clinging around her neck. One of the Sudanese workers wanted that baby monkey, so he set a trap, drugging the water and taking the baby boy away from its mother. Everyone loved that little monkey. Even the adults smiled as the children tamed it so we could play.

When we arrived one day, the baby monkey was nowhere to be found. My siblings and I looked everywhere. Then my father's cook came to me and whispered that the sweet little monkey was dead, that one of my father's men who had been sent to the farm to work had become enraged by the sight of the pet monkey. He had chased that monkey down to run it over with a water tanker.

We were furious, failing to understand how anyone could deliberately harm such a cute little creature who did nothing but bring much needed gaiety into our lives. Imagine our shock when we learned that the ex-warrior gleefully told everyone who would listen that the baby monkey was not a monkey at all, but was a Jewish person turned into a monkey by the hand of God. In his eyes, he had killed a Jew!

My entire body shook when I heard such ridiculous talk. I was young and admittedly unsophisticated, but I was a rational thinker who knew that monkeys were not Jews and that Jews were not monkeys. One had nothing to do with the other.

Like many Arab children, I was aware of the enormous dislike, and even hatred in some cases, between Muslims and Jews and between Muslims and Christians. Children are not born with prejudice, however, so although I knew that many Muslims considered Jews their bitter enemies, my thoughts did not go in that direction.

I was even more astonished when I was later told that it was my father who had convinced the veteran of the ridiculous Jew/monkey theory. I was hurt and angry that my father had caused such a thing to happen.

The life I was leading was becoming increasingly weird and intolerable, but being a child, I was helpless, carried along by a deluge of hate so strong I was struggling to save myself. To add to my worries, since Abdullah failed to return into the family fold, I noticed that my father's keen eyes began to fall on me more frequently. Was I the chosen son?

Soon there was talk that we might not be able to remain in Khartoum, that Saudi Arabia and other regional governments did not want Osama bin Laden in Sudan. We were told that even the U.S. president Bill Clinton and his government wanted us kicked out of the country. Why? I could not guess why the American president was sitting in his Washington office thinking about my father.

Of course, I had no knowledge of the ongoing schemes being fostered by al-Qaeda, or the other two radical groups so closely aligned to my father's organization.

In the beginning, my father was curiously unconcerned about the calls for his expulsion. He was intimately connected with the government, called the National Islamic Front, as well as the president, General Omar Hassan Ahmed al-Bashir. He was even more comfortable with a very powerful man in Sudan, Hassan al-Turabi. My father's businesses provided such huge financial benefits that he believed that the Sudanese government would never expel him, regardless of what pressure might be applied by Saudi Arabia or Egypt or even by the United States.

But my father was wrong. There were limits to the pressure that even a legitimate government could withstand. In fact, it was an event that had occurred the previous year that would eventually lead to the end of those previously carefree days in Sudan. On June 26, 1995, Egyptian president Hosni Mubarak had been in a motorcade en route to an African summit. They were driving from the airport to the Ethiopian capital of Addis Ababa when gunmen blocked the motorcade and opened fire on the Egyptian president's limousine. Two of Mubarak's bodyguards were killed, but Mubarak's driver was so skilled that he was able to spin in a circle and speed to the safety of the airport, saving his most famous passenger.

Two of the six assassins were killed in the gun battle. The subsequent investigation took some time, but eventually the investigators traced the assassins directly to the door of Omar Abdel Rahman's al-Gama'a al-Islamiyya group, the same men who were now living in Sudan and closely associated with my father's al-Qaeda group. This group had been working to overthrow the Egyptian government for years. They were even responsible for the assassination of Egyptian President Sadat in 1981. In fact, Showqi Islambouli, who was one of the assassins in the Mubarak hit team, was also the brother of Khalid Islambouli, the man who murdered Sadat. Khalid was later tried and executed by firing squad. Showqi, on the other hand, was not captured.

After this assassination attempt, nearly every government in the area joined in the chorus to "do something about Osama bin Laden." Although it took a year, the pressure accumulated until the Sudanese government was standing alone against all its neighbors.

We felt the pressure ourselves, although we were not privy to every detail. For some months before the end of our time in Sudan, our father was noticeably subdued. While he didn't speak with his sons about his troubles, we witnessed grim-faced Sudanese government officials coming and going. It didn't take a genius to realize that something big was afoot.

My brothers and I concluded that we would probably be leaving Sudan. A few months previously, our father had startled his older sons by presenting legal documents stating that Abdullah, Abdul Rahman, and Sa'ad would be his signatories, or the sons given the authority to act on his behalf should he be incapacitated.

I was furious not to be included, asking my father, "Why am I not a signatory?" He gave me a hard look but didn't answer. So there was something else to stew about.

The end came on a miserable late spring day in 1996 when we were all sitting dejectedly in our mother's apartment. I remember that day as being particularly boring. I felt the prison chains wrapped so tightly that taking an easy breath was difficult. I was becoming increasingly angry over every facet of my life. Our security guards had turned into hawks, their big eyes following our every move as though we were small birds to be devoured. During such times I felt our bin Laden lives would have been less miserable had we never tasted liberty. I can vouch for the fact that freedom lost is acutely missed.

We were sitting there bubbling with despair when our father came in. His face was so glum that for the first time in my life I felt sorry for him. He motioned for us to make a space for him to sit between us. There we sat with our eyes on the floor, for it is a sign of respect in my culture not to stare directly into an elder's eyes.

He hesitated, then said in his soft voice, "I have something to tell you. I am going away tomorrow." I glanced up temporarily, to see him looking in my direction. I quickly averted my eyes. He announced, "I am taking my son Omar with me."

All of us looked at him in bewildered shock, the same questions speeding through our minds: Going away? Where? Why? Taking Omar?

My brothers protested, "But why is Omar going? Why can't we go?"

Unaccustomed to his decisions being questioned, I braced myself for parental violence, but he did not raise his cane for once. Stern and unapproachable, he curtly replied, "You know not to question me."

Truly I did not know what to think, although the restrictions had raised my boredom to such a level that I had little concern where my father was taking me. The trip was the thing, not the destination.

My brothers remained silent as he issued instructions. "Omar, do not pack. Do not take a toothbrush. Do not pack a comb. Only you are going." He stood and turned away, motioning for our mother to follow him into her bedroom.

Mouth dry and head spinning, I sat like one paralyzed. I had been chosen! I was going away with my father!

My brothers glared at me without speaking, but I ignored their surly conduct.

I prepared my bedding and tried to rest. Who knew how we might travel? Knowing my father, we might leave Khartoum on horseback! Sleep escaped me as I speculated as to what the morning would bring. Where was I going? Would we return to Khartoum? If I could not remain in Khartoum, I wished to return to Jeddah, to a time when my father was a hero in the eyes of the world. Perhaps my father and the royal family had put their disagreements to the side. Yes. Jeddah would be nice. Besides, our extended families were there, and despite my unhappiness as a schoolboy, there was a unbreakable link between our family and Saudi Arabia.

I quickly put that thought behind me, for I was not stupid and I had not missed the increased tension between my father and the Saudi royal family. Revisiting our past would not be possible as my father was convinced that he would be imprisoned in the land of our birth.

I considered other places my father might select as our new home. Were we going to move to Yemen? I knew that my father had many contacts there and it was the ancestral home of both my maternal and paternal families. I had never been to Yemen so I wouldn't mind seeing it. Or perhaps we were returning to Pakistan? My father had built a huge network of associates in that country, and knew that Peshawar had become an exotic refuge for many disgruntled Muslim fighters. I was not keen to live in Pakistan, as I remembered too well the poverty and the isolation I had experienced there. Other than Pakistan and Yemen, I could not imagine where we might settle.

After sunrise prayers, I was mentally ready to depart Sudan, although I suffered intermittent pricks of regret about what I was leaving. What would happen to our horses? Would they be abandoned, like our horses in Saudi Arabia? How long would it be before I could see my mother? We had never been apart for any length of time. I loved my mother more than anyone in my life. My stomach churned at the thought of missing her daily presence, her calm demeanor, which brought peace to our entire family. When I said goodbye, I lifted her small hand into mine and affectionately brushed it with a kiss.

Her pretty face crinkled into a slow sweet smile. "Take care, Omar. Go with God." I took one last long look at my mother's face before turning to my siblings, who were standing nearby. In a rush to leave, I muttered a hasty farewell to each.

Chapter 14

Journey into the Unknown

OMAR BIN LADEN

Not knowing where I was going or how long I would be away, I followed my father's every move. We were both carrying the customary Kalashnikov weapons across our shoulders, even though we were encircled by heavy security, with guards standing shoulder-to-shoulder until we were safely inside an SUV with blackened windows. When everyone was seated in their assigned automobile, all the vehicles in the motorcade advanced at the same time. Picking up speed, the motorized procession sped from al-Riyadh Village with such haste that it was a miracle the lead vehicles didn't strike down Sudanese workers unwittingly crossing the narrow roads.

My father was in deep thought, and exchanged no words we me on the short drive to the airport. Once there, we were whisked to a chartered Learjet. My father and his party were treated as dignitaries, with no need for the formalities of passports and customs. Besides my father and me, there were only eight other male passengers making the trip, seven of whom worked for my father, staunch comrades during my father's hour of need. Some of the men I saw often around my father's guest house. Brother Sayf Adel, my father's security chief, and Mohammed Atef, my father's best friend and top commander, were traveling with us. An unexpected passenger was a Sudanese dignitary, a man my father called Mohammed Ibrahim.

I felt myself to be my father's guard, although in reality I was only a boy of fifteen, still small and so physically underdeveloped that a single whisker had not yet emerged on my smooth face. Yet despite my youth, I would have died to protect the man whose love I had sought since I was a toddler. I felt my position of favored son keenly as I stood aside in respect, inspecting our immediate area while my father climbed the five steps before entering what I hoped was safety inside the airplane interior.

I followed, pausing for a moment at the door to take in my surroundings. Everything in the airplane smelled like new leather. By chartering such an expensive plane, someone in the Sudanese government had made a great effort to demonstrate respect for my father. My father chose a seat on the first aisle at the front of the plane, keeping his weapon on his lap. Brother Sayf Adel sat nearest to my father, while I settled in the window seat behind him. Mohammed Atef and another of my father's trusted friends slumped in nearby seats. A third man I knew as Hatim sat nearby, his hands clutching a map and a compass. The other four men chosen to accompany us sauntered to the back of the plane.

My mind was racing, speculating as to where we might be going. Not wishing for those aboard to know that I was not privy to any information, I kept silent. My face was impassive, even as my excitement was building. We were definitely beginning an adventure.

Pricked with the memory of my left-behind brothers, I suddenly understood why my father had not named me a legal signatory. My father was not certain that either of us would survive the day's travel! If a tragedy occurred, my brothers would assume responsibility for his vast network of businesses.

Were we headed for trouble, even death? Death at age fifteen was a disturbing thought, despite the fact we Muslims are taught from our youth that to leave earthly life is only the first step to paradise if one is a true believer.

But I was not keen to go to paradise just yet. Remembering the armed men who had tried to assassinate my father, I wondered if another hit team might be surrounding the airplane even as we sat on the tarmac. I didn't catch an easy breath until the pilot pulled the airplane off the runway and into the sky. I raised my head and peered at what I was leaving. A temporary sadness settled as I silently muttered to myself, "Farewell Khartoum . . . Farewell."

The hectic African city soon disappeared from the porthole view and I saw nothing more of a city I had grown to love. One bitter thought swirled in my head: The life I had known for the past five years was swept away as suddenly as in the tide that rushes over the beach, washing away those unique years of my youth. For the first time I had tasted something akin to true happiness. But something told me that Omar bin Laden would never again know such carefree joy.

I sighed deeply, rubbing my chin with my hand, wishing I could instantly sprout a full-grown beard. If that were the case, I would be considered a grown man able to make my own choices, as had my older brother Abdullah. I knew that given the option, I would run away from the madness of our bin Laden lives. But along with my mother and younger siblings, I had no choice but to follow my father, wherever his actions might lead.

The tension on the airplane heightened with every minute. Being young, I yearned to ask what was going to happen, but my father's contagious silence spread to everyone on board. I did not dare to speak.

My father had never been open about his inner thoughts, even with members of his own family, yet I knew that his mood was unusually solemn, perhaps even angry. He had never believed he would be kicked out of Sudan, but it had happened.

There was a slight rustle of papers as Hatim folded and unfolded his regional map. In a flurry of hand and eye motions, he would look intently at the compass, then back at the map, and hastily make notations in the margins. Hatim was grimly meticulous in letting us know that he did not trust the loyalty of the two pilots—which must mean that my father suspected some sort of trickery from the Sudanese government.

My father was stunned when his formerly welcoming hosts had capitulated to the demands of the Saudis, the Egyptians, and the Americans. Once he realized that he had no choice, his focus quickly altered to where he might move his operations and what funds and goods he would be allowed to take with him.

Now those questions plagued me, too. Where would we go? Would we lose all our possessions? Remembering that I had been ordered to leave Khartoum without a toothbrush in my hand, I began to suspect that all was lost. I had not even been able to slip my bulky inhaler and asthma medications onto the plane. I hoped I could find an inhaler and some Ventolin when we arrived at our destination.

But first we faced far more urgent questions than the fate of our possessions: Had the Sudanese officials sold my father out? Had the pilots been ordered to transport us to Riyadh, or even to America, to face arrest and imprisonment? Or was someone planning to shoot our airplane from the sky?

Seeking reassurance, I shifted my position to look around the plane. My father revealed little, but the Sudanese diplomat, Ibrahim, was a soothing presence. His behavior was solicitous, even subservient, with no hint of concern that plans were in the works to shoot us down. Surely he would have refused to accompany us if he suspected treachery. His attendance on the flight was a good sign, I decided.

Hatim muttered quietly to my father that we had passed over the Red Sea, that watery connection between Africans and Arabs. Safe, thus far! While the good news was that no fighter planes had intercepted our journey, the bad news was that we had entered Saudi airspace. At that point my father spoke loudly enough for everyone on the plane to hear: "Let there be no more talk! Pray to God in silence until we leave Saudi airspace."

Apprehension thickened, with every man becoming stiff in his seat. Some prayed silently, while others stared fixedly out the porthole windows. I glanced once more at my father, and saw that he was quietly praying, putting everything in God's hands.

I prayed, too, although my thoughts continued to race. Being told that we were in Saudi airspace settled one question. We were not going to Yemen, which was south of Saudi Arabia. If that were our objective, we would have no cause to enter Saudi airspace, but would make the flight entirely over the Red Sea.

My next thought was of Pakistan, which would require us to cross the entire width of Saudi Arabia, Iran, and Afghanistan. Since Saudi Arabia is a huge country of empty sands, one-third the size of the United States, all the passengers remained in a state of high anxiety for a very long time.

After praying for a long time, my father finally asked Hatim, "Do you know where we are going?"

Hatim shook his head. "No."

My heart skipped several beats. Did Hatim really not know our destination? Or was my father asking because *he* did not know? This was not good. I wanted to blurt out my questions, but forced myself to remain silent.

I glanced at Mohammed Atef (called Abu Hafs by those who knew him best), finding his face free of worry. My father confided completely in Abu Hafs, who must surely be privy to our destination.

My father's security chief, Sayf Adel, seemed tense, occasionally slipping from his seat to step into the cabin to confer with the pilots. I attempted to see the pilots, but caught only a glimpse. One of the two was an olive-skinned man with dark hair. His coloring made me assume that he was an Arab, but I was not certain.

Hatim continued studying his map and compass. The minutes seemed like hours until he finally announced, "We are out of Saudi Arabia."

My father took one long breath before turning around to address me directly. "My son, I was praying that the Saudis did not know I was on this plane. Had they known I was crossing their territory, they would have ordered their jets to shoot us down. They probably thought a Sudanese diplomat was on board."

Happy shocks went through my body. Perhaps the most dangerous moments had passed and this day would end safely after all.

The moment we left Saudi Arabia, we passed another body of water, the Arabian Gulf, or the Persian Gulf, named according to whether you are from Saudi Arabia or Iran. I was surprised that our plane began a descent into Shiraz, Iran, for I had never considered Iran as a possible new home. But I soon learned that we were refueling only and that our stopover would be brief. As our wheels touched the tarmac, my father instructed, "Omar, the Iranians do not know there are bin Ladens on this plane. *Do not speak a word*."

Sure enough, Iranian officials came dashing to the plane, demanding to climb on board. Our escort, Ibrahim, jumped to his feet and rushed down the steps, meeting the men, blocking their way inside. I could see one of the officials stretching his neck, peering around Ibrahim, who was talking in his silky manner. The pilots never stepped out of their compartment.

My father's shoulders stiffened. I peered over the seat to see that he had his weapon ready to fire. Sayf Adel and Abu Hafs were both in a similar state of preparedness. I looked toward the back of the plane, seeing that all my father's men were tensed for battle. If those officials came on board, none would hesitate to kill anyone they felt a threat to our journey. I even eased my own weapon in a better position, telling myself there was a possibility of a shootout.

Thankfully there was no need for gunfire, for Ibrahim convinced the Iranian officials that we were merely important businessmen passing through their country. Since we were not going to place our feet on Iranian soil, he told them, a formal inspection was unnecessary. I'm sure Ibrahim pressed a large sum of money into the hands of those men, for soon I heard them chattering and laughing as though they had been friends since childhood.

After the fueling, I was uneasy to learn that Ibrahim would not be continuing on our journey. Although he exchanged no words with me, he and my father said a long farewell and off he went, just as our pilots revved the engines. My father told me that Ibrahim would board a commercial flight back to Khartoum.

I kept my silence, as always.

We were back into the air so soon that not a single member of our travel party had a chance even to stand and stretch our legs. From Iran our plane continued on its mystery course.

A range of mountains soon appeared through my porthole. My father addressed Hatim, a final time, "Do you know our destination now?"

I held my breath, knowing that I would soon know my future home.

"Well," Hatim said, "we have crossed Iran. We are over Afghanistan." He spoke with confidence. "I believe that our destination is Afghanistan."

My father nodded but did not confirm with a yes.

Abu Hafs nodded, too.

Moments later we began our second descent of the day. Finally my father verified, "You are right, Hatim. Our destination is Afghanistan. We will land in Jalalabad."

I grunted in surprise, taking a fleeting glance at the faces of my father's fighters. All were impassive because they never questioned my father's decisions.

I tried to absorb the idea. So! Now we were to live in Afghanistan. I didn't know what to think, but my stomach fluttered in anticipation. Afghanistan was the country of my father's warrior years. Since I was a boy, my youthful imagination had been fed by tales of Afghan death struggles in the historic battles of Jaji and Jalalabad. Now I would finally get the opportunity to see those battlefields myself.

Being young and uninformed, I could not imagine the implications of living in a country that had so recently passed through a debilitating ten-year war with a superpower, followed by a fierce civil war that would reduce the few surviving remnants of the old Afghanistan to shreds. Never having even been in a war zone, I was unaware of the daily challenges of surviving in a country made primitive by incessant war. I stupidly believed that my life would continue much as it had in Khartoum.

A Note Regarding Osama bin Laden's Political and Militant Activities

JEAN SASSON

While Najwa was raising her children in Sudan, and Omar and his brothers passed into their teenage years, Osama's militant activities greatly increased. Enraged at having to leave Saudi Arabia for good, he blamed both the Americans and the Saudi royal family. This fury increased his determination to strike terrorist blows at the United States, and at Saudi Arabia.

Grateful to the country that had offered him refuge, he developed plans to improve the economic situation in Sudan. Soon he was constructing factories, opening businesses, and building roads.

So angry with the Americans and the Saudis at his exile he was also in a rush to activate the military arm of his al-Qaeda organization. With the approval of his Sudanese hosts, he set up the first of his military training camps in various parts of the country, and began recruiting for holy warriors. His famous name was a popular draw for fighters and before long the training camps were filled to capacity.

After Osama transferred his base of operations to Sudan, the Egyptians followed. Dr. Ayman al-Zawahiri and his al-Jihad group along with Omar Abdel Rahman's al-Gama'a al-Islamiyya Group reestablished their relationships with Osama when they brought their fighting men to Khartoum. The combination of the three groups made for a hotbed of radicalism.

Osama had only been in Sudan for a short period before signs were clear that assaults upon America had begun. First there was an attack in Aden, Yemen. The American military was using the city as a base on their way to Somalia, where they were involved in a humanitarian mission. On December 29, 1992, bombs exploded at two hotels in Aden. While American soldiers were the target, none was killed; but two innocent Austrian tourists died.

Less than a year later, on October 4, 1993, there was coordination with Somali militia, who shot down two American Black Hawk helicopters, killing eighteen U.S. servicemen, the tragic event that was the basis for the book and the movie *Black Hawk Down*.

In 1994 the Saudi government not only rescinded Osama's citizenship and that of his family, but froze his assets, confiscating his children's heritage. While the exact figure is not known, it is believed that Osama lost many millions of dollars in one swoop.

His desire to attack Saudi Arabia and America increased with every personal blow.

While some plans organized from Osama's al-Qaeda bases were prevented by western security forces, others succeeded. But it was a June 26, 1995, terrorist plan gone awry that caused Osama and al-Qaeda to be expelled from Sudan. Ironically, Osama bin Laden was not involved in that particular attack.

When Abdel Rahman's al-Gama'a al-Islamiyya Group attempted to assassinate Egyptian president Hosni Mubarak, governments from the area, along with the United States, increased the pressure on the Sudanese government to expel the three notorious radical groups.

At first the Sudanese officials offered to turn Osama bin Laden over to the Saudi government. But the rulers of the kingdom knew that Osama was still highly celebrated as a war hero in their country. They were not keen on putting a war hero on trial.

The Sudanese then offered Osama to the United States. Since there was no indictment against Osama bin Laden at that time, the American government had no legal basis to arrest Osama.

At that point, the Sudanese officials informed Osama that he must leave their country. Unsure where he might be welcome, Osama sought and received an invitation from certain powerful parties in Afghanistan.

And so in May 1996, Osama, his son Omar, and other trusted advisers departed Khartoum to fly to the most lawless land in the world: Afghanistan, a place where he would not be bound by national or international laws. Osama bin Laden would be free to do as he pleased.

Afghanistan

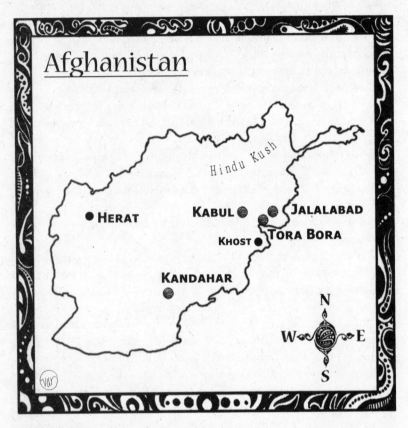

Hindu Kush

● **HERAT** **KABUL** ● ● **JALALABAD**

KHOST ● ● **TORA BORA**

KANDAHAR ●

N
W ⊕ E
S

Afghanistan:

Osama bin Laden moved his family to Afghanistan in 1996
Omar bin Laden fled Afghanistan in the spring of 2001
Najwa Ghanem fled Afghanistan on September 9, 2001

Facts on Afghanistan:

Full Name: Islamic Republic of Afghanistan
Ruled by: Provisional Administration
Head of State: President Hamid Karzai
Capital: Kabul
Area: 251,773 sq miles
Major Religion: Islam
Major Languages: Pashto, Dari (Persian)
Population: 27.1 million
Monetary Unit: 1 afghani = 100 puls

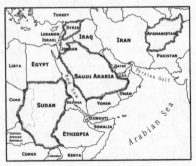

PART III

Afghanistan

A 1964 painting of Osama's father, Mohammed bin Laden. *(Courtesy of Omar bin Laden Family Photo Collection)*

Osama bin Laden, age 16, one year before he married his cousin, Najwa. Jeddah, 1973. *(Courtesy of Omar bin Laden Family Photo Collection)*

Left: Osama in Afghanistan fighting the Russians, 1984. *(Courtesy of Omar bin Laden Family Photo Collection)*

Right: Omar, age 3, in Jeddah, 1984. *(Courtesy of Omar bin Laden Family Photo Collection)*

Osama bin Laden wearing military garb during his period of fighting the Russians. Photo taken at a farm in Jeddah, 1985. *(Courtesy of Omar bin Laden Family Photo Collection)*

Above: Omar bin Laden, age 6, the year the family moved to Medina and Omar started school. *(Courtesy of Omar bin Laden Family Photo Collection)*

Right: Sa'ad, Osman, and Mohammed in Osama's study at family home in Jeddah, 1990. *(Courtesy of Omar bin Laden Family Photo Collection)*

Fatima, Sa'ad, Omar, (holding ball with Abdullah), Mohammed (yellow shirt), Osman, and Abdul Rahman in bin Laden family sitting room in Jeddah, 1989. *(Courtesy of Omar bin Laden Family Photo Collection)*

Omar and his baby sister, Fatima, at family home in Jeddah, 1990. *(Courtesy of Omar bin Laden Family Photo Collection)*

From left to right: Omar, Fatima, and Sa'ad in Jeddah family home, 1990. *(Courtesy of Omar bin Laden Family Photo Collection)*

Abdullah bin Laden in Sudan working on his father's heavy
equipment, 1993. *(Courtesy of Omar bin Laden Family
Photo Collection)*

Abdullah bin Laden on the Nile in Khartoum, 1993.
(Courtesy of Omar bin Laden Family Photo Collection)

Omar in his bedroom in Khartoum, 1993. *(Courtesy of Omar bin Laden Family Photo Collection)*

Happy days for Omar in Khartoum. *(Courtesy of Omar bin Laden Family Photo Collection)*

A small Afghan village Omar passed through on his way
from Jalalabad to Tora Bora. *(Hill Bermont)*

The burqa that women are forced to wear in Afghanistan.
(Hill Bermont)

Omar and his son, Ahmed, in Jeddah, 2005. *(Courtesy of Omar bin Laden Family Photo Collection)*

Omar bin Laden with his beloved horse in Jeddah, 2007. *(Courtesy of Omar bin Laden Family Photo Collection)*

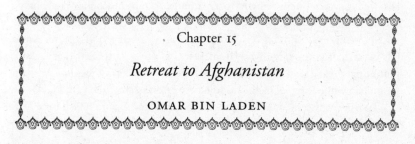

Chapter 15

Retreat to Afghanistan

OMAR BIN LADEN

An old friend was waiting for my father's return as we filed from the airplane, stretching our tight limbs. Mullah Nourallah, meaning "Light of God," rushed to my father's side, welcoming him as enthusiastically as if my father was a long-lost son. I was struck by a memory of my father telling us that the Pashtun are some of the most hospitable people on earth. If Mullah Nourallah was any example of routine Pashtun hospitality, then I felt better already.

With his powerful body and confident stride, Mullah Nourallah looked like a warrior. He wore his black beard long, although it was tinged with a streak of gray. As always, I remained unnoticed, standing to the side, observing. My father never introduced me as I tagged behind.

I soon learned that Mullah Nourallah was one of my father's oldest and best friends from the days of the Russian war, the two often fighting side by side. After the war, he had become one of the main leaders of Jalalabad, the capital and most important city of the Nangahar Province, the home of the Pashtun tribe. Nangahar Province was a significant area of Afghanistan, edging up to the Khyber Pass, which is the all-important gateway to Pakistan.

The Pashtun are the world's largest tribal society, with approximately sixty major Pashtun tribes. While Pakistan has the world's largest number of Pashtun people, or 28 million, Afghanistan is home to the second largest population, of thirteen million. The Pashtun speak the Pashto language, and follow a long-established code of conduct and honor, called the Pashtunwali.

The previous year, Mullah Nourallah had been responsible for bringing a brutal bandit to justice, putting the criminal to death. Since that time he had risen to a high rank, yet his life was in constant danger from the bandit's brother, who had sworn vengeance. The old adage of an eye for an eye and a life for a life was a common response in a tribal land. Mullah Nourallah brushed aside any warnings to be watchful, accepting as a true believer that his life was solely in God's hands. If God determined that Mullah Nourallah was to die at the hands of the bandit's brother, then so be it.

With Mullah Nourallah confidently pushing through the crowds, we slipped easily past all airport officials, walking rapidly to a group of double-cabin trucks with drivers waiting to take us from the airport. Mullah Nourallah's vehicle was a bright red and to my mind a shining beacon for the bandits stalking him.

No one seemed to have considered the danger of being so visible, for Mullah Nourallah sat openly in the front seat, his driver so relaxed that he was humming a tune and smoking a cigarette. My father sat behind Mullah Nourallah while I settled in the middle between my father and Abu Hafs.

Once properly settled, Mullah Nourallah appeared to notice me for the first time, peering into my face while asking my father, "Who is this boy? Is he your son?"

"Yes. This is my son Omar, the fourth boy."

Mullah Nourallah nodded and smiled, reaching out to touch the bridge of my nose approvingly. "It is a good nose, long and prominent." With a big smile, he announced, "You, Omar, have the nose of a strong man."

I couldn't think of anything to say. Truthfully, I had never thought of my nose as being long and was unsure whether or not I liked the idea.

With one ear on the conversation, I turned my eyes to my new surroundings. The Safed Koh Mountains hovered over the plain of Jalalabad. I had expected the city to be brown, but to my delight, the Pashtun city was a green oasis, watered by the Kabul River.

Everything else was disappointing. The people and the buildings appeared old and weary. As we drove through the city, I was stunned by the signs of poverty all around me. Instead of cars, many people were reduced to riding in horse-drawn or donkey-drawn plain, flat carriages. I saw young men dressed in shabby clothing riding bareback on emaciated horses and sad-eyed mules. I felt myself a time traveler, thinking that within the course of a few hours, I had gone back a hundred years.

Through the haze, I overheard Mullah Nourallah tell my father, "Of course, you will stay in one of my homes. After you have settled in, you are welcome to the palace." He explained, "The government owns the old palace in Jalalabad, once the home of the former royal family."

A palace sounded promising.

After observing other homes and businesses in Jalalabad, I was happily surprised when our driver pulled our car into the drive of the villa belonging to Mullah Nourallah. It was beautiful. Who would have expected such luxury in the midst of worn-out Jalalabad? The villa was painted a bright white and much larger than I had expected. We piled out of the truck for Mullah Nourallah to escort us inside.

The interior was spacious, with twenty-five rooms, and every room clean and attractive. I was hoping for a bedroom of my own, for I have always been a loner and, with so many brothers, rarely had the opportunity for privacy. Those hopes were dashed when my father agreed with Mullah Nourallah that until they learned of any possible dangers to my father, we would all be sleeping in the basement, which was cold and dark.

Mullah Nourallah's men arranged for two single beds to be set up in the basement room that I was to share with my father, along with a small bathroom. My father's men slept in nearby rooms in the same dark area. A cook was arranged to prepare our meals. I was disappointed, but not surprised, to hear my father give instructions for the simplest, blandest meals.

Although I was eager to explore the city, security concerns required my father and me, along with his men, to remain voluntary prisoners in the villa or walled garden for two weeks. Despite our isolation, Mullah Nourallah extended that famous Afghan hospitality, checking on us daily and trying to convince my father to accept lavish meals. But my father never did, of course.

In word and deed Mullah Nourallah never ceased showing his great affection for my father. Their days of war had created bonds impossible to break. Their conversations also created a better understanding of my father's former life.

My father obviously felt exceptionally close to Mullah Nourallah, opening up more completely than I had ever seen. He spoke briefly about his obligatory departure from Sudan, confiding in a disheartened tone that he had poured all his resources and energy into projects that benefited the country and the individual Sudanese. For the first time I heard him confess his worries. "My friend, I am apprehensive about my future. I have lost much. I have a large family. I have many followers, with wives and children also. All depend upon me."

It didn't take a genius to know that with three wives and many children, combined with his religious and political activities, my father required vast sums of money. Yet I had never given much thought to my father's problems, mainly because I found it difficult to get past my personal struggles.

Mullah Nourallah swore his loyalty to my father. "Osama, you are the only non-Afghan who has remained loyal to Afghanistan for all the long years of troubles." He paused to smile, "Let your worries fly away with the wind, Osama. You have a home in Afghanistan for the rest of your life. After you go to paradise, all the members of your family can count Afghanistan as their home. I guarantee your safety, and the safety of your family and followers. You are free to remain in the palace as long as needed."

To show his respect and affection, Mullah Nourallah then presented my father with a very large tract of land in the city of Jalalabad, suggesting, "Here is land that I want you to have. Build yourself a compound. Bring your family and friends to this place. You are an honorary Pashtun!"

As a final grand gesture, he even gave my father an entire mountain in Tora Bora!

My father was very pleased and grateful to the man who had never forgotten his contributions to the cause of freedom for the Afghan people.

Once Mullah Nourallah felt more confident about our safety, we were moved to the old palace. By that time, I was sick of the beautiful villa because we had been restricted within its walls. I was glad to try something new and found the palace most agreeable. It had been built in an ideal location next to the Kabul River, surrounded by grand old shade trees. There were ample grounds, with the palace circled by numerous delightful gardens. A riot of vividly colored flowers nestled in every available spot.

Although the old palace was in good condition, it was not a mansion that one would expect to be associated with royalty. Yet I was pleased, for if one compared the palace with other Jalalabad homes, we were living in the greatest luxury.

The palace was a rectangular building two stories high that hinted at a time long past when workers had painted it a bright white, the color of choice for most expensive villas in Jalalabad. The roof was flat, similar to homes in Saudi Arabia and in Sudan, which was useful, for my father liked to survey his surroundings from rooftops.

At the entrance there was a wide corridor, covered with a red carpet. The hallway was filled with fancy chairs. There were ten rooms along the corridor, nine of them decorated with classic and elegant furniture that looked expensive, but ancient. I assumed it had once been used by the royal family. The tenth room had been turned into a kitchen. Interestingly, each of the ten rooms had its own bathroom, which was unusual for the times that the palace had been built.

After taking a systematic look at the first floor, we climbed the indoor staircase to the second—a duplicate of the first, but without a second kitchen. All the interior rooms were whitewashed, all the floors covered with the same pattern of red as the corridors. Most handy to my mind, the electricity and water were in working order, although I knew my father would have preferred for us to haul water from the Kabul River and stumble around with flickering gas lanterns. He had become increasingly obsessed with the notion that anything convenient or modern was bad for a Muslim. Although I had known from the time we left Sudan that one day my mother and siblings and the other wives and children of my father would join us in Afghanistan, and I was eager for that day to come, yet I cringed at the idea that they would live on Tora Bora Mountain in substandard housing.

Just as I was imagining the enjoyment my brothers and I would have playing in the gardens and swimming in the river, that bubble was burst by my father. "Omar, our stay here is to be temporary. We will soon travel to Tora Bora to claim our mountain. That is where we will live."

I was speechless. While Jalalabad was reasonably safe at the moment, most of Afghanistan was still embroiled in a civil war, with every tribal warlord scrambling to rule the entire country. I had no clue if the Tora Bora mountain area was gripped by war or enjoying peace.

Even if the area was peaceful, from what I had heard, Tora Bora was little more than mountains with caves. How could my father consider taking his family to such a place? While we older boys could live roughly if necessary, what about my mother and aunties and the younger kids? The mountain life was not suitable for women and children.

Looking at my father, I knew that no one could dissuade him from moving us all into the desolate mountain ranges of Afghanistan. That was the precise moment that I realized that our bin Laden lives had dropped yet another level.

Despite my despair over my father's news, the following two weeks in Jalalabad proved fascinating once Mullah Nourallah and my father decided it was safe to explore the city. Much to my excitement, off we went. Almost immediately I realized that the street scenes of Jalalabad were comparable to what I could remember from summer visits to Peshawar, Pakistan.

In those long-ago days, Peshawar had been heavily populated with Afghan Pashtun, the dominant ethnic tribe from the east of Afghanistan, where we were now. Once more, I observed similar vendors selling similar street food, smelled familiar odors, saw comparable antiquated transportation, and admired the handsome Pashtun. For me, Peshawar and Jalalabad were alike in more ways than they were different.

I paid close attention to my father, who kept me by his side wherever he went. My father has a habit of averting his eyes whenever he is out in public. Whether this comes from a basic shyness or the fact that he takes extreme care not to look upon a woman not of his family, I do not know. I considered telling him that he could look as he pleased, for it would have been impossible to see a woman's face in Jalalabad even had he tried. Afghan females were cloaked in pale-colored burqas, the tentlike costume that billows over every part of a woman's face and body. I was glad to see that the heavy fabric of the costume was fitted with a tiny barlike screen over the woman's upper face so she wouldn't trip and fall. Some of the wrinkled old women were not dressed in the burqa but instead were wearing long-sleeved, ankle-length embroidered billowy dresses with long-tailed scarves over their hair. When those ancient women saw a strange man, they would yank the tail of the scarf over their face.

I gawked so openly at the people and the sights that I noticed some people stop in their tracks to give back stares. Most seemed interested in my father, who attracted attention for his unusual height; for his face, deemed by many to be exceptionally handsome; and for a certain aura that he had about him. After checking out my father, their eyes would turn to Abu Hafs, who was so tall he could look my father directly in the eyes, and to Sayf Adel, who surveyed everything around us, always looking for troublemakers. I garnered the least attention, a boy too young for a beard walking in the middle of a group of stern men. I'm sure those Afghans were wondering why well-dressed Arabs were in Jalalabad, because most Arabs had left their country when the Russians had departed nearly ten years before.

My father was keen to visit some of his old friends from the Soviet conflict. One I remember most distinctly was Younis Khalis, who had once been an important sheik in Afghanistan. Younis Khalis was the oddest-appearing man I had ever met. First of all, he appeared ancient to my eyes, already seventy-eight years old when I met him, though he still sported an eye-catching red beard. It was easy to see that he was slowly being defeated by old age.

His former soldiers were very loyal. Although we were visiting him in the late spring, the nights could be quite chilly. When the old man complained of cold, his men made determined efforts to keep him warm. His house was old-fashioned and had been built of mud blocks with a raised concrete floor. Under the floor there was a special open space and his men worked hard running back and forth to shovel hot coals under the concrete, keeping the room toasty warm.

I wondered if my father might agree to such a method of warming for our family. Since he was set against electrical heating, I was already dreading the cold of the mountain winters.

Sheik Khalis was an unusual man for tribal Afghanistan. He had been a highly regarded Afghan leader during the Russian war. But the moment a peace agreement was put into place, he threw his hands in the air and said that was it! He was finished with fighting. Ten years of bloodletting was enough for any warrior. To prove that he meant his words, he made a big point of giving away all his weapons, including a number of tanks, grandly presenting them to the Afghan central government. Afghan men feel tremendous love for their weapons, and by emptying his weapon's coffers, Sheik Khalis hoped to create a precedent. He thought that all warlords should donate their weapons to the government, return to their lands, and remain at peace with their tribal neighbors.

But no other warlord shared his good sense, so all others warred on without him. Civil war grabbed hold of the land, bringing a time of ferocious fighting between men who had recently been allies against the Russians. My father confided that he had tried to encourage cooperation between the warlords. "But, my son," he said, "Afghan leaders can be the most stubborn of men. Most were unwilling to compromise on anything, whether land, government, or law. Sadly, when they could not reach an agreement of the minds, they reached for their guns."

My father was disheartened that the Afghans had not banded as one to put the broken pieces of their country back together.

There were other famous warriors known to my father, and Sheik Khalis and my father discussed their whereabouts, but I can remember little for their hearts were so full of memories that anyone who didn't experience the war with them would have a difficult time following their conversations. After all these years I do remember the names of Ahmad Shah Massoud, Abdul Rashid Dustum, and Sheik Sayaff.

Ahmed Shah Massoud was the Afghan warrior most famous to the world. His father was a policeman, and the young Ahmad received a good education, becoming fluent in five languages. Because of his father's position, he developed a special interest in politics. From his school years he had opposed the communist movement to influence his country. Yet he disagreed with resorting to terrorist acts, declaring that such violence would only destroy Afghanistan. After the Russian army invaded in full force, Massoud became a leader against the intruders, becoming the greatest resistance fighter.

After the Russians were defeated, Massoud continued his participation in Afghan politics, meeting with many former warlords in an effort to bring true peace to his country. That's when the Taliban group won the support of Pakistan, who hated Massoud because he said the Taliban was too radical and that Pakistan should stay out of Afghanistan's business. Instead, he called for democracy.

Massoud was an important part of the Northern Alliance, which was fighting the Taliban. But the Taliban, with its backing from the powerful Pakistanis, was conquering most of Afghanistan. By the time my father and I arrived in Afghanistan, most believed that Massoud didn't have a chance of victory. That was when my father predicted that the Taliban would ultimately win the civil war and control all of Afghanistan. That was when he also knew he must embrace the Taliban if he wanted to live in peace in Afghanistan.

Of course, this meant that Massoud, a man he had once supported, would become my father's enemy. Nevertheless, I believe that my father had enormous respect for Massoud, saying once, "No Russian ever walked through Massoud's territory."

I personally met another former leader, the striking-looking Sheik Sayaff. The sheik must have been proud of his beard, which had remained black as night, because he intentionally kept it long and dressed it bushy—the longest, fluffiest beard I have seen to this day. I wanted to ask about his beard but never found my nerve. His huge size was a second surprise. He was very tall, although not so tall as my father, but was the broadest man I've ever seen in my life, although his body width was not composed of fat. His form was so unusual that I find him difficult to describe and I wish I had a picture. When in his presence, I tried not to stare but found it impossible. Considering his beard and his body contours, I decided that he was the most majestic warrior of his day, which is saying a lot when nearly every Afghan soldier I met appeared powerful and intimidating.

Then the day came that my father said, "Enough visiting. The time has come to prepare our new home in Tora Bora."

I had been hoping that the gift of land in Jalalabad would cause my father to forget about Tora Bora, which had the unpromising meaning of "black dust." I wanted us to remain at the old palace until he could build a compound for us in the city. But for some strange reason my father seemed in undue haste to return to the mountains. After only a month in Jalalabad, he announced that we were traveling to Tora Bora, to check out our very own personal bin Laden Mountain.

By this time I was suffering from asthma, but much to my despair, there were no medicines or inhalers in Jalalabad. I was foolish not to have sneaked my medicine past my father, for my breathing difficulties were becoming worse with each passing day. My father noticed my ragged breathing and ordered one of his men to raid some hardworking bees of their honeycomb. My father watched carefully as I breathed through the comb, but his home remedies had never relieved my asthma. Once he had his mind set on a thing, my father was not one to give up. After he saw that the honey had no effect, he had one of his men boil some onions and squeeze the juice into a pan, telling me to breathe in the onion juice. That had no more effect than the honeycomb. Finally he instructed me to pour olive oil onto the burning embers of a fire and to drop my head over the smoke and inhale as deeply as I could. All that smoke only exacerbated my asthma, and breathing became so difficult that I feared I might die. Once when gasping, I thought I caught the scent of "grave dirt." I was ready to trade my share of the bin Laden Mountain for a single puff from my inhaler.

Such was my condition when we started the dusty ride out of Jalalabad to the White Mountains where Tora Bora was located.

Chapter 16

Tora Bora Mountain

OMAR BIN LADEN

The roads to Tora Bora Mountain were unpaved, so the dust clouds were circling our white Toyota trucks, the vehicle of choice in Afghanistan. Since Jalalabad and its environs nestle on a flat plain, one would hope that even a dirt road would offer smooth travel, but that was not the case. I grumbled silently that the Afghan roads must surely be the most poorly maintained on earth. Other than one or two main city streets, all were dirt; therefore, passengers received teeth-rattling vibrations as the tires fought to escape potholes and roll over large stones. As I was tossed around the vehicle like a rag, I gasped in misery, regretting for the first time that I had been the son chosen to accompany our father on his journey.

I really could not believe that our lives had come to this. My father was a member of one of the wealthiest families of Saudi Arabia. My cousins were relaxing in fine homes and attending the best schools. Here I was, the son of a wealthy bin Laden, living in a lawless land, wheezing for air in a small Toyota truck, surrounded by Afghan warriors carrying powerful weapons, on my way to help my father claim a mountain hut for our family home.

I looked at my father. He did not seem to mind the trying conditions, but seemed exhilarated by them. Had his risky exploits as a warrior in Afghanistan created a lifelong need for stimulation? I hoped not! No matter what, my father was a tough man.

I caught a glimpse through the window of the Tora Bora mountains looming majestically thirty-five miles away. After leaving Jalalabad behind, the road became rougher still as it wound through little villages. The sights I saw were dismal, with meager bazaars lining the village streets, adolescent boys shoveling water on the roads to beat back the dust, and youthful boys pulling toys made of poppy husks along the roadway. As one might guess, females past the age of puberty were locked away in their homes, concealed from any strangers' eyes.

The vast poppy fields took my mind off my troubles, and even prompted my father to demand, "What is the meaning of this?" as he gestured at the endless green fields of poppies. We all knew they were used to make opium, which would be turned into heroin.

The driver shrugged. "Farmers here say that Taliban leader Mullah Omar has made a fatwa saying that the Afghan people should cultivate and sell the poppy plant, but only if it will be sold to the United States. The mullah said that his goal was to send as many hard drugs to the United States as possible so that America's money would flow to Afghanistan while America's youth will be ruined by becoming addicted to the drug heroin."

My father grimaced, his expression puzzled. He knew from all that he had heard that Mullah Omar, like most Muslims, avoided anything to do with drugs. When he mentioned this to the driver, the man said, "Yes. The good Mullah Omar has not been in favor of the drug trade. He made this fatwa only against the Americans."

My father said nothing else, yet I knew that such was not to his liking. Regardless of his growing hatred for everything American, he followed the Islamic belief that forbade believers from trafficking in drugs for any reason.

I wondered why the Taliban leader hated the Americans. I knew my father believed that if the Americans had kept their noses out of Saudi business, that he and his Mujahideen fighters would have saved Kuwait and Saudi Arabia, further establishing his reputation as the greatest Arab hero for all time. It was the Americans who had put him in an untenable position, causing him to flee his country—and eventually forcing his expulsion from Sudan.

I wondered if the Americans had targeted Mullah Omar as well. For certain, Mullah Omar had lived a hard life. He was an ethnic Pashtun of the Hotak tribe. After his father's premature death, Mullah Omar was born in 1959 in a mud hut in a small village in Kandahar Province. Born in a country where leaders come to power because of wealth, family lineage, or royalty, the peasant boy was not a likely candidate to one day rule the country.

Mullah Omar was schooled in Islamic studies at a Pakistani madrassah, or religious school, being taught the strictest interpretation of the Koran. Growing into a tall, rugged teenager, his youth was spent working to help support his struggling family.

When the Russians invaded Afghanistan, Mullah Omar joined the Mujahideen, reportedly fighting under the command of Nek Mohammad, a famous Afghan warrior. Omar was a superior marksman who quickly gained the respect of the fighters around him. He was wounded many times, losing an eye and scarring his face. Becoming too disabled to fight, he began to teach in a village madrassah near Kandahar.

After the Soviets withdrew from Afghanistan, the country veered toward civil war. It was said that Mullah Omar wished to stay out of the fray, but after hearing about the crimes committed by former Afghan fighters, violence that included kidnapping and the rape of young boys and girls, the pious mullah gathered a group of students, inspiring those young men to fight the criminals.

With success came the idea to install a purely Islamic state. Due to his piety and call for strict law and order, Mullah Omar easily gained support. A Taliban army resulted. With Mullah Omar as their leader, the Taliban entered the civil war and began defeating all opposing factions, including the Northern Alliance led by Ahmad Shah Massoud.

By the time my father and I arrived in Afghanistan, anyone who wanted to live in Afghanistan had to reach an alliance with Mullah Omar. My father was cautious as to where we traveled, for he had not met with Mullah Omar and did not know if the Taliban leader would welcome us into the country. For the time being, we had the support of Mullah Nourallah, who was the leader of his province, but at any time Mullah Omar could order my father out of Afghanistan.

After three bone-shattering hours, the rutted roadway grew even more jarring, but our uncomfortable journey was coming to an end. The peaks of Tora Bora loomed over us against the sapphire sky, so numerous that they appeared to fold into one another.

Where in that towering rock pile would my ill-fated family find a home?

We left the highway to climb a steep, winding track so narrow that there was barely room for our small vehicle. Our truck tires edged the cliffs. One misplaced jolt and we would have plummeted to our deaths over the razor rim.

Another hour of measured climbing revealed some structures perched on a rock ledge. Was this the mountain that Mullah Nourallah had so generously given to my father? Quite obviously it was, for the driver maneuvered our vehicle up against the stony mountain and we stepped outside to walk the final distance. My father led the way, a man proud of his new mountain. As was his usual custom, he prodded the rocky earth with his cane clasped in his right hand and his Kalashnikov slung over his left shoulder.

I often smile when I read journalists reporting that my father is left-handed, showing their lack of personal knowledge about Osama bin Laden. For the first time I will reveal a truth that my father and his family have carefully guarded for most of his life, for in our culture it is believed that any physical disability weakens a man. My father is right-handed, but he has to make use of his left eye for any task that requires perfect vision. The explanation is simple.

When my father was only a young boy, he was happily hammering on some metal when a piece of the metal flew into his right eye. The injury was serious, resulting in a hushed-up trip to London to seek the care of a specialist.

The diagnosis upset everyone. My father's right eye would never again see clearly. Over the years my father taught himself to conceal the problem, thinking it better for people to believe him to be left-handed rather than allow them knowledge that his right eye barely functioned. The only reason my father aims his weapon from his left side is because he is virtually blind in his right eye. Perhaps my father will be angry that I have exposed this carefully guarded secret, but it is nothing more than a truth that should hold no shame.

And so it came to be that, unlike my father, I was able to look upon Tora Bora with both eyes. The sheer size and complexity of the vista was more than I could have ever imagined. The dramatic view stretched endlessly, the flamboyant panorama spoiled only by the sight of some archaic mountain houses, fit for nothing more than sheltering livestock. I was hoping to hear my father say that those homes would be dismantled in order to build more suitable accommodations, a lavish mountain home perhaps.

Instead, he father motioned to the primitive dwellings and said, "We will live here, at least until the civil war concludes."

I sighed, thinking that the war in Afghanistan might last for years. Perhaps I would grow a gray beard on this mountaintop.

My father was suddenly struck with nostalgia about the huts now meant to house women and little children. "Omar, these structures served a great purpose for the brave fighters during the war."

I said nothing, yet I was wondering how my mother would abide living in such a wild and barren place. Not only was it primitive, but it was a treacherous environment for young children. On the opposite side of the homes was a dangerous descent of over three thousand feet. In my mind's eye I was already envisioning the toddlers in the family tumbling off the mountain.

In shock, I followed my father into the first building, which had a total of six very small rooms. My father announced, "Your mother and your aunties will have two rooms each."

I grunted, afraid that if I spoke I would be unable to control my growing anger. My father could not always restrain his legendary temper, although he was generally placated by hitting his sons with his cane. Perhaps if I offended him while we were standing so close to a precipice, he might toss me off.

So I kept quiet and feigned interest in the huts. All six rooms were constructed of blocks that had been cut, carved, and rudely shaped from the mountain granite. The flat roofs were made of wood and straw. Most surprising, the windows and doors were empty openings.

My father was attuned to my thinking, pointing with his cane and saying, "We will hang animal hides over the doors and windows."

Was he serious?

The abandoned structures were littered with the debris of war. There was rotten bedding, empty shell casings, bare tins, yellowed newsprint, cast-off clothing, and plastic containers. Not surprisingly, there was no electricity on the mountain, so we could forget even having the convenience of a few dim light bulbs.

I knew then that terrible times were upon us.

So, finally, the Osama bin Laden family would be a true mountain family, our activities lit by candles or gas lanterns. Most worrying, no pipes had been laid to bring water to the area. Would my delicate mother now balance a water jug on her head, struggling to climb a rock mountain to bring drinking and cooking water into her kitchen? Then I remembered that there was no kitchen. Where would our food be prepared? A second later I realized that there was no bathroom. I grimaced. Such would not do because my mother and aunties and sisters were often hidden away, unable to leave their homes if men not of the family were in the area. They must have an accessible indoor toilet!

Once again, my father seemed to read my mind. "We will build a small bathroom for each set of two rooms."

Pulled into a debilitating melancholy, as before I could only grunt in reply.

Once again, my father appeared euphoric when he should have been in despair. Something about the old times of war had triggered an unexpected enthusiasm. How I longed to argue with him, to point out that while the ramshackle buildings might look sweet to his warrior self, they were unsuitable for women and children. But I didn't, for I was not yet of an age when bravery came instinctively. I still felt myself a child in my father's presence, helplessly caught in the swift-moving vortex that was taking his family with him to a destructive end.

"Yes," my father said with a confident ring. "All will be well."

I glanced at Abu Hafs and Sayf Adel, who were accustomed to my father's way of thinking and maintained their usual composure. Two other soldiers were scratching their heads in bewilderment, but like me, they would never dare argue with my father. In fact, every man who served my father had a habit of requesting his permission before opening their mouths. "Dear prince, may I speak?"

At my father's command, his men and I spent the next few weeks tossing out the ten-year-old rubbish of war, sweeping the dirt floors, draping animal hides over the open doors and windows, and traveling back and forth to Jalalabad to buy ordinary supplies. We purchased three small portable gas cookers, each with one ring, for my father's wives. There was a need for metal pails for hauling water from the nearby spring and a few metal cooking pots for cooking. We gathered enormous quantities of plastic dishes and simple cotton bedding, along with a few military cots for the adults. I was glad that my father sent us back to the stores to find a bunch of cheap carpets to spread on the floors.

Even after our efforts to tidy up and furnish the buildings, the huts appeared bleak and inhospitable.

The most difficult job was to construct three simple bathrooms, yet we finally completed the task. I wondered if they could fulfill their purpose in the absence of a water supply, but my father said there was a company in a nearby village that could possibly deliver containers of water. Hopefully my mother would not be hauling drinking and cooking water from a mountain stream.

Once we had done all that we could do, my father announced that he had decided against bringing his wives and children for an additional three months. The war was still erupting in pockets and no one seemed to know what to expect. My father was apprehensive because he still had not received any message of welcome from the reclusive Mullah Omar.

Despite my relief that my father was being cautious, I was missing my mother. Perhaps her sweet presence might bring clarity to my father, helping him to understand the absurdity of women and children living perched on a mountaintop in stark, cold, and inferior dwellings.

My father, his men, and I mainly remained in Tora Bora, although there were trips back and forth to Jalalabad. My father met with various military men there, but he often told me to wait outside while he spoke to them.

As time passed, I became more familiar with the soldiers who had made the airplane trip from Khartoum. My favorite of all my father's men was Mohammed Atef. Like so many of the soldiers, Mohammed Atef was no longer welcome in his native land of Egypt. Although he had once been a police officer, after becoming disgruntled with the political situation, he had become a member of the Egyptian Islamic Jihad. Before long he was in political trouble in Egypt, fleeing his country to travel to Afghanistan to join the Jihad there. That is where he and my father forged a firm friendship.

Mohammed Atef was older than my father by thirteen years. His hair was dark brown, and he wore a full beard. He was a big man, less than an inch shorter than my very tall father, but slightly heavier built. I believe that my father loved Mohammed Atef as much as one man can love another. Due to their indestructible friendship, Mohammed became like a favored uncle to my father's children. Despite what he became later in life, he was always kind to me and later to my brothers.

Mohammed smiled, telling me, "Call me Abu Hafs," meaning "father of Hafs."

I politely inquired about his son, and that is when I learned that he had no son. Unlike my father, Abu Hafs said he was content with one wife who had given him several daughters, although he had a deep longing for a son. He said, "Since I know God will bless me with a son one day, I have already selected his name. I might as well take the honored title." He laughed and after looking to see that my father was not nearby, I laughed with him. Despite the fact I was a teenager and was expected to carry a weapon, my father was still likely to reprimand me for exposing too many teeth when smiling or laughing.

And that is why everyone called Mohammed Atef, Abu Hafs, father of Hafs, honoring him for a son that he never had.

My father was so prudish that I often wondered at their friendship, for Mohammed was carefree and quick to crack jokes. My father rarely smiled, and so seldom indulged in idle chatter that I can count the times on one hand. Yet somehow the two men connected, forming the tightest friendship of my father's life.

My father said that I needed responsibilities while on the mountain so I would serve as his personal tea boy. Believe me when I say that I was happy to have responsibilities, for the boredom of life on Tora Bora Mountain eludes description. Being by his side for nearly every moment of the day and night gave me a good insight into my father's true character. For all of my childhood, he had remained a distant figure, too busy to squander time with his children, but in Afghanistan I was the only family member with him, often one of only three or four people he felt he could trust completely. His trust was not misplaced, for although I hated what he did, and what his actions brought to his family, he was still my father. As such, I would have never betrayed him.

Over time, he began to relax and share his habits. Admittedly, I found some pleasure in those times and did all I could to please him.

I remember one afternoon when I washed his feet before prayer. Little did we know that a mullah who lived nearby was on his way for a visit, arriving to observe the rite that was becoming routine. Muslims must wash before every prayer, which is five times each day. One day when he was particularly tired, my father asked me to splash the water upon his feet. From that first time, I took up the custom.

The foot washing displeased the Mullah, who made a big point of telling my father that what I was doing was wrong in the eyes of Allah. No man is below another man. No man should wash another man's feet, or perform similar subservient acts. The mullah said, "Even if the king of Saudi Arabia comes for a visit, this boy should not wash his feet."

My father listened quietly, his face flushed with embarrassment, for he had enormous respect for most men of religion and the last thing he wanted was to appear ignorant of God's commands. My father turned to me, his voice sharp,

"Omar, you hear the mullah. He is right." From that time I was not allowed to wash my father's feet. I felt angry at the mullah, for the ritual was one of the few times in my life I felt a strong connection to my father. I longed to protest, but didn't.

There had been a number of unpleasant incidents involving the ritual of washing. One day in Tora Bora, when I was serving tea to my father and some of his friends, he reminded me of one of the most mortifying moments in my young life.

"Omar, do you remember the time when we were with that Egyptian general from the Russian war? I had fought with him here in Afghanistan."

My face turned red with the humiliating memory. We had been living in Khartoum at the time, and my father had ordered me to bring water for washing. Since the general was his honored guest, my father instructed, "First you must wash the hands of our visitor, Omar."

I bent down on one knee to do as my father ordered, but the general had other ideas, refusing the courtesy. He pulled away, saying, "I only want the jug. I will wash myself." I was young and didn't know what to do but to obey any adult giving orders, so I passed him the jug.

At the precise moment of the handover my father saw the general take the container in his hands, completely misinterpreting what was happening. Without asking what was going on, my father began to scream threats and insults, "Do you want me to beat you with my stick? Why do you embarrass me? How dare you expect the general to wash your hands! Why should he wash your hands? You are nobody!"

My father was so angry that spit spewed from his mouth. He seized the jug and personally washed the hands of the general, who had grown very quiet.

I had anticipated a severe beating when the general departed, but for once my father did not turn to violence. I assumed that my father had gotten so busy with his affairs that he had forgotten about the incident.

Now, several years later, I squirmed with disgrace as he recounted the story to his friends in every detail, shaming me in front of men I had come to know. At the end, he looked at me with approval, "You have learned much since then, my son."

I didn't know whether to laugh or cry. My father was still unaware of what had actually occurred on that day, that the general had been the one to take the jug out of my hands. But I didn't bother explaining, for I had learned long ago that once my father made up his mind, facts would not change it. If one disagreed, his mood could spark in only a second. Who wanted to incur his wrath?

I did my best to make his life easier. I prepared his tea in the way he liked it, boiling hot but weak, with two spoons of sugar, always poured in a small glass. I don't remember my father ever requesting coffee; his favored drink was tea, or at times honey in hot water, which he claimed had healing properties for the mind and body. My father scorned all soft drinks and would not allow ice to be put in any drink. He actually detested cold liquids and if some unknowing person presented him with a cold drink, he would let it sit until it naturally warmed.

He confessed that he was missing his favorite drink, which he had often prepared while living in Sudan. Dried sultanas (grapes) would be placed in a large jug, which would then be filled to the top with water. Left overnight, the sultanas and water would mix, leaving a very healthy grape juice that he would drink during the following day.

His food of choice was fruit and he looked forward to the mango season. He was a bread eater, but only ate enough to fill his stomach. He was not particularly fond of meat dishes, but preferred lamb above chicken and beef, all served over a plate of rice. Truthfully, my father cared little what was put before him, and often said he only ate enough to sustain strength. I can say that he spoke the truth.

My father kept two items with him at all times, his walking cane and his Kalashnikov. He demanded that other favored items be in easy reach: his prayer beads, a small copy of the holy Koran, a radio that picked up stations from Europe, including his preferred station, the BBC, and lastly, a small Dictaphone. Back in Khartoum my father had begun a habit of recording many of his thoughts and plans. He carried on with the practice after arriving in Afghanistan.

While I was keeping him company, he would often spend hours speaking into the Dictaphone, recording many thoughts, including historical facts, current politics, and stories from Islam. When frustrated at the recent changes in his life, he would thunder over past grievances or pose new ideas that he believed would alter the course of the world.

As I scurried about tending to his needs, I heard him rail against the Saudi royal family, other rulers in the area, and the Americans and the British. He seethed over the disrespect shown to our Islamic faith, which seemed to the basis of his growing discontent. My father's thoughts and words often triggered a flurry of emotions, resulting in a loud voice and an angry face, which was not his customary manner of speaking.

After a week or so of hearing his tirades, I shut my ears to his unpleasant rants, but now I regret my inattention. Many times I wish I had those tapes in hand so that I could better understand what it was that drove my father to hate so many governments and so many innocent people.

In truth, I learned more about my father's life during those three or four months than all the years of my early life combined. Although my father was so serious that he rarely spoke of personal events, there were times in Afghanistan when he actually relaxed, pulling me with him into his early life.

Since I now know that I will never again see my father, for his violent path has separated us forever, I often think about those times and the stories he shared. Some of his fondest memories seemed to date back to childhood visits to Syria, to the home of his mother's family, to the time when he was not so angry with the world.

"Omar, come," he would say in his low, pleasant voice, patting the colorful flat cotton mat beside him. "I want to tell you a story. When I was only a teenager and we were holidaying in Syria, I often went with your mother's brother Naji for long walks. The two of us enjoyed exploring the woods, checking out every turn in those narrow winding paths, very often leaping over bubbling streams. The trees in the hills of Syria were virgin. I believe that your Uncle Naji and I were the first to ever walk under their shady canopy. One day we were hiking in an area that had particularly dense undergrowth when we suddenly heard the noise of a snake. That snake was directly in our path, but I didn't wish to kill it, so we stood to observe what the snake might do. Not moving, the snake watched us with equal interest. Finally it slithered a bit to the side and I quickly passed by his spot, but your Uncle Naji was too curious, saying he wanted to examine the snake's colorful markings. I warned him, but your uncle was gritty-minded and so he inched closer to the long creature, when suddenly the snake became irritated by the human attention and coiled and hissed. Foolish Naji thought the snake's conduct interesting and edged closer, when that snake suddenly spiraled straight out of his coil and began to slide forward, causing Naji to break into a run." My father paused to smile and remember. "Naji was moving so fast that he quickly caught me and passed me. When I turned back I had a jolt of surprise. The snake had refocused his attention onto me. Off I went, your uncle and I struggling to outrun each other so that neither would be near that fast-moving snake."

My always too serious father chuckled once more, remembering that day and concluding, "I have too many times found myself in trouble as the result of the carelessness of others."

He enjoyed evoking memories of his mother, my Grandmother Allia, with whom he had shared the most pure and loving mother-son rapport from the time he was born. Even when I was a young child, I recognized their unique relationship. In fact, everyone in our close family circle knew that he loved his mother more than he loved his wives, his siblings, or his children. Anything she desired, he provided. If he was home, he visited his mother every other day. Anytime he spoke of or to his mother, a sort of glow came to his expression.

In Afghanistan, he revealed a few stories that I had never heard. "Omar, here is a story you must know about your grandmother. I remember once when our family was visiting in Syria and your step-grandfather Muhammad Attas had taken your grandmother and me for a short drive. We were on holiday and feeling leisurely. Muhammad failed to notice that our sluggish pace had irritated a minibus driver on the road behind us. That ill-tempered driver became so irate that he pushed his gas pedal hard, passing to block our car before leaping from his minibus and rushing toward us with a red, mean face. That man was so enraged that when Muhammad opened his door to receive him politely, to attempt to defuse the situation, the heated driver actually threatened him before giving him a rough push.

"Omar, you remember how gentle Muhammad has been for his whole life, never lifting a finger to harm anyone. Anyhow, wishing to avoid an altercation, Muhammad slipped back into the driver's seat, closing the door, leaving the man outside to rant, to wait him out. Although Muhammad remained calm, that man's behavior had so incensed my usually gentle mother that she jumped out just as Muhammad jumped in! She moved so quickly that neither Muhammad nor I could catch her. She rushed the rude man and hit him across the face before pushing him to the ground. Unsatisfied and furious that such a person was free to harass other drivers, she noted his minibus license tag and hurried to report the incident to my half-brother, who happened to know the Assad family, who as you know are the Baathist rulers of Syria. The result was that the man was arrested within a few hours."

He shook his head, smiling. "My mother is a strong, willful lady."

The stories I liked best of all had to do with his own father, Mohammed bin Laden, who had been killed when my father was only a child. My father, who had never emotionally recovered from the loss, kept the long-dead Grandfather bin Laden on a pedestal.

There was something odd that I had noticed from my youth. Never once did I hear my father call his father, "my father." Instead, he always referred to him as "your grandfather." I have no explanation for this, other than it seemed to pain him to use the words "my father."

There are many false stories regarding my father's relationship with his parents. For example, I read once that my Grandmother Allia was divorced by my Grandfather Mohammed bin Laden almost as soon as my father was born. Not true. In fact, my grandmother was the one who requested the divorce, although this did not occur until after she had become pregnant a second time.

Not so long after my father was born, Grandmother Allia found herself expecting another child. She has never said whether she was glad or sad, but in those early days the women living in Saudi Arabia did not have the soft life that came later. Although married to a man who was becoming one of the wealthiest in the kingdom, Grandmother Allia was not provided with domestic help, leaving her responsible for cleaning and washing. She had recently acquired one of the newest gadgets on the market: a wringer washer machine. It is thought that the machine had not been put together properly, because while washing the wringer part of the machine snapped loose to swing around to hit her in the chest and stomach. She fell to the floor in great pain. The following day she lost the child she was carrying, a child that would have been my father's full brother or sister.

Something about the loss triggered a desire for change in my grandmother. Shortly afterward, she asked her husband for a divorce. My Grandfather Mohammed, seeing that she was unhappy, graciously and freely gave her a divorce. He was very agreeable about the matter.

In those days a divorced woman was not allowed to live on her own, so she was soon married to Muhammad al-Attas, who became my father's stepfather, a gentle and wise man who regarded his stepson as he did his own children.

There is another rumor that when my grandmother left the bin Laden compound she did not take Osama with her. Some people have written that my father rarely saw his mother. This is not true. My father was only a toddler when his mother was divorced and remarried. When she stepped away from the bin Laden clan, her son was in her arms. Other than a few return visits to the bin Laden compound, my father never left his mother's home. Although Muhammad al-Attas worked in the bin Laden business, his personal life remained separate. Never again was my Grandmother Allia part of the bin Laden inner circle, and in reality, neither was my father until he was a teenager and came back into the family on a more routine basis.

"Omar, I have a few stories about your Grandfather bin Laden that you might like to hear," my father promised as he sat cross-legged on the floor, holding his teacup.

Eagerly I joined him, listening to every word.

"Omar, your grandfather was a genius who helped build the Kingdom of Saudi Arabia, bringing the country out of the sand. While your grandfather was working, some members, mainly Saud, one of the eldest sons, was foolishly squandering the early oil wealth. But my father was so loyal to the first king, Abdul Aziz, who happened to be a very fine man, that nothing could tempt him to say a word against the behavior of the king's son."

My father paused, a faraway look in his eyes, thinking, then said, "But of course that is not my story.

"Omar, your grandfather was a very tough man, because the times called for it. He was most inflexible when it came to his children. He had rules for everything.

"I remember once when your grandfather called his sons home for one reason or another. He had a strict rule that when he met with his sons, we must stand in a very straight line, organized according to height, rather than age.

We would nervously gather, from the tallest to the shortest. The half-siblings saw each other infrequently, so we spent a lot of time measuring ourselves against the other, taking care not to get in the wrong position, because it was easy enough for your grandfather to spot the one delinquent. Before I became a teenager, I was not the tallest, although I overtook my brothers later in life. On that day two of my older brothers, both taller than me, locked me between them. I really didn't know what to do. Being a shy boy, I stood silently, hoping against hope that your grandfather would not notice I had gotten captured between two taller brothers.

"Your grandfather noticed. Furious, he marched to stand in front of me and, without one word of warning, struck me with his strongest force across my face. I nearly fell backwards. I've never forgotten the pain of that blow, both physically and mentally.

"But you can be sure I never broke that rule again, but would dash back and forth until I found my proper place in the summit lineup.

"While your grandfather was too rough with his own children, he was the most generous man when it came to strangers. I remember once when he stuffed a canvas bag with money and made his way to a small village known for its poverty. He knocked on every door, distributing cash to surprised but happy villagers. It was the sort of effort the king himself often made. Most people who knew them both reported that King Abdul Aziz and your grandfather were like-minded.

"I remember my mother telling me one of the reasons she grew unhappy married to your grandfather. She recalled that his servants were usually young boys and men, and that he had a shocking habit of asking his wives to take off their veils and stand in a line, sending for his male servants to look upon their faces and point out his most beautiful wife. Of course, the male servants were terrified that their answer might anger their employer, or even rile the wives, who held some power within the confines of the household. Not surprisingly, your grandfather's wives were devastated to be treated thus, for in those days women wanted to veil, finding it humiliating to be lined up like harlots on view. But your grandfather was king in his household and everyone did as he told them to do. This might explain that a few years before he died, he made a rare confession that the one thing he regretted in life was the injustice he showed when it came to females. He was sad about that aspect of his behavior and said that he hoped his God would forgive him."

My father stopped speaking for a few minutes, quiet, with his eyes looking past me, reliving a memory that had occurred long before I had been born.

"Omar, I only had one personal one-on-one experience with your grandfather. This happened a year or so before he was killed.

"When I was only nine years old, I was struck by the strongest desire to have my own automobile. I had an early love for cars. I talked incessantly about automobiles, goading my dear mother and stepfather, Muhammad Attas, to desperation. As you know, Muhammad was never a man of wealth, and he could not afford to indulge me. But after months of my pestering my dear mother, Muhammad announced that he was going to ask for an audience with my biological father, so that I could express my wish to the only man who had the power to make it happen.

"When I heard the strategy, I was nervous but excited. I had never stood alone in front of your grandfather, as I only saw him when he summoned all his sons. Therefore, I didn't have the sort of relationship that eased the situation. But I was determined to carry it out.

"Finally the big day came. Muhammad Attas led me into your grandfather's office in Jeddah. There he was, sitting behind the largest desk I've ever seen. Unsmiling, he looked at me then said, 'What is it you want, my son?'

"Muhammad Attas squeezed my shoulder in encouragement, both of us relieved that I had been so easily acknowledged, because it was known that your grandfather never recognized his own sons. Always, he would ask the son before him to identify himself by naming his mother. But on that day my father knew that I was his son. I realize now that it was only because Muhammad Attas was accompanying me, and your grandfather knew who my mother had married. But I didn't think about the logical explanation at the time, and felt so very pleased that your grandfather knew exactly who I was.

"Your grandfather was looking me sternly in the eye. I dropped my own gaze because I would never lock eyes with him, careful not to show disrespect. I fixed my eyes to the floor, listening as he asked me to tell him why I was there. He asked the same question three times before I finally found my voice. I surprised myself with my steady tone. 'I want a car, Father.'

"He kept asking the same question and I kept replying with the same answer.

"Finally he asked me: 'Osama, why do you need a car?'

"I answered: 'I need a car so that I can drive to school.'

"He asked: 'Why do you think you deserve a car?'

"I replied: 'I like cars. I will be good at driving.'

"He asked: 'Are you good at school?'

"I replied: 'I am.'

"He asked: 'Are you an obedient child?'

"I replied: 'I am very good.'

"He sat silent for a moment, making his decision.

"I stood quietly, basically holding my breath.

"He broke the silence. 'I will not give you a car. I will give you a bicycle.'

"I was devastated, but knew I would be beaten if I protested his decision.

He returned his gaze to the documents laid out on his desk. I thanked him and walked away. He did not say goodbye, and neither did I. I believe that was the last time I ever saw your grandfather, although of course I did not know that was our final meeting at the time. Only God knew our future, that your grandfather would be dead within the year.

"My heart was so heavy that I could not speak. Muhammad Attas was the kindest stepfather, making every effort to cheer me up during the drive home, trying to excite me over the idea that I would soon get a new bicycle.

"A red bicycle was duly delivered but failed to spark joy in my heart. I think I rode it a few times and then gave it to one of my younger brothers. Then one day several weeks later I received the biggest shock of my life. A shiny new car was delivered to our home in Jeddah! For me!

"That was the happiest day of my young life. Although my mother and Muhammad Attas would not allow me to drive it alone for a few more years, our driver or Muhammad would take me out for a spin, to my immense joy.

"Of course, your grandfather was killed when I was ten years old, so I never had a second occasion to privately meet with him."

After hearing such childhood tales, I felt sorry for my father, yet I was puzzled. If after so many years he could recall how pained he was when his father struck him or ignored him, I could not understand how he could so easily, even eagerly, beat or ignore his own sons. I never got the courage to ask my father that question, although I am sorry now that my nerve failed me.

Although being on Tora Bora gave me the opportunity to spend time with my elusive father, it was far too challenging a place for human life. If any of us were struck by illness, we were far from any medical help. As fate would have it, one morning I was stricken with a high fever. Believing I had contracted a cold virus, I slept late, but sleeping failed to bring a cure. Restless, I became more ill with a splitting headache and body cramps. All I wanted was my mother, for she was always so reassuring when one of her children grew ill, petting us with kind words and preparing hot soups. But my mother was thousands of miles away in Khartoum, unaware that her son Omar was too sick to even cry out for help.

I became so unwell that my father's men grew alarmed, calling in one of the drivers, a man by the name of Shear. My writhing torment rushed Shear into action. He shouted out that he would transport me to Jalalabad.

I have no recollection of my father's whereabouts on that morning, but knowing him, he had probably taken a long hike. No man on earth enjoys a hike in the high mountains quite as much as my father.

So, without my father's knowledge, I was loaded into a car to be taken to Jalalabad. The drive there was the most miserable of my life. My fever gained in heat and I continued vomiting. I twisted and turned. Poor Shear, the driver, drove far too fast for the narrow winding roads. I'm surprised we didn't plunge off the mountain. In record time, he arrived at the hospital in Jalalabad, where a student learning to draw blood tested his poor medical skills on me. Eventually I was diagnosed with typhoid fever and malaria. Indeed, the doctor warned the men with me that I might die.

The doctor in charge ordered a number of injections and medications. My father's men refused to leave me unattended in the hospital, so I was discharged to be taken to the old palace. I was surprised to be told that there was no room for me at the palace, for by that time my father's war veterans from Pakistan, Yemen, and other countries were converging on Afghanistan, bringing their wives and daughters with them. Females had taken over the old palace. Due to our restrictive culture, men were no longer allowed inside with the women. I ended convalescing from two very serious diseases on a cotton mattress under a shade tree in the garden.

There I lay, slipping in and out of consciousness for three days. Youth was on my side and although greatly weakened, I slowly recovered. Before I was fully well, my father sent orders that I should return to Tora Bora to recuperate. Once there, I collapsed on the floor mattress. Within twenty-four hours my illness flared with a vengeance. The frantic run to the Jalalabad hospital was repeated.

I recall nothing of that second trip down the mountain, but I do have a dim memory of being treated by the same young doctor. He was small and slim with a thin beard, but I was doing so poorly that an older doctor was called to consult on my case. But all he did was prescribe additional medications. Once more I was returned to the palace to sleep under the same tree.

I think everyone was astonished that I didn't end wrapped in a shroud and buried in the sands of Afghanistan.

My father's health was another story. There has been much speculation about my father suffering from severe kidney disorders, including claims that his kidneys were so diseased that it was necessary for him to transport a dialysis machine on the back of a mule. Nothing could be further from the truth. The only explanation for the rumor is that my father, along with others in his extended family, had a tendency to suffer from kidney stones. Those stones caused immense pain until they had passed out of his body, but his kidneys were strong otherwise.

Although the Russians had deployed chemical gas against my father and his soldiers, the lingering effects were nothing more serious than occasional bouts of coughing. Later he had contracted malaria in Sudan, and like most malaria victims, he suffered some recurrences, but he made quick recoveries. Despite the chemicals and the malaria, he was physically healthy. He even out-hiked vigorous young men half his age.

In fact, while we were living in Tora Bora, my father thought nothing of hiking over the border and into Pakistan. Much to my dismay, he decided that I should accompany him, telling me, "Omar, we never know when war will strike. We must know our way out of these mountains." Discontented unless he knew every inch of the path, he insisted, "We must memorize every rock. Nothing is more important than knowing secret escape routes."

Without warning, he might wake me from a deep sleep to tell me that we were hiking to Pakistan. Although the border was not terribly far away, there was no set time limit for the trip and no set route. I've been with my father when the hike took seven hours, and other times when it took fourteen. Once I walked ahead, exploring new territory on a ledge higher than my father's path. Being unfamiliar with the lay of the land, I lost my footing, crashing through the crusty ground, nearly toppling off a high mountain. My father, as always, was calm at the sight of my desperate struggle, waiting patiently until I clambered back upon the path to resume the march.

When I asked him what he would have done had I fallen to my death, he calmly replied, "I would have buried you, my son."

After arriving in Pakistan, we would sleep on the hard ground. There were times I risked his ire by carrying along a single blanket for cover. He had not changed from the times in Sudan when he ordered us to cover our cold bodies with twigs or dirt.

I made those hiking trips to Pakistan more times than I care to recall. When my brothers arrived a few months later, they, too, were subjected to the harsh trudges. My brothers and I all loathed those grueling treks that seemed the most pleasant of outings to our father.

In late June or early July in 1996, approximately two months after arriving in Afghanistan, a messenger came running with unwelcome news. Bowing his head humbly, he said, "Dear prince Osama, there is bad news. Will you allow me to speak and to share this news with you?"

My father's face had whitened, but he gestured for the man to continue.

"Dear prince Osama, Mullah Nourallah has been killed."

My father's lips tightened, but he did not say a word, for any lament would be the same as criticizing God Himself, who had decided that Mullah Nourallah was ready for paradise.

We were all in shock as the messenger provided details of the unexpected death. "I was with him, dear prince. We were traveling from Jalalabad to Pakistan for some business there. We were midway on our journey when our enemies jumped from a hiding place, armed with Kalashnikov weapons. They began to shoot at everyone in the convoy. Mullah Nourallah, who was easily recognized in his red truck, was killed instantly. I would be in paradise with him, but God was with me. Just as bullets ripped over my head, I tripped and fell over a large stone. Without a weapon at hand, I lay there like the dead until the attackers ran away. I then jumped to assist those still living.

"We have since discovered that the killers were the bandit's brother and other members of the family. This was the bandit put to death last year by Mullah Nourallah." He shook his head. "Mullah Nourallah is already in his grave, dear prince."

I remembered the many times I had heard my father and others warn Mullah Nourallah to guard his precious life, but he was not a man to worry about what he could not control. He probably assumed that his destiny was to leave his earthly life in a hail of bullets, for that was the fate of most Afghan warriors. Killing was a revolving door in Afghanistan, where the most minor insult would not go unchallenged, even if it meant an act of revenge would reverberate on every man in the tribe.

My father sat down, too shaken to speak.

I had overheard enough conversations to know his worries. Mullah Nourallah had been our powerful protector in a country that grew more lawless by the day. His protection discouraged those who might take offense at an Arab living in Afghanistan. Now, without Mullah Nourallah's strong personality shielding us, anything could happen.

My father's men gathered, silent and sad, waiting for word from my father. For the first time in his life he didn't have a word left to speak or a plan of action remaining in his head. He sat strangely mute, paying no heed to anyone around him, staring into space.

But during this life on earth, good news often follows bad. Within a few hours, the silence was disrupted when my father's portable two-way radio receiver blared with an alert from our security men who were watching the mountain pass. "An automobile has arrived carrying three men. They are wearing the costume of the Taliban. What shall we do?"

The Taliban were distinctive in a country where it paid to know the tribe or the faction of the man facing you. While al-Qaeda are conservative Sunni Muslims, the Taliban are even more strict: They did not allow music or singing, kite flying, keeping pigeons, television, movies, or education for women. Shaving was banned, and all adult men were ordered to wear a beard that protruded further than a fist could clamp from the base of the chin.

Their automobiles were usually black in color, with tinted windows.

The al-Qaeda group, started by my father, followed the beliefs of the Wahhabi sect of Sunni Muslims. Although the Wahhabi are also extremely conservative, with the Islamic faith ruling every facet of their lives, they differ in various ways from the Taliban. The Wahhabi will destroy the graves of holy men, as they accept as true that believers should honor only God rather than mourn the dead, while the Taliban will not. The al-Qaeda Muslims do not believe in dreams, whereas the Taliban often base their decisions on them.

My father did not hesitate, ordering, "Let them pass. Welcome them. Bring them to me."

Very soon my father's security detail escorted the men to us. They were dressed in the purely Taliban way, with turbans on their heads, two twined together, with one end hanging loose over their shoulders. Their Pashtun traditional clothing consisted of long-sleeved shirts made of heavy cotton coming nearly to their knees but belted at the waist. Dark-colored waistcoats topped their shirts and loose-fitting trousers and boots popular to the area which were constructed of yak hide completed their attire.

By the second month of our arrival in Afghanistan, my father and I had discarded our traditional Saudi thobes and adopted the Pashtun dress, because the traditional clothing was well suited for the terrain and my father said that our life would be easier if we did not stand out in a crowd. We rarely wore the Taliban turban because it took a lot of skill to learn to wind that long band of fabric, but we sometimes topped our heads with the small rounded cap common to the Pashtun.

The head messenger approached my father, who held out his hand in welcome.

The Taliban representative went straight to the point. "Mullah Mohammed Omar has sent us to you. He says to tell you that he has heard of the death of Mullah Nourallah. Now Mullah Mohammed Omar welcomes you and wants you to know that you and your entourage are under the protection of the Taliban. This is a special invitation for you to visit Mullah Mohammed Omar at his home in Kabul anytime."

My father smiled the smile of the saved. Tea was served and the men made small talk about the various hot spots in the country and what might happen in the future, for the Taliban had nearly won most of Afghanistan.

After their brief visit, the messengers left with these words from my father. "Tell Mullah Mohammed Omar that I am very pleased and thankful for his welcome. I would like to visit soon, but first I must settle my family, who will soon be coming from Sudan."

When our visitors had departed the mountain, my father's mood lifted to pure ecstasy, his expression so joyful I thought he might embrace everyone on the mountain. He did not, saying merely, "Omar, this message was sent by God. This welcome from Mullah Omar is the answer to all my problems in this time of dire circumstances."

My father had never met Mullah Omar, although he followed the Taliban's progress very carefully. "Soon," he said, "you will see, Omar. The Taliban will soon rule the entire country. It is good for us to have this invitation from their leader."

After that day, my father visibly relaxed and for the first time in my memory, he rarely raised his voice to anyone, even those who accidentally displeased him. He was calm, knowing that he could bring his family to Afghanistan and would be free from assault by the Taliban. Within the hour my father had issued orders that we would leave for Jalalabad as quickly as possible. There was much to do to bring our family from Sudan.

Despite my father's inner relief, the return trip was hushed with gloom, for our thoughts turned to Mullah Nourallah and the fact we would never see his merry face again. We had never been to Jalalabad without his welcome. All who knew Mullah Nourallah loved him. He was always so affable and accommodating. Although we mourned his passing, we knew that he was celebrating in paradise. Despite our happiness at that thought, such did not mean we would not miss him on earth. He had been one of the kindest men in all of Afghanistan, sensitive to those around him, even to someone as unimportant as a young boy. Never would I forget that after a few visits to Tora Bora, he had arrived with a brown and white puppy under his arm, telling my father that a mountaintop was a lonely place for a young boy. He said, "Osama, this puppy is for Omar."

My father did not protest, although after our puppy experiences in Khartoum, I was certain that he was not overjoyed. But that puppy, whom I named Bobby in honor of my previous dog in Khartoum, was a good companion. Through many lonely hours Bobby snuggled by my side, sharing my lonely place in the world.

I didn't disclose my sad thoughts to my father because I feared his accusation that my sorrow meant I questioned God's decision, but even the idea of a party in paradise failed to wipe out the horrible image of a bloodied and dying Mullah Nourallah.

Perhaps to put my mind off Mullah Nourallah, my father began speaking about his mission in life. "Omar, I know you often wonder why I do the things I do. When you grow older, you will understand. But for now, Omar, just remember this: I was put on this earth by God for a specific reason. My only reason for living is to fight the Jihad and to make sure there is justice for Muslims." He had a stern look when he said, "Muslims are the mistreated of the world. It is my mission to make certain that other nations take Islam seriously."

He took my silence as interest and agreement, I suppose, for he launched into one of his speeches about the evil policies of America. "The American president sees himself as the king of the world, my son. The American government and people follow their king to invade Muslim countries even when the rest of the world says no. Kuwait was none of their business. The Iraqi invasion of Kuwait was a Middle Eastern problem, ours to solve. The Americans want the oil, of course, but another goal is to enslave Muslims. Americans hate Muslims because they love the Jews. In reality, America and Israel are one country, not two."

That's when I remembered that my father's men sometimes lightly grumbled behind his back that he ignored the dangers of Israel. The fighters hated Israel more than they hated America. They longed to attack Israel and speculated as to why such an order was never given. Yet none was brave enough to pose the question to my father's face.

My tongue moved before my mind could stop it. "My father, why don't you attack Israel rather than America?"

My father looked at me without responding.

I then repeated what I had heard the men say, "Israel is a small country near to us. America is a huge country far away from our shores."

My father paused before explaining it this way. "Omar, try to imagine a two-wheeled bicycle. One wheel is made of steel. The other wheel is made of wood. Now, my son, if you wanted to destroy the bicycle, would you destroy the wooden wheel or the steel wheel?"

"The wooden wheel, of course," I replied.

"You are correct, my son. Remember this: America and Israel are one bicycle with two wheels. The wooden wheel represents the United States. The steel wheel represents Israel. Omar, Israel is the stronger power of the two. Does a general attack the strongest line when in battle? No, he concentrates on the weakest part of the line. The Americans are weak. It is best to attack the weakest point first. Once we take out the weak wooden wheel, the steel wheel will automatically fail. Who can ride a bicycle with only one wheel?"

He patted my knee with his hand. "First we obliterate America. By that I don't mean militarily. We can destroy America from within by making it economically weak, until its markets collapse. When that happens, they will have no interest in supplying Israel with arms, for they will not have extra funds to do so. At that time, the steel wheel will corrode and be destroyed by lack of attention.

"That's what we did with Russia. We bled the blood from their body in Afghanistan. Those Russians spent all of their wealth on the war in Afghanistan. When they could no longer finance the war, they fled. After fleeing, their whole system collapsed. Holy warriors defending Afghanistan are the ones responsible for bringing a huge nation to its knees. We can do the same thing with America and Israel. We only have to be patient. Their defeat and collapse may not come in my lifetime. It may not come in your lifetime, but it will come. One day Muslims will rule the world." He paused. "That is God's plan, Omar, for Muslims to rule."

I sat mute, feeling not one jolt of passion for my father's life. I only wanted him to be like other fathers, concerned with his work and his family. I didn't dare tell him my truth, that never would I understand why his mission to change the world was more vital than his duty as a husband and father.

When I sat staring without expressing excitement for his ideas, my father glanced at me in disappointment. He was accustomed to the passion of his warriors, men who hung on his every word, men who slept, ate, and drank only for the destruction of others.

That same passion did not exist in my heart.

My father and I rode the rest of the stony highway in cold silence.

My father returned to Jalalabad with big plans. Now that he had the blessing of Mullah Omar, he would send for all of his former soldiers. Some of the men had been with him in Sudan and their return would be easy. In fact, they would arrive on the same plane with my mother and siblings.

Although governments in the area did not welcome my father to live in their lands, because his passion to fight the non-Islamic world brought unwelcome attention from the strong western leaders, ordinary people all over the Muslim world continued to celebrate my father as a great war hero. While Muslim governments distrusted, even hated him, their citizens loved him. In fact, as soon as the news spread that Osama bin Laden was setting up new training camps for Muslim warriors, there were many eager recruits, all rushing to join the Jihad. With new recruits following the old, I was a witness to the making of a new army of eager Mujahideen.

Before long, my father would have more men than ever bowing to his ideas, willing to die for his cause. As they arrived in Afghanistan, I met many of those soldiers, because I was ordered to be at my father's side. I discovered that the mature soldiers who had fought with my father against the Russians were for the most part very good men. They had given up their personal dreams in order to free a Muslim country from the grip of a world power. Their purpose had never been to kill innocent civilians. But I noticed that while they seemed to enjoy the camaraderie of former soldier friends, they no longer seemed to have a fire in their belly for fighting.

The younger soldiers were distinctly different, their eagerness to kill and be killed so acute they swaggered with determination through the camps, warriors in the making. But when one looked closer, the quality of their characters appeared questionable. Many seemed to be running away from problems in their home countries. Some had fled to avoid being punished for violent crimes; for example, one of the younger soldiers bragged about slitting his own brother's throat when he discovered that brother having premarital sex. Others had lived in such severe poverty that they had only eaten meat a few times in their lives. Most could not afford to marry. Since Middle Eastern society promotes young marriage and many children, these men felt themselves failures at the achievements their culture held dear. Many were so miserable they felt themselves living in hell on earth, and were easily swayed by the Jihadi message to seek death so that they might soon be boosted into paradise.

I felt sorry for those young men. I knew they believed death to be a great reward, yet I never felt the urge to die; in fact, I did everything I could to stay alive. Though my own life was unhappy, I wanted to live and to pursue God's blessing of life on earth.

One day, while sitting on the edge of the ledge of Tora Bora Mountain and feeling particularly dismayed by my situation, my spirits were instantly lifted when my father announced that my mother and siblings were departing Khartoum the following morning.

I jumped to my feet, knowing that soon I would see my mother's sweet face.

He said, "I will stay here in Tora Bora. They will be taken to the palace in Jalalabad. The following morning after their safe arrival, you will go there, stay for a few days before arranging transportation with my men to bring them all here."

So, he was set on his plan of making the women and children live the mountain life. Although cross at the idea of what my mother's daily existence was about to become, I was still excited because I had not seen my dear mother in nearly four months. I wanted to shout with glee across the mountain range, but I muffled my excitement because my father did not approve of emotional displays.

Two days later when Shear drove me away from our bin Laden Mountain, I turned back to see my father staring at my departure. Set against the backdrop of those bleak stone mountains, he appeared an aging, lonely figure. For the first time in my life I realized that he was of the past, and I was of the future. I felt myself a man.

Chapter 17

A Far, Far Country

NAJWA BIN LADEN

In Khartoum we waited in uneasy suspense for four long months, left to our lonesome selves to wonder what was going to happen to us. Perhaps I was melancholy because soon after Osama had left me I had discovered that I was pregnant for the tenth time. My husband did not even know. We had not spoken since he left. And, without Osama around, I was unable to leave the interior of my home even once during those four months. Our family driver organized provisions for the women and children.

My husband had taken long absences all through our married life, yet this time was different. I felt a slight shift, as though as I was being forewarned, something comparable to the alarm raised by frantic animals as a speeding tsunami moves quietly under the tranquil sea. My innate sense gave notice that our lives were changing, and not for the good. Even my smallest children, Iman and Ladin, became sad and listless.

Omar had never been away before, and over the years he had become the son I most depended upon. Although younger than three of his brothers, Omar was my most sensitive and mature boy. My two oldest sons still with me in Khartoum, Abdul Rahman and Sa'ad, seemed to miss him more than the other children, perhaps because they spent the most time with their brother. Abdul Rahman was generally a quiet boy, rarely stirring up the atmosphere, while Sa'ad couldn't stop chattering. Since Omar had been away, I realized for the first time that Omar was a calming influence on his siblings.

I thought of my husband and Omar every day they were away. I worked on my patience, but after they had been away from my sight for nearly 120 days, I began to despair of ever seeing them again. Then one happy day my husband's faithful employees suddenly informed us that on the following morning we would all be departing Khartoum to join Osama and Omar. I was not told where we were going and I did not ask. I was most surprised when I learned that my husband had ordered that we were to leave all personal items behind. We were instructed that we could only bring two changes of clothing for each person. We were not to take any household items. I was not even to take a sewing needle! I could only assume that our belongings would follow us later. My husband always organized everything just so.

There were other considerations more worthy of my worry: How would the move affect my children? My thoughts also drifted to Omar and his love for the horses. Once again his father's beloved horses were to be abandoned to an unknown fate. Since Osama's departure, some of my husband's men had taken Abdul Rahman, Sa'ad, Osman, and Mohammed to the stables, so the horses were still fit. But what would happen to those beautiful horses once my sons were unable to supervise their care? I did not know. Realizing how such news would afflict Omar, I felt sad for his sadness. I had many other questions but they remained private to me, tucked away in my heart.

The departure on the following morning was not as complicated as the time we moved out of Saudi Arabia because we had no personal items to pack. We walked away as if we were a family going on holiday, soon to return.

My husband's workers arrived at al-Riyadh Village in a convoy of mini-buses and automobiles. We were led to our assigned vehicles to be driven to the airport. I looked back only once as al-Riyadh Village disappeared from view. Another chapter of our lives was closed.

A large airplane had been chartered for our private use. Osama's family was not traveling alone, for his men and their families were going, too.

My husband's wives and children had assigned seats at the front of the plane. Every other seat was filled with Osama's men and their families. Without speaking to anyone, I settled in with my children. My sister wives and their children sat nearby, close enough to converse, although none felt stirred to idle chatter.

With Abdullah in Saudi Arabia, and Omar with his father, I departed Khartoum with only seven children. Khairiah and eight-year-old Hamza were on the plane with us, as were Siham and her four children. In total, there were fourteen members of Osama's family who were on the flight, four fewer than had first flown into the country from Saudi Arabia. My mind was calmer than you might think, for when one has no control, it does no good to fret, although I did pray for peace to envelop the entire world and for my little family to be settled nicely. I held that thought close to my heart.

Ours was a mystery flight, as no one on board had been given any indication of where the journey would conclude. From what we women were told, not even the men knew if we were returning to Saudi Arabia, or perhaps moving to Yemen or Pakistan.

From what I remembered of Pakistan, I would not be unhappy there. I knew little about Yemen, other than that both of our families had come from there, but felt it was a conservative Arab Muslim country that would be well suited to our traditional style of living.

The flight seemed to last forever, leading me to believe that perhaps we were going to circle the earth. But eventually the pilot began to lower the plane's height. That was when I first noticed some big mountaintops far below. Some more minutes passed and we could feel our altitude sinking even more. When I peered out the window again, I saw that we were close to landing on a plain, flat area of earth surrounded by mountains. Some trees came into view. My thoughts were befuddled. I remember thinking, "What is this far, far country?"

Suddenly a very small airport came into view and I caught a dim glimpse of the natives who lived in the land. Men dressed in what I believed to be Afghan costumes were dotted around the airport area. I recognized that native dress from the summers in Pakistan. Whether I was looking at an Afghan in Pakistan or an Afghan in Afghanistan remained to be seen.

My heart skipped a few beats before I calmed all uncertainties by reminding myself I should and would rejoice that our family would be together again, no matter where that might be.

Upon landing everything was a bit chaotic. Our entire party was quickly taken to a long line of minibuses and small Toyota trucks parked around the airport grounds. I remember little else about that exhausting day. I do recall that we were transported to a big white house called the old palace, where someone had organized the nicest rooms for my husband's wives and children. There were other ladies living there, women married to the men who worked for Osama.

I felt uneasy because I had not yet seen my husband or my son, who I had expected to be in attendance to greet us. Someone said that we had arrived in Afghanistan, but I wanted to hear that from them. I rested but did not sleep, because of all of the questions swirling around in my head.

But the following morning I was in for a lovely surprise when my handsome son Omar came calling, patiently waiting for me on the outside of the palace.

Dressed as a Pashtun Afghan, my son looked little like himself. Even with the loose-fitting clothes I could see that my already small son had lost weight. He was having difficulty breathing, reminding me of his troubling asthma. I would ask about those problems later, but for the moment I said nothing. The smaller children filled the silence with their teasing ways, laughing together about their brother's funny dress.

When he smiled his sweet, hesitant smile, I knew it was my Omar. Although he was still not so tall, Omar had a new maturity on his face. I supposed that the months spent with his father had taken him into the world of men.

My most kindly son gently lifted my hand, kissed it, and said, "Hello, my mother. How are you doing?"

I replied, "I have been well, Omar. The sight of your face is best of all."

My son kissed my veiled face more than once.

The suspense gathering, I finally asked, "Omar, where are we?"

"You are in Afghanistan, in the city of Jalalabad, not so far from the Pakistani border."

So, it was true, Osama had brought us to Afghanistan. There was nothing to do but to thank God for our safety and our togetherness. I asked two questions, "Our belongings? When will they follow?"

Omar looked in every direction but to me, finally saying, "I do not know."

I had a nibble of worry but asked nothing more. Soon I would see my husband and hoped that he would clarify everything for me.

I did not have a desire to stay in the palace, which was filled with many women and children I did not know. So I asked Omar, "What are our personal arrangements?" I assumed that my husband was waiting for me at a nice place that would be our personal home.

My son seemed a bit hesitant as he answered, "You are all coming with me, to Tora Bora. Father is waiting there for you."

I remembered the name Tora Bora. My husband had described it a few times when telling our sons about the battles he had once fought from that hideout. I could not imagine why we would be going there, but I had learned after many years of living with Osama not to ask questions, for all would be revealed when my husband thought it best.

I had trusted my husband from the first moment of our marriage, and he had always taken care of his family. I had no reason to believe that this time it would be different, although I could not imagine living so high that I might touch a cloud. I had always lived comfortably by the sea or on the plains.

The rest of that day I was very quiet, saying nothing as I cared for my smallest children.

The following morning Omar came for us with a caravan of small trucks. Omar shared our vehicle and, in his way, provided few details. Our talk was casual about the other children and what had happened in Khartoum since Omar's departure. I did not probe, but I felt that my son had a sense of trepidation about him, the cause not becoming clear until I saw what he already knew. I was relieved that Omar did not question me about his beloved horses, for I knew only that they had been abandoned, as had our horses in Saudi Arabia.

The geography of Afghanistan was as amazing as I had heard. My eyes were seeing a breathtakingly beautiful land. I had a thought that I would like to paint the striking landscape, but then I remembered that all my artist supplies had been left in Khartoum.

I was so weary that my eyes closed. My first months of pregnancy adversely affected my energy, but the road was so bumpy that sleep was impossible. Iman and Ladin soon exhausted themselves and napped fitfully.

Soon we were climbing a big mountain with our truck slipping and sliding across a dirt road not much larger than a pathway. For sure we would all perish! I was glad that I was wearing the veil so no one could see the alarm on my face, but Omar spotted my knotted hands. "My mother, the first time is scary. But our drivers are the best. No one has gone off the side yet."

My son wanted to make me feel better.

The mountains were so closely connected that they appeared as one. Omar, so sensitive that I accused him of being a reader of minds, said, "Soon you will be accustomed," before relating the very surprising news that one of those huge mountains had been given to my husband by the man recently killed in a tribal feud, Mullah Nourallah. I admit that information did not make me feel any better, as I was not fond of my husband becoming too personally attached to such a high mountain in such a distant land.

At that moment we passed a security checkpoint, my husband's men guarding the area with their big guns. Of course they were expecting us, so we passed freely. Once the trucks were parked, Omar shocked me with his words, "My mother, we must walk the remainder of the way."

Thankfully the walk was not so long. I had several worries. Perhaps I would stumble and harm my unborn child. Or perhaps one of the younger children might plunge off the tall mountain. I glanced back to see Khairiah and Siham following closely, and although we were all wearing our veils, I knew in my heart that their faces were filled with worry. Where on earth was our husband bringing us?

When I turned my face upward to the sky, I saw Osama's large figure standing on the edge of a ledge. His men had alerted him to our arrival and he was now intently watching as a human trail of women and children climbed his mountain. He appeared to be standing on a flat area of the mountain and I wondered if he had ordered his workers to chisel down the granite. I was surprised to see that Osama had company. There was a tall dog standing near my husband. Omar told me, "That is Bobby, my watchdog. Mullah Nourallah gave Bobby to me a few weeks before he died."

I began to wonder about that man Mullah Nourallah. He was a great giver of gifts, from dogs to mountains. Arabs honor those who are so charitable. A very generous man who cared about my husband and my son had been killed. I felt sorry for that, although most likely the man was in white paradise even as my children and I were in danger due to his generosity, braving the steep mountain he had so graciously given to my husband.

We moved closer to Osama. I could see some ramshackle buildings made of dark gray rock behind him. I admit those buildings did not excite me. While my heart was heavy by what I was seeing on the mountain, there was a spark of genuine gladness to see my husband's soaring figure.

Osama greeted each member of his family before leading me inside the largest of the buildings. Omar took his brothers over to introduce them to that long-limbed dog, Bobby. Everyone else stood quietly and waited.

The buildings were basically stone huts, haphazardly constructed of different-sized rocks that had been carved out of the mountain with a crude attempt to shape them into blocks. When Osama said that I was looking at my new home, I really could not believe him.

My husband had never apologized for anything that came my way. That day was no different. Instead he pointed out that my eight children and I would have two rooms and a bathroom. There was a sitting room combined with a cooking room; and one tiny bedroom, supplied with a wooden bed built especially for me. There was a very small bathroom that had been recently constructed. Never had I seen such a place in my life, but I was so numb with shock that I nodded and feigned an interest.

I would be living with my children in extremely small square rooms set on top of a very dangerous mountain. Knowing that my husband would not abide complaints, I mentioned the things that I knew were not normal for mountain huts, such as the walls painted white and most of the center floor recently covered in thin concrete. The edges of the floor that met the walls remained dirt, but there were some cheap nylon carpets softening the effect. I made no reference to the fact that there was no electricity on the mountain, even though Osama had always allowed me to use electrical lighting, while everything else of the modern world was forbidden. I guessed that we would be using lanterns, and I was right, for Osama pointed out some gas cylinders so we could replenish the lanterns when they went dry.

I saw no taps for running water, although I did not raise the topic. I spotted a new portable gas burner with only one ring, the kind that people use on camping trips, so I knew how I would be cooking our meals. My children would sleep on thin cotton mattresses on the concrete floor, as there was no furniture, other than the one wooden bed, although I did see some thin cushions stacked in the corner of the largest room.

Thinking of how we might heat the hut, I looked around and spotted a steel box in a corner. There was a pipe connected to that box that led through the wall. A bunch of rough-hewed logs were stacked nearby.

Osama's eyes followed my own and he said, "The mountains are filled with trees. The boys will provide you plenty of wood. You will be warm."

The mountain felt cold to me, even though we had arrived during the early part of September. Although I have lived my adult life in isolation, I knew enough to know that the mountains of Afghanistan were famous for fierce winter storms.

I shivered in anticipation of what was coming our way.

I waited until later that night to tell Osama that we were going to have another child. I can't remember his response, although by that time he was the father of seventeen children, so he was most likely immune to a lot of excitement.

And so my children and I came to live in Tora Bora, on a very tall mountain that belonged to my husband. Although I was happy that we were all together, those were difficult times in so many ways.

It was not long before all of us were weary of our limited diets. We had eggs, eggs, eggs, or potatoes, potatoes, potatoes, or rice, rice, rice.

For breakfast we had scrambled eggs, white salty cheese, bread, water, and green tea. For our midday meal we sometimes had rice mixed with vegetables, or potatoes, and on occasion okra and tomatoes, if we were lucky. We rarely ate meat. Normally I would not be concerned for myself, but I was pregnant and anxious about my unborn child. My growing children were another big worry, for I knew that they required protein in their diets. For supper we had to repeat our breakfast meal, with eggs and bread. On very rare occasions we might get a can of tuna each, a treat thrilling for my little children, who never received sweets or any special foods that are known to excite children.

My growing children were always hungry, but I tried to release our tension with a little teasing, once telling my boys that they would soon be clucking like chickens, for eggs were the only food in ample supply and my sons ate endless boiled eggs.

Lacking a built-in system of water was an inconvenience I shall never forget. In the beginning days we were forced to retrieve water from a mountain stream, but that was nearly impossible for such a large group of people. After a few weeks, Osama arranged for a small truck to deliver water. Since females should not be seen by men not of our family, someone bored a small hole in the wall of the building for the delivery man to poke a pipe through to let loose the water. My daughters and I jumped about in a funny way, as it was essential for us to be exceedingly nimble to take hold of empty plastic jugs to fill one then the other without spraying ourselves wet.

Never once did I complain to my husband, even as I washed our dirty clothes in cold water in a big metal bucket, or cooked rice on the paltry one-eyed burner, or cooled our perishable food in a mountain stream. I diligently swept the floor with an odd brush that someone had covered in a nylon mat. I had never seen such a broom, but it served the purpose.

I never complained even as I stifled screams when my smallest children ran recklessly on the mountain's edge.

I never complained although my left-behind possessions often came to my mind. I never mentioned how I longed for my little treasures, my beloved books, the beautiful golden coins given to me each time I gave birth to one of my children. My secret stash of photographs of my children was painfully missed. Since the day we had married, my husband's rulings on cameras and photographs swayed back and forth, first saying no to picture taking, then saying yes, and then no again. Picture taking was my one little sin, and from the early days of my marriage I always managed to capture the sweet images of my beautiful babies. Those pictures were some of my most cherished items that I knew were forever gone. I longed for some scented shampoos and soaps, but had to wash with the roughest detergents. I often thought about the pretty dresses that I had so joyously worn in the privacy of my home. I even missed my black abaaya and black veils and scarves, for as soon as our feet climbed the rock mountains of Tora Bora, Osama decreed that every member of his family must assume native dress. Even his wives would discard our familiar abaayas so they would not stand out from native women. And so he sent his drivers to the nearest village bazaar to purchase the Afghan chadris or burqas, those tentlike covers with a latticed slit for the eyes. I greatly preferred the black flowing abaaya with head scarf and face veil to the billowing pastel-colored burqa. But Osama said that I must become a burqa-clad woman, and so I did.

Every day was very similar to the next for my two sister-wives and myself. We three would pray five times each day, and after our chores we might meet to read the Koran, or to sit and look over the mountains to watch the forest animals around us, wondering what their lives were like. My little daughters, Fatima and Iman, spent much time with me and I entertained them by sharing fun tales about my childhood in Syria. The favorite times for my daughters, though, were when their brothers would take the time to sit in a circle and describe the life outside the rock walls of our home. My little girls mostly shared purdah with their mother, unless there were no strangers on the mountain and they were liberated to play with their brothers.

Even though I missed the life I had known before, there was nothing to do but to adapt. My life was for my family and so I did what I had to do. This did not mean that I blamed my husband, for I did not. He was in a situation where his presence was not allowed in most countries. He had to live where he could, and that place was Afghanistan.

Looking on a bright side of the situation, at least my children breathed fresh mountain air and the boys for the first time in their lives were free as the birds, running around on that mountaintop like little wild things. When there are so many children, life is never dull. Out of boredom, my oldest sons were gathering a nice collection of dogs and making plans to start a rabbit farm.

Although Muslims are not keen on dogs, my husband allowed them on the mountain because he felt their natural habit of barking would offer a good alarm system from intruders. In fact, when we lived in Khartoum my husband had purchased two big guard dogs, ordering them from a catalogue to be shipped from Europe. They were German shepherd dogs whom my husband named Safier and Za'ear. One of the biggest surprises of my life was when one of my boys told me that he had witnessed his father petting those dogs. Never would I have guessed that my cousin and husband, Osama bin Laden, would allow his fingers to caress a dog. My husband follows the words of our Prophet Mohammed, who warned Muslims that dogs are dirty and should not be touched. Sadly, those expensive dogs did not enjoy a happy ending as one was stolen and the other suffered terribly from a mysterious disease before dying.

Hopefully the dogs in Afghanistan would be more fortunate. Omar had his sweet dog, Bobby, tall, white and brown with skinny legs so long he created much conversation and hearty laughs. He had very long silky hair that many women would envy. Abdul Rahman had been given a midsized black dog that had a cute attitude. Sa'ad had gotten himself a dog, too, but the memory of that dog's face is left behind in Afghanistan. Osman had taken possession of two little brown dogs that were very amusing. I'm sure all those dogs had names, but for the life of me, I can only remember Omar's dog, Bobby.

Those dogs created some excitement from time to time. One day my husband was in the special room that he had set aside for his meetings with other men, as it is not proper in our society for strange men to come into a home where women are living. My husband's office was one ledge down the mountain, so nearby that we could see his rooftop from our vantage point, coming into contact with the flat area where the children played. On that day my husband had three important visitors, men that he had never before met, so I am sure he wanted them to leave with a good impression.

It happened that our oldest sons, Abdul Rahman, Sa'ad, and Omar, were working hard on that day training their dogs to protect our home. Something Abdul Rahman did spooked the dogs. Sa'ad, thinking to play a funny joke on his brother, yanked loose the restraints and off all five doggies went after Abdul Rahman's legs and ankles. Poor Abdul Rahman panicked when the dogs starting nipping at him, so he ran away. He was galloping like a race horse, running too fast for the terrain, failing to watch the path as he kept turning back to make sure he was leaving those dogs behind. As luck would have it, Abdul Rahman ran right off the ledge and onto the top of the wooden and straw roof covering Osama's office.

While my husband and his visitors were discussing the most serious world business, tree limbs and dried grasses suddenly rained on their heads. A child came next, arms flailing and legs kicking. My panicked son plunged straight through the roof, his fall interrupted by the hard floor. Stunned by the uncontrolled tumble, Abdul Rahman crumpled at the feet of my husband's astonished visitors.

Omar had very rapidly maneuvered his way down the mountainside by this time and reported that the sight would have been amusing if not so scary. My husband and his visitors moved not a muscle, sitting as still as stones as Abdul Rahman crashed in amongst them. Omar said he looked carefully at his father's face to see what would happen, preparing to run for safety if necessary, but Osama kept his business face, as though it was perfectly normal for a child to plummet through the roof.

After many long moments of silence, Osama slowly dusted the debris from his head and body, rising to his feet to step over to our dazed son. He brushed the roof bushes and splinters from Abdul Rahman's clothes before checking to make certain that our son had escaped without any broken bones. One of the visitors commented that it was lucky that the roof "very nicely broke" Abdul Rahman's fall.

Osama gently led a shaken Abdul Rahman out of the room and quietly told him, "My son, go home to your mother." My serious husband then peered up to the ledge to see a frightened Sa'ad and Osman peeking over the edge. Omar reported that his father spoke with enormous calm, "Sa'ad. Osman. Move the dogs from this area or I will kill them at the end of my meeting."

The boys gathered their dogs and scattered. Omar watched as his father coolly returned to his meeting and the four men resumed their business as though nothing out of the ordinary had occurred.

Omar was the son who most worried me. I saw that since coming to Afghanistan he had become very sad. I stirred around without speaking, but carefully observing as Omar spent too many long hours sitting in our home. Sometimes he would turn his back to the world and perch for hours with his ear next to the radio, leading me to believe that he had fallen asleep with that radio to his ear. But when I slipped around to get a view of his face, he would have eyes wide open like a corpse, although a breathing corpse. My most sensitive son was in trouble and his mother did not know what to do to help him. The only good advice I could offer was to remind him that everything was in God's hands and as such all would be okay.

Before the wives and other children had arrived in Afghanistan, Omar had his father all to himself. I believe that such closeness did my son good. Of all my children, Omar felt the keenest longing for a father's love. But now that the entire family had arrived in Afghanistan, Osama once again became distant, coming to his wives and children infrequently.

One day I was surprised when Abdul Rahman, Sa'ad, Omar, Osman, and Mohammed came to me, with Omar as their spokesman, saying, "Dear mother, we never see our father. Can you speak with him and tell him we need his attention?"

I was so startled that I could not speak. Some thinking was required, for since the beginning of my marriage I had never questioned my husband. Osama always had his mind on matters of the world, and did not appreciate input from his wives. But now my nearly grown sons were asking their mother for a simple favor.

"Yes. I will," I promised, pledging that I would find the strength to approach my husband.

The next occasion when Osama showed himself in my humble hut to take the evening meal with us and stay the night hours, I gathered my courage to tell him, "Osama, your sons need you now that they are becoming men. Please do spend some time with them."

Osama looked stunned, for never had I been so bold. He did not reprimand me, though, but said, "I will speak with them."

The hut was so small that there was nowhere for me to go so that my husband and boys might have their privacy. So when Osama called them in for a little talk, I was a witness.

My boys gathered to sit in a circle, and like good boys they sat in a respectable way with one leg under their body and the other knee touching their chests. There they sat without looking up. In our culture boys do not meet their father's eye in a daring manner, instead speaking while their eyes remain downcast. As usual, Omar was the one chosen by his brothers to convey the message. I was awed to hear Omar speak so clearly, and without fear. "My father, we are feeling ignored. You are *our* father but you spend all your time with your men."

Osama sat easily, sipping on his tea, studying his sons. Finally he spoke, "My children, it is not that I do not want to spend time with you. I would be very pleased if I could be with you all many more hours in each day, but you know my situation and how difficult our lives have become. You know the hours that I work. You must learn to be grateful for the brief times we see each other."

My boys did not say anything. I knew Osama's response was not the answer they were seeking. Sensing that additional talk was needed, Osama told them something that few people knew, for Osama is not a man who easily reveals the hurts in his heart. He spread his fingers and thumb of his right hand as though counting and said, "In my whole life I only saw your grandfather five times. Five times! Those very brief meetings, all but one with my large clan of brothers, were the only times my eyes saw your grandfather. And then he died." He made a clicking sound with his tongue. "Truly, we all must be grateful that we see each other as much as we do."

Our boys echoed their father, making little noises with their tongues, their minds clearly in sympathy with his nearly nonexistent relationship with his own father.

Osama gave the boys something important to think about. "You must understand. I have all of the world's business on my mind. I cannot be the perfect father who spends every minute of the day and night with my children. But from now on, I will try to spend more time with you, my sons."

Our sons nodded, recognizing that there was nothing further any of us could do.

How I hoped Osama would do as he said. Our sons appeared as lost boys.

That night I thought a lot about my husband and my children, and felt an overwhelming urge to escape the walls of my rock hut, to breathe the free air around me. After my children ate their boiled eggs and flat bread, they retired to their mattresses, tossing and turning until each slowly drifted off to sleep. Only then did I peek to make sure that I alone was still awake. Feeling comfortable that I would not be caught, I slipped on the unfamiliar burqa, taking soft steps to the edge of the ledge, gathering the puffy fabric of the cloak under and around me to sit quietly on the stony cold ground. There I sat in silence, a woman covered from head to toe, alone with my thoughts.

There were few sounds to be heard, for the mountain creatures had retired, yet I could see for many miles as there was a full moon, shining brightly over the world, little glimmers of moonlight flashing like a silent echo off the endless chain of rugged mountains. I sat there, peering through the burqa's latticed opening into the star-filled skies of Afghanistan. I was no longer a part of the hustle and bustle of earthly life. In fact, I knew that somewhere beyond the mountains of Tora Bora a busy world was passing me by. Such thoughts made me feel entirely alone in the world, a burqa-clad woman forgotten to all. Few people in the world even knew that Najwa Ghanem bin Laden existed. Yet who could deny that I had lived, for I was a woman who had given life to nine children, with a tenth child soon to be.

I sat quietly with my thoughts for many hours, the full moon highlighting my still, small figure. I felt myself to be nothing more than a stone on the mountain known only to Allah.

Chapter 18

My Father's Army

OMAR BIN LADEN

My father failed to keep his promise to devote more time to his sons. After our meeting, life went on as before, with our father totally involved with his "world business" and his sons hanging around the perimeter of his Jihadi life.

While in Sudan, he had maintained an interest in normal matters of life, such as his businesses, whether farming or factories, but once he lost the right to live and work in that African nation, his fury sparked a tremendous desire for revenge. That's when violent Jihad became his whole life, rather than merely a part of it.

After Mullah Omar sanctioned our presence, my father felt confident to send out the call for warriors for Jihad. Men began to swarm into Afghanistan, worker bees looking for "their queen," or in this case, "their king." And why not? My eyes were a witness to the overwhelming effect my father's mere presence had on tough warrior men.

That's the time when I took an active interest in the world of Jihad, and the evolution of my father's al-Qaeda organization from Abdullah Azzam's Services Office, which had been formed for the purpose of organizing resistance against the Soviet presence in Afghanistan. The need for such an organization as the Services Office was acute. With so many young warriors stomping around in unfamiliar territory, it was necessary to establish a registration process in order to keep track of their whereabouts. There were other needs. Those soldiers needed housing in Pakistan during the registration process, and in Afghanistan for the training process. Training was extremely important, for most were ignorant of what it took to be an effective soldier. Commanders had to be chosen to lead the soldiers.

The undertaking to establish a well-organized military force was enormously complex, for Abdullah Azzam and my father started with little more than large sums of money and an eagerness to fight a holy war.

In those days, my father was an enthusiastic student, learning much from Abdullah Azzam. My father soon founded his own guest house (House of Helpers) in order to assist the fighters, and in fact, created his own private army of Arab volunteers.

By the time the war drew to a close, my father was looking to expand his mission. Although ridding Afghanistan of the Russian invaders had consumed much of his energy for nearly ten years, he became increasingly passionate to change the face of the Middle East, wanting to rid the area of western interference, as well as overthrowing Arab kings and dictators, who were to be replaced by religious leaders. After his mission to change the Middle East was accomplished, his second mission would be to change the face of the world.

The entire world should be Islamic.

Now we know that the al-Qaeda organization was formed as a result of my father's world vision. Although there were other Islamic organizations with a similar vision, because of my father's wealth and passion for Jihad, his al-Qaeda organization became the main umbrella over Islamic Jihad ambitions. That's when the meandering tentacles of al-Qaeda first began to spread throughout the world with its new mission of violence.

After the Gulf War, my father's attention locked on the Americans and the British. His hatred for the Americans soon led to his unfortunate break with the Saudi royal family.

His position had further hardened since his exile.

My father began setting up training camps all over Afghanistan. Many were located in the abandoned Russian military camps, while others were constructed new. As I grew older, I was allowed to wander around the borders of my father's business. For the first time I began to hear alarming stories about how Americans hated Islam so much that they were sending their massive military all over the world for the purpose of murdering innocent Muslims. I remember being shown a map that displayed every country that allowed American soldiers to be based on their soil. The Americans had military bases in over fifty countries, and military personnel in approximately 150 countries.

I watched the faces of my father's soldiers as they began to point at the map, buzzing with talk that the Americans were everywhere. My father spoke out, "America is the only power in the world with an army capable of patrolling and controlling the world. They have gained a foothold in every region. And for what purpose? To destroy our Islamic society."

I didn't know anything of the world outside my immediate environment, so it was easy for such speeches to alarm me to the dangers I faced as a Muslim.

Jihadi leaders gave many lectures in which they told young Muslim men that the Americans had basically forced the state of Israel upon the Palestinians. We heard that every bullet the Israelis fired upon the Palestinians was a treasured gift from the Americans. Israeli gloves were covering American hands.

Of course, now I know that such views were not limited to al-Qaeda leaders, but had become common throughout the Muslim world. Because so many Arab governments cultivate these same beliefs, my father's soldiers arrived mentally prepped for such talk. The government of America is greatly hated by nearly everyone in the Arab world, despite the fact that individually the American people are viewed more favorably.

At meetings held in Kandahar, warriors were driven into a great fury by videotapes showing Israeli soldiers gleefully stomping on Palestinian women; Israeli tanks purposely destroying Palestinian homes; Israeli soldiers viciously kicking young Palestinian boys; and Israeli soldiers hatefully shooting to kill young stone-throwing Palestinian children.

At the end of such viewings, young men would burst from meetings, their hearts exploding in rage. My father's Jihadi warriors were ready for war, whatever form war might take. And who could blame them? That view was their only reality. Muslims must act before being attacked!

As a young and malleable boy, I came away from such meetings accepting as true that all Muslims were in dire danger, and it was only a matter of time before we would be forced to fight for our very lives. I began to understand why my father trained his family to sleep in dirt holes in the desert. Perhaps one day we might find ourselves in such a situation, and it was best to be prepared.

I had no idea that, in fact, the majority of the American people gave Muslims little thought one way or another. The American people have always lived in protective isolation, their oceans for the most part keeping the problems of the world at bay. The Israelis were another matter because they were a part of our Muslim neighborhood. It was clear that the Israelis thought of us more frequently and in more dangerous terms.

Very soon, my brothers and I became a more intricate part of my father's world vision. Soon after my mother and siblings arrived in Afghanistan, my father gave the order for us to be trained with weapons. Although we had been hunting for years, and had been presented with our own Kalashnikov guns after the assassination attempt in Khartoum, my father said that the time had come for serious training.

First of all, our father selected some of his most experienced soldiers to teach us everything about the Kalashnikov, telling us that we were forbidden to be without it, even when at ease in our home. For sure, I could not recall ever seeing my father at an arm's length distance from his weapon, even when he was visiting with my mother.

I was not unhappy to learn more about weapons, for we lived in a dangerous world. Unfortunately, despite our familiarity with the weapon, my brothers and I were irresponsible. Due to our age, our gun etiquette was appalling.
I remember an occasion when my brothers and I fired our weapons at each
other's feet, commanding, "Dance! Dance! Dance!"

Because we were our father's sons, we were never corrected, although I'm
sure that the fighters itched to give us a beating.

It was during this same time that our father suggested that my brothers and
I visit some of his al-Qaeda training camps. My father's suggestions were in
reality orders, so off we went. I was surprised to see that the living quarters
provided to the fighters were even worse than our own spartan accommodations. The buildings were small mud-block buildings with few necessities of
life. Of course, my father made sure there was no method of heating in the
winter or cooling in the summer.

The trainees were tough men, some old, but most were young, all unshaven,
with most wearing long beards. There was no specific camp uniform, so some
trainees were dressed as Taliban, others as Pashtun, and to my surprise there
were some soldiers strutting about in the uniforms of American or Russian
soldiers. I was told that when the Russians left, they had not bothered taking
their military supplies. Warehouses were discovered with uniforms, weapons,
and food. Those supplies had been put to good use by my father. Where my
father's fighters procured the American military uniforms, I never discovered.

Before the men could even begin their training, they were required to take
an oath of loyalty to my father. Their training routine was strict. The men rose
early for the first prayers of the day before being served a meager breakfast of a
boiled egg, bread, and tea. Training went on until 1 P.M., including special exercises organized to whip trainees into tip-top shape, from running on the flat
ground of the valley to sprinting up steep mountains. They were taught how to
fight in close combat. They had to run alongside automobiles, learning how to
assassinate the passengers. They would jump hurdles and end in a somersault,
learning how to get away if the mission went poorly.

They were taught how to take prisoners and what to do with those prisoners
once they were under control. Special interrogation methods were taught to
the soldiers who showed higher than average intelligence.

After the morning training session, they would break for a two-hour rest,
and then resume training until six in the evening, when they took their evening meal. Rice and vegetables was common fare for dinner, although on occasion the soldiers might receive a gift of a can of tuna. After the training day
ended, there were further requirements, because trainees had to attend lectures
on why Jihad was important, which basically consisted of verbal attacks upon
the United States.

After the last lecture, the soldiers were free to talk to others, or read the Koran. On rare occasions the men would play soccer, sparking my guilt with the memory of the time in Peshawar when I had ended with the fighter's ball in my hands.

Generally, the solders were so physically shattered at the end of their day that they fell asleep the moment their bodies stretched over their thin mattresses. I comforted myself with the thought that few were dreaming of playing soccer, or any sport.

Personal hygiene was not a priority, as none of the soldiers changed clothes while I was there, but instead trained and slept in the same garments. When the weather cooperated, soldiers might trek to a spring or river to wash their bodies with a cheap piece of soap, and try to wash their clothes still on their bodies. I noticed that all the soldiers were thin, yet their muscles rippled.

Weapons training was a big part of their program. There were so many weapons around the camps that it boggled the mind. There were stinger missiles, previously given to the Mujahideen fighters by the Americans. Trainees were taught how to make explosives and how to plant bombs. Most astonishing for me was that trainees were taught to drive tanks. From our time in Sudan, I had learned to operate some of the heavy equipment owned by my father, so I was familiar with huge equipment. For the fun of it, I volunteered to learn that skill, although I have never had the occasion to fight in a tank battle. When I wearied of the harsh camp, I returned on my own to Tora Bora, thankful that my father was too busy to ask questions. I'm sure he assumed that because I was his son I had inherited his love of fighting.

There were other stories about my father's fighters that I will reveal, although for the life of me I cannot recall the exact dates I witnessed the events. Our lives were so chaotic and no one kept a diary, or even referred to calendars. It is virtually impossible to look back and accurately date daily lives or events.

While many fighters bore an authentic desire to uphold Islam by fighting against the West, there were other very bizarre characters who appeared in my father's army. I remember one particular Pakistani man who came to join the Jihad. He was so religious that he made a name for himself by doing nothing but training, eating, and reading the Koran in a loud voice. One day he started a hugging campaign and made it his business to hug every tough fighter, which I admit was not met with a lot of cooperation. He refused to sleep until he had hugged each fighter.

The fighters tried to decide what was going on with the Pakistani. In our culture it is not unusual for men to hold hands or to offer a kiss at a greeting, but it is not customary to be a chronic hugger. The barracks were unheated and became so frigid during the winter months that, out of necessity, the fighters slept side by side, sometimes wrapping their legs around their nearest bedmate in order to generate heat. None of this meant that any of the men had any sexual intentions. Quite simply, they were freezing.

One night after the Pakistani had retired, a young man who spoke no Arabic came fleeing from the room where the Pakistani was sleeping. He was screeching at the top of his lungs that the man was hurt. Everyone dashed to see for themselves, finding the Pakistani with a large hole in his neck. He had been shot and had died instantly.

The young man with the hysterics claimed that it was an accident that he had been "playing with his gun." Of course, no one knew the truth of that night. Whatever happened, the result was tragic because two men lost their lives when the young shooter was hauled off by the Taliban, most likely to be executed.

There was a practical joker in every camp. I remember one specifically who created havoc by using Super Glue on his sleeping mates. One man had been injured, and the other men were sleeping closely, trying to keep him warm. During their sleep time, the joker glued their hands and legs together with the Super Glue. Surprisingly, his friends didn't beat him bloody, but it took many months before they saw the humor.

Although there have been many reports of men who claimed to be my father's driver, the truth is that he never had one specific driver. Wishing to avoid jealousy among his followers, my father had a habit of walking up to a trusted follower and saying, "Drive me to Kandahar" or "Drive me to the camp." None of the men who drove my father's vehicles knew when they might be asked to transport my father, although all were hoping to be chosen for the honor.

For this reason I was astonished to follow the 2008 trial of a man by the name of Salim Ahmad Salim Hamdan whom the Americans identified as my father's driver and bodyguard. Salim was charged with some serious crimes after he was arrested at a roadblock in Afghanistan in November 2001. Two surface-to-air missiles were allegedly found in his car, and the Americans believed he had been delivering weapons.

I have no idea if Salim was doing my father's bidding in transporting weapons, but what did surprise me was to hear Salim parrot one of the arrest charges, claiming yes indeed, he was my father's driver. The Americans had it wrong, and Salim admitted to something he never was. Perhaps Salim still so revered my father that he wanted history to remember him as a special follower of my father. He probably believed it impossible to have a fair trial and he might as well have some glory attached to his name. In the Arab world, Salim and his entire family would be highly praised and rewarded to be formally identified as Osama bin Laden's trusted driver.

I admit I was glad when the American jury found Salim innocent of the most serious charges of conspiring with al-Qaeda to attack civilians because I can say that Salim was never a member of al-Qaeda. Just because a former veteran took pleasure in hanging around my father did not mean he belonged to al-Qaeda. I was with my father for years, and along with my brothers I even observed the fighters' camps, but I never joined al-Qaeda.

Before my father's soldiers were allowed to appear in the camps, they were told to choose a fictitious name. The soldiers were also instructed to "forget their past," forbidden to share personal information about their former lives. My father said that it was necessary to create such smoke screens, making it impossible for captured fighters to reveal the real names of other fighters. How could they reveal a name they had never heard?

I believe that is why it has been so difficult for the American security to trace many fighters. Only the veterans of the Russian war knew the real names of other veteran fighters. All newcomers never revealed their true names to other fighters, or if they did, the names were quickly forgotten due to the common use of their bogus names.

For example, my brothers and I knew Salim as Sakhr al-Jadawi, meaning the "Eagle of Jeddah." Sakhr was born in Yemen and had the typical Yemeni appearance of a small but tough man, with dark skin, brown eyes, and black hair. Sakhr was short, a bit broad, but never fat. He sported a nice mustache with a stunted beard. Mostly I remember that Sakhr was a jolly soul who was often observed laughing and joking.

Sakhr became one of my favorite men in Afghanistan. I remember that he had been very young, only a teenager, when he first volunteered to travel from Yemen to Afghanistan to fight the Russians. After the war ended, he remained in the area, discouraged from returning to Yemen, as many Mujahideen fighters had been arrested by their governments upon their return home.

While Sakhr was not my father's designated driver, he *was* an exceptional driver, able to maneuver the narrow and winding Afghan highways better than anyone I knew. Sakhr was also my father's chosen automobile mechanic because no one could repair a car or truck with such skill. The position of auto mechanic was Sakhr's single job for the entire time I was living in Afghanistan, although I cannot swear to Sakhr's role once I left Afghanistan for the final time in 2001. I feel confident that Sakhr was never a bodyguard, because he didn't have the qualities necessary to serve in such a position.

Sakhr was also a favorite of the veterans of the war with the Soviets. He was a peaceful man, often proclaiming that he had finished his fighting duty against the Russians. He was not in typical soldier physical condition; and like the majority of the Russian veterans, never bothered to renew his soldier skills in the camps. He was more of a friend to my father, but never expressed awe or fear of Osama bin Laden, like so many of the fighters. Many times I witnessed

Sakhr sitting beside my father, the two of them reminiscing about one thing or another.

Sakhr spent much of his free time hanging around with the sons of Osama bin Laden. He would arrange barbecues in the flatlands and accompany us on horse-riding jaunts. By this time my father had acquired horses. Sometimes Sakhr would play games with us, or help us with our rabbits or dogs.

When I returned from my first trip to the training camps, I felt lost and confused. There were times I felt a great anger at the West, for propaganda is a powerful tool and few could withstand the constant half-truths. Without a competing message about the Americans, I believed that the United States was an evil nation with an evil agenda to kill Muslims.

Most of the men around my father were passionately committed to my father's message of hate, even if their support meant that they would die. I heard my father speak many times; and he never ordered anyone to go on a suicide mission, but instead instructed fighters that if they felt compelled to do so, to write their names on a piece of paper and leave it in the mosque. My father was adamant that no one would be pressured to give up life, even for a cause he believed to be worth any sacrifice.

While the soldiers enthusiastically embraced the message of hate, it drove me to despair, for I am not a natural hater. I knew that my father expected me to become a soldier, perhaps even to give up my life on a mission. Although I was a boy who relished outdoor activities, such as horseback riding and hunting, I was not and could never be a killer of men. My only real goal was to figure out how I might escape the life my father had ordained for me.

Desiring mental escape, I often listened to one of my father's old radios. He had many and kept his ear attuned to the BBC, rabidly following the news of the world as though he had a personal stake in every story. One day while I was sitting in the horse stables with a friend, both of us drinking hot tea and listening to the radio, suddenly a distinctive voice rang out, singing a song so beautiful it was like poetry raining from heaven. I moved quickly to twist the dial off because my father allowed us to listen only to talking voices, not singing voices. But the switch was stuck, and I could not turn off the haunting song. The emotion portrayed by the singer made me feel strangely soft inside, and I asked my friend, "Who is this man singing?"

My friend said, "That is not a man. You are hearing a woman, the famous Egyptian singer Um Kulthum, the 'Star of the East.' Everyone in the world believes her to be the greatest singer ever to live. I believe it, too."

"A woman?" I really couldn't believe it. Her voice was deep and mysterious, unlike any female voice I had ever heard. Listening to any kind of singing was strictly forbidden by my father, yet I was entranced, wanting so badly to hear more that I was willing to risk his wrath.

"She is dead, now," my friend reported, striking my heart with unexpected sadness, for the singer had been unknown to me until the previous moment. Instantly obsessed by her voice, the following day I sought out one of the religious sheiks in the area and asked him, "Is it forbidden in Islam for me to listen to poems set to music?"

That sheik brought hope and cheer into my bleak life when he replied, "One of the most important sheiks in Islam says that it is allowed, so long as the poem does not sing about the body, or the features of a woman, or does not contain any crude lyrics."

From that moment on, poems and songs became an important distraction to the backdrop of my miserable existence. I would spend every possible moment listening to Um Kulthum singing her woeful songs of love, longing, and loss. I was so inspired by the idea of love that I even felt compelled to write a few poems of my own.

Every desire created by those love songs and poems was wrapped around my desperate need to create a new life for myself. Um Kulthum's message brought me to the realization that there was a parallel world to our bin Laden universe of hate and revenge, a world previously unknown to me where people lived for and sang about love.

During this time of romantic dreams, my hopes soared that I might return to Saudi Arabia and marry one of my cousins, as my brother Abdullah had done. I spent hours thinking about a certain cousin, a pretty and sweet girl I remembered from my childhood, imagining us falling in love, getting married, and living in a lovely home filled with sweet-faced children. I will not identify her because it might bring her negative attention, since the children of my father are universally believed to be tarnished by my father's activities.

There are so many who avoid *us* because of *him*.

I did receive comfort from my dear mother whose instincts warned her that all was not well with me. When I accidentally discovered that she had started a nighttime habit of relaxing by sitting on the ledge outside our hut, breathing in the cold, fresh mountain air and watching the twinkling stars hanging in the night sky, I joined her. Peaceful hours passed as we sat quietly or, when a talking mood struck, discussed our lives, and how strange it was that we had started out in a palace in Jeddah and ended in a rock hut on a mountain in Afghanistan. I had always loved my mother more than I loved anyone else, and through those talks, our mother-son relationship grew closer than ever.

A few months later when I overheard talk about my father's plans for an important change, my mother was the first to know. I had discovered that my father no longer confided in her as he had during the early years of their marriage. He was a man pulled into so many different directions that his personal relationships slowly shriveled to the size of a dried fig, even his once loving rapport with my mother.

After living in the country for nearly a year, my father finally traveled to Kandahar for a meeting with the Taliban leader, Mullah Omar. During their first visit, my father and Mullah Omar discovered that they held mutual ideas about Islam. The two men had agreed that my father should return to Jalalabad for a brief time while arrangements were made for us to visit Kabul, the former capital of Afghanistan, and then perhaps move to Kandahar where Mullah Omar lived.

I liked the idea of seeing something more of Afghanistan. I was so bored on the mountain that even an invitation to visit an active war zone held appeal, for all of Afghanistan was still boiling.

My mother said little when I told her that we were leaving the bin Laden Mountain to return to a life in the city. My mother refuses to condemn my father, even to me, her son, yet I saw her small shoulders lift and I believed that motion signified a lifting of stress. I hoped that her worries lessened. I could tell that she was troubled regarding the safety for her youngest children, particularly her two young daughters. By this time my mother was heavily pregnant with her tenth child, so I prayed that we would be off the mountain before the time came for the child to join us.

Despite the fact that the civil war had exploded, I believed that any kind of life would be better than the life we were living. For the first time in months, my spirits rose. A nice thought went through my mind: Perhaps after escaping Tora Bora, I might even find a way to flee the country.

While living on my husband's mountain, I watched my oldest sons stretch into their adult years. Abdul Rahman was a man at nineteen years, while Sa'ad followed closely at eighteen. Omar, who seemed many years older than the actual time he had spent on earth, would soon be sixteen. Osman, who was growing as tall as a mountain, was fourteen. It appeared that Osman would be the son that achieved his father's lofty stature. Sweet, quiet Mohammed was twelve, striving to keep up with his older brothers.

I spent many hours with my youngest children, for we were mainly isolated in our living quarters. Fatima was a serious ten-year-old girl, shadowed by seven-year-old Iman. Ladin, still called Bakr by Osama, was my youngest son, an active toddler at three. My daughters adored their little brother and took pleasure in being little mothers, the way many little girls pamper toddler siblings.

My daughters and I had managed to acquire some sewing supplies from my sons, who sometimes were allowed off the mountain to go to the villages below to purchase supplies. So my girls and I sat together and chatted while we darned old clothes and tried to make new ones without the benefit of a sewing machine or electricity.

The nighttime was spooky on the mountain. Other than moonlight, we only had gas lanterns to light our way. I was still cooking on a one-eyed burner, which was nearly impossible with so many hungry children to feed.

Hunger and cold were our two most vexing problems. There were many people that my husband must feed, yet his resources were few. Although there were times that I swayed from weakness because there was not enough food, my main worries were for the unborn child I was carrying and the lively children at my feet. Never had I imagined that I would see my children cry from hunger pangs. A more helpless feeling I have never known.

The cold mountain weather was a big problem. Our only heat was supplied by the wood-burning metal stove, and no matter that we kept the fire burning day and night, Tora Bora Mountain was subject to terrible blizzards. With snow piled up to the top of our roof, it was difficult to heat even three tiny rooms. Many were the hours that my children and I hovered close to that metal stove, shivering with cold, and wondering how we might survive without frostbite.

My sister-wives faced the same challenges, and I do not know what we would have done without each other. Our husband had so many business matters that he was away as much as he was on the mountain. Thank goodness my sons were old enough to take over some of Osama's duties of looking out for their mother, aunties, and siblings.

The isolation brought me closest to my son Omar. For the first time I had the opportunity to closely observe all my children, and Omar's behavior revealed that he had grown the strongest personality and had become a man in all ways. Yet he had many facets to his character. My good son was trustworthy, faithful, and decent, yet he could be short-tempered, reaching quick decisions that he stubbornly held to even in the face of evidence that he might be wrong.

Our sleeping quarters were close on that mountain, with all my children crammed into a very small space. There were many times I woke in the middle of the night to see Omar kneeling to his God, feverishly praying. I knew that my son was unhappy. But there was nothing I could do but to tell him that our lives were in the hands of God, and as such, we should not worry.

Despite his misery, Omar thought mainly of others. He could not bear to see anything with life mistreated, whether human or animal. He was the one to come to the defense of all, even snakes, a scary species that has frightened me since my childhood.

One night there was a terrifying storm that sat down on my husband's mountain. The storm was blowing with such intensity that our windows and doors lost their animal covers and we were caught without any protection from the strong winds and rain. My smallest children were squealing with terror. Being on top of the mountain gave a feeling of being tossed into the maelstrom of the storm. Never had any of us seen such natural violence. We were accustomed to little more than sandstorms, which can be frightening, but nothing matched the power of crashing thunder, lightning flashes, high winds, and torrential rain. Finally my older sons managed to hang a blanket over the door and towels over the windows. My smaller children and I huddled against the wall at the greatest distance from the doors and windows.

My older boys dashed away to check on their aunties. I suddenly heard a very strange hissing sound, which I believed to be gas leaking from one of the cylinders that held fuel for our lanterns. When I went to check on the problem, my eyes caught sight of an enormous snake coiled by the hut's opening, acting as though she had been invited to visit, although I realize now she was simply seeking shelter from the storm. I called God's name out loud and tried to walk backwards very slowly. My husband and sons had warned me to be alert because those mountain snakes carried poison so deadly one would not have time to rush down the mountain and drive the highways to the hospital in Jalalabad. I did not want to die and leave my little children without their mother.

I was tottering with fright. I am a woman whose childhood fears have increased to the level that that I cannot tolerate even the image of a colorful snake on the pages of a book. Having nowhere to run in that small hut, I cried out for my boys. Omar quickly came running to me with his Kalashnikov in his hand. For the first time I was happy that my husband made my boys carry that bad weapon.

I shouted, "Omar, be careful! There is a giant snake. There, by the door! Kill it!"

Omar took a look at the snake and teased me. "Poor snake. You want to kill it? Leave her alone, let her live."

By that time I was yelling very loudly, "Kill that snake!" There was no way I was going to allow that snake to run away to come back to possibly crawl under my blanket while I slept.

My son kept repeating that he did not want to kill the snake.

I kept screaming, "Kill the snake!"

Finally Omar saw that his mother meant business and he used his big weapon to hit the snake on its head. I watched the snake's body slowly deflate, to my immense relief.

Omar felt guilty for the snake's life, lifting the limp snake in his arms even as I screamed in terror for him to take it away, for even a dead snake makes me quiver. Omar was sad when he said, "You should not have made me kill this snake."

Off my son went, a big dead snake in his arms, and to where I do not know, and at the time, did not care.

Omar had a way with animals. I remember once when I was watching my husband attempt to deliver a baby camel. There was trouble, but nothing helped the desperate mother. The baby was stuck half in and half out, and the mother camel was in the greatest pain.

Omar heard about the problem and came to assist. Though my husband told him to go away, Omar did not respond, but reached to lift the baby head of the camel, helping the mother. Finally Omar got the baby out alive and prayed some verses over mother and baby. My husband did not know what to say because it was becoming clear that Omar was blessed by God to feel the pain of every animal, and had a bit of magic in communicating with them.

There are many other stories. The life lived by the men around us was often so brutal that they did not notice cruelty. Even my own sons, and sons of the men who worked for my husband, were known to abuse animals. But Omar was willing to fight to protect them, telling the others, "Hey, leave that animal alone. I order you to stop." Even the older boys would obey because they knew that Omar would not hesitate to take further action on behalf of the animal.

After months of life on that mountain, the days were beginning to feel like years. Then a good day arrived when Omar gave me the news that we would soon be leaving, to move to a city called Kandahar. Omar said, "My mother, your daily life will improve." Although I was careful not to speak of my happiness, my heart fluttered with joy to hear that the time had come for us to leave the mountain life. I knew my child was nearly due, and I did not know what might happen, for I had not seen a doctor once since arriving at Tora Bora. I was no longer a young woman having easy pregnancies. I prayed that I would be in the town of Jalalabad or at Kandahar when my child decided to come.

Soon we were loading into my husband's vehicles and making our way down the mountain. The move did not come a moment too fast, because soon after arriving in Jalalabad, I went into labor. My husband was not with me, but my three oldest sons transported me to a small hospital in Jalalabad. No one could be with me, because that was not the way it was in Afghanistan, but my sons waited outside to hear that our family had another little girl to love. And so it came to be that I had Rukhaiya, a lucky baby who was never subjected to life on Tora Bora.

Although life would remain difficult in so many ways, God granted my wish that my feet would never again walk the peaks of my husband's Tora Bora Mountain.

Chapter 20

The Violence Escalates

OMAR BIN LADEN

The thing I had wanted most had happened. Our family finally departed Tora Bora, and from that time on would never live on the mountain again. I could see that my mother and siblings were pleased, too. Although life anywhere in Afghanistan was a challenge, nothing could match Tora Bora for sheer misery.

The previous month had been filled with activity. When my father gave the order for his family and the main leaders of al-Qaeda to vacate bin Laden Mountain, my brothers and I were so cheerful that we had to struggle to keep ourselves from laughing aloud. For the first time, the grueling four-hour drive from Tora Bora to Jalalabad met with no complaints.

We remained a few weeks in Jalalabad so that my father could organize his new plans with his lieutenants. That was an opportune time because my mother gave birth to a little girl named Rukhaiya almost as soon as we arrived, giving her a few weeks in Jalalabad to rest before we had to load up once again to make a car trip to Kabul.

When we left for Kabul, we saw that at every point the scenery was dramatically beautiful. Yet we could hardly enjoy the spectacular vistas because the roads were so rough that our vehicles bucked like wild broncos. Kabul was only a hundred miles west of Jalalabad, but the bad road meant that the trip took eight hours. I could think of little beyond my mother, her infant daughter, and my other young siblings.

I was relieved that we all arrived in Kabul in one piece. The city was located in a small plain, divided by the Kabul River and ringed by the dramatic mountains of the Hindu Kush.

Most importantly, my mother and the new baby made the trip without any medical complications. The family remained in that broken city for several weeks so that my father could inspect the area and meet with individuals there. While waiting on him to conduct his business, our family lived in rented two-story houses that were rather ordinary, yet we were happy to have a roof over our heads, for few in Kabul had that luxury.

Kabul was an example of what total war will do to a country. Factional fighting since the Russians left Afghanistan had left the once prosperous city a pile of rubble. Although there were a few livable homes scattered about, most of the suffering population lived in blown-out concrete shells that little resembled homes.

The city was so dismal that my mother, siblings, and I were happy to leave, and most pleased to hear that we would traveling the more than three hundred miles to Kandahar by air. By that time, we all had our fill of the roadways in Afghanistan.

My father refused to board any kind of aircraft, declaring that the equipment was in such disrepair that he didn't trust any of the Afghan planes to stay airborne. So when the time came for us to depart, he bid us farewell and left with a few of his men in vehicles. Despite his concern about the safety of air travel, traveling across Afghanistan on appalling dirt roads during the middle of a ferocious civil war would not be a picnic. Ignorant of his plan at the time, I now know that he was surveying military bases abandoned by the Russians. Those military compounds had been built near every major Afghan city. Mullah Omar had told my father that he could make use of any of the complexes not occupied by the Taliban.

Still hugely embittered by his exile from Sudan, which he continued to blame on the Americans, my father was in a heated rush to set up training camps. He was obsessed to train many thousands of fighters to unleash on the western world.

The airplane used for our transport was owned by the Taliban, but generously placed at my father's disposal. When we boarded I could see that every passenger seat had been removed. There were so many of us that everyone had to sit bunched together on the floor. The women automatically filed to the back of the plane, while the men settled in the front. All the men were heavily armed, with guns looped across their shoulders and grenade belts around their waists. That was standard practice in Afghanistan, where one never knew when a fight might ensue and every man felt the need to be equipped for battle.

We were told that the flight would last for only a few hours. We gathered collectively in groups, pleased to have an excuse to be social. Young men sat with young men while the older fighters banded together. I was in a rare good mood, excited about the move to Kandahar. I had never been there and was hoping that there was one place in Afghanistan that I would find agreeable.

I was sitting with a friend of mine named Abu Haadi, who was older than me by fifteen years. He had grown up in Jordan, but seeking a higher purpose, had traveled to Afghanistan to join the Jihad. My older brother Abdul Rahman was in my view, and I noticed that he was playing with his grenades, but I thought nothing of it at the time.

An hour or so into the trip, Abu Haadi urgently nudged me, whispering loudly, "Omar! Look! Look at your brother!"

One glance and my heart raced. Abdul Rahman had accidentally armed one of his grenades. The pin was on the floor and the grenade was in Abdul Rahman's hands! Any moment the grenade would explode, bringing down the plane and killing everyone on board.

Abu Haadi moved more quickly than I've ever seen a grown man move, grabbing Abu Hafs and hurriedly telling him the problem. Abu Hafs was the man my father had entrusted to deliver his entire family safely to Kandahar. Abu Hafs seized the grenade from Abdul Rahman, then solicited the help of one of the grenade experts on board. The two men stabilized the grenade before dashing into the cockpit. It happened that the plane was flying low, and somehow they tossed the grenade out a window. They claimed the grenade detonated in midair, although none of us heard it explode.

No one ever related the story to the women on board.

After that high excitement, we landed safely in Kandahar. The airport was small with only one main building and one runway. There were vehicles waiting to take us to our Kandahar homes. We didn't know what to expect but we were driven quite a long way, at least twenty-five miles from the airport.

Our vehicles turned in to an immense complex that had been built by the Russians during their time in Afghanistan. The compound was enclosed by a high wall with sentry posts at each corner. There were around eighty medium-sized pink shaded concrete homes inside the confines of the wall, buildings that my father's men had been repairing for some weeks. After the Soviets had left in 1988, the buildings had been ransacked. Even after the houses were patched, I saw missile damage and bullet holes.

My father finally had his own military base. Of course, there was no electricity or running water; my father refused to modernize the compounds, reiterating his belief that his family and fighters should live the simple life. With the memory of the stone huts of Tora Bora flickering in our minds, no one complained.

My mother and aunties were all moved into their own homes inside the compound. Their homes were side by side, which was convenient, as they had no other companions. Soon my father's men would construct walls around each house, providing needed privacy for my father's wives.

There were twenty large villas outside the wall that I heard had once been used by the Russian generals. There was also one huge building that had housed the lowest-grade military men. Fighters who were married with children lived in the large building outside the compound walls. Villas for the unattached fighters were outside the walls as well. There was a huge military building outside the walls where special ground-to-air missiles were placed on the roof.

Of course, there was a small mosque inside the walls, as well as various offices for my father and his high-ranking soldiers. Stables for our horses were constructed beside the bachelor quarters.

Kandahar was far from a perfect haven. We were still living in a country at war. There were times we could hear bombing and fighting, although the war never entered the compound. There was also the danger of dying from disease in a land where the citizens had dealt with war and death for so long that many former habits regarding health and hygiene had lapsed.

Although we generally remained at our compound, some months after moving to Kandahar my brothers and I, along with a few friends, grew bold enough to venture to the city. It was in Kandahar that we witnessed the various problems disturbing the well-being of many Afghans.

I remember a time when my friends and I pooled our funds so that we might go to a popular restaurant in Kandahar. Accustomed to food so bland that even the stray dogs ate it reluctantly, we were filled with anticipation. After ordering, one of my companions noticed some jugs sitting near the table area. Being the curious sort, he lifted the container to peer inside. After a sniff, he gagged. The waiter explained that prior to starting a meal Afghanis were partial to clearing their throats of expectorant. To discourage customers from spitting on the floor, the restaurants provided spit jugs.

Such an unappetizing image ruined our meal.

The city itself was polluted, with open sewers in the city streets. Most of the sewage came directly from the homes along the sidewalks and streets. Although most homes had indoor toilets, there was no running water. In order to dispose of the waste, toilets were built with exposed seats that opened out to the street below where the human waste was emptied. Better on the street than in the house, was the common answer to our questions.

Although we did not live in such housing, my father had rented a number of buildings in the city to use as guest houses. There were times my brothers and I, or our friends, utilized the houses, so we saw for ourselves the unsanitary method of waste disposal. Most troubling for us, pedestrians could easily look upward to see the toilet user's bare bottom.

There were times when we found this funny, as when we had a visitor from Saudi Arabia who was accustomed to the finer things of life, for the Saudi government had used oil money to modernize most of the country. This particular friend was experiencing intense stomach cramps after eating in the local restaurants. When we pointed out the toilet, we purposely did not alert him to the open hole. Soon he ran to us in a frenzy, reporting that a dog was barking at him from the street below. This was something new, so we dashed to see for ourselves. We sneaked a quick look through the toilet opening to discover the barking culprit. There sat a mother dog and her puppies curled beneath the toilet. The mother had found a nice street corner to place her puppies. When they were splattered from above, she commenced complaining. Needless to say, my friend's tummy ache immediately subsided. He refused to use the indoor toilet from that time, thinking it best to relieve himself in a nearby field or empty lot.

Those toilet seats created havoc on humans as well as dogs. Human waste had nowhere to go but down. Of course, when pedestrians walked on the narrow sidewalks, they found it was necessary to navigate mounds of human waste. The odor was so strong it was paralyzing. Despite the fact farmers came into the city several days a week to collect the waste to use on their fields for fertilizer, the stench of human waste hung over the city.

Afghanistan proved to be a dangerous place for the bin Laden sons. My brothers and I came close to death more than once. Most of our near misses came with the mishandling of grenades or other explosives, for weapons were everywhere and not always in expert hands.

Once we moved from Tora Bora to Kandahar, my father set up weapons training classes within the compound, ordering us to return occasionally for a refresher class. We didn't complain, for we were often bored and looking for something to do.

On one particular day my brothers and I decided to check in on a grenades class run by certain general. One of his rules had to do with "what to do with a grenade when the pin is removed." Well, as fate would have it, he dropped the grenade while talking. He reassured the class, "Don't worry, it's not activated."

I examined the grenade rolling around on the floor. Seeing that the pin was separate from the grenade, I immediately ordered my brothers, "Get out of here!"

Several of us ran for the door, but Abdul Rahman froze in place, merely covering his head with his hands, which, of course, would have given him no protection from a blast. I struggled to get him moving when the general started to laugh. He, too, had noticed the danger and had quickly replaced the pin or deactivated the weapon, one or the other.

To reassure the wary class, the general related a small story about how teachers often used such tactics to frighten students, to see how they might react, looking for students who kept their cool in such a situation. He said chaos had ensued not so long before in a class that was packed with gullible students. On that occasion so many students tried to run out the door that they had tightly wedged their bodies in the door frame, the result being that no one could get out and no one could get in. Another soldier, still physically fat from the good life in Saudi Arabia, had made for a small window exit. Unfortunately, his body was larger than the opening, so he had become jammed with his head and shoulders outside and his chest and lower body inside.

Thankfully the exercise was only a ploy, or all those trapped in doors and windows would have been blown to bits.

In another class we were observing, the situation became more serious. My brothers and I were trying to hide our laughter because the teacher looked more like a scholar than a soldier. Most troubling to me, he appeared to be half-blind, even though he was wearing very thick glasses with double lenses that made his eyeballs seem huge. That nearly blind instructor was holding a lighter in one hand and an explosive in the other, telling us it was important for a soldier to know how long a fuse would burn. He moved the lighter so close to the fuse that it started smoldering. Unaware that he had accidentally lit the fuse, he threw it into the box with the other explosives.

I was about to warn my brothers to run to safety, when I remembered the first teacher's instruction that many of these situations were designed as tests for students. I forced myself to sit still, keeping a close watch on the box of explosives. Well, the box caught fire and smoke billowed. The teacher panicked, grabbing and tossing the box to the floor, stomping on the flames. Just as I stood to make a quick exit, some battle-trained soldiers heard the commotion and dashed inside. Seeing the teacher and the burning box, several soldiers bravely seized the box and dashed outdoors. Although two men suffered hand burns, they escaped life-threatening injuries.

Yet another time a teacher was demonstrating the workings of a small bomb when he accidentally ignited it. Too late the teacher saw that the fuse was shorter than usual. He screeched for us to run and we all did, with our teacher on our heels. At the precise moment we reached safety, the bomb exploded.

Another kind of incompetence endangered us during one of our daily religious classes, which were held at the mosque inside the compound. The classes were large, because sons of al-Qaeda men attended with us.

Our teacher was a pleasant-faced man named Abu Shaakr, an Egyptian in his early thirties. He was thin but muscled and fit. He had a short beard and an appearance difficult to describe because he possessed no atypical physical features, such as a big nose or small eyes. He was happy to be with students and always kind, a favorite of all the schoolboys.

The mosque was old, originally constructed of mud bricks. The roof, as was usual in Afghanistan, was made of wood, grass, and mud bricks. Because of the mud in the bricks, water dripped from the ceiling every time it rained. A repairman would be called in after each rain. Rather than take the time to properly repair the school, the repairmen would pour a little sand on the roof, a recipe for disaster, due to the accumulated weight. His technique was unknown to my father, of course, who was an expert when it came to building or repairing any kind of structure.

Our usual routine meant that the smaller boys left at eleven in the morning while we older boys remained an extra hour for additional study. One day, my brothers and I were sitting in back of the mosque. Hamza, the only child of Auntie Khairiah, my mother's best friend and a sister-wife, was the last of the little kids to leave, slamming the door behind him.

When my brother slammed the door, the mosque roof cracked and collapsed. Heavy mud bricks fell on our heads, followed by sand, grass, and wood.

The weight on our heads and bodies stunned us, although we remained conscious. We could hear Abu Shaakr shouting loudly, calling out our names. The poor man was probably terrified, thinking that the elder sons of Osama bin Laden had perished on his watch.

My brothers and I were alive, although stuck in position, because the wood and mud bricks had locked us in place. But we were strong boys and started pushing as one. Over the din we could hear our little brother Hamza crying loudly, realizing that something very dangerous had just happened. Hamza feared that he would be blamed since he was the last one out of the building.

Within minutes, we heard our father's commanding voice, followed by the voices of other men. My father and his men were frantically removing the rubble with their bare hands while we were pushing from below. With two ends meeting in the middle, we soon saw the light of day. Later we were told that we created quite a frightening sight for the young children. Our eyes were closed from dust, our faces yellowed by sand, and our headwear pierced with large wooden splinters. One of my brothers said that with our bloodied hands reaching out like the living dead we reminded him of ghosts and goblins described by one of our father's fighters.

Dr. Ayman al-Zawahari made an appearance and studiously checked us over. He announced that we were all free of serious injury.

That was the first time that Dr. Zawahari had ever laid a hand on me. I had felt disquiet from the first moment my father had introduced me to the man. And in Sudan, after he murdered my young friend, the son of Mohammed Sharaf, I avoided him whenever possible. I knew from the beginning that Zawahari was a negative influence on my father, taking him further down the road of violence than he would ever have gone on his own. Zawahari, who was a very intelligent man, picked up on my feelings. I sensed his dislike for me, formed perhaps because I was the only son of my father who was sometimes bold enough to speak my mind.

For example, I remember once when Zawahari, my father, and Abu Hafs were sitting and drinking tea. The three men were all leaders, although my father was the head, and they knew it. Even Zawahari would ask permission to speak. I never once heard him say a single word without that permission. He would say, "Sheik Osama, may I please speak?" Or, "Sheik Osama, please, may I say something to the men?" All the other men were the same; no matter their stature in their organizations, none dared utter a single thought without my father's permission.

But on that day they had my father's permission to talk and were involved in a complex conversation about their goals to save the world from American power. My father was saying, "All the weight and injustice has been put on the Islamic world. Do you put all the weight on one end of a seesaw? No, if you do, the seesaw cannot rise normally, in the way it was intended. Everything must be evenly distributed in life. Because Muslims are blamed for everything, we receive all the injustice in the world. It is wrong. "

I was expected to be a silent server, but on that day I had heard quite enough. Before I knew what was happening, my foolish tongue moved and I blurted out my thoughts. "My father, why have you brought us to this place? Why do you make us live like this? Why can't we live in the real world and have a normal life, with ordinary things, surrounded by normal people? Why can't we live in peace?" Never before had I spoken out so boldly, yet I was so desperate to hear my father's response that I looked brazenly into his eyes for the first time in my life.

My father was too shocked at my audacity to respond. He sat there without looking, or speaking to me. Remembering my tone and attitude, I'm surprised he didn't cane me in front of the men.

Finally Abu Hafs relieved my father, saying, "Omar, we want to be here in this country. We have come out of our own desires so that we might escape the real life. We no longer want to be a part of that world. That is why your father is here. As his son, you belong with your father."

I longed to protest further, but I didn't. I well remember the hateful way that Zawahari glared at me, probably wishing he could put a bullet in my head, just as he had done to my innocent friend in Sudan.

By this time and age, I was losing my polite personality. My father wanted his sons to be aloof from all men, to follow his direction, a man whom few people really knew. He said, "My sons must be the fingers of my right hand. My thoughts must control your actions in the same manner my brain controls the movement of my limbs. My sons, your limbs should react to my thinking as though my brain was in your head."

We were to be robots, in other words, without opinions or actions of our own.

Over time he would send us out with his orders, commanding us to be strong and forceful, and to avoid becoming too friendly with any of the men. Thus my brothers and I were afforded some of the princely status of our father. The men even starting calling the older sons of my father "the big sheiks," which I admit was not unpleasant to my ears, for I had never had any recognition. My desire to create my own shadow increased with age. Over time my brothers and I became arrogant, feeling ourselves above all the others, because that is the way we were regarded.

Our father abused us as his robot slaves and his men indulged us as young kings. As a result of our distorted lives, each of us developed personality problems. Only Abdullah had escaped the worst. Abdul Rahman had not changed much since childhood, comfortable mainly with the friendship of horses. With every passing day, Sa'ad became more impractical, chatting nonstop. The tough soldiers around us were unaccustomed to any man who couldn't control his tongue, but because Sa'ad was the son of their champion, my brother was quietly tolerated.

After we moved to Kandahar, Sa'ad had gotten into a habit of prattling endlessly about food. No one knew why, although I believe it was because we were often hungry and when we did eat, our food was so inferior. One bad meal repeated the last, bringing Sa'ad to an obsession with cuisine. One day in Kandahar he managed to get a sweet cake, from where we never knew. Sa'ad discussed it so incessantly that even today I remember that cake as if I ate it myself! That cake had sweet shredded wheat covering the top and dripping with sugar and honey.

Sa'ad had eaten the whole cake, refusing to share even a crumb. For weeks afterward, Sa'ad would approach strangers on the street to launch into a detailed description of what the cake looked like, tasted like, and how he believed it had been baked. Grown Afghan men backed away, thinking that my brother was not right in his head. My father's soldiers listened to Sa'ad babbling about that cake until they began to run away when they saw him approaching. I finally threatened to beat him if he didn't shut up. But he carried on regardless until one day he got hold of a special pudding and began to describe that pudding as he had the cake. Not even my father's disapproval could stop Sa'ad's tongue from wagging.

My father's choices for our lives had begun to drive his sons crazy!

Osman had a difficult time maintaining a normal friendship with anyone, primarily because he wanted to control their opinions, in much the same manner as our father.

Today when I read news reports that my brothers are important leaders in my father's organization, I question those reports. By the time I left, they had formed their adult personalities, and none of them was capable of organizing a fighting force.

Baby brother Mohammed is the only sibling that *might* have risen to a high rank, for he was of a quiet and serious character. Even before I left Afghanistan, I could see my father transferring his hopes from me to Mohammed for the title of the "chosen one." Once he had Mohammed photographed with him, while my brother was holding a rifle in his lap. In our world, this is a message that the father is passing his power to his son.

Before then, however, his confidence and trust grew in my direction. I remember when he came to me about a growing problem, the shortage of food and other provisions. We all knew by that time that my father was no longer a wealthy man. Although a system was in place to procure funds from those who supported Jihad, for there were a number of friends, family, and royals who still offered financial support, there were times the cash coffers were bare.

During one week when family members were going hungry, my father came to me and said, "Omar, I have noticed that you are a just man. I need someone I can trust to ration the food. From now on, it will be your job to calculate the amount of food necessary for each wife and her children. Take into account that teenagers need more than most, for they grow so rapidly. You must sort out all the food supplies and divide fairly."

I speculated that my father knew that Abdul Rahman could not be considered for the job because his personality so craved isolation that he would have found it impossible to interact with others while distributing the food. Sa'ad was not suitable because we all knew that he would eat the tastiest morsels for himself.

I took the job seriously. I could not bear for my mother and aunties or the children to be hungry. Although our diet was generally bland and sparse, there were a few times when visiting royals who traveled to Afghanistan to go with my father on hunting trips would bring gifts consisting of large boxes of fruit, fish, red meat, and vegetables. Those were the happy days, when the smallest children would receive a special food treat. My father said he received reports that I was so fair there were no complaints from anyone. Soon after this episode, my father confided that I was the son he had chosen to be his second-in-command.

My father's face paled when I replied, "My father, I will do anything to help my mother, aunties, and siblings, but I am not the correct son to assume your life's work. I am seeking a peaceful life, not a life of violence." Even with my words, my father failed to back away from the idea that I was his rightful replacement. Soon afterward he took me to the front fighting lines. I can only guess that he hoped if I got a taste of the fighting excitement, I might become passionate for war, as he had done when fighting the Russians. He was to be sorely disappointed.

Over time I became much bolder than I had ever dreamed possible, speaking confidently against my father's decisions. But our relationship-breaking conflicts would come later.

A few months after my family settled in Kandahar, I was visiting with my mother when one of my brothers came to tell me that our father wanted me by his side. Obedient to my father's commands, I slung my Kalashnikov over my shoulder, adjusted my grenade belt, and walked away.

At the time I assumed that my father had a question about our food resources, or wished to give orders regarding family matters. Although I was only sixteen years old, I had assumed a large share of responsibility for the wives and children.

I was informed by a passing fighter that my father was in the building he used as his office. I found him there, sitting cross-legged on the floor, with a group of his fighters. I approached softly and without speaking because that was our way.

My father looked up, looking neither pleased nor displeased to see me, saying only, "My son, I am leaving now to go to the front lines. You are to come with me."

I nodded without comment. I was not afraid, but excited. After more than a year of living in the warring country, I was curious about the front, as I had heard many tales of valor from returning soldiers. The Taliban was still battling the Northern Alliance, headed by Ahmad Shah Massoud, a warrior known for his military genius and a Mujahideen hero from the Russian war days. Upon my father's return to Afghanistan, the two heroes of the Russian campaign had become foes. After Mullah Omar provided his shield of protection, my father had committed his fighting force to Mullah Omar's army. Mullah Omar and the Taliban were deadly enemies of Massoud.

Everything about that day was casual. The men chosen to make the trip had no assigned vehicles or seats. My father randomly selected a vehicle and driver and I followed, riding with Sakhr al-Jadawi (Salim Hamdan). The ride was short, no more than thirty or forty minutes, but uncomfortable and bumpy, as are all trips on Afghan roads. I can't recall anything specific about the journey, other than Sakhr's tall stories kept me laughing, bringing me out of my usual serious state. Sakhr was the sort of man who constantly joked, enjoying his life more than most. It was difficult not to loosen up when in his company.

Once we arrived at the front, everyone found something to do while my father met with some of the lieutenants holding the line. Sakhr and I wandered off, and out of boredom Sakhr decided to do some target practice.

Sakhr set up an empty tin can and began shooting.

We discussed his prowess for a while and then he shot some more.

Sakhr fired once again.

We were in for a big shock, because the blast was so loud that we were instantly confused. What had occurred? Neither of us had ever heard a Kalashnikov make such an earth-shattering noise.

Just as we were examining Sakhr's weapon and discussing the strangeness of the situation, a missile broke through the air around us, exploding nearby. That's when we realized that the Kalashnikov was *not* the source of the noise.

Within seconds we were under a full-blown bombardment with missiles raining down. There was a short break in the attack, and I heard my father's voice shouting, "Move back! Move back!"

I sat crouched with Sakhr. I was too startled to move and Sakhr was too cautious. He was plotting how to move out without running into a missile.

Our minds were racing, neither of us understanding how Massoud's men had gotten so close. We were behind the front line, for God's sake! How had Massoud's men slipped in between the Taliban line and us without being seen?

Squatting there, expecting to die any moment, I looked back to see that my father and his friends had taken cover in a concrete building, where they looked helplessly at Osama bin Laden's son, so openly vulnerable. With missiles whistling past my head, dirt and small stones peppering my face, and deep craters appearing all around me, I truly believed I was living my last moments of earthly life. My big regret was the sorrow I knew my death would cause my mother. Strangely enough, I did not feel a sense of true fear. I suppose that an adrenaline rush was creating a deceptive sense of courage.

I looked back once more to see my father, possibly for the last time. He was now standing at the entry of the improvised shelter, risking his own life, beckoning with his hands for me to run to him. Finally I got the nerve to dash to the shelter, where my shaken father appeared very happy that I was alive.

We were not prepared for a full-fledged battle, so we had no choice but to retreat. After recovering from the initial shock, my father suddenly realized that we were not under attack from Massoud's men, but instead it was the Taliban firing upon us! We were the victims of friendly fire.

Never have I seen my father in such a violent rage. "Sakhr," he ordered, "get your car. Drive around this area. Get to their launching spot. Tell them to stop it now or they will kill us all!"

Sakhr arrived safely, thank God, and the Taliban commander was told that he was firing upon Osama bin Laden, and had nearly killed the sheik's son. Sakhr said that commander almost had a heart attack. When he had heard Sakhr firing his weapon, he had believed that he was under a surprise attack from his back. He thought that Massoud's men had somehow evaded his look-out.

His explanation didn't satisfy my father, who remained as furious as I've ever seen him, saying that in such a situation, a commander checks first before bombarding an area believed to be safe territory.

I never forgot that trip to the front, but neither did it inspire me as my father had hoped.

Chapter 21

Real War

OMAR BIN LADEN

There were so many factions battling in Afghanistan that war fronts bordered most cities and villages. It was not unusual for my father to reinforce the Taliban forces, particularly when the Taliban got caught up in pitched battles with the Northern Alliance led by Massoud. I sensed that my father enjoyed putting his men up against those of a man whose military skills he so admired. Nothing gave him more pleasure than to be told that he had outwitted the brilliant commander.

I'm happy to report that for a while my brothers and I dodged being sent on the front lines, but then one day for no good reason I can think of, my father ordered me to report to one of our al-Qaeda bases located high in the mountains of Kabul, on the outskirts of the city. My father said, "Go, my son. Go and discover the soldier's life."

I believe that I had just reached my seventeenth year at the time. Fighting on the front lines was the last item on my list of things I desired. I had seen too many seriously wounded and dying men brought back from the front. Generally a war wound meant death because there were no base hospitals or even temporary medical clinics to treat the injured. Efforts were sometimes made to take the wounded to the nearest city, but that rarely happened. Although we had Dr. Zawahiri for true emergencies, his main duty was not to be a physician, but to plan attacks.

But there was no choice but to do as ordered, as I had not yet reached the age where I could rebel against my father. In fact, once I was on the road, I felt little flickers of excitement.

When I arrived at the base in the Kabul mountains, I could see Massoud's men facing my father's men. The fighters on the front line were set up with machine guns and other close-range weapons. There was an artillery line directly behind, between the front line and the base. I spotted some functioning Russian tanks left over from the last war, camouflaged by tree limbs and grasses and hidden in corners on some of the flat areas. Tank battles were not too common, which was disappointing because I had a few tank operations skills and like most teenage boys would have relished a chance to drive one of those tanks.

I saw massive supplies of weaponry, from stinger missiles to machine guns to artillery. I was amazed at the complexity of the war, for like most people I had imagined that the war in Afghanistan consisted of guerrilla warfare. But the battle lines were drawn in much the same manner that I imagined the huge forces had faced off during confrontations between world powers. Seeing the vast array of highly trained men manning mostly modern equipment, I remembered hearing that once my father and his soldiers had joined with the Taliban, the military professionalism he had learned during the ten-year war with the Soviets had fully altered the conduct of the present conflict.

The battle had quieted upon my arrival. For the first five days I mainly observed, thinking that being at the front lines was not the worst thing that could happen to me. There were occasions when I would fiddle with my portable handheld receiver. Most of the soldiers on the front line had one. The common soldier's receiver was not sophisticated, like the ones used by my father and the high-ranking leaders.

I was bored, and found that if I took my time, I could generally find the band being used by Massoud's men. I began engaging them in conversation, asking them where they were from, and other nonmilitary chatter. Of course, I never relayed that I was the son of Osama bin Laden, or those men might have made a full-fledged attack to capture such a prestigious target, little knowing that my father would do nothing special to get my release.

Once I asked a friendly soldier, "Why are you trying to kill us?"

The Massoud soldier replied, "I have nothing against you. This is a war over land. We have orders to shoot anyone on the land. You are on the land. I will have to shoot you if I get the chance."

That soldier was speaking the truth. Every warlord wanted to rule the country. Although there was a shortage of homes, hospitals, schools, food, clothes, and other necessities, there was no shortage of warlords, each striving to assume the top position. Yet another bitter war was the result of a group of stubborn and uncompromising men.

The front line around Kabul linked to a village area. Modest huts dotted the mountainside. Since many of the houses had been deserted due to the close combat, my father's soldiers opted to sleep in the huts rather than hunker down on the stony ground. During the sleeping hours, my father's soldiers stationed lookouts along the mountain trail. The night came when it was my turn to serve as a lookout, for my father had sent word that I should be treated no differently from any other soldier. "No better, no worse," was his order.

Almost instantly after positioning myself on an advantageous lookout point, I felt the whistle of a bullet fly past my right ear. Then a second bullet soared past my left ear. Soon many bullets were flying. Enemy soldiers had spotted my position. With bullets zipping past on both sides, I couldn't settle on which way to jump.

I'm still not certain how I avoided being shot. Conceivably the moonless night skewed the enemy's marksmanship, or perhaps my figure was so fixed in place that the enemy shooter determined that his target was a mountain rock. My soldier comrades finally heard the racket and crept out to join the battle at the precise moment the firing ended. When the light of dawn appeared, they were amazed to see many bullet shells surrounding my position. God was with me on that night.

On the sixth day the battle commenced, and I instantly gained a new respect for the soldiers. I was sent to the artillery line where the clatter of war damaged my eardrums. Of course, I slowly grew accustomed to the noise of war, but never to the sight of war. The carnage of useless death was hideous, with wounded and dying men all around, most of them no older than me.

I was sorry to continually disappoint my father, but I came away with renewed determination that war was the most useless exercise imaginable. While perched on that mountaintop, I had pledged to spend the rest of my life speaking out against the very thing my father so loved.

The only thing my father loved more than war was Islam. While a Muslim can pray anywhere, on the street, in his home, in his office, in the desert, or even in an airport, it is best if a Muslim—at least a Muslim man—has the opportunity to pray in a mosque. But there were times when my brothers and I wearied of going to the mosque. This was not due to lack of faith, because we were believers, but because the mosque was utilized for so many things that my brothers and I spent more time there than in our homes. There were too many tedious gatherings that persisted for many hours. Often the most uninspiring Islamic speakers lectured until our eyelids drooped and our heads swayed with boredom. Our father had no pity on our situation, expecting his young sons to sit still and appear enthusiastic over countless variations on the same theme.

Over time, word got around that anyone who felt the urge to lecture was allowed to do so. Those enthusiastic lecturers detained reluctant spectators, keeping them captive for hours. Nearly every adult clamored to address the audience, to convince the others of his special understanding of Islam. Most were not Islamic scholars, but ignorant men who felt themselves elevated by the ceremony of endless talk.

Already my brothers and I spent more hours than most in the mosque, where we were taught verses of the Koran, the history of Islam, the reasons for Jihad, the facts we needed to know about the wickedness of the non-Muslim world, along with my father's future plans to destroy the West. It was in the mosque that we received the message that the United States feared that Islam was closing in on the Christian faith. We were told that it was God's holy plan for all religions, including those practiced by Christians, Jews, Hindus, and others, to yield to Islamic rule. All the people of the world would come together under an Islamic caliphate.

After two years of being subjected to lengthy harangues from the mouths of uneducated bores, I wrote an anonymous letter, cautious to alter my personal handwriting.

Here is what I remember of that letter:

"No one should be allowed to stand up and speak in the mosque without the permission of Sheik bin Laden. It is unfair that the congregation should be subjected to a continuous barrage of lectures. There are many things in life worthwhile for men to do rather than sit hours in the mosque to listen to un-learned speakers.

"The mosque should not be used in such a careless manner. Such boring lectures, which are generally the opinion of a single individual, do nothing to further Islam. Islamic lecturers should be inspiring for believers, but the majority of the lecturers who have hijacked our mosque are creating discord and dissatisfaction. Believers should not be put in a position of total boredom, as such will discourage believers from attending many worthwhile events at the mosque."

Not wishing to be discovered, for I had no desire to incite my father's anger, I slipped into the mosque during a quiet time to nail my letter to the wall.

When the next prayer time arrived, I was there with my father. One of the older men came to us to speak frankly. He said, "The men have been talking. They say that only a son of the prince [meaning my father] could be brave enough to post such a message. We thought about this and discussed the sons of Sheik Osama, and all agreed that this letter had to come from one hand, the hand of the son Omar."

I said nothing.

My father said nothing.

Finally the older man asked me openly, "Omar, did you write this letter?"

I met his eyes, without admitting to anything. I didn't say yes and I didn't say no.

My father continued to sit quietly. He didn't look at the older man. He didn't look at me. I think he was looking at his hands.

The old man finally said, "Why did you write this letter, Omar?"

Knowing that he would never go away if I didn't respond, I replied, "Even if I didn't write it, I agree with it. All the young men are fed up."

Not sure as to what my father's reaction might be, the old man nodded and walked off without further words.

My father didn't move. I dreaded what he might say, for I had never lied to my father. I felt that his heart told him that, indeed, his son Omar was the perpetrator, but oddly, he left the topic closed. For a while the speeches diminished, but most men like nothing better than the sound of their own voices, so it was not long before they were once again thrusting themselves onto the podium to preach their personal brand of Islam.

A week later I came to see that my father had more serious problems than boredom in the mosque. He was without *any* money for the first time in his life.

Although we had been poor since 1994 when the Saudi government froze my father's assets, there were new problems. Once my father lost access to his personal funds, his huge organization began to exist on charity. Sympathetic royals, ordinary Saudi citizens, or even members of my father's immediate family had been generously donating to the cause of Jihad. Up until that time, there were no rules against such giving. But the government had recently forbidden Saudi charities from donating to my father's cause. Everyone was being watched to make sure they did not contribute.

We were truly desperate for the first time, at such a low state that there was no money for food for our family, or for the enormous band of people who had gathered around my father.

My memories are keen about that day, because I was famished, as were all the men. I had personally given the last of the food, consisting of eggs and potatoes, to the women and children. Hunger pangs were pricking our bellies.

My father was discussing the problem with Abu Hafs and a few other men he trusted as I sat and listened. My father spoke in a sad, disappointed manner, "If only I had five million dollars, I could win this war today." We all knew that he was speaking of the all-consuming civil war that was continuing to plague every man, woman, and child living in Afghanistan, a conflict that was delaying him from what he thought of as his real mission in life, which was to make war with the West.

I felt a surge of anger. My father did not possess one Saudi riyal, or one Afghanistan afghani. If we didn't get funds soon, we might all die of starvation. Now, I was hearing my father fret because he had no money to make war. I kept my mouth closed, however, for it was not the time to start a disagreement with my father. He was surrounded by men who loved him to the point they would happily plunge a dagger into my heart for criticizing my father.

After a few moments, his attention returned to the problem at hand. He looked at his men, instructing them, "Go to every lock box, look in every hiding place, search for some forgotten funds that we might have tucked away during our time of plenty."

His men did as told, with one after the other returning with the unwelcome message that the boxes once crammed with money were now bare. One man said, "There's not even dust."

Suddenly, one of the men rushed into the room, beaming. He presented my father with a bundle of American dollars, telling him, "Sheik, I discovered this money in a long-forgotten lock box."

My father quickly made a count, announcing, "There's five thousand dollars here!"

Reprieve! Such a sum would go a long way in the food bazaars of Kandahar. Now we could buy provisions to feed our hungry. Despite the happiness on my father's face, there was enormous sorrow in his voice when he said, "Never in my life had I imagined that finding a modest five thousand dollars would bring me such joy."

The incident had taken my father back in time, to the days when he believed that all his dreams would come true. After defeating the Russians, he had settled into a time of arrogance, convinced that the remainder of his life would be filled with victories. That had not happened. In fact, his dreams had evaporated.

My father first looked at Abu Hafs, his dear friend for many years, and then glanced to some of the older men in the circle, the Russian veterans, before gesturing at me and saying, "Look at my young son! When we first arrived in Afghanistan so many years ago we were fresh-faced young men, too. We were vibrant warriors, tall, muscular, fit, and healthy. Our beards were black and our heads were full of bushy hair, without a white hair to be seen!"

His voice became wistful. "Who could have dreamed that our lives would have taken this path? We lost so many friends in the Jihad. They are in paradise, while we are still struggling on earth, fighting for justice for Islam. Although we know that life on God's earth is nothing more than a stepping-stone to heaven, the journey is often too hard to bear. When we so eagerly came to Afghanistan we arrived as young men. We felt sorry for the old warriors, barely able to get about. Now look at us! We are the old men! Now it is our sons whose feet are planted in our footsteps."

I squirmed, knowing that if my father was counting on me to carry out his dreams, he would be sorely disappointed. At my first opportunity, I would lift my feet from my father's footprints and make my own.

I knew for certain that my father was thinking of me as the chosen one when he announced that a British journalist, Robert Fisk, was coming to Afghanistan to interview him and that I would be in attendance. Fisk had interviewed my father once or twice before, but this was the first time I would meet him.

Although Abdul Rahman was not taken for the interview, Sa'ad went along. I only hoped that Sa'ad would not start talking about the tasty eggs and bread he had just eaten. Although I was proud to be one of the two sons chosen to be with my father at such an important interview, I am sorry to say that I remember little of the actual discussion. Those interested can find Fisk's work and read it for themselves. Mainly I recall that Fisk was a very pleasant man who even gave me a little attention, turning to me with a genial expression to ask me if I was happy.

I was stunned by his question. During my entire life few people had ever really cared about my feelings, and certainly no one had ever asked whether or not I was happy. For a split second I wondered if Fisk was simply being polite, but he seemed so sincere that I wanted to please him with my response. I finally replied, "Yes, I am happy."

Fisk didn't question me further, but my tongue ached to take back those words—to confide the truth, that I was the most miserable boy alive, and that I hated the hatred and violence my father was promoting. I wanted to pull Fisk to the side and tell him that one day I would find the courage to speak out against my father and work for the cause of peace. I was bursting, but too cowardly to speak out yet.

Fisk pleasantly asked my father if we would like a photograph taken with me. I was excited when my father agreed, because he was not a fan of photography, and his approval to be in a picture with me meant more than the photo itself.

After Fisk left us I found the nerve to ask, "Father, are you nervous about what this reporter might say?"

My father shrugged and said, "No. He will be fair."

Later I was able to get a copy of Fisk's interview and felt strangely disappointed that I was not mentioned in any way, even though I knew that my father was the only person that mattered in our family. The world had no reason to be interested in me, although I had reason to be interested in the world. The time to be on my way was drawing near.

Chapter 22

Jihad Vacation

OMAR BIN LADEN

As time passed, our bin Laden lives became even more bizarre. This was because my father's passion for making Jihad connected with people who were lost in life and had a longing for war, rather than with those who sought the ordinary pleasures of living. While some of the recruits were temporary visitors, their stay in Afghanistan more of a "Jihad vacation," most of the soldiers quickly became addicted to the Jihadi life. They were seeking violent Jihad because they believed the cause was the purest for a Muslim. They felt that their lives had great meaning because they wanted to give that life to God.

Those young men became the companions of my father's sons, exposing us to many strange happenings.

My father was always a source of awed conversation because his men were so overcome by his presence that they believed every little thing was a sign from God. One day several of the men were struck by a strange phenomenon. Each summer the birds of the region would flock to Kandahar on their migration. Arabs like birds, so we made special efforts for the birds to be comfortable. My brothers and I even opened the glass above the door so that the birds had a nice place to nest. Once their eggs hatched into baby birds, they would leave. The men began to notice that one particular bird was a return visitor for several years in a row. She had a distinctive twelve-inch red tape on one of her legs. No other bird wore such a tag.

One of the soldiers speculated that the bird was being used by the Americans to track my father. Soon he decided that was not the case, but still there were many laughs about how a little bird repeatedly found my father's home while the technically advanced American military could not.

There was a military trainer who was especially pleasant to me, always greeting me with a ready smile and offering a helping hand. I never heard his true family name, of course, because he was forbidden to use it, being known as Abu Zubair to everyone in my father's army. Abu Zubair held a high-ranking position in my father's organization, going back and forth between Kandahar and the training camp near Kabul.

There was one incident with Abu Zubair that I will never forget. He was the proud owner of a handsome black and white cow, which won him the envy of many of soldiers because food and drink were so carefully rationed. Soon the cow gave birth to a male calf, which was another source of pleasure for Abu Zubair, for he had plans for the calf.

One night he suffered a bizarre nightmare. He dreamed that two of his soldiers had secretly milked his cow, taking the milk that belonged to the baby calf. The following morning he couldn't get the dream out of his mind. Even after saying his first prayers of the day, the message of the dream still lingered. Abu Zubair called in another trainer, a man by the name of Abu Atta, and the two discussed the dream with great seriousness. Knowing that he couldn't relax until he got to the bottom of the troubling business, Abu Zubair finally sent for the two men in his dream.

The men appeared, visibly nervous.

Abu Zubair cleverly questioned them. He knew them to be very superstitious. "Did you commit a sin last night?"

The soldier named Abu Walid broke down immediately, confessing that the two of them had sneaked into the cow shed to milk Abu Zubair's cow. They had already drunk the evidence, so no one but the hungry calf would have known about the illegal milking if not for Abu Zubair's dream.

Of course, Abu Zubair was furious at the breach of trust and his punishment was severe. Both soldiers had to run up and down the mountains until they swore they had learned their lesson. Of course, word spread that if anyone committed a sin, God so favored my father's work that He would alert his leaders as they slept.

There were other amusing stories. I remember when I accompanied my father and some of his highest lieutenants on a driving tour to survey the land, confirm particulars regarding the fighting, and check the status of the latest recruits who were training in the camps. My father was in one of the lead cars, and I was a passenger in a rear vehicle. As usual the journey was strenuous due to inferior roads and lack of amenities available to Afghan road travelers. Many of the fighters were cranky with fatigue, so my father called for frequent stops to break up the trip. When approaching small villages, he would have his vehicle pull over so that we might fill our water containers from the village spring, consume some simple village fare, and of course, relieve ourselves.

Since there were no public toilets, or for that matter, private toilets, available to villagers, it was necessary for the fighters to scatter to seek privacy in isolated corners in the fields. After finding relief, fighters would return to the caravan to wait under a shade tree for the other soldiers. We seldom objected to the delays because no one was particularly eager to get back on the rough roads of Afghanistan. We liked having extra time to sit and exchange gossip.

I remember a certain soldier who had waited to the very last minute, and rushed off to be gone for so long that we began to wonder what had happened to him. We lingered under the tree, taking our time enjoying the breeze, when suddenly he came hurrying through the tall grasses, grinning widely.

When he saw his mates, his grin turned into laughter. Interested in anything amusing, we pushed for information, but he couldn't reveal his story for laughing. Finally he choked out, "There I was doing my business when I heard footsteps. I used the signal to alert the intruder that I was occupied in a private matter. Imagine my shock when the intruder picked up speed, coming directly at me. I kept making the signal, 'Huh, hum, huh, hum,' but nothing stopped the approach.

"I was frantic, for I was not in a proper position to be seen!"

By this time we were all laughing.

"All of a sudden, a tall man appeared in front of me! He placed his hand on my shoulder and looked down at my squatting figure to ask, 'Are you all right, my friend? I heard some very strange noises that so worried me that I had to come and make certain the man behind the noise was okay.'"

The soldier fell over laughing, "All I could do was grunt some more! What was I to do? There I was with my drawers around my ankles, squatting miserably, having a conversation!"

By this time a huge circle of fighters had gathered, and for some reason that story struck everyone as hilarious. No one could speak. Tears of laughter were streaming down the hardened faces of every fighter.

While my life was bleak in so many ways, I tried to console myself with the thought that I was better off than many others. At least I was not living the life of a disabled child in a country racked with civil war. Poor Afghans had no manner of properly handling a handicapped or mentally deficient child. Some of the soldiers had seen cases where the mentally challenged were shackled like dogs, with heavy chains linking them to a tree or to a chair.

In fact, there was one such boy I identified with, for we were of the same age. He lived in a village near our compound in Kandahar, surviving in chains. Over the years he had become adept at escape. After breaking out of his restraints, he would sometimes make his way to our compound. One day a security guard saw a male figure approaching, and shouted, "Stop! Identify yourself!"

Unable to understand, the poor boy ambled along, following the sound of the human voice. Convinced that a suicide bomber was coming for the compound, the guard began firing above the boy's head. The boy kept rambling forward, undeterred by the gunfire.

Finally the guard got a good view and saw that the visitor was the poor chained boy of the village. Other guards, who had rushed to the front gate at the sound of gunfire, hurried to collect the boy and return him to his life of chains.

As time passed, I noticed that my father had bouts of sadness, though he failed to enlighten me to his innermost thoughts. Yet his unhappiness would pluck at my heartstrings and, as his son, I would look for reasons to excuse him for his behavior. I wanted my father to give up war and violence. Of course, those were the days before he had crossed a line that would ensure he could never again live normally.

Just when I was feeling more kindly toward my father, certain cruelties came to light that solidified my aversion to al-Qaeda and my father's life work forever.

My brothers and I had kept puppies as pets from the day of our youth in Khartoum. After Mullah Nourallah presented me with my first pup in Afghanistan, Bobby, our dog population increased. There was no such thing as intentionally controlling pet populations in the world we lived. In fact, in my Muslim world, it is considered cruel to "fix" dogs so that male dogs cannot have the pleasure of mating and female dogs miss out on the pleasure of motherhood. The Muslim mind-set is such that we leave nature as God made it. Therefore, puppies became abundant around our compound.

Shortly after we moved to Kandahar, I heard that my father's training camps had become more sophisticated, with the men testing deadly chemical and biological weapons.

One day when I was tending to my female dog and her young pups, several of the fighters came and asked to borrow my puppies. I didn't like that idea, but thought they were searching for pets for themselves. So I allowed them to take the puppies, who were of an age they could live without their mother's milk.

Such requests became commonplace and raised my curiosity as to where all my puppies were going. I had lived in Afghanistan for a number of years by that time, and had noticed few people had affection for dogs. In fact, most Afghans actively looked upon dogs as pests in the manner that many people think of rodents. Rather than running to embrace a cute puppy, they would shoot it. My world had no connection to the great love I am told that people in the West have for their pets.

A friend soon confided that the puppies my siblings and I adored were being sacrificed for the Jihadi cause. My father's soldiers were using our puppies as test subjects, gassing them to see how long it would take them to die.

Shock ran the length of my body. I wept, but nothing could move my father or his men. They must have test subjects, I was told, and our puppies were ideal for that purpose. My father gave no indication of concern that I cared deeply enough to plead for the lives of my puppies. Several of the new soldiers, young men who had been born without sensitivity, enjoyed describing the death throes of those cute little animals. They insisted on telling me of their terror trembles, sitting tied in a cage, suffering throughout the ordeal. The gas was not as fast as one might have imagined.

I never again allowed myself to become attached to any newborn puppies, because while looking at their cute faces, I realized they were dead, they just didn't know it yet. The gas tests were ongoing even as I left Afghanistan.

After I learned about the puppies, I turned even further away from my father, recognizing that his path led to nothing but pain, disappointment, and death. In fact, the image of suffering dogs was so painful that I pushed it to the deepest corner of my mind. Today I am speaking about this story for the first time in my life.

My emotions were tossing about as if in a fierce wind. I decided that my only chance at happiness lay in becoming independent and finding a suitable bride with whom to start my own family. In March of 1998, I turned seventeen, which was a landmark because I had always believed that would be the age that I should marry. Perhaps this age stuck in my mind because my father had married at age seventeen, as had my brother Abdullah. Both Abdul Rahman and Sa'ad wanted to marry, too.

The three of us asked our friends what fighters had daughters of an appropriate age for marriage, as puberty is considered a requirement. At that time, there were no suitable prospects on the compound. My greatest desire was to marry a cousin in Saudi Arabia, as Abdullah had done, because I knew I would never return to Afghanistan. But none of my aunties or uncles would allow their daughters to marry the son of Osama bin Laden. Abdullah had been lucky enough to marry before our father's reputation became so tarnished that it blackened his children's name.

I decided that I should travel to Sudan to find a proper bride, and Sa'ad resolved to accompany me. Since Sa'ad was nineteen years old and I was seventeen, our father did not forbid the journey. Our dear mother was not one to forbid anything, but said, "My sons, I pray to God to look over you, keep you safe, and bring you the happiness you want."

Sa'ad and I packed a few things and traveled by taxi to Pakistan, where we boarded a plane for Syria via Iran. When we passed through Iran, I reminisced about the day I had accompanied my father from Khartoum to Jalalabad. Although that trip had occurred only two years before, to me it felt like a hundred lifetimes. The dreary life in Afghanistan had a way of expanding time.

It was fun to be in Syria, especially when we surprised my mother's family by walking through their door unannounced. We stayed for only a few days, but were there long enough for me to realize that my grandmother suffered greatly from my mother's prolonged absences. It had been so long since my mother had been in a position to call them over the telephone or to write letters that the Ghanem family had not known about my mother's last daughter, Rukhaiya. They were so eager for details regarding my mother and her children that they couldn't stop asking questions. Mainly they were worried about my mother's health and physical safety once they heard the barest details about life in Afghanistan.

They asked few questions about my father and his current activities. Some topics in life are best left unexplored. After a very pleasant visit, they bade us farewell and we boarded an airplane to Sudan.

When Sa'ad and I finally arrived in Khartoum, I felt a surge of affection for the land and the people. I felt myself a prodigal son returning home, for I had never forgotten the friendly people and the joy known during our time there.

My father had provided us with some names of government officials who might offer us some protection. I could feel their fondness for the sons of a man they had known as a magnanimous friend. They expressed sorrow that the government had been forced to expel our father, and gave us official permission to travel to any part of the country, which was unusual in those days.

Sa'ad and I quickly parted company. He found a family to stay with, as did I. Such was best, for Sa'ad's endless chatter quickly grates on the nerves. We conducted individual searches for our wives, relying on old friends to ask around if there were any attractive young women from good families whose parents might approve their daughters marrying one of the bin Laden sons.

But before looking seriously for a bride, I sought out the horses we had left behind. I had thought often of our horses, praying that someone kindly had purchased them and treated them well. I took a quick trip to my father's stables, where the horses had been left.

I entered into a nightmare. I was told all the horses but two had either starved or died of untreated illnesses.

Adham and Lazaz, two of the strongest, were still alive. But poor Adham was sick to the point of death, so weak that his once muscular legs would no longer support his body. It didn't take a horseman to know that Adham would not live out the week.

Lazaz, the proudest horse I had ever known, was so scrawny that his bones were poking at his flesh, trying to break through. The horse with a spirit so proud that he nearly defeated my dominant father now seemed confused, unsure of who or where he was. He had no memory of me.

Sorrow wrapped around me. I attempted to save Lazaz's life. I failed. The subject is so painful that I find I cannot return to those memories. After that horrifying discovery, my heart was so heavy that the joy of the trip was destroyed.

I found some of my old school friends and we mused over the good times we had enjoyed together. Many of those boys had never known what happened to the bin Laden boys, just that one day we were at school and the next we were not. They had not heard of the assassination attack against Osama bin Laden, which was the reason our father withdrew us from the school. A few admitted that they had later learned we had left Sudan entirely. Most assumed we had returned to Saudi Arabia, to the good life, and were surprised to hear that we had gone to Afghanistan. A few of the boys looked at me sadly, smart enough to know that our bin Laden lives were not as they should be.

Afterward I went to visit the businesses my father had formed and the lands he had purchased, all with our bin Laden inheritance. Many businesses had once borne our family name, including a large leather-processing factory where my father had taken his sons on several occasions, proudly noting that it was one of his most successful business ventures.

I arrived to see that the leather factory was closed and the building had been given to a nearby college, which was using it as housing for teachers. I grew angry at the idea, for that factory belonged to the bin Laden family, and no one had the right to present it as a gift to others.

I wasted so much time at that factory, pacing about and wallowing in anger, that I suddenly realized that it was growing dark. Knowing I should return to Khartoum quickly, before the night made the journey unsafe, I decided to swim the Nile, rather than take the long route over roads to get to a bridge.

Such a decision was not as foolish as it might seem, for my brothers and I had swum the width of the Nile many times. There was no reason to feel foreboding. Although the sun had disappeared from the sky, the full moon lit the night, reflecting light off the river's waves. By my calculations I could swim to the city within ten or fifteen minutes. Walking would take several hours because the nearest bridge was out of my way.

I sat on the edge of the river to remove my shoes, thrusting them between the waist of my pants and my flesh, then waded into the cold, dark water. I could see the palm trees swaying on the opposite shore, reminding me that I had but a short distance to swim.

Within minutes I was in trouble. The current was deceptively strong, pulling me away from the shore, pushing my body down the river. Rather than float to conserve my energy, I kept fighting the current, thinking that if I only tried harder I would make it to the shore. My futile efforts were exhausting. Soon I grew so tired that every muscle in my body pulsated with pain.

Hours passed as I bobbed on the Nile, my thoughts drifting incoherently. I cursed myself. I should have brought Sa'ad with me to the factory. I had not even told him where I was going. In fact, no one knew where I was, not even the fine family who had offered me a place to stay. No one had a clue that I was floundering in the Nile. I would most likely be eaten by a crocodile, disappearing without my family knowing my fate.

I prayed to Allah, begging him to send me a single piece of driftwood, something to hold on to until I could reach the shore. Allah answered my prayer; at that moment I caught a glimpse of an object floating past, and when I surged forward to grab it, my feet touched the bottom. I was at a spot where the river runs shallow. I had been flailing when I could have stood and walked out of the water.

Feeling rather foolish, I scrambled to the sandy bank thankful to be alive, yet not knowing where I was, for I had drifted a very long way. I would have to wait for the sun to find my way back into Khartoum. The night air was freezing. I searched the edges of the Nile until I found a big stick, probing the sand until I found a good place, not too soft and not too hard, plunging the stick into the dirt until it was firmly planted. I then removed my wet clothes and hung them from the stick. My shoes had been lost.

Never had I been so cold, not even in the deep snows of Tora Bora Mountain. I remembered my father saying that when in such a dilemma, go down, down into the earth. I scooped sand with my hands until I dug a hollow large enough for my body. I crawled into the crater, using my hands to pull the excavated sand onto my body. Within minutes I felt the heavy sand creating warmth. Exhausted from my near drowning, I slept soundly.

Before the sun appeared in the sky, I was awakened by voices. Startled, I looked up to see a large group of angry men peppering me with questions, "Who are you? Where did you come from? Why are here?"

I told them my story, which they didn't seem to believe. I was becoming afraid, for I was only a teenager, lying naked in a hole, and the men had a roughness about them that alerted me to danger.

For what reason I will never know one of the older men began shouting, "He is a ghost! He is a ghost!" Several of the men flinched and pulled away from me. Another one gasped. Ghosts obviously frightened them, for they turned and fled up the shoreline.

I was still for a few moments, thinking about what had just happened. Realizing that a calmer head might think better of the ghost idea and convince his comrades to return to beat and rob me, I cautiously crept out of my hole, dressed, and searched for a better place to hide. After a few miles of walking, I dug another hole and tried once again to capture some much needed sleep. As fate would have it, a different group of men soon arrived, as suspicious as the others. They, too, demanded to know who I was and what I was doing in their territory.

Remembering the reaction to the mention of a ghost by the other gang, and knowing that most rural people are often superstitious, I shouted loudly, "I am a ghost! I am a ghost!"

Those men froze in place, then, taking me at my word, the whole group ran like the wind. From such reactions, I sensed that I must be in a very dangerous, lawless region, and decided to look for a village where I would find a cleric.

Luckily I soon found a village with a mosque where a kindly man of God gave me food and a place to rest. Afterward, he guided me to the best place to find a way back into Khartoum. I managed to catch a ride on the back of a wagon, which was sheer misery, for the dirt road was so dry that grit blew into our faces.

When I reached the outskirts of Khartoum I took a taxi to the home of the family where I was staying. My host was waiting for me, frantic for my safety. Surprisingly, when I told him my story, he became furious, shouting accusations, saying that I was a bad Muslim! Then he accused me of spending the night with a woman. My true experience of swimming the Nile, nearly drowning, spending the night in a hole, being accosted by ghost-fearing natives, and finding sanctuary in a village mosque, was so implausible to his ears that he never believed the truth he was hearing, remaining annoyed up until the day I departed Khartoum.

His reaction disheartened me.

After such unhappy experiences, I settled down and tried to find a bride. Everywhere I turned, I met with rejection. Perhaps my host had warned his friends that I was prone to wild nights, I'll never know. But no one wanted their daughter to marry me.

Imagine my surprise when I learned that Sa'ad had accomplished the impossible. With single-minded purpose, the same as when he looks for food or describes a delicious meal, my brother had focused and found himself a pretty bride. Knowing Sa'ad, he probably harassed everyone he knew until they grasped that the only way to shut my brother up was to find him a bride. The girl was sixteen years old, old enough for marriage with her family's permission.

Sa'ad was elated that his wedding was set. The wedding was not a big affair, but decidedly joyful because the groom was so excited. The wedding was held at the girl's home, with the women inside and the men outside. Afterward, her papers were prepared and arrangements were made for her to accompany her new husband back to Afghanistan.

Wifeless, I returned to the comfort of my mother and siblings in Afghanistan. Although my family was most interested in Sa'ad and his new wife, I was welcomed back with the greatest happiness, too. It seemed that everyone had missed me, which was unexpected. Still, I had so liked being out of Afghanistan that I began thinking of excuses to make another trip as soon as possible.

Over time I had become closer to some of my father's Russian war veteran friends than to my own brothers. When I returned from Khartoum, my good friend Sakhr seemed particularly pleased to see me. He even agreed for me to practice my driving, which was not something I got to do every day. I climbed into the driver's seat and Sakhr sat beside me, advising me to be careful; the last time he had driven, the bad roads had damaged the steering. Sakhr was so patient, doing all the things most fathers do for their sons, guiding me, allowing me to drive all the way into Kandahar, teaching me the tricks of maneuvering single-lane roads, watching out for all the donkey carts and horse-drawn carriages. In many ways the scenes of Kandahar were enchanting, even though we both knew that war and terrible poverty had reduced the Afghan people to substandard life.

Such lighthearted occasions were about to end, for an event was on the horizon that would take us one step closer to hell on earth.

Chapter 23

True Terror

OMAR BIN LADEN

During the summer of 1998, the Kandahar compound reminded me of a disturbed beehive. Leaders were coming and going without explanation. Whatever they were doing, it excited the fighters, who set about testing their weapons, monitoring the roads, and peering at the skies, all with equal intensity. I searched the skies, too, for what I did not know. I sensed a great conspiracy, but no one would tell me anything. I approached my father gingerly, asking if something big was at hand.

He replied, "My son, it is not for you to know. It is the family business." That was his code for al-Qaeda business, his usual barbed response when his sons became too inquisitive for his liking.

The secret was well kept. Even my friend Sakhr was unaware of the exact nature of affairs, although he agreed with me that my father and his commanders were as prickly as porcupines.

Time passed slowly until August 7, 1998, when those of us out of the loop finally discovered the reason behind the energized activity. I had risen early as usual, gone to the mosque to say my prayers, and then walked over to my father's main office within the Kandahar compound.

My father did not speak; he was listening intently to the world news on the radio. Soon afterward, he announced, "All men of fighting age prepare to leave Kandahar." We rushed to do his bidding, discovering that we were going to a nearby training camp to await some important news.

The camp was only an hour away, and once there, all the leaders tuned their radios to the news. I did the same, eager to discover what it was my father was waiting for. Around 12:30 P.M. local time in Afghanistan, and 10:30 A.M. local time in Africa, the news reported that there had been simultaneous car bomb explosions at the United States embassies in Dar es Salaam, Tanzania, and Nairobi, Kenya. According to the report, there was massive loss of life.

The breath left my body. I studied my father's face; in my life, I had never seen him so excited and happy. His euphoria spread quickly to his commanders and throughout the ranks, with everyone laughing and congratulating each other. I soon heard someone shout that a successful strike had been made against the enemy: America!

After a few moments of shock, I expressed gladness as well, mirroring the reactions I was seeing, especially since I had been taught since childhood that Americans were determined to murder me because I was a Muslim.

With reports coming in about the terrific damage and loss of life, the fighters celebrated by firing their weapons into the air. I heard some of the fighters boast about how the explosives for the bombing had been prepared in one of the homes of the ammunition experts and then hidden in the gardens where al-Qaeda children played.

One proud fighter claimed, "My own children's footprints could be seen in the sand covering the boxes of dynamite and TNT. Other explosives were hidden under a jungle gym climbing set. My little ones played happily, and I was at ease as well, knowing that God would not let anything happen to our children."

Those men had risked the lives of tiny children to hide their explosives. Nothing much shocked me after that.

I can't remember exactly how long we remained at the training camp near Kandahar, but it was long enough to hear that 213 people had been killed in Nairobi and at least a dozen in Dar es Salaam. I listened carefully, and learned that most of the bloodied and dead were African civilians who had been passing by when the bombs exploded. Looking back, I wonder why some of the men didn't raise a question about all the Muslims killed in Africa.

My father had no regrets for the action, even for the death of Muslims. If any of his fighters had raised such concerns in the past, he had answered, "We are in a war. If the enemy mounts a wall of civilians in front of government or military offices, they must be killed first. How else will you get to the enemy? Besides, their civilians would be safe if their governments would leave us alone."

Any facility bearing the American flag was a viable target. If Muslims were killed, then so be it. Besides, my father was of the belief that God decides all things and had it not been the time for those African Muslims to die, they would not have been there when the bombs exploded.

Within a few days my father began to hear news reports that President Clinton might retaliate. He received a few secretive communications over his two-way radios, then met with his head commanders before announcing we would go north, to an area near Kabul.

238

I worried about the women being left behind at the Kandahar compound, but my father said, "No. They will be safe. Clinton will never strike where there are women and children."

I was less comfortable about leaving my mother and younger siblings unprotected, but there was nothing I could do. We left the area, driving many hours north through a country that was still in the throes of civil war. Shortly before arriving near Khost and the Farouk training camp, we ran into a street battle between the Taliban and members of the Forse tribe. The fracas had closed the road, so my father stopped the convoy to ask what was going on.

The Taliban commander recognized my father and came to attention. He answered that one of the Forse men had made a crude gesture, sticking his middle finger up at the Taliban group. The insult was so great that the Taliban arrested the finger man and beat him with big sticks and the butts of guns, then threw him into an open truck. I knew that the man was being taken away to be executed. The Taliban were experts in executing civilians. Besides, such a thing as execution or violent death had become so common in Afghanistan that few seemed to care. We waited for a short time for the Taliban commander to clear the area, then continued on to the Farouk training camp, one of the more famous camps my father had organized.

Our journey felt like a victory lap. When we arrived, the men at Farouk, who were already thrilled about the bombings in Africa, began celebrating in earnest. Revenge against America was on every tongue. All the years of hearing lectures and watching videos about American brutalities against Muslims had incited such hatred that even one American death was cause for jubilation. This was why the men had joined al-Qaeda in the first place, why they didn't complain at the long days and nights of training, and why they were willing to risk their lives.

After a few days at Farouk, my father received a highly secret communication, then declared, "Quickly, we must change our location," he said. "We will go to Kabul, to a guest house there." My father rented a number of guest houses in every major city, using them as plush accommodations for special guests from Saudi Arabia or Dubai or other oil-wealthy nations.

And so it was that on August 20, 1998, we said our goodbyes to the fighters at Farouk and went to Kabul.

The guest house was a detached, three-story white villa surrounded by a beautiful green garden with lots of trees. I was hoping that we would remain there, but soon after we arrived, the head of security came rushing to my father, saying that he had received the most dreadful news over his handheld transmitter. Farouk, the camp we had left only two hours before, had just been hit. In a massive attack, U.S. cruise missiles had rained down on the camp, killing or wounding many of the men we had so recently left behind.

My father soon discovered that the missiles had been launched from U.S. warships in the Red Sea. Khartoum had been hit as well, although we couldn't imagine why.

I had left several good friends in Farouk. I silently prayed they had survived the attack.

My father usually accepted bad news with a calm countenance, but upon hearing about the damage and death at Farouk, he was struck with the most violent, uncontrollable rage. His face turned red and his eyes flashed as he began rushing about, repeatedly quoting the same verse from the Koran, *"The God kills the ones who attacked! The God kills the ones who attacked!"* Punching the air wildly with his fists, he shouted, *"May God kill the ones who attacked! How could anyone attack Muslims? How could anyone attack Muslims? Why would anyone attack Muslims?"*

At that moment I agreed with him, but then later in life I recalled the many times he had proclaimed that Americans were on a mission to kill Muslims, which made me ponder his genuine astonishment that Muslims *had* been killed. Curiously, none of us considered that it was my father who had caused the bombing of his camp by first bombing the American embassies. An eye for an eye.

We soon learned that there had been strikes at numerous training camps throughout Afghanistan. I felt physically ill until we learned that the Kandahar compound escaped attack. My mother, aunties, and younger siblings were safe, at least from what we heard.

Once my father composed himself, he thanked God that the Americans had failed to kill him. Certainly, we would have lost many more men had the Americans fired their missiles only two hours earlier.

My father's mind whipped from one idea to another until he finally decided that the guest house was no longer safe. We would go underground in the way that American Mafia bosses drop out of sight during their turf wars. You might say that my father, his top leaders, and his sons "went to the mattresses" when we rushed from the guest house in Kabul to a safe house in the same city.

Even his sons did not know the location of the safe houses my father maintained in all the major cities of Afghanistan, but we were quickly transported to the one nearby. The safe house was more ordinary than the guest villa, but more secure because it was set in the middle of a large, populated area. We were concealed among the innocent because my father had often noted that the Americans were cautious not to kill civilians.

We hid there for over thirty days. Knowing the Americans were desperate to find my father and his leaders, everyone stayed out of sight, even from our neighbors, who had no idea that the top-ranking al-Qaeda commanders were dangerously close. The only freedom my father would allow his sons was an occasional peek out the front windows. Opening the curtains no more than a tiny bit, my brothers and I would study the nearby houses and watch the Afghans walking past. Meanwhile, my father and his top men were learning which fighters had died and calculating the damage to the organization, yet taking time on occasion to savor the death tally from the bombings at the American embassies.

Our Muslim deaths were lamented, African deaths ignored, and American deaths celebrated. I was too young to understand the full madness of such thinking.

That dreary month passed too slowly. We were all eager to return to Farouk and the other bombed training camps, to look for our friends, to mourn the dead, and then to return to Kandahar to reassure ourselves that our families were indeed safe.

On September 19, 1998, my father finally gave the order for us to leave the guest house in Kabul. We were going to Khost, to see the damage for ourselves.

The passengers in our vehicle were quiet as we drew close. The last time we had seen the camp, it was bustling with activity. Classrooms were filled, men were sleeping in bunkers, and others were praying in the prayer halls. There were numerous training and storage facilities.

We could not believe our eyes. Where a camp once stood, there was nothing but ruins. It was amazing that anyone had survived.

We piled out of the automobiles and followed my father as he surveyed the damage. By then we had heard that the Americans had fired over seventy cruise missiles into the country.

The attack had been so violent that tough fighters were still shaken even after a month. They told us they had continued celebrating after we left. Everyone, instructors and trainees, had been abuzz with the events, on an emotional high, discussing the visit of the sheik. Then, without warning, the world went bizarre. At first they believed that stars were springing from their place in the sky, hurling their heavenly glowing bodies to earth, falling bright and white.

My father explained, "What you were seeing was the heat rushing from the missiles."

The air was suddenly full of menace, with bright flashes and crashes so loud that their eardrums were bursting. They recognized the danger too late. Men met grim deaths as they rushed in one direction and then the other. Friends were pulverized before their eyes.

Wherever the missiles hit, life was obliterated. Buildings evaporated and large craters opened the earth. I was told that my Saudi friend was dead, his remains splattered in a large crater. When I asked about Abu Mohammed, a good friend I had met through Abu Zubair, I was told that he, too, had received a direct hit. Led to the crater that held small pieces of his body, all my anger concentrated into a dark ball in my heart. Confused by the messages I had heard all my life, I had no reign over my emotions, one second furious with the Americans and the next second angry with my father. Another friend had been thrown about, the whirling, metallic storm tossing him from one point to another, finally leaving him after piercing his body with large chunks of shrapnel. I was shocked to discover that he survived, although with massive wounds.

Animals had suffered, too. Abu Zubair wailed about his black and white cow and her baby calf, both of whom had been blown to bits. Witnesses had reporting seeing the cow flying through the air. Although the mother cow dissolved into nothing, not even the hide of her body was ever discovered, the upper half of the baby calf was found crumpled in the training camp.

Life can be very perplexing. Many tough fighters discussed their sorrow at the loss of the cow and her calf for many days to come.

After finding out more details about the American embassy bombings, I became even more agitated. I imagined that governments in the West were plotting my family's demise even as my father charted more strikes. Anytime I looked at my mother or the youngest children in our family, I worried that they, too, one day, would simply evaporate as a result of a powerful missile.

My father was devastated at the losses, yet he collected his emotions and, like the leader he was, surveyed the damage, plotting his revenge, I am sure.

My mind had been turning on the subject of killing and death for days when I was with my father and a few men. I decided that I was going to raise the topic of killing. I had matured and didn't launch directly into a subject that I knew would anger my father. Rather than discuss the current violence overtaking our lives, I eased into the conversation by first asking him, "My father, how many men did you kill in the Russian war?"

My father ignored me.

I persisted, determined not to accept silence as an appropriate answer. "My father, I really want to know how many men you killed in the Russian war."

My father continued to take no notice, until I childishly repeated the question over and over, in a rapid, nearly comical manner. "How many men did you kill in the Russian war? How many men did you kill in the Russian war? How many men did you kill in the Russian war?"

I sounded half mad, but was smoldering inside, for once not caring if he punished me. "You must have killed someone, my father!"

The leaders and fighters surrounding us were so stunned they didn't speak, but gawked at me as though I was one of the insane, someone to be shunned. No one ever talked to the sheik in such a disrespectful tone, not even one of his own sons.

Exasperated, my father finally turned to me and said in a firm voice, "I did. I am a leader! I gave orders to kill and I killed people myself! I killed so many that I do not know the final figure. Many died at my own hand or on my orders."

I was not surprised to hear his answer. Wanting more details, I continued like a wound-up toy, unable to stop myself. "My father, my father, when is this killing and war going to stop? You have been at war since before I was born! Why can't you find another way? Why can't you sit and talk? Why can't there be a truce? I hate this fight! This can't continue!" I even started to moan and groan. "I want to leave this land! I want to live in the real world. Please, can't I just leave?"

Tough warriors began to shuffle away, not knowing what to do, probably believing that I was in the throes of a mental breakdown, which, in truth, I probably was.

My father kept his cool. "My son! It is your duty to stay by my side. I need my sons with me! I don't want to discuss this subject again!"

My father left me sitting, but I had the fever of discontent and knew that I would never give up until I received permission to leave. Looking back, my actions tell me that indeed I was on the verge of a breakdown. I started lurking in various areas in the Kandahar compound, waiting for my father. If he went into an office, I waited until he came out, then I would leap from my hiding place pleading like a mantra, "I want to leave this place! I must leave this place!"

Never did my father raise his voice, only repeating what he believed to be best, "No. You must stay. Who will take my place, if not you, Omar? You are my right arm. I need you. You will be my second-in-command."

"No! I am not a commander, my father. I want to live in a world of peace. I want to be educated. I don't want to fight. I want to be free." Remembering friends whose remains were so small they could not be buried, I said, "I don't want to be killed!"

A few days later when I was walking behind my father, feeling as though I were going to burst as surely as Abu Mohammed's body had been ripped open by the cruise missile, I began speaking to myself, yet loud enough for him to hear every word.

"I wonder when my father is going to stop this fight? My father! When are you going to stop this war?"

Finally my father had had enough. He whirled around angrily, glowering at me. "Omar! How can you keep asking me this question? Would you ask a Muslim when he was going to stop praying to his God? I will fight until my dying day! I will fight until I breathe my last breath! I will never stop my fight for justice! I will never stop this Jihad!" He turned and walked away as rapidly as he could, speaking more loudly than I had heard him, "This subject is now closed!"

I had pushed my father to his limit. He would never turn his back on Jihad, even if it meant that everyone he loved, including every wife and every child, was killed because of his actions. To extricate myself from his Jihadi life would require boldness and careful planning.

After causing my father much grief and shame with my unruly behavior, I felt guilty when he was seriously hurt in a riding accident. One day not long after our final heated exchange, my brothers and I, along with a few of my father's men, including Sakhr, were riding our horses within the Kandahar compound. Our father had taken my brother Osman's horse, a gray called Sekub, out for a gallop when he saw us. After our father joined us, we started racing in an area only about a half mile long. His unseeing right eye made him miss a ditch about a yard deep located adjacent to the perimeter wall, a hollow used for rubbish disposal. Aiming to catch up to us, our father raced Sekub at a high speed, running straight into that ditch, pitching headfirst off the horse.

A good friend to my father cried out a warning, "Abu Abdullah has gone down!" A few of my father's closest called my father Abu Abdullah, meaning father of Abdullah.

Everyone reacted quickly, making our horses sprint to get back to him and quickly dismounting. I passed everyone, arriving by his side first, lifting his head, fearing that he had broken his neck. My father did not speak. From his pale, grimacing face, I knew that he was in great pain, but as is his way, he refused to acknowledge any discomfort. Sakhr ran back to his horse, shouting, "I will get a truck," then disappeared in a flash of hooves.

By this time my father was struggling to stand, refusing to allow anyone to lift or support him. He stood quietly, refusing to answer our questions, until Sakhr rushed back in a red truck and said, "Dr. Zawahiri will meet us at Um Hamza's home," meaning Auntie Khairiah's home, which was nearest to us.

Still refusing assistance, Father eased himself into the truck while Sakhr raced the engine, zooming off the moment our father was seated. Without wasting a second, we riders mounted our horses and pushed them to gallop at their highest possible speed. Someone thought to grab the reins of Osman's horse, Sekub, who had escaped unharmed.

We arrived as our father was walking into Auntie Khairiah's home. Dr. Zawahiri was impatiently urging us to get our father to the nearest bed. Once Father was in Dr. Zawahiri's care we could do nothing but stand around in shock.

Zawahiri finally reported that in his medical opinion our father had escaped life-threatening injuries, yet he noted, "There is acute pain in the rib cage area," and recommended X-rays and further investigation. It was decided that one of the drivers most familiar with Pakistan would drive across the border to find the best doctor and bring him back with his medical equipment so that our father could be treated without leaving Kandahar.

The following day a renowned Pakistani surgeon was brought to my father's side. As Dr. Zawahiri suggested, arrangements had been made to bring the latest medical equipment with him. Soon tests confirmed that my father had broken ribs, as Zawahiri had suspected. As everyone knows, the only treatment for broken ribs is to wait for the healing. My restless father stayed in bed for one month, with my mother and two aunties caring for his needs, the longest any of my father's wives had been with him since the early days of their marriages.

My father reacted to the incident with disbelief, having been a skilled horseman since childhood. I remember sitting by his side as he chuckled ironically. "My son, America has been trying to kill me for years now, using the most accurate and deadly weapons available. The mighty United States cannot harm me, while one little horse nearly killed me. Life is very mysterious, my son, very mysterious."

When he emerged from his recuperation, he looked gaunt and drawn. The injuries and inactivity had depleted his once powerful energy. Many months passed before he fully recovered.

While Sekub was unharmed, none of us desired to look upon that horse's face again. He was presented as a gift to some Afghan whom I did not know personally.

There were many complicated aspects to my father's life, including his association with the head of the Taliban, Mullah Omar. Afghanistan was such a dangerous place that my father had concerns that Mullah Omar would meet with the same fate as Mullah Nourallah, once again leaving my father without a strong support. No Afghan ever forgot that my father was an Arab not of any Afghan tribe. This fact weakened his position.

While my father kept his enemies guessing by moving constantly, rarely sleeping in the same bed more than one night, Mullah Omar was a solitary man who seldom left his home in Kandahar. Any determined assassin could easily find him.

After his near assassination in Khartoum, my father often reminded us that the price for Jihad was eternal vigilance. In fact, he tried to convince Mullah Omar of the importance of remaining a moving target. But the Taliban leader shrugged off my father's advice. Mullah Omar was an admitted fatalist, believing whatever God decreed would happen, and declaring that he slept peacefully, never giving potential assassins a moment of worry time.

Then one day a large water tanker truck appeared outside Mullah Omar's home in Kandahar. Such a truck was unusual because the mullah had a piped water supply, but no one thought to mention its appearance. Soon there was a huge explosion, ripping through the mullah's home, killing two of his three wives, two of his brothers, and many members of his staff. There were many body parts flung over a large area, but Mullah Omar was only slightly injured.

Even after that close call, Mullah Omar retained his old habits. Staff members reported that the mullah still slept through the night like a contented baby, knowing in his heart that the deaths had been God's will.

Not so long after the American embassy bombings and the Clinton attack on the training camps, the United States, Saudi Arabia, and various other nations began to pressure the Taliban to expel my father from Afghanistan. Remembering the trauma of being expelled from Sudan, I believed that history was repeating itself.

All wanted a chance to arrest my father and put him on trial followed by execution. I could see my father's tension when such talk reached his ears. There were few places of refuge left. If he was kicked out of Afghanistan, he was unsure where he might land, although secluded regions of Pakistan and Yemen were still a possibility.

While Mullah Omar was not the sort of man to allow outside intervention in his business, the American attack upon Afghanistan had caught his full attention.

I was loitering in my father's Kandahar compound office one day when he received word that Mullah Omar was coming to visit later in the day. We had only a few hours to prepare, Anxious to make a proper impression, my father peppered his men with instructions to prepare a feast and set up one of the largest and nicest garden areas for the meeting area.

My father dressed in his formal Saudi robes to wait. This was an important occasion, the first time that Mullah Omar had left his home to pay my father a visit. Picking up on the apprehension of men like Abu Hafs and Zawahiri, who were usually cool and calm, my brothers and I waited nervously with our father.

Soon my father's lookouts informed us that a caravan of twelve black Land Cruisers with dark-tinted windows was coming our way. No one spoke as the cruisers pulled into the compound. When the caravan stopped, the doors opened and heavily armed Taliban soldiers stepped out. Notoriously secretive, Mullah Omar had few known photographs of him taken, so my brothers and I had no idea what he looked like. But when he stepped from the vehicle, all identified him instantly from the aura of power and invincibility that set him apart from his followers.

I found myself looking at a man taller and slimmer than my own father, which was a big surprise. I had never met anyone who was taller than my father.

Mullah Omar was wearing distinctive Taliban dress consisting of a black waistcoat and a white shirt, so white and shiny that we knew it was made from the finest cotton. He had a black turban twisted around his head, with only a small part of jet black hair peering from under the turban. He had a handsome masculine face with olive skin. Unkempt, bushy brows gave him an intense look. His healthy beard was thick and reached mid-length. A full mustache covered his upper lip.

As we had heard, he bore facial injuries from fighting the Russians. There was a depression of his right eye socket and other scars disfiguring his right cheek and forehead. In a violent country like Afghanistan, such wounds were a man's badge of honor.

Despite his mutilation, Mullah Omar looked youthful. The knowledge that he had lost his right eye brought thoughts of my own father, whose right eye, although intact, was basically useless, other than to maintain an attractive appearance. I felt certain that the two men had never discussed their common affliction.

I was surprised that when my father walked to meet Mullah Omar, the Taliban leader rudely walked away, not giving my father a chance to greet him in the usual Islamic manner, saying *Salam Alaikum*, followed by a handshake and customary cheek kisses and embraces. Such greetings are a sign of great respect in my culture.

Some of my father's men led Mullah Omar and his entourage to the garden next to my mother's home, the nicest garden in our Kandahar compound. My father and his followers walked behind. Of course, there were no women present.

My brothers and I followed the crowd of men, for as the sons of Osama bin Laden, we had the right. Much to everyone's surprise, Mullah Omar called out for a western-styled chair to be found for him to sit on. A chair left behind by the Russians was found in one of the houses. That is where Mullah Omar sat, indicating that although he would sit high in that chair, everyone else should sit on the ground, including my father. Additionally, Mullah Omar had the chair placed at the opposite side of the garden, ordering his men to sit between him and my father. My father calmly settled himself on a Persian carpet that had been placed on the ground, sitting crossed-leg Arab style.

This is not a good sign, I thought to myself. The display was surreal, with Mullah Omar perched high on his chair, while my father was a good distance away, sitting low on the ground. The rebuke could not be missed. Mullah Omar was letting my father know that he was nothing to him. His actions also indicated that he was furious.

The insults continued when Mullah Omar failed to address my father directly, instead speaking in the language of his Pashtun tribe, Pashto, using his personal translator to interpret his message into Arabic. My father spoke Pashto fluently, so I did not understand the reason for the disengagement during such an important conversation.

Despite the social snubs, my father sat quietly, respectful and patient, waiting to hear what Mullah Omar had to say. It was a strain to listen to the translated conversation because both men spoke in low voices, Mullah Omar's voice even softer than my father's. The similarities between them struck me more and more.

Mullah Omar did not waste words or time, but launched into the reason he had come out of his habitual seclusion. The Taliban leader was displeased at my father's militant activities. Concerned only with the internal affairs of Afghanistan, Mullah Omar had no desire to attract interference from the outside world. Already there were rumblings from human rights organizations about the treatment of women under the Taliban.

"The political situation is heated," Mullah Omar concluded. "It is best if you and your men leave Afghanistan."

My father's face remained impassive, even though I knew the last thing he wanted was to be expelled from his sanctuary. He was very slow to respond, choosing his words carefully, then speaking softly at last.

"Sheik, I have spent many years of my life in Afghanistan, from the time I was a young man, fighting for your people. Never once did I forget this country, returning to build a village, even moving my wives, children, and close friends here. Now we are this large group numbering many hundreds of people. How can I move such a large group of people easily? Where would I move them?"

Mullah Omar repeated, "The time has come for you and your fighters to leave Afghanistan."

My father paused, careful, careful, careful, softly requesting, "The Sudanese government allowed me to live there for five years. Would you offer me the same courtesy? Will you allow me to remain in Afghanistan for another year and a half?"

Mullah Omar remained quiet for a very long time, his face thoughtful. When he finally answered, he spoke for a very long time. I cannot remember his exact words, but he carefully detailed the pros and cons of my father's continued presence in Afghanistan.

Just as instinct whispered to us that Mullah Omar's next words would be for my father to leave, my father ever so lightly rubbed a Muslim nerve, saying, "Sheik, if you give in to the pressure of infidel governments, your decision will be against Islam."

Mullah Omar, who was known for his total devotion to Islam, gave a little twitch. He would be hesitant to go against Islamic teachings. He paused.

In that moment Mullah Omar chose his religion above all, above the good of his country and the well-being of the world. He nodded.

"Sheik Osama, I will fulfill your request. I will give you the same courtesy as did the Sudanese government. You have my invitation for another year and then a half a year. During that year and another half year, make arrangements for your move. Do find another country for your family."

My father was saved once again, because he had outwitted Mullah Omar. Once he realized that the mullah was going to expel him despite his loyalty to the Taliban, my father had oh so carefully chosen the perfect words to change his mind, at least temporarily. No good Muslim would ever bend to the infidel's will over the good of a Muslim, even if the infidel was in the right and the Muslim was in the wrong.

My father was a brilliant man in many ways.

Few onlookers realized exactly what had transpired, knowing only that all was well. A feeling of celebration flashed through the crowd of men.

When my father called for the food to be displayed, many men began bringing whole sheep on platters, with rice and vegetables. Although our food supplies were low, somehow my father and his men had managed to put on a huge feast. As is our Arab way, my father ordered the servers to present the choicest pieces to the Taliban leader.

But we were in for a final shock. Mullah Omar stung my father with a parting insult, brusquely declaring that he was not hungry. With that, the leader of the Taliban marched away, without speaking a word of farewell to my father. The large number of men with their big guns jumped into their assigned vehicles. Mullah Omar's caravan quickly left.

Many of my father's men exchanged baffled glances, for such an insult could bring a tribal war in our Arab world. Yet there was nothing to do but to accept his disrespectful behavior. Mullah Omar was the most powerful man in all of Afghanistan. He controlled most of Afghanistan, and his men, the harsh Taliban soldiers, brought fear into nearly every heart. Despite the strength of my father's al-Qaeda organization, he could not afford to get into a battle with the Taliban. He would lose, and he knew it.

Although humbled by the day's events, my father was relieved that he had some time to work out the details of his future. When he had been expelled from Sudan, he had only a few months to organize. Now he had over a year to make his plans. Anything could happen in a year. Refusing to eat, he retired to meet with his top lieutenants. My brothers and I went to our mother's home to be certain that the females and the children received a share of the feast. It was rare that we had such delicious food on our table.

I admit to a feeling of pride that my father had saved the day yet again, although I also thought that nothing would have been better for me personally than for the mullah to force my father's departure within the hour. Either way, I know now that nothing would have stopped my father from his Jihad. If he could not remain in Afghanistan, he would go to Pakistan. If Pakistan pulled the welcome mat, he would go to Yemen. If Yemen threw him out, he would journey to the middle of the most hostile desert where he would plot against the West. Violent Jihad was my father's life; nothing else really mattered. Nothing.

My only hope was that Mullah Omar's withdrawal of support would decelerate my father's Jihadi activities. Surely, after such a close call, he would become more cautious. But that was not the case. Following the ominous meeting with Mullah Omar, my father increased his activities. His journey down a dead-end road continued. He was still the driver and we were still the passengers. But the destination became clearer to me with each turn of the wheel. This was going to be a one-way trip.

Very shortly after Mullah Omar's visit, my father received word from one of his contacts in Pakistan that his mother had flown from Jeddah to Dubai and that she and her husband, Muhammad al-Attas, were soon to arrive. The details of her trip had been carefully coordinated by my father's brothers, who lived in Saudi Arabia, although my father was unaware she was coming until she was in Dubai.

My grandmother had visited once or twice when we lived in Khartoum, but that was a long time ago and much had happened since then. Everyone was pleased by the news that we would soon see a favored and lovely face in our Afghan home, but none more than my mother, who at forty years of age was pregnant with her eleventh child. She loved her Auntie Allia as a second mother, so she was more excited than I had seen her in a long time.

On the day of their arrival, my father announced that he would drive to the airport himself and I would accompany him in his vehicle. Other brothers and fighters would follow in a caravan. Since we left Saudi Arabia, my father had rarely driven himself. So I knew he was displaying the highest honor for his mother.

As usual, we were fully armed with our Kalashnikovs and grenade belts, thinking nothing of how that might appear to our family visitors who were un-accustomed to our militant world. In Saudi Arabia, civilians will land in prison for carrying weapons, although during his years of fighting the Russians, the Saudi royal family had allowed my father flexibility for his personal security.

My father and I stood together and watched as the airplane landed. While I emulated my father's quiet, serious demeanor, in my heart I could barely contain my excitement. Just then, my grandmother and her husband appeared at the open door of the airplane and gave a little wave before starting their descent down the roller-style stairs.

My grandmother was a woman of normal height and build. My father had inherited his height from his biological father. Grandmother was attractive, very smart, and spoke with confidence. My father's stepfather, Muhammad al-Attas, was a short man, about five feet eight with a medium build, gray hair, and a mustache but no beard. He had a very pleasing appearance and a quiet, kindly nature.

My father and I walked rapidly to meet them. Once Grandmother was halfway down the stairs, my father apparently noticed for the first time that she was unveiled, her face revealed for any stranger to see. He quickly motioned with his hands for her to cover her face. She seemed surprised, but took the edge of her head scarf and looped it over her face and eyes. Of course, that made it difficult for her to maneuver the steps, causing her to stumble, nearly toppling down. We made an instinctive jump to save her from a fall, but she managed to catch her footing at the last minute.

His mother glided gracefully to her son, locking her hand into his and the two of them were in a world of their own. Never had I seen perfect happiness before, but on that day I knew that my father was as happy as a man could be.

My father escorted his mother and Muhammad to the cab of the newest truck in his fleet, telling me to ride in the back, in the open air, as there was not room enough for four to be comfortable. The other automobiles would follow. I leaned over the side of the truck, feeling so good that I wanted to celebrate. By this time I had acquired some of the habits of the fighters in the camps, and thought nothing of discharging my gun in celebratory firing, shooting many times into the air.

My father was not pleased, banging on the back window of the truck, motioning for me to stop. When we arrived at our compound, he told me that poor Muhammad had believed us to be under attack and was noticeably shaken, even after my father assured him that it was only my foolishness creating the noise.

My grandmother and her husband were settled in the nicest of the guest houses, then escorted to my mother's house. My grandmother had brought gifts of chocolates. My siblings and I were thrilled; we had not seen chocolates since we lived in Khartoum. Some of the smallest children did not even know what candy was, so it was fun to watch their little faces when they ate the sweet treats.

My father was proud to fete his mother and stepfather with good-quality provisions that he had somehow managed to acquire. Usually the food available to us in Afghanistan was repugnant. He even relented when it came to cooling fans, for there was still no electricity in the Kandahar compound and most guests sweltered in the summer heat. After a few high-ranking guests had nearly fainted, my father had ordered a few battery-powered fans for his most honored guests.

Although my grandmother and her husband did not make use of the fans, I had witnessed a number of guests struggling to hold the spinning blades close to their faces while trying to have a conversation or enjoy a meal, reminding me of those wealthy guests in Khartoum working those woven hand fans.

The first evening was the only night that our family was all together, and was so enjoyable that my father began to recall some delightful tales from his youth. Looking sweetly at my grandmother, he asked, "My mother, do you remember when I was very young, long before my school days, when my only goal in life was to have a pet goat?"

Grandmother Allia nodded in pleasure. "Yes, my son," she replied, "I remember everything of that incident."

"Your husband would not allow your son to have a goat. I asked him again and again, and every time he would say no, definitely there would be no goats at his home in Jeddah. After the third or fourth time, your husband became weary of your son, and said, if you want a goat, Osama, you will need to grow one for yourself. I was truly confused, asking your husband how I might go about such a task as growing a goat."

Muhammad laughed heartily, calling to mind the long-ago incident.

"My mother, your husband told me that the next time my mother served goat for our dinner meal, that I was to take the cooked leg bone of the goat, and then plant it three inches in the ground. He cautioned me that if I did not give the goat leg a daily watering, I would not grow a goat.

"Sure enough, the next time you served goat, I saved the leg bone and very earnestly carried it into the garden to dig a hole and plant it, diligently watering the goat bone daily. After a few weeks, I began to wonder what I might have done wrong, for nothing resembling a goat broke through the garden soil. After weeks of tending that goat bone, your husband finally told me the truth, that it was only a joke, and that the bone would never grow into my very much desired goat!"

My father glanced my brothers and me. "And, that, my sons, is why I have always granted your every wish when it came to your desire for animals."

I suddenly remembered all the goats my father had bought us when we were small in Saudi Arabia. I understood for the first time that in presenting his sons with those goats, he was fulfilling his own childhood desires.

Muhammad enjoyed the little story, finally saying, "Osama, I had no idea that you would take me seriously. I am sorry if I caused you any grief."

My father smiled. "No. It was a good and funny joke for a small boy."

The goat story led Muhammad to remember yet another family tale. "Osama, do you remember when you rode the bull?"

My father smiled. "I do." He seemed very happy at the memory. "My dear family, you know my love for horses. From the time I was very young, I wanted a horse more than I wanted anything, even a garden-growing goat! I pestered my mother and Muhammad endlessly, but no one took me seriously. Once when we were holidaying in Syria, at the home of your mother's parents, I was hiking with your mother's brothers when I noticed a big breeding bull in a field. Something nudged me to slip through the fence and approach the bull.

"It was a magnificent specimen, the most powerful animal I had ever seen. I had a plan to ride the bull, thinking to myself that it couldn't be much different from riding a horse. If my family would not allow me to have a horse, perhaps I could have a bull! I slowly approached, but the bull didn't react to my presence. I assumed that he was accustomed to human hands. The bull remained indifferent, chomping on green grasses, content in his bull world.

"I quietly approached from the side, then, in a flash, I leaped from the ground and onto the back of the bull. The bull was instantly determined to throw me from his back. I wrapped my arms around his neck, making him even more defiant. He bolted, first one way, and then another, running as fast as a bull can run. He twisted. He turned. It was the wildest ride of my life. I hung on, but realized that I was going to be seriously harmed. I braced myself, then pushed off, tumbling over and over, smelling the new grass as my face and body skidded helplessly across the field.

"Najwa's brothers were watching. Other people had walked past to witness my attempt at bull riding. Your mother's brothers made it their business to dash to your mother's family home, shouting that Osama had been tossed from a bull's back.

"Of course, my mother and Muhammad were terrified by my caper. They decided then that I needed something to ride and that a horse would be much less dangerous."

Muhammad al-Attas nodded. "You know your father, once he sets his mind to a thing, never thinks about turning back. He will not stop until he gets what he wants."

Yes, we knew that aspect of our father's character. Such a trait can be good, or it can be bad. From what I knew of my father's life, his stubbornness had brought him many problems. Once he wished for something, he never gave up, even when his wish had a twin, and that twin was called ruin.

But that evening was a rare opportunity for us to be a real family, and I was not complaining. It did me good to see my mother's serene, happy face, and to watch my serious father enjoying himself for a change. While he was usually so stern about everything, in his mother's presence, he seemed an ordinary son, father, and husband. My mother and grandmother exchanged many affectionate glances, and I could tell that my grandmother was very worried about my mother.

Although that first night was perfection, the remainder of my grandmother's visit did not go as well. We learned later that hers was not simply a family visit. She had been sent to my father by King Fahd, who hoped that my father's great affection for his mother would work a charm. Grandmother Allia had come to Afghanistan to plead with my father to give up his Jihadi path, to come home, to make amends. It was not too late, Grandmother Allia said. King Fahd was making one last effort, promising my father that he would not be imprisoned or turned over to the Americans, but would be guaranteed a quiet life if only he returned to Saudi Arabia.

Although he understood that his mother truly believed the king's promises, my father did not. He was convinced that if his feet touched Saudi sand, he would be imprisoned for the rest of his life, or given to the Americans so that they could have a show trial, the way they did for Omar Abdel Rahman, the Egyptian blind cleric who had been convicted of seditious conspiracy and sentenced to life imprisonment. Over the years, my father had repeatedly declared that he preferred death to the filthy grasp of the hated Americans.

He so loved his mother that he felt no anger at her words, but merely replied that he could never return to the kingdom. His eyes would never again see Saudi Arabia. His feet would never again walk on the streets of Jeddah. He was finished with the country he loved.

Thus that joyful evening ended on a somber note. My grandmother and Muhammad al-Attas departed Afghanistan two days later.

My grandmother's visit increased my desire to leave my father and the life he had chosen for me. Such ideas grew more urgent after my closest friend, Abu Haadi, took me aside and warned me earnestly, "Omar, you need to leave Afghanistan. I have heard talk that there is something very big in the works. You need to leave, Omar. You are a young man. You have never harmed anyone. You need to leave, seek out a normal life. Do not stay here any longer."

So, even after the attack from America, even after Mullah Omar's warnings, my father and his men were still sculpting violence. And, from Abu Haadi's words, they were intending something even larger than the deadly attacks upon the American embassies. More innocents would be killed, as they had been in Africa and Afghanistan, for some of the men killed in the camps were not training to be fighters, but had come to visit friends, or out of simple curiosity.

Abu Haadi was not a man who would lie. If he thought I should leave, I should leave. Later that day, I gathered my father's sons around me. "Listen, my brothers, I have heard confidential information. Something big is in the works. Here is the simple truth. If we leave, we live. If we stay, we die."

They were quick to agree, with one saying, "If our father makes other attacks, all of Afghanistan will be destroyed."

"We must escape," I said.

My brothers concurred, but how? Our departure must be a secret. Our father had become so extreme that he might imprison us if he knew our plans to escape.

I suggested, "When our father goes away on business, we will dash to Pakistan. On our horses."

My brothers nodded. All the sons of Osama bin Laden were excellent horsemen, and we had easy access to our father's stallions. We had the added advantage of being intimately familiar with the mountainous terrain. All those forced hikes to Pakistan from Tora Bora might be good for something after all.

Yes, we would ride our horses to Pakistan, sell the horses to a wealthy landowner, then use the money to fly to Sudan. After a pleasant visit in Sudan, we would take a trip around the world! We would enjoy ourselves for a change.

We dreamed big dreams. We were so serious about escaping that we began to slaughter some of our father's camels, drying the meat so that it would not spoil, packing a few supplies. Only Abu Haadi knew of our plans, and he was in complete agreement.

Of course, guilty feelings regarding our mother and younger siblings flitted into our minds. Yet all understood that our mother would never consent to leave without her husband's permission. And should he inquire, our mother would find it impossible to lie. Our plan would be foiled.

None of us wanted to imagine our father's reaction to our disloyalty. We knew he believed we should follow his Jihad with the greatest passion. We should take up arms and attack the Americans, or anyone else he deemed his enemy.

Our worries were soothed somewhat by the knowledge that our mother and younger siblings had the advantage of sex and age. Our father would make efforts to protect them. And, even if the Americans attacked again, we remembered our father's words that the Americans never intentionally strike women and children.

Soon we had enough food for the journey. I was excited, for I had been thinking of leaving for several years. But the idea was new for my brothers, and one by one, they began pulling back.

One brother said, "Our father's long arms reach many places. He will kill us, for sure."

Another said, "Afghanistan is so dangerous. Behind every bush is a bandit. We will be robbed and murdered on the trail."

"Those are chances we must take," I argued. "We will die if we remain with our father. Information I have received leaves no doubt that we must go!"

All were quiet, contemplating. Soon each of my brothers drifted away from the plan. All began to avoid me.

I thought of going alone, but common sense told me that fewer than two travelers could not survive. Lookouts were essential. A single traveler alone would be attacked and, most likely, murdered. Life was so cheap in Afghanistan.

I finally approached Abu Haadi and asked if he would be willing to go with me. Although he wanted me, a young boy, to escape, he said, "No, Omar. I cannot. My place is with your father."

I sat silent and sad, nibbling on that dried camel meat for weeks, dreaming of my lost opportunity to escape. Yet I did not give up on the idea.

That's when my mother caught my full attention. Watching her one day when she was laboring in a steaming hot kitchen, cooking a simple meal of rice on a single gas burner, I was struck by the dreadful idea that perhaps my mother might not live through her upcoming delivery.

Pregnant for so many times and now enduring an older pregnancy without medical care or proper nutrition, my long-suffering mother appeared unwell. Not that she complained, because never once during all those years did I hear my mother voice displeasure about anything. She lived without air-conditioning in the hottest weather, without proper heating in the coldest weather, without modern appliances to store or cook food or wash her family's clothes, without proper food for her children, without medical care for anyone, and without a way of communicating with her mother and siblings. She accepted all these circumstances with the sweetest composure, always voicing positive thoughts to her husband and children. Yet surely she must have had many silent doubts about the path my father had chosen. She had started her marriage with great hope, traveling to a wealthy country to live out her life with the man she loved. I knew that her girlhood dreams had not come true, even if she refused to acknowledge it.

Suddenly I was glad that I had not run way and left her. With my father so occupied with his Jihad and other business, my mother mainly depended upon me.

That's when I knew that *someone* must take my mother out of Afghanistan. She should return to her mother in Syria, where she could have proper medical care. Her youngest children must go with her. There were three youngsters between the ages of three and nine years. Pretty Iman was nine, cute Ladin was six, and adorable Rukhaiya was three.

Thinking that perhaps the dried camel meat would be useful after all, I began to hatch a second escape plan, focusing this time on the safety of my mother and youngest siblings.

Little did I know that other shocking ideas were brewing in my father's mind, plans that would push me away forever.

Chapter 25

Young Marriage

NAJWA BIN LADEN

I knew that my boys were growing up when I overheard them discussing marriage. Osman and Mohammed were both too young for the marriage talk, but were influenced by the eager discussions they overheard among their older brothers.

Abdullah and Sa'ad were the only two sons who had married. Abdullah had now been gone for five or six years. When Auntie Allia visited, she brought the welcome news that our eldest son was a father. I had not enjoyed any happy occasions to meet with my first grandchildren, although those babies were in my daydreams.

Sa'ad and Omar had actually traveled to Sudan to find brides, but only Sa'ad was successful, bringing his wife back to live near us. Within a year Sa'ad and his wife had a son they named Osama, which greatly pleased my husband.

I could scarcely believe that my husband and I were grandparents. Where had the years gone?

During that time Osama called the older boys together and presented them with some land, telling them that they should till the earth and produce food as he had taught them to do in Sudan. My husband believed that our boys could become financially self-sufficient by harvesting this land. Such a business enterprise would put fresh vegetables on the table as well as providing extra cash from any sales.

None of my sons was enthusiastic about farming, although they were respectful as always, each one replying, "Thank you, my father. We will tend to this matter." His sons did not inherit Osama's great love for agriculture.

Omar was yet unmarried, although he keenly wanted a wife, frequently inquiring if any fighters knew of a marriageable girl from a suitable family.

Becoming discouraged at ever finding a bride, Omar became even more sub-dued than usual. There were nights that Omar disappeared for many hours, horseback riding in the desert. I waited patiently for our son, until the dawn if necessary, for as his mother I worried about his safety. Perhaps one of those poison snakes might bite him, or his horse might fall in a hole.

With seven sons, accidents were not uncommon. I remembered the time when little Mohammed was running and playing in the desert, and dropped from sight. He had fallen into a deep hollow carved in the earth, and was un-conscious for a full day. Thanks be to God, Mohammed's brothers were in the area and after a day began a big search, finally finding him in that burrow. Had his general location not been known, no one could have guessed where to look and perhaps wolves would have gotten him. Another time Sa'ad was driving recklessly and flipped his automobile. Ladin was sitting in the backseat and crawled out with a broken hand.

My thought was that if Omar were to meet with disaster, no one would know where to begin a search. My husband did not object to Omar's solitary rides in the desert, reminding me that he been the same way when he was a young man in Saudi Arabia. My husband seemed to love Omar more for his lonely spirit, giving his son the nickname of Omar "Alfarook," which is an Arab name that means "sword."

Many people were recognizing Omar's special traits. One of my sister-wives thought so highly of Omar that when she would see him walking to us she would say, "Here is the father of wisdom." Another named him, "Omar the generous," because he was known to be the most charitable of all my sons, sav-ing what little money he could get to help others worse off.

Although I was pregnant again, I had many more things on my mind than myself.

In fact, it was in early 1999 that Osama decided the time had come for our daughter Fatima, who was born in 1987, and his daughter Kadhija with Siham, who was a year younger than Fatima, to be married. It is not unusual for girls of such a young age to wed in our culture. Besides, such decisions were Osama's alone. I was glad to hear that he conferred with Omar, asking my wise son for his advice regarding the fighting men Omar knew best. My husband instructed Omar to find good husbands for both his daughters.

Omar took the search seriously, carefully observing the men who were at-tached to my husband's work. Finally Omar recommended two Saudi soldiers, Mohammed and Abdullah, whom he believed to be intelligent and kindly men. Both potential grooms were from Saudi Arabia, which seemed to please Osama, and were nearing the age of thirty. One was a bodyguard for my hus-band, so Osama knew him better than most.

Omar recommended that Fatima be married to Mohammed and that

Kadhija be married to Abdullah. Once the choice was made, everything was handled in the traditional Islamic way. Osama discussed the matter with me, and with Siham. We both accepted our husband's decision.

As is proper, Osama then called in each daughter separately, telling her about the husband he had selected. Osama was careful to go by our religion and to advise his daughters that if she was not in favor of this husband, that the marriage would not go forward. If that was the case, there would be a search for another groom.

Both daughters very shyly said yes, they would be pleased to marry the men selected for them by their father. At that time Osama arranged for the grooms to have a chaperoned meeting with his daughters. Once our daughters and the potential grooms said that they agreed to each other, their engagements were announced.

My daughter's wedding would be first. And so it came to be that my darling Fatima was married to a Saudi man named Mohammed. Fatima's wedding was very simple, held in our home at Kandahar. Of course, the men and the women did not mingle. Food was scarce during that time, so we had nothing special to serve guests, only rice and vegetables, the same as we ate every day of the week.

After the wedding, my daughter and her husband moved into a compound house close to me, which brought me joy. I remembered years before when I had married Osama, and my mother had balked at her daughter moving so far away. For the first time I understood my mother completely.

Omar appeared strangely subdued. Although glad to have the chance to recommend the best grooms, Omar confessed that during the weddings that he had been struck by apprehension at seeing his baby sister Fatima become a wife at such a young age.

After Omar said those words, I confessed that worry nibbled at my heart as well. Fatima was so young and innocent, completely protected by her mother. She had never known anyone outside her family. On the other hand, in our culture, a woman needs a good husband to protect her. I could only pray that her husband, Mohammed, would be the best husband for my young daughter.

A few weeks after Fatima's wedding, Omar came to me in a very serious state of mind. My son said, "My mother. I would like for you to travel to Syria to have this child. I will take you." He paused. "We will take the youngest children with us."

I was so surprised that I did not know what to say. None of Osama's wives was in the habit of leaving Afghanistan, for any reason. In fact, I had already given birth to one child in the country, my youngest daughter, Rukhaiya.

Truthfully, I had not once considered leaving.

Omar appeared obsessed, pushing for me to agree. He said, "My mother, if you will not ask your husband for permission to leave, I will do it for you."

I stared at my handsome son, his brown eyes flashing with determination. Who could have guessed that of all my sons the most sensitive Omar would be the one whose courage would soar with each passing year? It was not easy for anyone to stand up to Osama's tremendous force. My son was a brave man, and I loved him doubly for his care for me and his younger siblings.

Chapter 26

The Beginning of the End

OMAR BIN LADEN

During those tense days, it was impossible to find an opportunity to have an easy exchange with my father. By his very nature, he was an obstinate man, always quick to say no when one of his sons had an idea. So I knew that I needed time alone with him to state my case, to choose my words carefully. I could not mention Abu Haadi's warning, or my friend would be severely punished. I must speak only of my mother's health, and the need for her to have special attention for the upcoming birth. But gaining a private time with my father was difficult, for he was always surrounded by his loyal men, men who reeked with the desire to hover closely.

Then one day my father called a meeting with all the fighters. My brothers and I tagged along, wondering what the urgency might be.

My father's talk was about the joys of martyrdom, how it was the greatest honor for a Muslim to give his life to the cause of Islam. I looked around the room as my father spoke, studying the faces of the fighters. I noticed that the older fighters looked a bit bored, while the young men newest to al-Qaeda had a kind of glow on their faces.

When the meeting ended, my father called for all his sons to gather, even the youngest. He dismissed the men who generally hung by his side, so I was thinking that I might have the perfect opportunity to discuss my mother's health, and her need to have a good doctor to deliver her eleventh child.

My father was in a rare good mood, having come off a successful talk with the fighters. Certainly, he had the power to inspire young men to give up their lives, for as we filed out of the meeting room, I saw several of the younger fighters scrambling to put their names on the martyr paper.

In an excited voice, my father told us, "My sons. Sit, sit, gather in a circle. I have something to tell you."

Once we were at his feet, my father said, "Listen my sons, there is a paper on the wall of the mosque. This paper is for men who are good Muslims, men who volunteer to be suicide bombers."

He looked at us with anticipation shining in his eyes.

For once we did not keep our gaze to the ground, but stared at our father, although no one spoke. As for me, I was too shocked to cry out the words that were on my tongue.

Although our father did not tell us that we must add our names to the martyr's list, he implied by his words and his expectant face that such would make him very happy.

No one moved a muscle.

My father repeated what he had said. "My sons, there is a paper on the wall of the mosque. This paper is for men who volunteer to be suicide bombers. Those who want to give their lives for Islam must add their names to the list."

That's when one of my youngest brothers, one too young to comprehend the concept of life and death, got to his feet, nodded reverently in my father's direction, and took off running into the mosque. That small boy was going to volunteer to be a suicide bomber.

I was furious, finally finding my voice. "My father, how can you ask this of your sons?"

Over the past few months, my father had become increasingly unhappy with me. I was turning out to be a disappointment, a son who did not want the mantle of power, who wanted peace, not war. He stared at me with evident hostility, gesturing with his hands. "Omar, this is what you need to know, my son. You hold no more a place in my heart than any other man or boy in the entire country." He glanced at my brothers. "This is true for all of my sons."

My father's proclamation had been given: His love for his sons did not sink further than the outer layer of his flesh. His heart remained untouched by a father's love.

Such a truth was no small pain to me. I finally knew exactly where I stood. My father hated his enemies more than he loved his sons. That's the moment that I felt myself the fool for wasting my life one moment longer.

I knew then that I was leaving, and leaving soon. When I did, I would not give my father any more thought than he gave me. My only challenge was how to get my mother and her children out with me.

My brothers and I slowly walked away, with only the smallest boy having given my father's Jihadi pride a boost.

I waited a few more days until my father was walking from one building to another. I had been lurking, trying to find a time that I could at least be near to his side without five or six men between us.

Although he refused to acknowledge me, I spoke. "My father. I am worried about my mother's health. She has come to a dangerous age for having children. Will you allow me to take her to her mother? Perhaps she will be safe there."

My father did not answer, although he took a quick look at my face. I knew from that look that his father's love for me had weakened to a dangerous point.

Yet nothing would stop me. I was becoming obsessed, the same as a few years back when I had harassed my father about the unwanted violence surrounding my life.

And so the following day, I made the same appeal.

My pleas were always the same, asking to take my mother to a better place for her delivery. I made certain to speak with him at least once a day, sometimes twice, always in the presence of his men, for never could I find an opportunity for a private session.

After ten days of stalking my father, he sent one of his men to get me. I followed the man warily, wondering if my father was so fed up with me that he might have me locked up.

When I entered his office, I was met without affection, yet my argument had touched a nerve. "Yes, Omar," he finally said, "your mother can travel to Syria for the birth of this child." He gave me an unpleasant look, a final chance for me to change my mind.

"Yes, my father. I will take her."

He threw both hands up in the air. "Remember Omar, this is between you and your God."

In other words, my father believed that by leaving him that I was not being true to my faith. I repeated, "Yes, my father. This is between me and my God. I will take her."

My father sighed, then called for one of his men to give him a small amount of money. He motioned for me to take it from his hands. "If you are frugal, this will get you to Syria. Your mother's safety is your responsibility."

"And the children? Can my mother take her youngest children with her?"

My father sat silently, then gave a limited permission. "She can take Rukhaiya. And Abdul Rahman."

Rukhaiya was only two years old, so that was not a surprise. And Abdul Rahman needed to be with his mother. But there were others who required our mother too.

"Iman? Ladin?" Iman was still a young girl, only nine years old, and Ladin was only five, although soon to turn six. Both children were timid, afraid to be without their mother. I did not want to leave them, because once I had my mother out of Afghanistan, I had hopes of convincing her not to return.

My father was too cunning, for he knew that my mother could not bear to part permanently from Iman and Ladin. "No. Iman and Bakr [as my father called Ladin] must stay with me. Only Rukhaiya and Abdul Rahman. No more."

I started to speak again, to plead for those little children, but he held up one hand. "No. You know better than to question me. Do not ask me again. Only Rukhaiya and Abdul Rahman."

I nodded. I had done what I could. I would worry about the other children later. For now, I would get my mother to safety.

Once given his approval, I moved rapidly, rushing home to tell my mother that we were leaving soon. Although she had never expressed a desire to leave, I saw the relief wash over her face, though she turned sad when I told her that Iman and Ladin would have to stay behind.

But I couldn't think about that at the moment.

We were leaving Afghanistan.

Bitterness accompanied the pleasure. When my mother and I told Iman and Ladin that she must be away for a while, both became nervous and frightened. After some explaining, little Iman accepted her fate passively, for she was accustomed to doing what others told her, but Ladin was a different story. He wept pitifully, inconsolable that his mother was going away without him. Even the thought of a new baby sister or brother did nothing to ease his anguish.

I was plagued by the idea of the big plan Abu Haadi had warned me about. I prayed that the plan would be canceled, or at least postponed until I could arrange to bring out Iman and Ladin.

The day we departed was nerve-racking. Ladin was continuing his campaign to go with us. Finally he broke down altogether, crying noisily, following my every step, tugging on my trousers, pleading, "Brother, take me. Brother, take me."

I had a quick thought to grab Ladin when no one was looking, to whisper for him to be very quiet, to snuggle him under the bedding in the back of the vehicle, but I never had the chance. My father and his men were watching, their eyes as keen as hawks, missing nothing. Besides, my father had decided that my sister Fatima and her new husband, Mohammed, were going with us to the border of Pakistan.

Truthfully, I was pleased. The road was dangerous; Afghanistan had more than its share of bandits, but they might think twice before attacking three armed men.

I called out to my mother that the time had come to leave. She slowly walked toward me, with Fatima by her side. My sister was holding little Rukhaiya in her arms. I would be the first to drive, so I settled at the wheel. Mohammed and Abdul Rahman sat in the front, while my mother and the girls got into the back.

That's when I saw my father walking up to the automobile. My heart skipped a few beats, worried that he had changed his mind. But he was only there to tell my mother goodbye. They exchanged some quiet words that I did not hear.

I felt no sadness at leaving my father, for I had begun to defy him years before. The tragedy for me was to leave Ladin and Iman behind. Abandoning my small siblings to an unknown fate was the most difficult thing I have done in my life.

As I drove away from my father and the violence of his life, I took one final look at his tall figure, disappearing into the distance. That's when I knew that I was not leaving Afghanistan to look for happiness. I was searching only for peace.

Chapter 27

To Syria

NAJWA BIN LADEN

I felt Osama's eyes upon me as I walked past to settle myself in the black SUV. I wondered if my husband would say goodbye, because he had been strangely quiet about my departure. As soon as I settled in the backseat of the vehicle, my husband moved in my direction, stopping to peer intently into the window and at my burqa-clad self.

My husband surprised me with his words.

"Najwa, no matter what you might be told, I will never divorce you."

Wordless, I stared. Divorce? I had not been thinking of divorce. I was only going to Syria to have my child.

Osama next said, "As soon as you can travel, return with the baby."

"My husband, I will," I replied. "I will return with the child as soon as I can."

Osama smiled, knowing that I meant what I said. In all our years of marriage, I had never lied to my husband.

The ill feeling was palpable between Omar and Osama. Omar did not turn back to speak with his father and Osama did not make any effort to talk to his son. I was not privy to what had happened between my husband and my son, because neither speaks easily of private matters, but something serious had created a schism. Since Omar had become a teenager, his path had swerved from his father's. I only hoped that time would bring them close. I knew from his earliest days that Omar had loved his father with more feeling than any of my children, but that love had been damaged.

Just then Omar started the engine of the car. He drove away, his neck strong and rigid, determined to leave without any emotions, but at the last minute I saw my son's neck rotate when he relented to take one final look at his father. I looked back, too, although I am sorry I did, for my eyes could see nothing but my tiny son Ladin standing lonely by the side of the road, weeping for his mother. Iman was standing nearby her older brother Mohammed, keeping her brave facade. But little Ladin's face showed all the emotion of his heart. Unable to restrain his himself, Ladin began running along beside our vehicle, still crying out to Omar, *"My brother, please take me with you. Please let me go with my mother. My brother, I beg you."*

Omar let down his car window and waved, shouting, "We will take you next time, Ladin. We will."

My mother's heart was broken. My two youngest were clearly frightened. But the evening before I had talked with them both, and had given them my heartfelt promise: "I will be back. Be brave. I will be back."

And I would. I had no intention of leaving my children forever. I would return.

I sighed deeply and turned my attention to Fatima. I knew that Fatima and her husband were going no farther than the Pakistani border, where Omar, Abdul Rahman, Rukhaiya, and I would transfer to a taxi to take us to a Pakistani airport. From there we would fly to Syria. "Fatima," I said, "take special care of Iman and Ladin."

"I will, my mother. Do not worry."

All were quiet for long periods, for any automobile journey in Afghanistan is dangerous and exhausting, and passengers tend to keep their attention on the hillsides hugging the road. Although Osama had arranged for us to travel in his newest and best vehicle, a big and good SUV, the roads were so dreadful that within a few miles we felt as though we had been beaten with big sticks.

My pregnancy of seven months was no fun. I felt awkward, unable to find a comfortable position. Rukhaiya was only a toddler so she required much attention, climbing over my body from me to Fatima and back. Fatima had been assisting with her younger siblings for as long as she could remember. I knew that my Fatima would make a wonderful mother, but due to her youth, I hoped any pregnancies would be delayed.

Fatima's husband, Mohammed, reported that the driving trip would take three days, and those days would be hazardous. Afghanistan remained an unruly land with ongoing tribal squabbles and gangs of bandits lurking to rob travelers. We had heard that bandits often murdered their victims. I put worry out of my mind as best as I could, knowing that all three of our men were proficient with their Kalashnikov assault rifles. In addition, each carried a pistol and plenty of grenades. Of course, every man in Afghanistan was armed thus, so anyone who attacked us would be equally prepared.

None of our men carried on a conversation, but spoke in short bursts, reporting what they could see out the windows of our automobile. Omar insisted on driving, so Abdul Rahman looked for signs of danger on our left side, while Mohammed looked to the right. Fatima took a lot of care to stare behind us, to make sure no one was coming up from behind. I felt myself in good hands, to tell you the truth.

I tried not to think about what we might do if criminals came after us, although I went over in my mind what Osama had taught me about weapons. Several times after moving to Afghanistan, he had taken me and my sister-wives to an isolated place to show us how to hold a gun in our hands and what levers to push to make the bullet fly out of the barrel. Each of us had held our husband's heavy gun and done as we were told, but Osama soon saw the reality, that it was nothing more than a little fun for us to try to hit the targets he placed against the big rocks. I don't believe that any of us ever came near those targets. Now that the day had come when I might actually need such skills, I wish I had tried harder to become an accomplished gun-woman.

Omar was so worried for our safety that as soon as the sunlight began to fade, he insisted we take our automobile well away from the road. Darkness brought the greatest danger for travelers. And so we left the road and climbed a few high hills, with Omar parking the vehicle on a high spot so that our men could take turns looking out over a wide area.

My darling Fatima insisted that she and her husband sleep on the ground outside the car. Abdul Rahman slept with them. Omar refused to rest, keeping watch with his big gun. Little Rukhaiya and I slept as comfortably as a heavily pregnant woman and a small child can in a small space inside an automobile.

And thus we traveled for three days and two nights. We were not alone in that car, I'm sorry to say, because fear, danger, and discomfort were our constant companions.

At the end of three days, we were all in need of a good bath, but none cared, for we had arrived safely. The sad part was that we had to say goodbye to Fatima and Mohammed. Mohammed said that he was going to take a rest on the Pakistani side of the border, then drive straight through. How he would manage that, I had no clue, but my daughter had married a strong man with a lot of determination. If anyone could do it, that would be Mohammed.

Omar, Abdul Rahman, Rukhaiya, and I took the rest of the Pakistani journey in a taxi. I couldn't help but compare how our family used to travel in long black cars with escorts. Now we were poor and no longer enjoyed special treatment. Life had changed in many, many ways.

We went to the airport and boarded an airplane to Syria. We were pitiful-looking travelers, soiled and tired, but I was still under the burqa, so no one knew that it was Najwa Ghanem bin Laden under the billowing cloak. There were advantages to the garments of a Muslim woman.

Words cannot describe the joy in my heart at seeing my dear mother and my beloved siblings after seven long years.

Syria was a world of calm after life in Afghanistan. There was no excitement for a change, which was good for me. I visited my family, and I rested. By the time I had my eleventh child, two months after arriving in the country, I felt myself healthy and fit, the woman I once was. I told Omar that he had been right, that I needed greater care for this birth. My child born was a little girl, and she would be Nour, the name Osama had chosen, in honor of his half-sister Nour, who had died in 1994.

While gazing at little Nour in my arms, I was struck by the thought that after twenty-five years of marriage, and at age forty-one, I was the mother of eleven children. As a young teenage girl in my mother's home, never had I dreamed of having eleven children, although I loved each child with a pure mother's love.

During this time, my son Omar was making plans. My son had never accepted the loss of his heritage, and his goal was to be reinstated as a Saudi Arabian. His father's family was offering their kind help, and it seemed Omar would succeed, although time was needed for his application to be approved.

That's when I discovered that my son was not only making personal plans, but had ideas about other members of our family. Omar wanted to return to Afghanistan only in order to bring Iman and Ladin out to live in Syria.

I took my time speaking, for I wanted Omar to understand that I could not abandon my children. Finally I replied, "My son, Iman and Ladin must remain where they are. I am going to them. They are not coming to me." I paused, glancing at little Nour. "When Nour is three months, I will return with her to Afghanistan."

Omar pleaded, "My mother, I have heard talk. Great harm is coming. You must remain out of Afghanistan."

I had heard Omar's warning more than once, yet I was but a miserable fragment of a woman without those six children I had left behind in Afghanistan. I was also the wife of a man whom I had never disobeyed. "Omar, I will be returning to Afghanistan, my son. That is where my husband and children are."

Omar was persistent. "My mother, please stay far from Afghanistan. A great harm is coming."

"Omar, if danger is coming, then I must return. I have small children there. They will need their mother."

Neither of us could erase Iman and Ladin from our thoughts, for Omar blurted, "I cannot sleep. If only I had stopped the vehicle and seized Ladin as he was running along beside me. If only I had grabbed Ladin."

I looked at my son, a feeling of sadness gripping my heart. I knew my place in life. I was the wife of Osama bin Laden, and I had many children with him.

I had to return to my place in the world, which was with my children. But Omar was another story. My most sensitive son had never accepted the life he had been given. He would never be happy with his family, yet I feared he would never be happy without his family.

Osama soon called me, to know that the child had arrived safely. He asked when Omar was bringing us back to Afghanistan. That's when I told him that Omar might not return. Osama paused, but said nothing other than I should arrange to fly from Syria to Pakistan. He would have Osman, our fifth son, there to meet us. If Omar was not returning to our family, then Osman would be responsible for his mother.

The day arrived that I said goodbye to my family in Syria. Omar was still there, waiting for approval for his Saudi passport, at which time he would go to Jeddah, to resume his life there, as had my eldest son, Abdullah.

Before I left, Omar made one last appeal, but my answer was the same: "I must return to my place in life, my son, and that place is with my children."

And that was that.

The return trip was so unpleasant that I have mainly blocked it from my memory. I missed Omar more than I had imagined, for my fourth son had been my staunch protector since he was a teenager, but now he was in Syria, and I was traveling without him. I did have Abdul Rahman and Osman with me, but both were involved with the dangers of the road journey. I, alone, cared for a tiny baby and a toddler. Both babies cried many tears during that nightmarish journey.

Despite the danger Omar warned was awaiting in Afghanistan, nothing had ever looked quite so welcoming as the walls of our compound in Kandahar.

My husband came quickly to see me and the new baby. Little Ladin was a jumping bean, so excited that his mother had returned. Darling Iman was equally pleased, but stood quietly, waiting for her mother's touch. My sister-wives were all well, happy that I was back so that we could catch up with our news. By this time it was early in the year 2000, and I spent the rest of that year enjoying my children, although I missed the ones who were not with me, especially Omar.

The biggest surprise came late in the year when my young son Mohammed, who had just turned fifteen, started pushing to marry.

Mohammed claimed to be in love with the daughter of Abu Hafs, my husband's closest friend and highest-ranking commander. Although Mohammed had had no occasion to spend time with Abu Hafs's daughter, he had seen her, and had fallen into an obsessive love.

My husband and Abu Hafs told Mohammed, no, that he was too young, as was the bride, who was several years younger than my son.

But my son had inherited his father's willpower, refusing to take no for an answer. He so annoyed his father and Abu Hafs that the men conferred, agreeing to allow the youngsters to have a chaperoned meeting, which is considered proper in our society. The two children were so delighted by each other that the two fathers agreed upon an engagement, a long engagement. Or at least that was the plan.

So the engagement was announced and the proper papers were signed. Of course, the marriage was not consummated due to the immaturity of Mohammed and his bride.

Everyone hoped that the formal arrangements would soothe Mohammed into waiting until he became seventeen in 2002, a suitable age for a groom, according to my husband.

Our son had other ideas.

One night in October of 2000, while everyone was sleeping, my restless son slipped from his bed, sneaked to my husband's stables, and took a horse. He galloped that horse over a dangerous territory for six hours, traveling more than thirty miles from our country compound to the city of Kandahar. He arrived at the home of Abu Hafs shortly before dawn.

Abu Hafs was startled by a loud banging on his door.

He crept to see if he needed to use his gun.

But there was Mohammed, so bold that he loudly proclaimed, "I am here to claim my bride."

Mohammed was braver than most young teenagers, for Abu Hafs was a huge man, a fearless warrior, and a father who took the honor of his family seriously.

Mohammed was lucky not to get a caning, but instead was invited into Abu Hafs's home, where he would not stop talking, speaking strongly to convince his future father-in-law that the wedding should be held sooner rather than later.

Abu Hafs traveled back to our compound with Mohammed to meet with Osama. The two men were concerned that Mohammed had taken a chance with his life to make that midnight ride alone.

The two fathers finally relented, convinced that a great love existed between their children.

And so it came to be that the two men who had been close friends since the days of the Russian war planned a big wedding for their son and daughter. Our children were so happy that the event spiraled into a huge occasion, taking several months to plan. Even family members from Saudi Arabia were invited. It was decided that Mohammed's wedding would be in the month of January 2001. Osama's mother, her husband, and one of her sons would travel to Kandahar for the affair.

January came quickly. My son Mohammed's wedding was a big event with much gaiety and laughter. Never have I seen Osama so pleased, for he loved Abu Hafs as a brother, and their two children were linking our families forever.

As always, men and women celebrated separately. After the wedding, Mohammed and his bride settled near to me, where they gave every appearance of being the happiest of couples. I loved my son's wife as I love my own daughters.

I was so glad to be back in Afghanistan with my children that I hardly ever gave Omar's warning of coming doom a single thought.

Chapter 28

Return to Saudi Arabia

OMAR BIN LADEN

For the four months I was in Syria in late 1999 and early 2000, I accomplished little, other than to learn the art of waiting. I was determined to reclaim my rightful heritage as a Saudi citizen. I had never accepted the sham of my Sudanese citizenship. I was a Saudi Arabian, period.

My efforts to keep my mother and the youngest two siblings out of Afghanistan had failed. My mother could not keep herself away from her other children, or from the only life she had known since the day she married my father, twenty-six years before.

Once she left, I fell into a listless state, anxious that each day I would hear of a terrible calamity brought about by my father. Thankfully, the early months of 2000 passed quietly, with no news of any attacks coming out of Afghanistan. I was lulled into thinking that perhaps Abu Haadi had been mistaken, or perhaps my father had become more cautious, concerned that Mullah Omar would force him to leave Afghanistan immediately if there were any more missions against the United States or Saudi Arabia.

A good day arrived when I was told that my Saudi passport application had been approved. I was happier than I had been in years to learn that I had regained my birth name and real heritage, for I had never accepted my father's decision to change my official records prior to our leaving Sudan. In fact, I smiled so widely that all my teeth were exposed. Fortunately there was no one around who objected or who took a count.

The force of the emotion I felt at being a Saudi Arabian once again was greater than I could have imagined. I quickly made plans to return to the land of my birth. To the land I loved.

Arriving in Jeddah was the best moment. I had not seen the city of my childhood for eight long years. I relished everything, the scenery, the smells, the people. I visited my father's family, who had been instrumental in helping to make my dreams come true. Besides, who else could I turn to, if not to my family?

There was so much I wanted to do, but my first trip was to the holy mosque in Mecca. I thanked God that I had not been tempted by my father's path, that I had been successful in resisting a life of violence, even when I was young and malleable.

After that wonderful experience, I traveled back to Jeddah, enjoying every day as a step toward building my new life. I met many of my bin Laden relatives for the first time, for our father had intentionally kept his children on the perimeter of his father's family.

One of those relatives was Randa Mohammed bin Ladin, my father's half-sister and my dear auntie, who was a few years younger than my mother. Not holding my association with my father against me, Auntie Randa took me under her protective wing.

This auntie was one of the smartest ladies I've ever known, and had accomplished so much with her life. She was not only the first woman in Saudi Arabia to obtain a license to fly an airplane, but had gone on to become a medical doctor, taking care of family members when they were ill.

For some reason, my auntie took a big interest in my life. Although my bin Ladin relatives had given me a menial job, she said that in order to achieve any success, I must go back to school. She was so serious about it that she telephoned the Ministry of Education and arranged for me to go in for an interview. I told her that I would, although I was not certain that I could carry it through. School days triggered such terrible memories.

For years I had carried around a seething anger at the teachers at the Obaiy bin Kahab School in Jeddah, particularly one who was so cruel that he had no business working with young children. I decided to return to that school to confront the man. He had beaten me repeatedly, and I thought perhaps I might lure him from the school and cane him, to teach him what it felt like.

The humiliations there had been so great that when I walked up to the entry of the school, I suffered a rush of dread throughout my body. Although I was nineteen years old and had finally grown to be a big, strong man, I felt as if I were a helpless child.

But I would not let it stop me from telling that cruel teacher what I thought of him. To my disappointment, I soon learned that he had retired years before. No one would tell me where he lived; in fact, I could not locate any of the teachers who had mistreated my brothers and me. Realizing that revenge was going to be impossible, I stormed away.

That school made me think more seriously about the appointment my Auntie

Randa had made. I had to admit that I was uneducated. My father had interrupted our formal schooling, except for religious instruction, when I was only twelve years old. While religious schooling was important, I knew that formal education would be a requirement for a good career in business. And I had noticed that my bin Ladin cousins were highly educated and knowledgeable of so many things of which I was unaware. It bothered me that I felt less prepared for life than my cousins.

I decided to follow my Auntie Randa's recommendation.

On my way to the appointment at the Education Ministry, I became confused, because there were so many big buildings in the area, and I ended up in a building that housed several television companies. Unaware that I was in the wrong place, I walked around, checking the doors for the name of the education department.

A security officer became suspicious and asked to see my identification. Thinking nothing of it, I presented my ID. Well, the sight of my name caused the man to go into a frenzy. When I admitted that I was the son of Osama bin Laden, he arrested me!

I was taken to the Haras al-Watani, which is an office for the Saudi army, and put into a small room to be interrogated.

Two men arrived, with one talking over the other, asking why I was in the television offices, where was I going, and why was I going there. The security officer who had arrested me began lying, telling the army officer that he had realized I was up to no good when he saw me surveying the building in a very suspicious manner. I could see he was already imagining himself receiving an award for stopping a terrorist act!

That's when everyone panicked. I was moved to a more secure place and locked in a cell. I waited there for six hours, not knowing what to do, while people kept walking back to stare at me. Not wanting them to think of me as a troublemaker, I was too embarrassed to ask to call my family.

Finally a general arrived, and I was lucky that he was intelligent. He calmly asked me questions, and I told him the truth, which was simple. I had an appointment at the Education Ministry and had gotten lost. I had no idea I was in the wrong building, and was simply going from office to office, hoping to find the right department.

That kindly general smiled and said, "You don't look like a terrorist to me. I believe you." He stood up and shook my hand, and left to order my release.

The following day I returned to the area to find the correct building. The minister of education was agreeable, and registered me in a school where the students were aged seven to twelve, although there was a separate department for older students like me who had never had the opportunity to finish school.

The day came for my first classes. Never have I been so ashamed. There I was, a man over six feet tall, entering a school where all other students were children. The headmaster made it clear that he didn't like me, demanding, "What are you doing here? You are too old for this school, even the special class. Stand aside." And so he made me stand outside until every child was directed to the proper classroom and seated. Only then was I allowed to enter the school building.

Later that day, when the headmaster discovered that I was the son of Osama bin Laden, his displeasure multiplied.

With every passing day, the headmaster made it more difficult for me to attend school. He made a rule that if I was not seated in my classroom by the starting bell, then I must go home. Yet he ordered me to wait outside until all the other students had entered, often making it impossible for me to get to class on time.

I will say that I was not the only student mistreated. Any student older than twelve years old was clearly unwelcome, despite the fact his was the school with the special classroom for older students!

I told myself, "This is what my father brought me."

I refused to allow that teacher to discourage me. I accepted his humiliations with an impassive face, finishing that difficult year, taking the exams for grade six, passing and receiving my diploma.

After that, I left school for good, realizing that the teachers in Saudi Arabia would never allow me to graduate. I was too old, too big, and I was the son of Osama bin Laden.

I would have to work my way up in the business without a formal education.

Then came October 12, 2000, and the attack on the U.S. ship USS *Cole* at the Aden harbor in Yemen. While the *Cole* was waiting to be refueled, a small boat approached, with the men on board pretending to be friendly fishermen, waving at the American sailors on the boat, who started waving back. When the boat reached the port side, a huge explosion occurred, killing seventeen sailors and wounding thirty-nine others.

I felt a wave of nausea. Was my father celebrating, as he had after the bombings in Africa? Of course, I had no way of knowing the full truth, no more than any other ordinary Saudi citizen. I was no longer on the inside looking out, but was on the outside looking in. In truth, I preferred my new viewpoint, although I never stopped worrying over my mother and siblings.

Before too many days had passed, international news reports were saying that my father's al-Qaeda organization was behind the *Cole* bombing. Was this the big attack Abu Haadi had warned me about? Instinct told me it was not, for despite the damage done and the lives lost, the *Cole* attack was much less destructive than the American embassy bombings. Abu Haadi's words had implied that the coming attack would be so gigantic that few could imagine it.

My nerves were shattered, and there was no one with whom to share my worries. My father's family in Saudi Arabia had an unspoken agreement not to speak about such awkward matters as my father and his activities. Even my full brother Abdullah rarely spoke our father's name. My half-brother Ali was living in Mecca with his mother, but Ali and I had little to say to each other. Our childhood memories were so painful we had no desire to revisit those days.

So I agonized in private, with Abu Haadi's words ringing in my ears, yet hoping that the big event my friend had warned me of would never occur.

During December 2000, my Grandmother Allia and her family received an invitation to travel to Afghanistan for my brother Mohammed's wedding. She was excited about seeing her eldest son.

Not surprisingly, I did not receive an invitation. I was amazed, however, to hear that my young brother Mohammed was going to marry the daughter of Abu Hafs; to me, both the bride and the groom were still children.

My younger brother's wedding also brought my own unmarried status to mind.

When my grandmother returned from the wedding, she summoned me to her home. I was eager to hear the details of family life in Afghanistan, and although she told me little, she did reveal that the wedding was one of the grandest, and that Mohammed was the happiest groom. She reported that all members of my family were doing well, which brought me a nice feeling of relief.

Then my grandmother surprised me by saying, "Omar. Your father is very angry with you for leaving Afghanistan. He commands you to return."

Dazed and startled, I asked for further details. "Why is he angry? He was not angry with Abdullah for returning to Saudi Arabia. Why is he angry at me?"

She would only say, "I do not know the reason for my son's anger. He is your father. Go back, Omar, go back and find out. Your father commands it."

The unexpected message plunged me into turmoil. No son could ignore such a direct command from his father, but what had happened to cause him to issue the order?

I thought about many possibilities. Perhaps the command had something to do with my friend Abu Haadi. Had my father called a special investigation as to why I failed to return from Syria? Had someone discovered that Abu Haadi had warned me of a secret mission? Although Abu Haadi had refused to say more than that I should run away, even that information could get him into such serious trouble that he might be executed for treason.

Had my father asked my mother to reveal our conversations? While my mother would never volunteer information about me, should my father ask a direct question, my mother would never lie to him.

After a week of vacillating, I decided to do something I said I would never do: return to Afghanistan.

But the trip would be brief. Quickly in, and quickly out.

The journey was so fraught with difficulties that I nearly turned around at the Afghan border. As I waited three weeks to make travel arrangements, I almost convinced myself to forgo the journey. Why should my father have any influence over me? Our heart ties had been cut long before. Yet I felt myself pulled against my will.

Perhaps our final goodbye was not final enough.

After the most grueling trip, my eyes once more saw our Kandahar compound.

My mother and siblings leapt with pure joy at my return, wrongly believing that I was back to stay. I pulled my mother aside and told her, "My mother, Grandmother told me that my father had ordered me to return. Do you know anything of this?"

She shook her head. "I have not heard of this command."

After a nice visit, I went to look for my father. Because of my grandmother's words, I dreaded a dramatic scene.

I looked for a day or two and could not locate him.

Finally, I spotted him going in to wash for prayer. I walked rapidly, not wanting to miss him. "Father," I said, "I have returned. Grandmother told me that you must see me."

"My son," he replied with an unexpected smile, "there was no need for you to return. You took a dangerous risk for nothing."

My father turned away and washed his face, hands, and feet, before entering the mosque to say his prayers.

I stood in shock. What had just happened? I had traveled a long distance, over the most dangerous roads, for nothing? Surely my grandmother would not have relayed such a message unless my father had given it to her.

I shook my head, puzzled. I walked away, looking for my friend Abu Haadi.

He was not overjoyed to see me. "Omar! What are you doing in Kandahar?"

I told my friend about my grandmother's message and my father's reaction.

Abu Haadi thought for a few minutes, looked around to make certain we were alone, then whispered, "You know your father, Omar. When your grandmother was here for the wedding, your father probably missed you, thinking that he was losing too many of his sons. He most likely had a moment of anger, and expressed his annoyance. By the time you got the message and returned, many other things had come to his mind and his anger was long forgotten."

Abu Haadi's explanation was as good as any other, I supposed.

That's when Abu Haadi turned back to his original warning. "Omar, don't think of staying here. Go back to your new life. The big plan is still ongoing. It will happen. You need to be far, far away. It is my belief that many of us will die."

Once again my friend used his hand to explain. "Remember, Omar, past missions were this size," and he held his hand low to the ground. "The new mission is this size," and he held his hand as high as he could, over his head.

I was convinced. "But my mother?" I reminded him.

"Try again to convince her to leave. I do not know when the big event will occur, but I believe the time is drawing near."

I believed Abu Haadi: I must leave, and this time for good.

I did remain for a few weeks, speaking seriously to my mother. This time we did not have a pregnancy on which to hang our appeal. Yet I told her, "My mother, if you cannot leave with me, you must leave soon. Please ask my father for permission. Perhaps he will give it to you."

For the first time my mother's eyes reflected concern. I hoped my warning had penetrated her naive perspective that everything in life would turn out well.

I wanted to see my father one last time, to have a final word with him, to plead with him to send my mother and her children away, but my father was always going or coming. Never was there an opportunity to get close, to have a private conversation. I had never seen my father so occupied, both with visitors and with his own men, even during that very busy summer in 1998 leading up to the bombings in Africa.

I wondered if my father was so industrious because he was in the planning stages of the big event Abu Haadi feared.

I said a final goodbye to Abu Haadi. That hardened warrior had wet eyes as he told me, "Omar, we will not meet on this earth again, but I will see you in paradise."

The most difficult leave-taking came when I bid farewell to my mother and siblings, struggling with a sinking feeling in my heart that I might never see any of them ever again.

When I left my mother, I told her for a final time, "Please leave this place, my mother. Come back to real life."

Chapter 29

Leaving Afghanistan Forever

NAJWA BIN LADEN

My son's visit had renewed my worries. All I could think about were his words of warning. For the first time, I felt that Omar had been speaking a truth, that it was best for me to leave Afghanistan. In fact, for the first time during my marriage to Osama, I wanted to take my children and return to my family home in Syria. Yet I was not brave enough to approach my husband.

I found myself thinking about leaving all the time, becoming obsessed with the idea that I must get out of Afghanistan. However, I did not want to leave without my children, at least my children who were unwed. That would be Abdul Rahman, and my four youngest, Iman, Ladin, Rukhaiya, and Nour.

Osman had recently married a daughter of the one of the fighters, so I had four children, Sa'ad, Osman, Mohammed, and Fatima, who were bound with their spouses to Afghanistan. I knew that they would not go with me.

I fretted until I was exhausted. Omar's worries became my worries. With this worry ballooning into a huge fear, I finally realized that I would be happier if I at least made an effort. If Osama said no, then there was nothing to do, and I would accept whatever God sent my way. If Osama said yes, then I would take it as a sign that I should go.

The hot summer passed from us in August, and that is when a good time arrived for me to approach my husband. Not wanting to lose my nerve, I asked without hesitation, "Osama, can I go to Syria?"

Osama did not move. He stared at me, thinking. During all the years of our marriage, Osama had always said that any of his wives were free to leave anytime they felt the desire to do so. He said, "You want to go, Najwa?"

"Yes, my husband. I want to go to Syria, to my mother's house."

My husband and I did not speak of divorce, because that was not what I was asking. I only wanted to go to Syria, with my youngest children.

Osama said, "Are you sure you want to go, Najwa?"

"I want to go to Syria."

He nodded, his expression a bit sad. He said, "Yes, Najwa. Yes, you can leave."

"Can our children leave with me?"

"You can take Abdul Rahman, Rukhaiya, and Nour."

"And Iman? And Ladin?"

"No. Iman and Ladin cannot go. They belong with their father."

I nodded, knowing that I would be unable to change Osama's mind on those two, but why, I will never know, for both were very young.

"All right. I will take Abdul Rahman, Rukhaiya, and Nour."

Osama said, "I will arrange it. You will leave in a few weeks." Then my husband turned and walked from the door, as though we were discussing the most mundane matters.

Doubts stirred. Perhaps Omar was wrong. Perhaps there was no reason for me to go away.

Osama saw me several times before I left. He took a special occasion to tell me, as he had when I had gone to Syria to give birth to Nour, "I will never divorce you, Najwa. Even if you hear I have divorced you, it is not true."

I nodded, believing my husband. I knew that our family ties would ensure Osama's loyalty. Besides, I was not seeking a divorce.

In fact, on the morning I was leaving, I presented my husband with a round ring, a token of our years together. Osama had always been in my life, my cousin before he was my groom, my groom before he was the father of my children.

Early in September 2001, my son Osman drove me out of Afghanistan and far, far away from my sons Sa'ad, Mohammed, and Ladin and my daughters Fatima and Iman. My mother's heart broke into little pieces watching the figures of my little children fade, fade away.

But I did save Abdul Rahman, four-year-old Rukhaiya, and two-year-old Nour.

For that entire journey across the rough terrain of Afghanistan, I never stopped praying that everything of the world could be peaceful, that all lives might return to normal. I believe that wish is universal for every woman who is a mother.

For all the horrible happenings that have occurred since I left Afghanistan, I can only think and feel with my mother's heart. For every child lost, a mother's heart harbors the deepest pain. None can see our sons grow to men. None can see our daughters become mothers. No longer can we see the smiles on their faces, or wipe away their tears. My mother's heart feels the pain of every loss, weeping not only for my children, but for the lost children of every mother.

Chapter 30

September 11, 2001

OMAR BIN LADEN

A weird wail, followed by an excited voice, woke me from a deep sleep. I was at my grandmother's home in Jeddah when my uncle came crashing into my room, his voice high, his words confusing. "Look what my brother has done! Look what my brother has done! He has ruined all our lives! He has destroyed us!"

He continued to shout, "Come quickly! Come and see what my brother has done! See what your father has done!"

I dressed hurriedly and followed him into a room with a television screen. I saw flames belching from tall buildings. I had no idea what I was looking at.

I knew soon enough, however: America was under a serious attack.

The words and the images were too horrific to comprehend. Although my uncle had expressed his worst fears, none of us could truly believe that someone we knew, someone we had loved, had anything to do with the catastrophic events we were watching.

Despite Abu Haadi's warnings, it seemed impossible for my father to be the one responsible for the chaos and death going on in America. The attack I was seeing was far too vast, something that only another superpower could organize. This was far bigger than my memory of Abu Haadi's words and gestures, first holding his hand only a few inches from the ground, telling me, "Omar, this is how big the Embassy bombings were" then, raising his hand as high as he could reach, "This is how big the next mission will be."

Was this the mission? Surely not!

Then I remembered a surreal moment. The night before, I had received a surprise telephone call from my mother, saying that she had taken my advice and had built her courage to ask my father for permission to leave. She had left

Afghanistan and was now in Syria. She had her two babies with her, along with Abdul Rahman. Her other children had been left behind in Afghanistan.

"Ladin?" I asked.

My mother paused, then said, "He is with his father."

That little boy's plight tugged at my heart.

In light of the current calamity, the implications of my father allowing her to leave struck me like a big stone. Had he let her go only because he knew what was coming?

After seeing the New York towers, I called my mother, to learn that she was watching the television from Syria. But she was too distraught to have a normal conversation. The phone call was brief.

The members of the huge bin Laden family reacted in the same way as my mother. Everyone shut down. No one spoke of the incident. My uncle never again addressed the possibility that my father was behind the attacks. My grandmother refused to consider the idea that her son had anything to do with the burning buildings.

I, too, fed my own uncertainties with a million reasons why he could not have done this terrible deed. I did not want my father to be the one responsible.

Only much later, when he took personal credit for the attacks, did I know I must give up the luxury of doubt. That was the moment to set aside the dream that I had indulged, feverishly hoping that the world was wrong and it was not my father who brought about that horrible day. After hearing an audiotape of my father's own words taking credit for the attacks, I faced the reality that he was the perpetrator behind the events of September 11, 2001.

This knowledge drives me into the blackest hole.

Everyone knew that the American president, George W. Bush, would not let the day go unanswered. We were waiting and wondering as to when the mighty American military would send their response. Truthfully, I lived in dread, thinking of my younger siblings and the horror they would experience beneath those massive American bombs.

No one in the family heard from my father, although in the past he had always managed to make contact when he wanted to.

Everyone in our bin Laden family became so subdued that we rarely spoke about any topic. Each was lost in his or her thoughts.

Finally, the suspense was over when the United States started their attack. On October 7, 2001, the Americans retaliated in the most massive bombing attacks anyone in that country had ever seen, which continued all through October and into November.

Thousands of people in Afghanistan were dead. People were running for the borders, desperate to escape the bombings. Several of the Arab newscasters carried reports of the dead fighters because many were Arabs. I saw the image of Abu Hafs and heard that a bomb had demolished his home. Supposedly many people died along with him. I wondered if my brother Mohammed and his young wife were among those dead.

Later I saw a fuzzy image of Abu Haadi flash across the television screen. He, too, was dead. My thoughts kept drifting back to the day that Abu Haadi said that I should leave, or I would die with him. He had been right; he was dead, and I was alive. I remembered that he had prepared his burial shroud, and kept it handy. I wondered if anyone had had time to wrap him in it for the burial.

I could discover nothing about my brothers and sisters, although there were constant reports of sightings of my tall father. Knowing that Osman was the same height, I wondered if the satellites were picking up images of my younger brother.

Supposedly, my father had returned to Tora Bora, to the mountain where he felt most at home. He would be hard to find there, I knew. No one knew those mountains like my father. I remembered that he recognized all the big boulders, knowing exactly the distance from one to the other. I heard reports that my father had sent his wives and children to Pakistan, and that he had followed.

I will forever be haunted by the image of poor Ladin. My baby brother was the most nervous and easily frightened of all the children in our family. He had recently turned eight years old, too young to be without his mother. Was Ladin scrambling over those huge boulders and hidden paths I had maneuvered so long ago when my father forced me to hike to Pakistan? My greatest anger was reserved for my father for forbidding Iman and Ladin to leave with their mother.

Much time has passed since those awful moments. I have experienced many disappointments and I have known joy. Some people have tried to harm me, and those I will not name, while others have graciously offered a helping hand, including my bin Laden relatives, my mother's relatives in Syria, the Egyptian government, led by President Hosni Mubarak, Sheik Hamad bin Khalifa al-Thani, the emir of Qatar, and King Abdullah bin Abdul Aziz al-Saud, the king of Saudi Arabia.

My mother is alive and well. She wants to say a special thanks to all the people who have helped her since she returned to Syria. She wants to thank her family, my father's family, and most importantly, the Syrian government headed by President Bashar al-Assad. President al-Assad and his family have been gracious and kind to her and her children. My mother is very busy caring for her young daughters.

During these years of loss and sorrow, I have had to reconcile myself to the truth about my father, Osama bin Laden. I know now that since the first day of the first battle against the Soviets in Afghanistan, my father has been killing other humans. He admitted as much to me, back in those days when I was his tea boy in Afghanistan. I often wonder if my father has killed so many times that the act of killing no longer brings him pleasure or pain.

I am nothing like my father. While he prays for war, I pray for peace.

And now we go our separate ways, each believing that we are right.

My father has made his choice, and I have made mine.

I am, at last, my own man.

I can live with that.

Final Comments

JEAN SASSON

As a writer who mainly focuses on stories about the lives of women who have lived through dramatic, even dangerous, times, I frequently receive inquiries from men and women who hope I might bring their stories to the attention of the world. On rare occasions I find myself immediately intrigued.

This was the case during the spring of 2008 when I saw an e-mail sent through one of my publishers' Web sites claiming to be from a member of the Osama bin Laden family. Omar bin Laden was the fourth-born son of Osama bin Laden, the notorious al-Qaeda leader who had finally admitted his role in the September 11, 2001, attacks upon the United States. Omar said that he wanted me to reveal his personal story, to tell the world his experiences of growing up as the son of Osama bin Laden.

Truthfully, my initial reaction was not positive. The images of 9/11 created such horror in my heart that I could barely think of Osama bin Laden without anger. But out of curiosity, I placed a telephone call to Egypt to speak with his son Omar.

I quickly learned that Omar's childhood had been miserable. Soon after our first conversation, I began to search the Internet for information on Omar. Despite my empathy for any child of a ruthless father, my initial discoveries were not encouraging. This son of bin Laden was making headlines for two reasons. First, the media was most interested that he had married a woman nearly twice his age. The British tabloids were frenzied by this bit of unusual news, unsympathetically taunting the couple.

Secondly, and more interesting, Omar was pitting himself against his father. The son of a man who routinely called for death for non-Muslims was bravely promoting peace and not violence. This was a big surprise. From my knowledge of Saudi men, sons *never* speak out against their fathers. I have personally witnessed high-ranking royal princes tremble in anticipation of the arrival of their aging fathers. Saudis highly honor their fathers, a wonderful aspect of the Saudi culture, at least in most cases.

Omar's call for peace even as his father called for violence caused me to reconsider my initial inclination to refuse the writing project. My curiosity increased. What kind of father and husband had Osama bin Laden been? Had he loved his wives and children? If so, how could he not consider the effects of his reprehensible conduct on his innocent children? Indeed, after several more telephone conversations, I made many surprising discoveries about the private life of Osama bin Laden and his family.

Omar had been a young boy of ten when his family had been forced to flee Saudi Arabia. He was a teenager when the family was told to leave Sudan. From there the family traveled to live in war-torn Afghanistan, then ruled by the brutal Taliban. Due to his father's activities, Omar had lived an isolated life without the opportunity for an education. For years he was unable to visit his extended family.

Omar seemed a natural peacemaker, yet he had no choice but to grow up around terrorist training camps. He had been forced to abandon his beloved horses each time the family had to flee. He had watched his beloved mother endure pregnancy after pregnancy while living in increasingly primitive environments. On three or four occasions, Omar had nearly lost his own life. He had been separated from his brothers and sisters, whom he loved dearly, leaving six siblings behind in Afghanistan.

The questions in my mind continued to fester. Had Osama's sons been forced to participate in fighting? Had his young daughters been married against their will? Was Osama bin Laden cruel, or kind, to his wives and children? What *really* went on in the Osama bin Laden household?

Certainly, Osama bin Laden had always been extremely private about his personal life. Suddenly here was an opportunity for the world to discover the unknown truth about a man who had lost the right to maintain that privacy.

I discovered that no books written about Osama bin Laden or his family had the cooperation of a single bin Laden family member. Although Carmen bin Ladin's book, *Inside the Kingdom: My Life in Saudi Arabia*, was a wonderful read, Carmen had married into the family. Her best-selling and very interesting story was more of a personal account of life in Saudi Arabia and her ongoing divorce dispute with Osama's half-brother.

Steve Coll's highly praised book, *The Bin Ladens*, was meticulously researched and well written, yet the author received no cooperation from any primary bin Laden source. As the author himself puts it, "In response to numerous requests for interviews over a three-year period, bin Laden family members offered only very limited cooperation, other than those in Yemen; senior family members based in Jeddah granted no extensive or substantive interviews . . . Nonetheless, after the manuscript was substantially drafted, Julie Tate and I attempted to fact-check material about living bin Ladens with family representatives. Through their lawyers, the family declined to respond to the great majority of written questions submitted."

I soon learned that Omar's mother was Osama's first cousin and first wife. In fact, the couple had never divorced, although Najwa was no longer living with her husband. I was surprised to receive a letter from Najwa, telling me about Omar. Her letter touched my heart, for I realized the effort it took for her to write a letter to an American woman whom she did not know. I had learned through Omar that his mother was a highly conservative Muslim woman who had always lived in seclusion. Such a woman does not easily reach out to a westerner.

But Najwa was a mother proud of her sensitive son, revealing sweet little stories about Omar's character and life. As I read Najwa's letter, I felt compelled to ask Omar if his mother would agree to her story being told as well.

Much to my surprise, Najwa agreed, but only because her son asked her to participate. Najwa had no desire to attack Osama through this book. In fact, there were limits to the topics she agreed to discuss. As a woman who had led her married life in total isolation, she was not privy to accounts of war, or of her husband's participation in Jihad. Yet I knew that others would share my fascination to learn what life was like for the first and most important wife of Osama bin Laden.

Suddenly I was struck with the thought that Omar's story would be the first book by a *real* bin Laden. It would be the only story to tell the truth of life in the home of the infamous terrorist.

I spoke with Omar several more times, asking Omar's true feelings about his father's activities and the deaths of innocent people. I did not want to participate in the book if Omar believed that his father had valid reasons for his murderous behavior. I was concerned, too, when I read a number of Internet articles in which Omar seemed inconsistent about his father's cruel actions. Indeed, while Omar proclaimed his hatred of violence, for a long time he seemed unable to accept as true that his father had been the man responsible for 9/11 and other despicable acts of violence. Then I reminded myself that most people would find it difficult to believe that someone they loved could be capable of terrorism.

The fact that a son could not fathom his own father ordering the deaths of innocent civilians was easy to comprehend. Moreover, conspiracy theories dominate public opinion in much of the Arab world. Much of the convincing evidence of Osama bin Laden's participation in 9/11 came from the American government, a government hated by most of the Arab world. In fact, few Arabs believe any reports that originate in Washington, London, Berlin, or Paris.

After Osama bin Laden released various audiotapes and videotapes, some taking responsibility for 9/11 and other violent acts, Omar finally admitted that it appeared his father had indeed ordered the attacks. Omar seemed understandably shell-shocked by some of his father's recordings. As much as he had wanted to believe the best of his father, he could no longer cling to the hope that his father was not guilty.

After learning many details about Osama bin Laden, his family, and the al-Qaeda commanders and soldiers who were an ever-increasing presence as Omar was growing up, my heart told me that this was an important story that should be told. I believe we should demand to know everything about the man behind the death of so many innocents, and it would be impossible to get any closer to the private world of Osama bin Laden than through his first wife and his fourth-born son.

When we look back, it becomes clear that the acts and accomplishments of human beings are the signatures of history. Human signatures have created an enormous chasm between the joyeous light of the age of the Renaissance to the dark shadow of September 11, 2001. Those of us living on that fateful day experienced the lower depths of mankind. As an author, avid reader, world traveler, and person of enormous curiosity, my life experiences have taught me that discord often erupts from a lack of knowledge and education. To discourage future dark moments, I believe we must nourish the minds of our young with learning that creates understanding between ethnic and religious groups. Perhaps understanding will lead to a marvelous day when we take a last fleeting look at violence so harmful to so many. I sincerely believe that nothing will further the cause of peace more than the education of our young. I would like for readers to know that a percentage of the profits from the sale of this book will be devoted to the cause of education.

May all roads lead to peace.

—*JEAN SASSON*

Postscript

Since the first publication of this book in late 2009, there have been many surprises. The first was its initial reception by the media. Omar, Najwa, and I were astonished when several reviewers questioned whether Osama's wife and son had participated in the writing of the book. Fortunately, once Omar had sat for various interviews, confirming that indeed he and his mother had revealed the stories of their lives to this author, any doubts about the authenticity of this book were laid to rest.

Despite much drama, nothing has been more exciting or important than the welcome news about lost members of the family, children Najwa has pined for since she left them behind in Afghanistan in 2001. Shortly after this book was published, Najwa, Omar, and other bin Laden family members received surprising telephone calls from Tehran, Iran. Osman bin Laden, Najwa and Osama's fifth child, was the caller. Everyone was stunned and overjoyed to discover from Osman that several family members they had not heard from for almost a decade had been living in Iran since late 2001. A delighted Najwa learned that the following children and other relatives were alive and well in Tehran: Osman, who at the age of twenty-six now has two wives and three children; twenty-four-year-old Mohammed, whose wedding had been videotaped and shown around the world, was also living with his wife and three children in Iran. Najwa's greatly cherished eldest daughter, twenty-two year-old Fatima, whose first husband, Mohammed, had perished in October 2001, is alive. Fatima has since remarried and has a daughter whom she named after her mother, Najwa. Najwa was overcome with relief to learn that her youngest son, Ladin (Bakr), and his sister Iman had also survived. Readers will recall Najwa and Omar's devastation when Osama refused permission for seven-year-old Ladin or eleven-year-old Iman to leave Afghanistan with their mother. Questions were also raised about thirty-year-old Sa'ad. In 2009, it was widely reported that he had been killed by an American drone, but since then there have been accounts from family members that suggested he was living with his wife and three children in Iran. As of this date, news is still unconfirmed regarding Sa'ad.

Other family members, along with Najwa's children, were heard of, including Osama's third wife, Khairiah, and her son, Hamza. Hamza, now twenty years old, is also married with two children.

A compelling question one might ask is how had the family ended up in Iran. When Najwa departed on September 9, 2001, they were still living at the military compound in Kandahar, Afghanistan. Some details remain unclear because phone calls are necessarily brief, but this is the account they shared with Najwa and Omar.

After September 11, 2001, Osama bin Laden callously abandoned his family in Kandahar and fled to safety in the Tora Bora mountains. Left to fend for themselves, the family formed a group with other followers of Osama and fled across the border into Pakistan. Once in Pakistan, the men of the family concluded that after 9/11 relatives of Osama would not be safe in either Afghanistan or Pakistan, and a decision was made to cross the border into Iran. They traveled on foot, and the journey took many weeks. Once at the Iranian border, they presented their Sudanese passports, the same passports that the government of Sudan had given Osama and his family when the Saudi government revoked their original passports in 1994. Osama had changed the names of his family at that time; therefore, the Iranian officials had no idea that they were admitting one of Osama's wives and a large number of his children and grandchildren into the country. At that time, hundreds of Afghan refugees were flooding over the border into Iran, and the family was taken with the other refugees to guarded compounds set up by the Iranian government. Osman reported that, while the family had been treated with generosity and courtesy, the time passed slowly. Government officials provided all the refugees with food and clothing, and on occasion refugees would be escorted to the souk to shop for necessities. However, it was not long before the refugees became extremely restless, with Najwa's children desperate to be reunited with their mother.

To this end, Iman and Ladin devised an escape plan, both agreeing that a female might have the best chance of success. While on a shopping trip, Iman slipped away from the family and ran through the streets of Tehran, pleading with a kindly faced man to take her to the Saudi embassy. When Iman arrived at the embassy, she informed Saudi government officials of her identity. The startled officials allowed a phone call to Najwa. Iman remained at the Saudi embassy in Tehran while Najwa and Omar talked to many Iranian and Saudi officials about the family and how to secure their passage out of the country. In a surprising move, the Iranian government booked sixteen-year-old Ladin on a flight to Syria. The teenager arrived unexpectedly at his mother's home in Syria, and they were finally reunited after a separation of almost nine frightening years. Now desperate to see her young daughter Iman, Najwa was invited to travel to Iran to collect her. Their reunion brought boundless joy.

A few months later, Mohammed and his wife and children joined Najwa in Syria, bringing hope that perhaps Najwa might one day be reunited with all her children.

At the time of this update, Najwa is living in Syria with six of her eleven children, including sons: Abdul Rahman, Ladin, Mohammed, and daughters: Iman, Rukhaiya, and Nour. All of her eleven children are accounted for other than Sa'ad, who may or may not be with the family in Iran. Omar, Najwa, and other family members continue to work tirelessly to find a country that might extend an invitation for the remaining family members to permanently settle. At that time, Najwa can be reunited with Osman and eldest daughter Fatima, and their children and, hopefully, with Sa'ad.

Belief in innocence and hope for justice are alive in my writer's heart. While I pray for justice for the victims of terrorism all over the world, it is my belief that the wives and children of Osama bin Laden are innocent of any wrongdoing. It is my hope that the world agrees that no innocent person should be punished for acts they did not commit.

Most amazingly to this author, Osama bin Laden failed to produce a single son who embraced his belief that violence is the answer to disagreements between governments or individuals. And so, may these women and children live peacefully in the world, becoming a force for good despite the efforts of Osama bin Laden to persuade his family to embrace evil.

—*Jean Sasson*
(2010)

Appendix A

Osama bin Laden's Family:
Who Were They? What Happened to Them?

A note about the spelling of the family name: According to Omar bin Laden, his father's name is routinely misspelled, and "Ossama Binladen" is correct. For the sake of ease, however, the decision was made to use the preferred spelling adopted by most of the world's publications, which is Osama bin Laden.

Osama bin Laden's Parents

ALLIA GHANEM

Osama's mother, Allia, was born in 1943 in Latakia, Syria. After marriage to Mohammed bin Laden in 1956, she moved to Saudi Arabia, where their only child, Osama, was born in Riyadh on February 15, 1957. When Osama was only a year old, Allia became pregnant a second time, but lost the child after a freak accident when she was injured by a faulty wringer-washer machine. Shortly after the miscarriage, Allia asked her husband for a divorce, which was granted. Living in a world where divorced women cannot live alone, Allia married for a second time, to Muhammad al-Attas, a kindly man and respected employee of her former husband's rapidly expanding construction company.

Allia and Muhammad al-Attas became the parents of four children, three sons and a daughter. Osama lived with his mother, stepfather, and four siblings in the Mushraf neighborhood of Jeddah, Saudi Arabia, where he grew up, and where he brought his first cousin and first bride, Najwa.

It is said that Allia, a loving mother, cannot accept the fact her son was involved in the September 11, 2001, attacks. Up until early 2009, Allia and Muhammad resided in the same villa where Osama grew up.

MUHAMMAD AL-ATTAS

Osama's stepfather is of an old Jeddah merchant family. Omar says that his step-grandfather is a gentle and kind man, loved and respected by all who know him, including his stepson, Osama.

MOHAMMED BIN LADEN

Although there are no official birth records, it is believed that Osama bin Laden's father was born between 1906 and 1908 in Rubat, Hadramaut, located in southeastern Yemen. After Mohammed's father died unexpectedly, he traveled with his younger brother, Abdullah, to seek employment outside Yemen. After a series of misadventures, the two brothers settled in Saudi Arabia, where Mohammed won the trust of the first king of Saudi Arabia, Abdul Aziz al-Saud, for his work on various construction projects. With the backing of the king, Mohammed soon formed the Saudi bin Laden Group, which grew to be one of the largest companies in Saudi Arabia. Later the company spread into other countries in the region. The increasingly prosperous Mohammed bin Laden married many women and became the father of numerous children, twenty-two sons and thirty-three daughters. Omar says that his father is the eighteenth of the twenty-two sons. Mohammed bin Laden died in 1967 as a result of injuries sustained in an airplane crash.

Wives

NAJWA GHANEM, MARRIED IN 1974

Najwa Ghanem was born in 1958 in Latakia, Syria, to Ibrahim and Nabeeha. Ibrahim married five times before marrying Nabeeha, but his were monogamous marriages. He had only one son from his previous marriages, a boy named Ali. Nabeeha was his sixth and final wife. Ibrahim and Nabeeha were the parents of five children, born in this order: Naji, Najwa, Nabeel, Ahmed, and Leila. Najwa married her seventeen-year-old cousin Osama in 1974 when she was fifteen. After four or five months, Osama, Allia, and Muhammad al-

Attas traveled to Syria to escort Najwa to her new home in Jeddah, Saudi Arabia. Ibrahim went with his daughter and remained in Jeddah for a visit.

Najwa and Osama became the parents of eleven children. Najwa moved with her husband from Saudi Arabia to Sudan, and then to Afghanistan. Between September 7 and 9, 2001, Najwa left Afghanistan for good.

For years, Najwa was haunted by the unknown fate of her children left behind in Kandahar. Najwa enjoyed unexpected surprises in late 2009 and early 2010 when her missing children contacted her from a compound in Tehran, Iran. While she was sad to learn that after she departed Afghanistan on September 9, 2001, that her husband Osama abandoned her children along with the two wives remaining behind, as well as their children, she was jubilant to learn that most of the children were together. After Osama ran away, leaving his young children to an uncertain fate, the children joined adults who fled the compound in Kandahar. After the release of the book about Najwa and Omar's lives, Najwa received a telephone call from Iman who had run away to the Saudi embassy. Later, after Iman's release, Osman, the eldest of her children living in Tehran, was allowed to call his mother. Osman gave few details at the time, other than the remainder of her children other than Sa'ad were living in a compound in Tehran. Additionally, Najwa's sister's wife, Khairiah, and her son, Hamza, were with the group. Over the course of six months, three of Najwa's children were released and joined their mother in Syria. Those children were Iman, Ladin, and Mohammed. At the time of this writing, only Osman and Fatima remain in Tehran, and it is hoped that they will soon join their mother in Syria. Najwa's third son, Sa'd, is still missing.

KHADIJAH SHARIF, MARRIED IN 1983

Nine years older than her ex-husband, Osama, Khadijah is from a family descended from the Prophet. A highly educated woman, she had worked as a teacher before marrying Osama bin Laden. After giving birth to three children, and while living in Sudan, she divorced her husband and returned to live in Saudi Arabia where she still lives. Her eldest son, Ali, is in prison in Saudi Arabia, having been sentenced to fifteen years for allegedly possessing an illegal weapon.

KHAIRIAH SABAR, MARRIED IN 1985

Khairiah's family is also descended from the Prophet. Educated to teach deaf-mute children, Khairiah became Osama's third wife after Najwa arranged the marriage. The mother of one son, Hamza, Khairiah remained in Afghanistan with her husband after the events of September 11, 2001. It is now known that Khairiah and her son, Hamza, survived the American bombing of Afghanistan after 9/11 and escaped with Najwa's children to Iran. Both are now living in a compound in Tehran, and both have hopes they will soon depart to live in another Middle Eastern country.

SIHAM SABAR, MARRIED IN 1987

Siham's family is also descended from the Prophet. She is Osama's fourth wife and the mother of four children. She remained in Afghanistan with her husband and children after the events of September 11, 2001. Najwa's children have reported that Siham and her children survived the United States retaliatory strikes that followed 9/11. Their information is that Siham and her children are living in Pakistan.

FIFTH MARRIAGE (ANNULLED)

Osama's fifth marriage was held in Khartoum, Sudan, shortly after his second wife divorced him and returned to Saudi Arabia. However, according to Najwa bin Laden, this fifth marriage remained unconsummated and was annulled within forty-eight hours.

AMAL AL-SADAH, MARRIED IN LATE 2000 OR EARLY 2001

Dismissing the marriage that was annulled, Amal is Osama's fifth wife and bore him one daughter, named Safia. No one knows if Amal and her child returned to Yemen after September 11, 2001, or if they remained in Afghanistan during the American bombings.

Children with First Wife, Najwa Ghanem

ABDULLAH

Najwa's first child and eldest son was born in Jeddah in 1976. As the eldest son, Abdullah held the most honored position of all the children of Osama bin Laden. When he became a teenager, Abdullah began to speak his opinion on matters affecting the family. Abdullah left the family in Khartoum in 1995 when he traveled to Jeddah, Saudi Arabia, to marry his cousin, Tiayba Mohammed bin Laden. Abdullah chose not to return to Khartoum, instead remaining in Jeddah with his wife and children where he operates a small business. Abdullah lives a quiet life, shunning all publicity, although he remains close to his mother, Najwa, whom he visits in Syria. Abdullah was thirty-three years old in 2009.

ABDUL RAHMAN

Najwa's second child and second son was born in Jeddah in 1978. According to Omar, his brother Abdul Rahman was an exceptional child who had to face unique personal trials. Abdul Rahman departed Afghanistan with his mother in September 2001. Since that time, Abdul Rahman has been unable to reinstate his Saudi nationality and has found it difficult to find employment or to marry without official papers. A talented horseman, Abdul Rahman lives quietly with his mother and two youngest siblings in Latakia, shunning all publicity like his elder brother. Abdul Rahman was thirty-one years old in 2009.

SA'AD

Najwa's third child and third son was born in Jeddah in 1979. A garrulous child, Sa'ad remained overly talkative even as an adult, often exasperating his brothers and other acquaintances. Osama refused permission for Sa'ad, his Sudanese-born wife, or their son, Osama, to leave Afghanistan with Najwa in 2001. Najwa's children tell her that Sa'ad was detained in Iran with the rest of the family, but that one day during a supervised outing to the shopping bazaar, he ran away. He has never been seen or heard of since that time. There were reports in 2009 that Sa'ad was killed in an American drone air attack, but there is no evidence to support Sa'ad's death. Therefore, Najwa still does not know the fate of her third born son, who would be thirty-one years old in 2010.

OMAR

Najwa's fourth child and fourth son was born in Jeddah in 1981. Omar was the son closest to his mother and the son who most vigorously rebelled against his father and his Jihad. In fact, it has been Omar's dream to counter his father's violent Jihad by organizing a peace movement that will find a better way to solve cultural and religious differences.

After leaving Afghanistan for the final time in 2001, Omar has met many challenges. Although successful in having his Saudi citizenship restored, it has been difficult for Omar to find his place in the business world. Omar married and had one son, Ahmed. When traveling in Egypt, Omar met a British woman. The couple fell in love, bringing his first marriage to an end. Since that time, Omar has become even more passionate in calling for an end to violence, longing for the bin Laden name to become linked with peace rather than with terrorism. Wishing to join his wife to live in the United Kingdom, where he believes he will find it easier to form a peace movement, Omar applied for a routine marriage visa. Problems arose with his visa application, resulting in a determined quest for political asylum. Finally, through the generosity of the government of Qatar, Omar and his wife settled there while waiting for his visa. As of the writing of this book, Omar has returned to Saudi Arabia, the country he most loves.

As of the writing of this book, Omar admits that he suffers from depression. In mid-2010, after a mix-up with his medication, Omar spent one day in a hospital to stabilize his antidepressant drugs. Although he appeared to be rational and lucid, there were tabloid reports that he was suffering from mental illness. Other than chronic depression, Omar has functioned normally. During this same time, Omar made a public statement that he and his second wife, Zaina al-Sabah, are divorced. He is hopeful that they can remain on friendly terms but says that the marriage is over. Omar often visits his mother and siblings in Syria, and travels back and forth to Saudi Arabia. Omar has hopes to make a visit to the United States in 2010 or 2011. He still calls out for peace in the world and hopes that he can do more to foster peace. Omar was twenty-nine years old in 2010.

OSMAN

Najwa's fifth child and fifth son was born in 1983 in Jeddah, Saudi Arabia. In 2001 Osman married the daughter of Egyptian Mohammed Shawky al Islambouli, a high-ranking member of Sheikh Omar Abdel Rahman's al-Gama'a al-Islamiyya group and who was closely affiliated with Osama bin Laden's al-Qaeda group. Osman's father-in-law, along with 107 other defendants, had previously been indicted in 1997 by the Egyptian government in the conspiracy to assassinate President Hosni Mubarak of Egypt, as well as other Egyptian leaders. Al-Islambouli's brother, Khalid, was infamous for being the lead assassin of President Sadat on October 6, 1981. Khalid had shouted, "Death to Pharaoh" as he ran toward Sadat to shoot him. Khalid was arrested and at trial found guilty of the crime and executed the following year, in April 1982.

Osama would not allow Osman or his wife to depart Afghanistan with Najwa. Rumors have circululated that Osman escaped Afghanistan during the October/November 2001 bombings by the American government, along with Dr. Ayman al-Zawahiri, but there is no firm evidence of this. As of this writing, Osman is still living in Tehran, Iran, but has asked to be allowed to leave and live with his family in Syria, or perhaps settle in another Middle Eastern country. Osman was twenty-seven years old in 2010.

MOHAMMED

Najwa's sixth child and sixth son was born in 1985 in Jeddah. Omar reports that Mohammed was his father's second choice for his successor as head of al-Qaeda. (Up until he expressed his disapproval of violence, Omar had been his father's first choice.) Omar also says that of all his brothers, Mohammed is the only brother possessing some of the qualities necessary to assume an important position in his father's organization. After marrying the daughter of Abu Hafs in 2000, Mohammed was the most content of the sons to remain behind with his father. At the time of this writing, Mohammed was allowed to depart Iran and travel to Syria to be with his mother and other siblings. Mohammed and his family are living a very quiet life in Syria. He does not wish to be featured in any media stories, and this author respects his wishes. In 2010, Mohammed was twenty-five years old.

FATIMA

Najwa's seventh child and first daughter was born in Medina in 1987. After Omar suggested a groom, Osama then arranged for the marriage of Fatima to a Saudi fighter named Mohammed in 1999 when Fatima was twelve years old. Her husband was killed in the American attacks of October and November 2001. Najwa now knows that her daughter, Fatima, survived the Afghan bombings after 9/11, escaped to Iran, and has been living there with her siblings. Fatima remarried during her years of exile in Iran, and she has a daughter named after Najwa. Sadly, at the time of this writing, Fatima is still living with her husband and child in Iran, although it is hoped that she can soon see her mother. Fatima was twenty-three years old in 2010.

IMAN

Najwa now knows the fate of her second daughter. Iman traveled with her siblings and others when they escaped Kandahar, and lived in Iran since that time. Iman was a very brave young girl and approached her younger brother Ladin and decided that one of them should attempt an escape. It was decided that Iman had a better chance because she was a young girl who might receive more assistance. Therefore, while the family was on a supervised outing at the shopping bazaar, Iman ran as fast as she could to escape their attendant, running through the streets of Tehran until she saw a man she felt had a kindly demeanor. She approached the man and told him that she was a Saudi and she had to get to the Saudi embassy. That man took her home to his wife and children and there they heard the story before Iman was driven to the Saudi embassy. After Iman's arrival at the embassy, the Saudi authorities allowed her to call her mother in Syria. There was a joyous reunion and plans were made for Iman to return to her mother. Several months passed before the Saudi and Iranian governments agreed to allow Najwa to travel to Iran to meet with her daughter and take her home. Their reunion was a huge celebration between mother and daughter, for they had not known of the other's fate for eight long years. As of this writing, Iman is twenty years old.

LADIN, ALSO KNOWN AS BAKR

Najwa's ninth child and seventh son was born in 1993 in Jeddah when Najwa left Khartoum to fly to Saudi Arabia especially for his birth. Ladin was only seven years old when Najwa left Afghanistan on September 9, 2001. Osama would not allow Najwa to take her youngest son with her.

The story of young Ladin pleading with his mother and brother Omar not to leave him was heartrending. However, as of this writing, Najwa is reunited with her young son. For the past eight years, Ladin was with his siblings in Iran, but after Iman was brave enough to flee their Iranian attendant, Ladin pleaded with Iranian authorities to join his sister and mother. Najwa had no clue what might have happened, but one day at three in the morning, there was a knock on Najwa's apartment in Syria. When the door was opened, Ladin was there, having been released by the Iranians and put on an airplane to join his mother and sister. Happily, Ladin is now living with his mother. Ladin was seventeen years old in 2010.

RUKHAIYA

Najwa's tenth child and third daughter, Rukhaiya was born in Jalalabad, Afghanistan, in 1997. Because of her extreme youth, Osama allowed Najwa to take Rukhaiya with her to Syria in 1999 when she left to give birth to her eleventh child. Najwa was also allowed to take Rukhaiya with her when she left Afghanistan for the final time on September 9, 2001. Rukhaiya is a happy young lady living with her mother and newfound siblings in Syria. She was thirteen years old in 2010.

NOUR

Najwa's eleventh child and fourth daughter was born in Latakia, Syria, in 1999. Osama had granted Najwa's request to take Nour, along with her sister Rukhaiya and one brother, Abdul Rahman, when she left Afghanistan in September 2001. Nour, like her older sister Rukhaiya, is delighted to have met her older siblings. She was a lovely young girl of ten years old in 2010.

Children with Second Wife, Khadijah

ALI

Khadijah's first child and first son with Osama was born in Jeddah, Saudi Arabia. After Khadijah and Osama divorced, Khadijah left Khartoum and returned to live in Saudi Arabia. Ten-year-old Ali accompanied his mother to Saudi Arabia, but returned the following year for one visit to Khartoum to see his father and half-siblings. A few years ago, Ali was arrested by Saudi security and charged with the illegal possession of a weapon. In 2008, after spending years in prison without trial, Ali was sentenced to fifteen years in prison. The family believes Ali to be innocent of any crime. In 2010, Ali was twenty-four years old.

AMER

Khadijah's second child and second son with Osama was born in Jeddah in 1990. When Khadijah left Khartoum to return to Saudi Arabia, Amer went with his mother, never seeing his father again. Today Amer is living in Saudi Arabia. In 2010, Amer was twenty years old.

AISHA

Khadijah's third child and first and only daughter with Osama was born in Khartoum, Sudan, in 1992. In 1993, when Khadijah left Khartoum to return to Saudi Arabia, Aisha went with her mother, never seeing her father again. Today Aisha is living in Saudi Arabia. In 2010, Aisha was sixteen years old.

Child with Third Wife, Khairiah

HAMZA

Khairiah's first child and first son with Osama was born in 1989 in Jeddah, Saudi Arabia. As of 2001, Hamza was Khairiah's only child. Remaining with his mother and father in Afghanistan, it is not known if Hamza survived the American attacks of October and November 2001. In 2008, there was an al-Qaeda audiotape released, crediting Hamza as the speaker. Omar says that the recording was made years before September 11, 2001, when Hamza was still a young boy and Osama asked for volunteers to make the recording. Hamza was the only son who volunteered. It is now known that Hamza and his mother survived the bombing attacks against Afghanistan after 9/11. He is living with his mother (and his family) in a compound in Tehran. He is hoping that he will be allowed to leave with his family to live in another Middle Eastern country. Hamza turned twenty-one years old in 2010.

Children with Fourth Wife, Siham

KADHIJA

Siham's first child and first daughter with Osama was born in 1988 in Jeddah, Saudi Arabia. At her 1999 wedding arranged by her father, Kadhija was married to a Saudi al-Qaeda fighter named Abdullah in 1999, when she was only eleven years old. Kadhija remained in Afghanistan with her mother and Siham and was there during the American bombings of October and November 2001. Najwa's children say that Kadhija and her mother and siblings survived the Afghan bombing attacks but that they did not go into Iran with the other family members. Instead, they remained in Pakistan. Kadhija was twenty-two years old in 2010.

KHALID

Siham's second child and first son with Osama was born in 1989 in Jeddah, Saudi Arabia. Little is known about Khalid, although he remained with his mother in Afghanistan. Khalid survived the 2001 bombing attacks and is with his mother and sisters in Pakistan. He issued a statement about his siblings in Iran in 2009. Khalid was twenty-one years old in 2010.

MIRIAM

Siham's third child and second daughter with Osama was born in 1990 in Jeddah, Saudi Arabia. Born prematurely, and on the same day as Najwa's daughter Iman, Miriam had a challenging early life. Little is known of Miriam other than she remained with her mother in Afghanistan. Miriam, like her siblings, survived the 2001 bombing attacks and is with her mother, sisters, and brother in Pakistan. Miriam was twenty years old in 2010.

SUMAIYA

Siham's fourth child and third daughter with Osama was born in 1992 in Khartoum, Sudan. Little is known about Sumaiya other than she remained with her mother in Afghanistan. It is believed that her father would have arranged a marriage to one of his fighters at the onset of puberty. Sumaiya survived the 2001 bombing attacks and is living in Pakistan with her mother, sisters, and brother. She was eighteen years old in 2010.

Child with Fifth Wife, Yemeni Amal al-Sadah

SAFIA

Amal's first child and first daughter with Osama. Although Safia's mother married Osama bin Laden in Kandahar, Afghanistan, prior to Najwa's leaving the country, unlike his other marriages, Najwa knew little of Amal. Today there is no firm information about Amal al-Sadah or her daughter, Safia. Some reports have Osama sending Amal and Safia back to Yemen and out of danger before the September 11, 2001, attacks on the United States, while others say that Amal and Safia remained with Osama and his extended family, fleeing Afghanistan into Pakistan. Since Najwa and Omar are no longer in contact with the family, there is no current factual information to report. But if Amal and her child remained in Afghanistan through the bombings and survived the attacks, Safia would be nine years old in 2010.

Appendix B

Osama bin Laden Chronology

The following are important dates in Osama bin Laden's personal, political, militant, and Islamic life from 1957 to 2009.

1957: Friday, February 15, 1957: Osama bin Mohammed bin Awad bin Aboud bin Laden al-Qatani* is born in Riyadh, Saudi Arabia, in the early hours of the morning to Mohammed Awad bin Laden and Allia Ghanem. He is the eighteenth of twenty-two sons that will be born to Mohammed Awad bin Laden, and the first child born to Allia Ghanem. His paternal and maternal families hail from Hadramaut in Yemen. A young Mohammed bin Laden settled in Saudi Arabia and became a Saudi citizen. Allia Ghanem's family settled in Syria and became Syrian citizens. Their only child, Osama, is born a citizen of Saudi Arabia.

1959: Mohammed Awad bin Laden and Allia Ghanem divorce. Allia keeps physical custody of her son, Osama, although he remains a part of his father's family.

1959: Allia Ghanem marries Mohammed al-Attas and will have four children with her second husband.

1963: Osama is registered at the primary school at the Al-Thager Model School in Jeddah, considered to be one of the most progressive schools in Saudi Arabia.

*Omar bin Laden reports that his father told his family that their real family name was al-Qatani, but that his father, Mohammed bin Laden, had never registered the name. This is not documented by any other sources.

1966: Osama's father purchases the family's first airplane.

1967: On September 3, there is an airplane crash at Oom, Saudi Arabia, and Osama's father, Mohammed bin Laden, is killed.

1974: Osama marries Najwa Ghanem. Najwa is fifteen and Osama is seventeen. Najwa is his mother's niece, and Osama's first cousin. A simple wedding is held in Syria, at the home of Najwa's parents. According to Najwa, media reports are wrong that she was coerced into the marriage. Her marriage with her first cousin Osama was a love marriage. After receiving official documents, Najwa joins her husband, Osama, in Jeddah, Saudi Arabia. The young couple resides in the home of his mother and stepfather while Osama continues with his schooling.

1974: Osama assumes part-time duties in his father's huge multinational construction business, the Saudi bin Laden Group.

1976: Osama enrolls as a student at the King Abdul Aziz University in Jeddah. He studies economics and management. (Najwa says that her husband never studied engineering, although that is a popular myth.) During these years the Muslim Middle East undergoes an Islamic awakening, called the Salwa, which came about after the 1967 war with Israel, when Egypt, Jordan, and Syria suffered a demoralizing military defeat. Osama came of age during this political change.

1976: Osama and Najwa welcome their firstborn, a son they name Abdullah. From that time Osama will be known as Abu Abdullah, meaning father of Abdullah, to his closest friends and associates. Najwa become known to family and friends as Um Abdullah, or mother of Abdullah.

1978: Osama and Najwa welcome their second-born, a son they name Abdul Rahman.

1979: On the Muslim calendar, 1979 is the first year of a new century.

1979: Osama, Najwa, and their two sons travel through England and to the United States for Osama to meet with Abdullah Azzam, the man many call Osama's first mentor. Abdullah Azzam was on a speaking tour in America to recruit for Jihad. Osama, who had recently awakened to the passion of Jihad, met with Abdullah Azzam to discuss and make plans for his role in the movement. While on this trip, Abdul Rahman becomes ill, and Osama and Najwa consult a medical specialist for their second-born son.

1979: Osama and Najwa welcome their third-born, a son they name Sa'ad.

1979: Muslims the world over received a terrible blow on November 20, 1979. The annual Haj pilgrimage had ended and Haj worshippers were preparing to depart Mecca. Since there are always foreign Muslim worshippers in Mecca, the Grand Mosque was filled with people. At the moment the Imam concluded the first prayer of the day, gunshots were heard and worshippers attacked.

Three hundred rebels led by Juhayman al-Uteybi, a formal corporal in the National Guard of Saudi Arabia, quickly overtook the men of religion and the worshippers, declaring them all as hostages. The rebels seized total control of the Grand Mosque, broadcasting their goals over the loudspeakers throughout Mecca.

The Saudi Army and National Guard poured into Mecca, ordering an evacuation of the city and surrounding the Grand Mosque. Since the Koran forbids violence within the Grand Mosque, the Saudi royal family first sought approval from the religious authorities to use deadly force against the insurgents, which was given.

The ensuing battle lasted for two weeks. Control of the Grand Mosque was finally achieved on December 4, 1979. Official reports say that 255 fanatics, troops and pilgrims were killed, while 560 were injured. The rebels who survived were imprisoned or beheaded, with reports claiming 63 beheadings.

1979: On December 26, Russia invades Afghanistan.

1980: Osama responds to what he calls the invasion by "Godless communists" by organizing charities to benefit the Afghan resistance fighters, known as the Mujahideen. His friend and mentor, Abdullah Azzam, founds an organization for this purpose. Osama, backed by his family wealth and the Saudi government's encouragement, becomes a chief financier.

1980: Osama begins the first of his travels to Pakistan to deliver supplies and offer assistance to his Afghan Muslim brothers. From this time on, Osama is heavily involved in the Afghan struggle against Russia, coordinating his trips to fit around his schooling and family responsibilities.

1980 or 1981: Due to his Jihadi responsibilities Osama drops out of the university, although he lacked only one semester to graduate.

1981: Osama continues to raise funds and to deliver supplies to Pakistan for the Afghan resistance against the Soviets.

1981: During the month of March, Osama and Najwa welcome their fourth-born, a son they name Omar.

1982: Osama bin Laden becomes more involved with the conflict in Afghanistan. The war between Russia and Afghanistan changed, with the Russians occupying the main cities and the Mujahideen (which were divided into many groups) waging a guerrilla war. From 1980 until 1985, there were nine main Russian offensives resulting in heavy fighting. While his friend and mentor, Abdullah Azzam, recruits Arab fighters to join the war, Osama bin Laden becomes further involved, collecting millions of dollars from wealthy Gulf donors for the purpose of contributing to the Mujahideen.

1982: While in Pakistan and Afghanistan, Osama meets some of the Egyptian Jihadists who will inspire the young Saudi. Later, they will become his followers. Five of these men are Mohammed Atef (Abu Hafs), Dr. Ayman al-Zawahiri, Abu Ubaidah al-Banshiri, Abdullah Ahmed Abdullah, and Omar Abdel Rahman.

1983: Osama purchases a large twelve-apartment building in Jeddah, where he moves Najwa and their children.

1983: Osama marries a second wife, a Saudi woman from Jeddah named Khadijah Sharif. The Sharif family is descended from the al-Hussain line. (The Prophet's daughter had two sons, one named al-Hassan and the other named al-Hussain. When a Saudi family is descended from the Prophet, they always clarify from which line, al-Hassan or al-Hussain.)

1983: Osama and Najwa welcome their fifth-born, a son they name Osman.

1984: On occasion, Osama takes both wives and his children with him on trips to Pakistan, where they live in a spacious villa in the city of Peshawar, close to the Afghanistan border.

1984: Osama and his second wife, Khadijah, welcome their first child, a son they name Ali. From that time Khadijah will be called Um Ali, although Osama will forever be called Abu Abdullah.

1984: Osama helps Abdullah Azzam to set up the Services Office, which carries out placement of Jihad fighters from Arab nations into Afghan fighting units, or with relief organization responsible for collecting food and weapons for the Mujahideen.

1984: Osama further expands his participation in Jihad, helping to establish fighter training camps across the Afghanistan border. He begins to build tunnels, roads, and training camps needed to help his Muslim brothers fight the Russian invaders.

1985: Osama and first wife, Najwa, welcome their sixth-born, a son named Mohammed.

1986: Osama becomes even more involved in the Afghanistan-Russia conflict. He sets up his first military base in eastern Afghanistan, near a village called Jaji, which is located only ten miles from the border of Pakistan. The military base is for his Arab fighters, and is named the Lion's Den. During his frequent trips to Pakistan he routinely crosses the Pakistan border into Afghanistan to fight as a guerrilla commander, leading his Arab troops in a number of battles with the Russians.

1986: In order to introduce his firstborn to Jihad, Osama takes his eight-year-old son, Abdullah, with him to the fighting base near Jaji. He receives unexpected criticism from family and other Jihadi leaders for exposing his young son to the danger of war. This is only the first of many instances when Osama will push his unenthusiastic sons to the forefront of his personal passion for Jihad.

1986: With many Muslim radicals joining the struggle in Afghanistan, Osama becomes more politically aware and active, leading him to think about his mission in life, which will expand to fighting for Islam on every front.

1987: Osama marries his third wife, a Saudi woman from Jeddah named Khairiah Sabar. With Osama's encouragement, Khairiah was selected by his first wife, Najwa.

1987: In the spring of 1987, Osama gains his reputation as the leading Saudi hero after the battle of Jaji, where his Arab fighters are pitted against the Russians.

1987: Osama marries his fourth wife, a Saudi woman from Medina named Siham whose family is from the al-Hassan line of the Prophet. Siham is the sister of Saad, a Saudi soldier under Osama, who was married to one of Osama's nieces in the bin Laden family.

1987: After undertaking a big bin Laden family construction project in Medina, Osama moves his three wives and children to that city.

1987: Osama and Najwa welcome their seventh child, a girl they name Fatima. Fatima is the first daughter born to the family.

1988: Osama and Siham, his fourth wife, welcome their first child, a girl they name Kadhija.

1988: In August of 1988, Osama turns to a global crusade, founding al-Qaeda al-Askariya (translates to "the military base," later shortened to al-Qaeda, "the base," or "the foundation"). By this time Osama has achieved hero status in the Arab press. Due to Osama's prominence, fighters for his organization are easily recruited.

1988: Osama replaces his friend and mentor, Abdullah Azzam, as the leader of the Arab fightens in Peshawar, training for the conflict in Afghanistan.

1989: The Soviets withdraw from Afghanistan.

1989: Osama returns to Saudi Arabia, bringing approximately one hundred of his veteran fighters to live in Saudi Arabia.

1989: Abdullah Azzam and one of his sons are assassinated when they are targeted by a roadside bomb in Peshawar. With Abdullah Azzam's death, Osama bin Laden is the undisputed leader of the Arab fighters.

1989: Osama and his third wife, Khairiah, welcome their first child, Hamza.

1989: Osama and his fourth wife, Siham, welcome their second child, Khalid.

1990: On August 2, 1990, Saddam Hussein invades Kuwait. Osama approaches the Saudi royal family, volunteering his military expertise and holy warriors to fight and defeat Saddam Hussein. Confident of his ability to convince the royal family of the wisdom of his plan, Osama prepares his forces to defend the kingdom.

1990: The Saudi government allows the United States to form a coalition of many countries, including many Muslim countries, to battle Saddam Hussein. The United States begins sending troops to Saudi Arabia.

1990: Osama is so enraged at what he considers a royal slight in allowing infidel troops on Islamic holy land that he begins to speak out and write treatises against the Saudi regime, leading to an end to their previous friendly relationship.

1990: Osama and his first wife, Najwa, welcome their eighth child, a girl named Iman.

1990: Osama and his fourth wife, Siham, welcome their third child, a girl named Miriam. (This child is born on the same day as Iman, Najwa's daughter.)

1990: Omar and his second wife, Khadijah, welcome their second child, a son named Amer.

1990: The Saudi government warms Osama to cease his criticisms of the royal family and their decisions. Osama refuses, increasing his opposition. The ruling family limits Osama's freedom, ordering that he confine himself to the kingdom.

1991: A coalition, led by the United States, fights the Persian Gulf War. Afterward, the United States establishes a permanent military presence in the kingdom. Osama and other intellectuals within the kingdom object to the infidel presence in the land of the two most holy places in Islam, Mecca and Medina. Opposition to the ruling family increases, resulting in the arrest and detention of a number of intellectuals.

1991: Osama flees the kingdom after convincing one of the royals to approve a one-time trip to Pakistan in order to complete and close down his businesses there. Osama promises that he will return to Saudi Arabia.

1991: Osama breaks his promise, and instead he arranges a move to Khartoum, in Sudan.

1991 or 1992: In late 1991 or early 1992, Osama moves to Khartoum, Sudan. His wives, children, and approximately one hundred of his veteran fighters who were living in Saudi Arabia join him there.

1992: With the approval of the Sudanese government, Osama sets up many businesses in Sudan.

1992: Osama begins to bring more Afghan veterans living in Pakistan into Sudan to work in his businesses, as well as setting up his al-Qaeda organization for future missions.

1992: Osama and his second wife, Khadijah, welcome their third and last child, a girl they name Aisha.

1992: On December 29, 1992, there is a terrorist attack in Aden, Yemen, on a hotel where American troops generally stay. On that day, however, the American soldiers had checked out of the hotel on their way to Somalia where the United States was conducting a humanitarian mission. The people killed were two Austrian tourists. Terrorism experts believe that this was the first attack organized by Osama bin Laden and his al-Qaeda organization, although it has never been proven.

1992: Osama and his fourth wife, Siham, welcome their fourth child, a daughter they name Sumaiya.

1993: In October, the U.S. government humanitarian mission is ambushed in Mogadishu, Somalia, and eighteen U.S. soldiers are killed. After the attack, Osama bin Laden admits that some of his fighters were involved in the attack. Osama ridicules the United States for withdrawing from Somalia after the ambush.

1993: Osama and Najwa welcome their ninth child, a son they name Ladin. Najwa is escorted to Saudi Arabia by her son Abdullah. After the birth, Najwa returns to Khartoum. Osama changes his mind and renames their son Bakr. From that time on the children and Najwa call their sibling Ladin, while Osama calls him Bakr, leading to much confusion.

1993: Other militant groups began to congregate in Sudan with Osama bin Laden's al-Qaeda, one of the few countries who would welcome them. There was the al-Jihad group, headed by Dr. Ayman Muhammad al-Zawahiri. There was also the al-Gama'a al-Islamiyya group, led by Omar Abdel Rahman. (After he was arrested and imprisoned in the United States, his son became the local organizer.) All three militant groups came together for the purpose of restoring Islamic Jihad. Their goal was to have the world ruled by Islam.

1993: Osama's second wife, Khadijah, asks for a divorce. Osama agrees and allows her to leave Sudan with her three children. Khadijah moves back to Saudi Arabia.

1993: The World Trade Center in New York is bombed. Six people are killed and one thousand injured. Authorities believe there is a link to al-Qaeda, but no charges are brought against Osama bin Laden or his organization for lack of evidence. However, Omar Abdel Rahman, a blind cleric and one of Osama's associates, is recorded issuing a fatwa encouraging acts of violence against U.S. civilian targets. (Omar Abdel Rahman is arrested on June 24, 1993, tried and convicted of seditious conspiracy. In 1996 he was sentenced to life in prison.)

1993 or early 1994: After his divorce from his second wife, Khadijah, Osama bin Laden marries for the fifth time while in Khartoum. However the marriage is annulled before it can be consummated. The family does not want to say why the marriage was annulled, considering it a private matter.

1994: The government of Saudi Arabia revokes Osama bin Laden's Saudi citizenship. His bin Laden brothers renounce him. Osama's bank accounts in the kingdom are frozen.

1994: The Sudanese government gives Osama bin Laden and his family Sudanese citizenship and passports.

1995: On June 26 the two Islamic groups associated with bin Laden's al-Qaeda allegedly try to assassinate Egyptian president Hosni Mubarak when he was in Ethiopia for a meeting of the Organization of African Unity. The assassination attempt fails but brings pressure from the Egyptians, Saudis, and Americans for the Sudanese government to expel Osama and the other Islamic groups from the country.

1995: Osama bin Laden writes an open letter to King Fahd of Saudi Arabia. In the letter he calls for a campaign of insurgent attacks in the kingdom against the United States forces still stationed there.

1995: In Riyadh, Saudi Arabia, there is a truck bombing of a U.S.–operated Saudi National Guard training center. Five Americans and two Indians are killed. Although Osama denies responsibility, he praises the attackers.

1996: In May of 1996, the Sudanese government bends to international pressure and expels Osama bin Laden and his associates.

1996: In May of 1996, Osama bin Laden, his top commanders, and his son Omar fly out of Khartoum, to Jalalabad, Afghanistan. Regardless of other media reports, Omar bin Laden says he is the only son that accompanied his father. He also reports that their plane crossed Saudi Arabia, and that their only stop was for the purpose of refueling the airplane in Iran.

1996: Four Saudi men are arrested for the truck bombing in Riyadh that killed the Americans and Indians. They confess that they were motivated by Osama bin Laden's militant activities. They are beheaded in Riyadh's Deira Square, more commonly known as "Chop-Chop Square."

1996: President Bill Clinton signs a top secret order authorizing the CIA to use any and all means to destroy Osama bin Laden's organization.

1996: A second truck bomb destroys Khobar Towers in Dhahran, killing nineteen U.S. soldiers. There is never any evidence that Osama and al-Qaeda were responsible, although the U.S. government believe he inspired the attack.

1996: Osama bin Laden signs and issues his "Declaration of Jihad," which outlines the goals of his network. He calls for the removal of the Saudi government from power; for the liberation of the Muslim holy sites from all foreigners; for the support of all Islamic revolutionary groups; and for driving the U.S. government out of the Arabian Peninsula.

1996: In September 1996, Osama bin Laden brings his wives, children, and Afghan veterans and their wives and children from Sudan to Jalalabad, Afghanistan. (Important note: Najwa and Omar were unclear as to the exact dates that the family lived in the various locations in Afghanistan, or to the exact timing of Rukhaiya's birth. Arabs do not celebrate birthdays in the same manner as in the West. They do know that the personal events listed below were in the general time line of late 1996 to mid-1997.)

1996: Osama bin Laden moves his wives and children to Tora Bora Mountain, in Afghanistan.

1997: Osama's family temporarily moves to Jalalabad. While there, Osama and Najwa have their tenth child, a girl they name Rukhaiya. The child is born in a hospital in Jalalabad.

1997: Osama moves his family to the airport compound in Kandahar, where they live until October 2001. (The family did live for very short periods in other areas in Afghanistan, including Kabul and Jalalabad, during this same period, but their main residence was the airport compound at Kandahar.)

1998: Although Osama bin Laden is not a cleric, he issues a fatwa calling for attacks on Americans. His signed statement calls for the killing of Americans saying it is the "individual duty for every Muslim who can do it in any country in which it is possible to do it."

1998: On June 8, a U.S. grand jury investigation of Osama bin Laden, which was opened in 1996, finally issues a sealed indictment, charging Osama bin Laden with "conspiracy to attack defense utilities of the United States." The United States prosecutors charge that Osama bin Laden is head of a terrorist organization named al-Qaeda, and is also a major financier of Islamic organizations around the world.

1998: A group calling themselves the Egyptian Jihad sends the Americans a warning, saying that they will soon deliver an important message to the Americans, "which we hope they read with care, because we will write it with God's help, in a language they will understand."

1998: On August 7, there are simultaneous bombings at the United States embassy in Kenya and the United States embassy in Tanzania. A total of 213 people are killed in Kenya, including twelve Americans. More than 4,500 people are injured. There are eleven people killed in Tanzania, and eighty-five injured. (There are no Americans killed in Tanzania.)

1998: U.S. intelligence agencies say that they have intercepted the telephone calls of two of Osama bin Laden's commanders implicating al-Qaeda in the August 7 embassy attacks.

1998: Mullah Omar, the head of the Taliban, the group in charge of Afghanistan, turns down a Saudi extradition request for Osama bin Laden.

1998: On August 20, the United States retaliates against Osama bin Laden and al-Qaeda, sending cruise missiles into al-Qaeda training camps. Two hours prior to the attacks, Osama, his sons, and commanders left one of the training camps near Khost to travel to Kabul to a safe house. Sources say that only six fighters were killed. Omar bin Laden reports that thirty fighters were killed.

1998: The United States issues a new indictment against Osama bin Laden, Mohammed Atef—listed as bin Laden's chief military commander—and others. Osama and his commanders are charged with the bombing of the two United States embassies and conspiracy to commit other acts of terror against Americans living abroad. Rewards of $5 million each are offered for Osama bin Laden and for Mohammed Atef.

1999: Omar bin Laden, Osama's fourth son with his first wife, Najwa, is warned of an attack by Abu al-Haadi, one of Osama's trusted fighters. Haadi believes the attack is going to be so big that the United States will retaliate with the intention of killing everyone associated with Osama bin Laden. After many heated discussions with his father, Omar takes his pregnant mother, brother Abdul Rahman, and baby sister Rukhaiya out of Afghanistan to Syria.

Late 1999: Osama and Najwa have their eleventh and final child, who is born in Syria. The baby is a girl whom Osama names Nour in honor of Osama's half-sister, who had died a few years before.

Early 2000: Najwa returns to Kandahar with her two small daughters and son Abdul Rahman. Omar remains in Syria, seeking the return of his Saudi citizenship, which is forthcoming in four months.

2000: On the 12th of October, there is a terrorist attack on the U.S. warship *Cole* at the Aden, Yemen, seaport. The explosion kills seventeen American sailors. President Bill Clinton does not retaliate, saying there is no concrete evidence that al-Qaeda was behind the attack, although that is believed to be the case.

2000 (late) or early 2001: Osama bin Laden marries for the sixth time to Yemeni Amal al-Sadah. It is said that his bride is only seventeen years old. The marriage was held in Kandahar, Afghanistan. As of this writing it is thought that Osama and Amal have one daughter, named Safia.

2001: In early 2001, a worried Omar returns to Kandahar, Afghanistan, after his grandmother in Saudi Arabia tells him that his father is angry and has ordered him to return to Afghanistan.

2001: Late April 2001, after a brief stay, and a repeated warning of a big attack in the making, Omar tries to convince his mother to take her children and leave Afghanistan. Najwa remains in Kandahar while Omar leaves his father and Afghanistan for the final time.

2001: Between September 7 and 9, Najwa departs Afghanistan for the final time. Osama forbids her from taking her other children. A distraught Najwa travels to Syria to live in her mother's home. Najwa's other children, their wives, and grandchildren remain in Afghanistan with their father.

2001: On the 11th of September, approximately three thousand people lose their lives when nineteen al-Qaeda suspects hijack four American passenger planes and fly them into American targets. Two fly into the World Trade Center, killing thousands and destroying the buildings. One flies into the Pentagon near

Washington, D.C. The final plane is stopped from its mission by the brave passengers who fight their hijackers. That plane crashes into a field in Pennsylvania.

2001: On October 7, six weeks after the attacks on American soil, the United States military begins a fierce air assault upon Afghanistan. The bombing attacks are so devastating that they cause a complete disruption of al-Qaeda and the training camps located in Afghanistan. Osama bin Laden, his commanders, and fighters hide in the mountains of Tora Bora before fleeing to Pakistan. It is believed that many hundreds of al-Qaeda fighters perished, including Mohammed Atef (Abu Hafs), who is killed at his home in Kabul. Osama bin Laden and Dr. Ayman al-Zawahiri make an escape into Pakistan. (Nothing is known of the fate of Najwa's children, or Osama bin Laden's other wives and children.) During this same assault, the notorious Mullah Omar and his Taliban government collapse, with Mullah Omar and his followers fleeing to Pakistan.

2004: In October, Osama bin Laden releases a recording taking credit for the September 11, 2001, attacks.

2008: Osama bin Laden releases an audiotape condemning the publication of drawings that he said insulted the Prophet Mohammed, and warned Europeans of a severe reaction to come.

2009: In January, Osama bin Laden releases an audiotape urging Muslims to launch a Jihad against Israel. The head of al-Qaeda vows to open new fronts against the United States and its allies. The twenty-two-minute audiotape includes an appeal for donations to support the fight he is waging.

2010: During the year 2010, there were the usual speculations about Osama bin Laden and whether he was alive or dead, with various media reports claiming both possibilities. But no concrete evidence came to light, although Omar bin Laden feels certain that if his father had been killed, the world would be informed. Therefore, it is Omar's opinion that his father is alive somewhere in the hinterlands of Pakistan.

Appendix C

Al-Qaeda Chronology: 1988–2008

With the end of the war with Russia in sight, Osama and the men around him began to dream of a global Jihad to spread the message of God and to bring the world under Islamic rule.

Osama's mentor, Abdullah Azzam, a leading Palestinian Sunni Islamic scholar and theologian, was the first to recognize the necessity for an organized foundation from which believers could launch their struggle for a perfect Islamic world. But while the orator Azzam talked, the military man acted. Osama called for the first planning meeting that would be named al-Qaeda to be held at his family home in Peshawar, Pakistan. Al-Qaeda was formed in August 1988.

Osama's al-Qaeda organization has both an Islamic arm and a military arm, with the military arm growing in prominence. As new Muslim fighters arrived in Pakistan, they were sent to training camps inside Afghanistan, then dispersed to the various fighting fronts.

As the war with Russia slowed, Osama had more time to devote to the Islamic goals of al-Qaeda. The planning to make Islam the religion of the world increased after he moved from Saudi Arabia to Sudan, and finally to Afghanistan. The organization slowly became a threat to innocent people around the world.

The following attacks are believed to have been conducted by, or inspired by, al-Qaeda:

December 29, 1992: Aden, Yemen: In an attack targeting American servicemen on their way to Somalia, bombs explode at two hotels in Aden. No soldiers are killed, but two Austrian tourists are.

October 3–4, 1993: Somalia: Somali militia shoot down two American Black Hawk helicopters, killing eighteen U.S. servicemen.

June 25, 1996: Dhahran, Saudi Arabia: The Khobar Towers building, a U.S. military housing complex, is bombed, killing nineteen U.S. servicemen.

August 7, 1998: Kenya and Tanzania: The U.S. embassies of both African nations are car-bombed. More than 222 people are killed, most of them Africans.

October 12, 2000: Aden, Yemen: Two suicide bombers ram a small boat into the USS *Cole* while it is docked. The death toll is seventeen American sailors.

September 11, 2001: Nineteen al-Qaeda suspects hijack four domestic American planes. Two planes are flown into the World Trade Center buildings in New York City. One plane is flown into the Pentagon near Washington, D.C. The fourth plane crashes into an open field in Pennsylvania when the passengers resist their hijackers. There are various postings of the number of victims, but the most accepted figure seems to be 2,986 innocent people murdered.

February 1, 2002: Karachi, Pakistan: American journalist Daniel Pearl is kidnapped and beheaded.

April 11, 2002: Djerba, Tunisia: The Ghriba synagogue is bombed by a natural gas truck. The attack kills fifteen tourists (fourteen Germans and one Frenchman) and six Tunisians. Thirty others are wounded.

October 12, 2002: Bali, Indonesia: Suicide bombers and car bombs detonate in or near the busy nightclub area, killing over 200 people; 164 tourists and 38 Indonesians. Over 200 others are seriously wounded.

November 28, 2002: Mombassa, Kenya: A car bomb crashes into the lobby of the Israeli-owned Paradise Hotel and kills sixteen people. During this same time, two surface-to-air missiles are fired at an Israeli charter plane. The missiles miss the plane, saving many lives.

May 12, 2003: Riyadh, Saudi Arabia: Thirty-four people are killed in a series of bomb attacks targeting housing for foreign nationals and a U.S. office.

May 16, 2003: Casablanca, Morocco: A series of suicide bombings strike a Spanish restaurant, a hotel, a Jewish center, and the Belgian consulate, killing thirty-three people.

August 5, 2003: South Jakarta, Indonesia: A car bomb explodes outside the JW Marriott Hotel lobby, killing twelve people and injuring over 150. The dead are four tourists and eight Indonesians.

November 15, 2003, and November 20, 2003: Istanbul, Turkey: Four car bombs explode at Jewish synagogues, killing fifty-seven and wounding over seven hundred.

2003–2008: Iraq: There are hundreds of al-Qaeda attacks in every region of Iraq, killing thousands of innocent Iraqis.

March 11, 2004: Madrid, Spain: Ten bombs explode on commuter trains in Madrid, killing over 190 people and wounding 1,800.

May 29, 2004: Khobar, Saudi Arabia: Four terrorists attack oil industry installations and the Oasis Compound, a housing compound for foreign workers. The terrorists take fifty foreign nationals hostage, killing twenty-two, some of whom have their throats slit.

June 18, 2004: Saudi Arabia: American Paul Johnson is kidnapped and held hostage and later beheaded.

July 7, 2005: London, England: Four suicide bombers attack the mass transit system in London, killing fifty-three and wounding seven hundred.

November 9, 2005: Amman, Jordan: Simultaneous bombings in three different American-franchise hotels kill fifty-seven people and injure 120 others.

April 11, 2007: Algiers: Two bombs explode, one at a police station and the other at the office of the Algerian prime minister, killing thirty-three people.

June 2, 2008: Pakistan: The Danish embassy is struck by a car bomb, killing six people and injuring many others.

2009/2010: During the years 2009 and 2010, there was a disturbing growing resurgent al-Qaeda presence in Afghanistan, Yemen, Pakistan, Iraq, and Somalia. Although the U.S. military, along with the British military and other assisting countries tried to dislodge al-Qaeda from power in Afghanistan, the movement proved impossible to eradicate. In fact, during the year 2010, al-Qaeda appeared to gain power in the areas outside major cities. As of this writing, there is a huge effort underway, led by U.S. General Petraeus, to give new life to the efforts against Afghan al-Qaeda. During this same time, Yemen showed signs of becoming a regional base for al-Qaeda. While the new Pakistani government entered into an alliance with the United States against al-Qaeda, success was mixed, with drone attacks creating enormous anger after numerous civilian deaths. Iraq was a hotbed of al-Qaeda activity during the year 2009, but seemed to be slowing during 2010. During this same time, al-Qaeda seemed to be drawing closer to Somali insurgents in the hopes of turning Somalia into a launching pad for Islamic jihad.

All of these signs point to the tragic fact that al-Qaeda is thriving and the mission to eliminate the danger from the terrorist group may not succeed for many years to come.

Index